Thackray's 2013 Investor's Guide

THACKRAY'S
2013
INVESTOR'S
GUIDE

Brooke Thackray MBA, CIM, CFP

Published in 2012 by: MountAlpha Media:
alphamountain.com

ISBN13: 978-0-9782200-8-2

Printed and Bound by Webcom
10 9 8 7 6 5 4 3 2 1

To my wife Jane

Acknowledgements

This book is the product of many years of research and could not have been written without the help of many people. I would like to thank my wife, Jane Steer-Thackray, and my children Justin, Megan, Carly and Madeleine, for the help they have given me and their patience during the many hours that I have devoted to writing this book. Credit must be given to Don Vialoux and Jon Vialoux. The three of us work together with the Horizons AlphaPro Seasonal Rotation ETF (ticker HAC:TSX) and many of the ideas and strategies that we have shared have found their way into this book. Thanks must be given to Wade Guenther for helping me source and filter a lot of the data in this book. I would also like to thank the proofreaders and editors, Amanda ODonnell and Jane Stiegler. Special mention goes to Jane for the countless hours she spent helping with writing, formatting and editing. This book could not have been written without her help.

INTRODUCTION

2013 THACKRAY'S INVESTOR'S GUIDE

Every year I add new features to the latest edition of the Investor's Guide. Many of the new features are based upon reader feedback – thank you.

Technical Commentary

The seasonal strategies that I have included in my previous books have proven to be very successful. The buy and sell dates are based upon iterative comparisons of different time periods measured by gain and frequency of success. Although the buy and sell dates are the optimal dates on which seasonal investors should focus on making their investment decisions, the markets have different dynamics from year to year, shifting the optimal buy and sell dates. Combining technical analysis with seasonal trends helps to adjust the decision process, allowing seasonal investors to enter and exit trades early or late, depending on market conditions.

The universe of technical indicators and techniques is huge. It is impossible to use all of the indicators. Only a small number of indicators and techniques that suit an investment style should be used. In the case of seasonal investing, a lot of long-term indicators provide very little benefit. For example, the standard Moving Average Convergence Divergence (MACD), is far too slow to be of any use. In this book I have chosen to illustrate the use of three technical indicators that have provided a lot of value in fine-tuning the dates for seasonal investing: Full Stochastic Oscillator (FSO), Relative Strength Index (RSI) and Relative Strength. The indicators are used in conjunction with the price pattern and moving averages of the security being considered. Investors must remember that technical analysis is not absolute and there will be exceptions when utilizing indicators and price patterns.

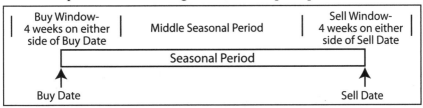

To combine technical indicators with seasonal trends, the indicators should only be used within the windows of the buy and sell dates. The indicators should be ignored outside the seasonal buy/sell windows. The only exception to this occurs when an indicator gives a signal during its seasonal middle period, which is in the seasonal period, but after the buy window and before the sell window. In this case a technical signal can support selling a full position based upon a fundamental breakdown in the price action of a security. By itself, a FSO or RSI indicator showing weakness in a security during its middle seasonal period, does not warrant action, it can only be used to support a decision being made in conjunction with underperformance relative to the broad market, or a major price action break.

Below are short descriptions of the three technical indicators that are used in this book and the metrics of how they are used with seasonal analysis. Full evaluation of the indicators and their uses with seasonal analysis is beyond the scope of this book.

Full Stochastic Oscillator (FSO)

A stochastic oscillator is a range bound momentum indicator that tracks the location of the close price relative to the high-low range, over a set number of periods. It tracks the momentum of price change and helps to indicate the strength and direction of price movement.

I have found that generally the best method to combine the FSO with seasonal trends is to buy an early partial position when the FSO turns up above 20 within four weeks of the seasonal buy date. Additionally, the best time to sell an early partial position occurs when the FSO turns below 80, within four weeks of the seasonal exit date.

For practical purposes in this book, %D, a 3 period smoothed %K, has been omitted. The standard variables are used in the FSO calculation (14 day look back period, and a 3 day simple moving average smoothing constant).

Relative Strength Index (RSI)

The RSI is a momentum oscillator that measures the speed and change of price movements. I have found that the best method to combine the RSI with seasonal trends is to buy an early partial position when the RSI turns up above 30 within four weeks of the seasonal buy date. The best time to sell an early partial position occurs when the RSI turns below 70, within four weeks of the seasonal exit date. Compared with the FSO, the RSI is less useful as it is slower and gives too few signals in the buy/sell windows.

Relative Strength

Relative strength calculates the performance of one security versus another security. When the relative strength is increasing, it indicates the seasonal security is outperforming. When the relative strength is declining, the seasonal security is underperforming. When a downward trend line is broken to the upside by the performance of the seasonal security, relative to the benchmark, this is a positive signal. This action carries a lot of weight and can justify a full early entry into a position if other technical evidence is positive. Likewise, if an upward trend line is broken to the downside, a negative technical signal is given and can justify a full early exit from a position if other technical evidence is negative.

THACKRAY'S 2013 INVESTOR'S GUIDE

You can choose great companies to invest in and still underperform the market. Unless you are in the market at the right time and in the best sectors, your investment expertise can be all for naught.

Successful investors know when they should be in the market. Very successful investors know when they should be in the market, and the best sectors in which to invest. *Thackray's 2013 Investor's Guide* is designed to provide investors with the knowledge of when and what to buy, and when to sell.

The goal of this book is to help investors capture extra profits by taking advantage of the seasonal trends in the markets. This book is straightforward. There are no complicated rules and there are no complex algorithms. The strategies put forward are intuitive and easy to understand.

It does not matter if you are a short-term or long-term investor, this book can be used to help establish entry and exit points. For the short-term investor, specific periods are identified that can provide profitable opportunities. For the long-term investor best buy dates are identified to launch new investments on a sound footing.

The stock market has its seasonal rhythms. Historically, the broad markets, such as the S&P 500, have a seasonal trend of outperforming during certain times of the year. Likewise, different sectors of the market have their own seasonal trends of outperformance. When oil stocks tend to do well in the springtime before "driving season," health care stocks tend to underperform the market. When utilities do well in the summertime, industrials do not. With different markets and different sectors having a tendency to outperform at different times of the year, there is always a place to invest.

Until recently, investors did not have access to the information necessary to analyse and create sector strategies. In recent years there have been a great number of sector Exchange Traded Funds (ETFs) and sector indexes introduced into the market. For the first time, investors are now able to easily implement a sector rotation strategy. This book provides a seasonal road map of what sectors tend to do well at different times of the year. It is a first of its kind, revealing new sector-based strategies that have never before been published.

In terms of market timing there are ample strategies in this book to help determine the times when equities should be over or underweight. During a favorable time for the market, investments can be purchased to overweight equities relative to their target weight in a portfolio (staying within risk tolerances). During an unfavorable time, investments can be sold to underweight equities relative to their target.

A large part of the book is devoted to sector seasonality – the underpinnings for a sector rotation strategy. The most practical rotation strategy is to create a core part of a portfolio that represents the broad market and then set aside an allocation to be rotated between favored sectors from one time period to the next.

It does not makes sense to apply any investment strategy only once with a large investment. Seasonal strategies are no exception. The best way to apply an investment strategy is to use a disciplined methodology that allows for diversification and a large enough number of investments to help remove the anomalies of the market. This reduces risk and increases the probability of a long term gain.

Following the specific buy and sell dates put forth in this book would have netted an investor large, above market returns. To "turbo-charge" gains, an investor can combine seasonality with technical analysis. As the seasonal periods are never exactly the same, technical analysis can help investors capture the extra gains when a sector turns up early, or momentum extends the trend.

IMPORTANT: *Strategy Buy and Sell Dates*
The beginning date of every strategy period in this book represents a full day in the market; therefore, investors should buy at the end of the preceding market day. For example the *Biotech Summer Solstice* seasonal period of strength is from June 23rd to September 13th. To be in the sector for the full seasonal period, an investor would enter the market before the closing bell on June 22nd. If the buy date landed on a weekend or holiday, then the buy would occur at the end of the preceding trading day.

The last day of a trading strategy is the sell date. For example, the Biotech sector investment would be sold at the end of the day on September 13th. If the sell date is a holiday or weekend, then the investment would be sold at the close on the preceding trading day.

What is Seasonal Investing?

In order to properly understand seasonal investing in the stock market, it is important to look briefly at its evolution. It may surprise investors to know that seasonal investing at the broad market level, i.e. Dow Jones or S&P 500, has been around for a long time. The initial seasonal strategies were written by Fields (1931, 1934) and Watchel (1942), who focused on the *January Effect*. Coincidentally, this strategy is still bantered about in the press every year.

Yale Yirsch Senior has been largely responsible for the next stage in the evolution, producing the *Stock Trader's Almanac* for more than forty years. This publication focuses on broad market trends such as the best six months of the year and tendencies of the market to do well depending on the political party in power and holiday trades.

In 1999, Brooke Thackray and Bruce Lindsay wrote, *Time In Time Out: Outsmart the Market Using Calendar Investment Strategies*. This work focused on a comprehensive analysis of the six month seasonal cycle and other shorter seasonal cycles in the broad markets such as the S&P 500.

Don Vialoux, considered the patriarch of seasonal investing in Canada, has written many articles on seasonal investing. His writings on this topic have developed a large following, via his free newsletter available at www.timingthemarket.ca.

Seasonal investing has changed over time. The focus has shifted from broad market strategies to taking advantage of sector rotation opportunities – investing in different sectors at different times of the year, depending on their seasonal strength. This has created a whole new set of investment opportunities. Rather than just being "in or out" of the market, investors can now always be invested by shifting between different sectors and asset classes, taking advantage of both up and down markets.

Definition – Seasonal investing is a method of investing in the market at the time of the year when it typically does well, or investing in a sector of the market when it typically outperforms the broad market such as the S&P 500.

The term seasonal investing is somewhat of a misnomer, and it is easy to see why some investors might believe that the discipline relates to investing based upon the seasons of the year – winter, spring, summer and autumn. Other than some agricultural commodities where the price is often correlated to growing seasons, generally seasonal investment strategies use the calendar as a reference for buy and sell dates. It is usually a specific event, i.e.

Christmas sales, that occurs on a recurring annual basis that creates the seasonal opportunity.

The discipline of seasonal investing is not restricted to the stock market. It has been used successfully for a number of years in the commodities market. The opportunities in this market tend to be based upon changes in supply and/or demand that occur on a yearly basis. Most commodities, especially the agricultural commodities, tend to have cyclical supply cycles, i.e., crops are harvested only at certain times of the year. The supply bulge that occurs at the same time every year provides seasonal investors with profit opportunities. Recurring increased seasonal demand for commodities also plays a major part in providing opportunities for seasonal investors. This applies to most metals and many other commodities, whether the end-product is industrial or consumer based.

Seasonal investment strategies can be used with a lot of different types of investments. The premise is the same, outperformance during a certain period of the year based upon a repeating event in the markets or economy. In my past writings I have developed seasonal strategies that have been used successfully in the stock, commodity, bond and foreign exchange markets. Seasonal investing is still relatively new for most markets with a lot of new opportunities waiting to be discovered.

How Does Seasonal Investing Work?

Most stock market sector seasonal trends are the result of a recurring annual catalyst: an event that affects the sector positively. These events can range from a seasonal spike in demand, seasonal inventory lows, weather effects, conferences and other events. Mainstream investors very often anticipate a move in a sector and incorrectly try to take a position just before an event takes place that is supposed to drive a sector higher. A good example of this would be investors buying oil just before the cold weather sets in. Unfortunately, their efforts are usually unsuccessful as they are too late to the party and the opportunity has already passed.

By the time the anticipated event occurs, a substantial amount of investors have bought into the sector – fully pricing in the expected benefit. At this time there is little potential left in the short-term. Unless there is a strong positive surprise, the sector's outperformance tends to slowly roll over. If the event produces less than its desired result, the sector can be severely punished.

So how does the seasonal investor take advantage of this opportunity? "Be there" before the mainstream investors, and get out before they do. Seasonal investors usually enter a sector two or three months before an event is anticipated to have a positive effect on a sector and get out before the actual event takes place. In essence, seasonal investors are benefiting from the mainstream investor's tendency to "buy in" too late.

Seasonality in the markets occurs because of three major reasons: money flow, changing market analyst expectations and the *Anticipation-Realization Cycle*. First, money flows vary throughout the year and at different times of the month. Generally, money flows increase at the end of the year and into the start of the next year. This is a result of year end bonuses and tax related investments. In addition, money flows increase at month end from money managers "window dressing" their portfolios. As a result of these money flows, the months around the end of the year and the days around the end of the month, tend to have a stronger performance than the other times of the year.

Second, the analyst expectations cycle tends to push markets up at the end of the year and the beginning of the next year. Stock market analysts tend to be a positive bunch – the large investment houses pay them to be positive. They start the year with aggressive earnings for all of their favorite companies. As the year progresses, they generally back off their earnings forecast, which decreases their support for the market. After a lull in the summer and early autumn months, they start to focus on the next year with another rosy forecast. As a result, the stock market tends to rise once again at the end of the year.

Third, at the sector level, sectors of the market tend to be greatly influenced by the *Anticipation-Realization Cycle*. Although some investors may not be familiar with the term "anticipation-realization," they probably are familiar with the concept of "buy the rumor – sell the fact," or in the famous words of Lord Rothschild "Buy on the sound of the war-cannons; sell on the sound of the victory trumpets."

The *Anticipation-Realization Cycle* as it applies to human behavior has been much studied in psychology journals. In the investment world, the premise of this cycle rests on investors anticipating a positive event in the market to drive prices higher and buying in ahead of the event. When the event takes place, or is realized, upward pressure on prices decreases as there is very little impetus for further outperformance.

A good example of the *Anticipation-Realization Cycle* takes place with the "conference effect." Very often large industries have major conferences that occur at approximately the same time every year. Major companies in the industry often hold back positive announce-

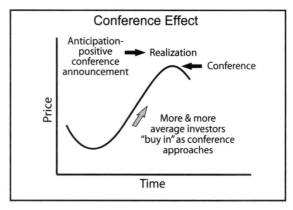

ments and product introductions to be released during the conference.

Two to three months prior to the conference, seasonal investors tend to buy into the sector. Shortly afterwards, the mainstream investors anticipate "good news" from the conference and start to buy in. As a result, prices are pushed up. Just before the conference starts, seasonal investors capture their profits by exiting their positions. As the conference unfolds, company announcements are made (realized), but as the potential good news has already been priced into the sector, there is little to push prices higher and the sector typically starts to rolls over.

The same *Anticipation-Realization Cycle* takes place with increased demand for oil to meet the "summer driving season", increased sales of goods at Christmas time, increased demand for gold jewellery to meet the autumn and winter demand, and many other events that tend to drive the outperformance of different sectors.

Does Seasonal Investing ALWAYS Work?

The simple answer to the above question is "No." There is not any invest-ment system in the world that works all of the time. When following any in-vestment system, it is probability of success that counts. It has often been said that "being correct in the markets 60% of the time will make you rich." Investors tend to forget this and become too emotionally attached to their losses. Just about every investment trading book states that investors typi-cally fail to let their profits run and cut their losses quickly. I concur. In my many years in the investment industry, the biggest mistake that I have found with investors is not being able to cut their losses. Everyone wants to be right, that is how we have been raised. Investors feel that if they sell at a loss they have failed, and as a result, often suffer bigger losses by waiting for their position to trade at profit.

With any investment system, inves-tors should let probability work for them. This means that investors should be able to enter and exit posi-tions capturing both gains and losses without becoming emotionally at-tached to any positions. Emotional attachment clouds judgement, which leads to errors. When all of the trades are put together, the goal is for profits to be larger than losses in a way that minimizes risks and beats the market.

If we examine the winter oil stock trade, we can see how probability has worked in an investor's favor. This trade is based upon the premise that at the tail end of winter, the refineries drive up demand for oil in order to produce enough gas for the ap-proaching "driving season" that starts in the spring. As a result, oil stocks tend to increase and outper-form the market (from February 25th to May 9th). The oil stock sector, rep-

XOI vs S&P 500 1984 to 2012

Feb 25 to May 9	S&P 500	positive XOI	Diff
1984	1.7 %	5.6 %	3.9 %
1985	1.4	4.9	3.5
1986	6.0	7.7	1.7
1987	3.7	25.5	21.8
1988	-3.0	5.6	8.6
1989	6.3	8.1	1.8
1990	5.8	-0.6	-6.3
1991	4.8	6.8	2.0
1992	0.9	5.8	4.9
1993	0.3	6.3	6.0
1994	-4.7	3.2	7.9
1995	7.3	10.3	3.1
1996	-2.1	2.2	4.3
1997	1.8	4.7	2.9
1998	7.5	9.8	2.3
1999	7.3	35.4	28.1
2000	4.3	22.2	17.9
2001	0.8	10.2	9.4
2002	-1.5	5.3	6.9
2003	12.1	5.7	-6.4
2004	-3.5	4.0	7.5
2005	-1.8	-1.0	0.8
2006	2.8	9.4	6.6
2007	4.2	10.1	5.8
2008	2.6	7.6	5.0
2009	20.2	15.8	-4.4
2010	0.5	-2.3	-2.8
2011	3.1	-0.6	-3.7
2012	-0.8	-13.4	-12.5
Avg	3.0 %	7.4 %	4.4 %
Fq > 0	76 %	83 %	79 %

resented by the Amex Oil Index (XOI), has been very successful at this time of year, producing an average return of 7.4% and beating the S&P 500 by 4.4%, from 1984 to 2012. In addition it has been positive 24 out of 29 times.

Investors should always evaluate the strength of seasonal trades before applying them to their own portfolios.

If an investor started using the seasonal investment discipline in 1984 and chose to invest in the winter-oil trade, they would have been very happy with the results. If they had chosen almost any other year, other than the last three years, to start the winter-oil trade in the last 29 years, they would have also been very pleased with the results. The years 1990, 2005, 2010, 2011 and 2012 produced losses of 0.6%, 1.0%, 2.3%, 0.6% and 13.5% respectively.

The fact that the trade has not worked in the last three years does not mean that the seasonal trade no longer works. All seasonal trades go through periods, sometimes multiple years where they do not work. An investor can start any methodology of trading at the "wrong time," and be unsuccessful in a particular trade. In fact, if an investor started the oil-winter trade in 1990 and had given up in the same year, they would have missed the following successful twelve years. Investors have to remember that it is the final score that counts, after all of the gains have been weighed against the losses.

In practical terms, investors should not put all of their investment strategies in one basket. If one or two large investments were made based upon seasonal strategies, it is possible that the seasonal methodology might be inappropriately evaluated and its use discontinued. A much more prudent strategy is to use a larger number of strategic seasonal investments with smaller investments. The end result will be to put the seasonal probability to work with a much greater chance of success.

Measuring Seasonal Performance

How do you determine if a seasonal strategy has been successful? Many people feel that ten years of data is a good sample size, others feel that fifteen years is better, and yet others feel that the more data the better. I tend to fall into the camp that, if possible, it is best to use fifteen or twenty years of data for sectors and more data for the broad markets, such as the S&P 500. Although the most recent data in almost any analytical framework is the most relevant, it is important to get enough data to reflect a sector's performance across different economic conditions. Given that historically the economy has performed on an eight year cycle, four years of expansion and then four years of contraction, using a short data set does not provide for enough exposure to different economic conditions.

A data set that is too long can run into the problem of older data having too much of an influence on the numbers when fundamental factors affecting a sector have changed. It is important to look at trends over time and assess if there has been a change that should be considered in determining the dates for a seasonal cycle. Each sector should be judged on its own merit. The analysis tables in this book illustrate the performance level for each year in order to provide the opportunity for readers to determine any relevant changes.

In order to determine if a seasonal strategy is effective there are two possible benchmarks, absolute and relative performance. Absolute performance measures if a profit is made and relative performance measures the performance of a sector in relationship to a major market. Both measurements have their merits and depending on your investment style, one measurement may be more valuable than another. This book provides both sets of measurement in tables and graphs.

It is not just the average percent gain of a sector over a certain time period that determines success. It is possible that one or two spectacular years of performance skew the results substantially (particularly with a small data set). The frequency of success is also very important: the higher the percentage of success the better. Also, the fewer large drawdowns the better. There is no magic number (percent success rate) per se of what constitutes a successful strategy. The success rate should be above fifty percent, otherwise it would be better to just invest in the broad market. Ideally speaking a strategy should have a high percentage success rate on both an absolute and relative basis. Some strategies are stronger than others, but that does not mean that the weaker strategies should not be used. Prudence should be used in determining the ideal portfolio allocation.

Illustrating the strength of a sector's seasonal performance can be accomplished through either an absolute yearly average performance graph, or a relative yearly average performance graph. The absolute graph shows the average yearly cumulative gain for a set number of years. It lets a reader visually identify the strong periods during the year. The relative graph shows the average yearly cumulative gain for the sector relative to the benchmark index.

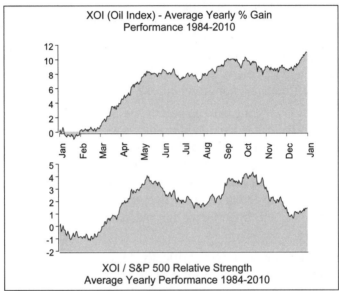

Both graphs are useful in determining the strength of a particular seasonal strategy. In the above diagram, the top graph illustrates the average year for the XOI (Oil Index) from 1984 to 2010. Essentially it illustrates the cumulative average gain if an investment were made in the index. The steep rising line starting in January/February shows the overall price rise that typically occurs in this sector at this time of year. In May the line flattens out and then rises very modestly starting in July.

The bottom graph is a ratio graph, illustrating the strength of the XOI Index relative to the S&P 500. It is derived by dividing the average year of the XOI by the average year of the S&P 500. When the line in the graph is rising, the XOI is outperforming the S&P 500, and vise versa when it is declining. This is an important graph and should be used in considering seasonal investments because the S&P 500 is a viable alternative to the energy sector. If both markets are increasing, but the S&P 500 is increasing at a faster rate, the S&P 500 represents a more attractive opportunity. This is particularly true when measuring the risk of a volatile sector relative to the broad market. If both investments were expected to produce the same rate of return, generally the broad market is a better investment because of its diversification.

Who Can Use Seasonal Investing?

Any investor from novice to expert, from short-term trader to long-term investor can benefit from using seasonal analysis. Seasonal investing is unique because it is an easy to understand system that can be used by itself or as a complement to another investment discipline. For the novice it provides an easy to follow strategy that makes intuitive sense. For the expert it can be used as a stand-alone system or as a complement to an existing system.

Seasonal investing is easily understood by all levels of investors, which allows investors to make rational decisions. This may seem obvious, but it is very common for investors to listen to a "guru of the market", be impressed and blindly follow his advice. When the advice works there is no problem. When the advice does not work investors wonder why they made the investment in the first place. When investors do not understand their investments it causes stress, bad decisions and a lack of "stick-to-it ness" with any investment discipline. Even expert investors realize the importance of understanding your investments. Peter Lynch of Fidelity Investments used to say "Never invest in any idea that you can't illustrate with a crayon." Investors do not need to go that far, but they should understand their investments.

Novice investors find seasonal strategies very easy to understand because they are intuitive. They do not have to be investing for years to understand why seasonal strategies work. They understand that an increase in demand for gold every year at the same time causes a ripple effect in the stock market pushing up gold stocks at the same time every year.

Most expert investors use information from a variety of sources in making their decisions. Even experts that primarily use fundamental analysis can benefit from using seasonal trends to get an edge in the market. Fundamental analysis is a very crude tool and provides very little in the way of timing an investment. Using seasonal trends can help with the timing of the buy and sell decisions and produce extra profit.

Seasonal investing can be used by both short-term and long-term investors, but in different ways. For short-term investors it provides a complete trade – buy and sell dates. For long-term investors it can provide a buy date for a sector of interest.

Combining Seasonal Analysis with other Investment Disciplines

Seasonal investing used by itself has historically produced above average market returns. Depending on an investor's particular style, it can be combined with one of the other three investment disciplines: fundamental, quantitative and technical analysis. There are two basic ways to combine seasonal analysis with other investment methodologies – as the primary or secondary method. If it is used as a primary method, seasonally strong time periods are established for a number of sectors and then appropriate sectors are chosen based upon fundamental, quantitative or technical screens. If it is used as a secondary method, sector selections are first made based upon one of three methods and then final sectors are chosen based upon which ones are in their seasonally strong period.

Technical analysis is an ideal mate for seasonal analysis. Unlike fundamental and quantitative analysis, which are very blunt timing tools at best, seasonal and technical analysis can provide specific trigger points to buy and sell. The combination can turbo-charge investment strategies, adding extra profits by fine-tuning entry and exit dates.

Seasonal analysis provides both buy and sell dates. Although a sector in the market can sometimes bottom on the exact seasonal buy date, it more often bottoms a bit early or a bit late. After all, the seasonal buy date is based upon an average of historical performance. Depending on the sector, buying opportunities start to develop approximately one month before and after the seasonal buy date. Using technical analysis gives an investor the advantage of buying into a sector when it turns up early or waiting when it turns up late. Likewise, technical analysis can be used to trigger a sell signal when the market turns down before or after the sell date.

The sell decision can be extended with the help of a trailing stop-loss order. If a sector has strong momentum and the technical tools do not provide a sell signal, it is possible to let the sector "run." When a trailing stop-loss is used, a profitable sell point is established. If the price continues to run, then the selling point is raised. If, on the other hand, the price falls through the stop-loss point, the position is sold.

Sectors of the Market

Standard & Poor's has done an excellent job in categorizing the U.S. stock market into its different parts. Although the demand for this service initially came from institutional investors, many individual investors now seek the same information. Knowing the sector breakdown in the market allows investors to see how different their portfolio is relative to the market. As a result, they are able to make conscious decisions on what parts of the stock market to overweight based upon their beliefs of which sectors will outperform. It also helps control the amount of desired risk.

Standard & Poor's uses four levels of detail in its Global Industry Classification Standard (GICS©) to categorize stock markets around the world. From the most specific, it classifies companies into sub-industries, industries, industry groups and finally economic sectors. All companies in the Standard & Poor's global family of indices are classified according to the GICS structure.

This book focuses on the U.S. market, analysing the trends of the venerable S&P 500 index and its economic sectors and industry groups. The following diagram illustrates the index classified according to its economic sectors.

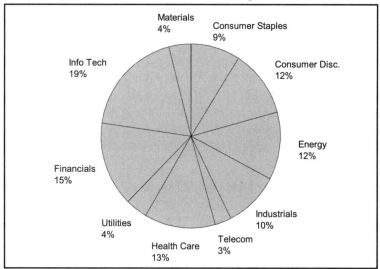

Standard and Poor's, Understanding Sectors, June 30, 2010

For more information on Standard and Poor's Global Industry Classification Standard (GICS©), refer to www.standardandpoors.com

Investment Products – Which One Is The Right One?

There are many ways to take advantage of the seasonal trends at the broad stock market and sector levels. Regardless of the investment products that you currently use, whether exchange traded funds, mutual funds, stocks or options, all can be used with the strategies in this book. Different investments offer different risk-reward relationships and return potential.

Exchange Traded Funds (ETFs)

Exchange Traded Funds (ETFs) offer the purest method of seasonal investment. The broad market ETFs are designed to track the major indices and the sector ETFs are designed to track specific sectors without using active management. Relatively new, ETFs are a great way to capture both market and sector trends. They were originally introduced into the Canadian market in 1993 to represent the Toronto stock market index. Shortly afterward they were introduced to the U.S. market and there are now hundreds of ETFs to represent almost every market, sector, style of investing and company capitalization. Originally ETFs were mainly of interest to institutional investors, but individual investors have fast realized the merits of ETF investing and have made some of the broad market ETFs the most heavily traded securities in the world.

An ETF is a single security that represents a market, such as the S&P 500; a sector of the market, such as the financial sector; or a commodity, such as gold. In the case of the S&P 500, an investor buying one security is buying all 500 stocks in the index. By investing into a financial ETF, an investor is buying the companies that make up the financial sector of the market. By investing into a gold commodity ETF, an investor is buying a security that represents the price of gold.

ETFs trade on the open market just like stocks. They have a bid and an ask, can be shorted and many are option eligible. They are a very low cost, tax efficient method of targeting specific parts of the market.

Mutual Funds

Mutual funds are a good way to combine market or sector investing with active management. In recent years, many mutual fund companies have added sector funds to accommodate an increasing appetite in this area.

As the seasonal strategies put forward in this book have a short-term nature, it is important to make sure that there are no fees (or a nominal charge) for getting into and out of a position in the market.

Stocks

Stocks provide an opportunity to make better returns than the market or sector. If the market increases during its seasonal period, some stocks will increase dramatically more than the index. Choosing one of the outperforming stocks will greatly enhance returns; choosing one of the underperforming stocks can create substantial loses. Using stocks requires increased attention to diversification and security selection.

Options

Disclaimer: Options involve risk and are not suitable for every investor. Because they are cash-settled, investors should be aware of the special risks associated with index options and should consult a tax advisor. Prior to buying or selling options, a person must receive a copy of Characteristics and Risks of Standardized Options and should thoroughly understand the risks involved in any use of options. Copies may be obtained from The Options Clearing Corporation, 440 S. LaSalle Street, Chicago, IL 60605.

Options, for more sophisticated investors, are a good tool to take advantage of both market and sector opportunities. An option position can be established with either stocks or ETFs. There are many different ways to use options for seasonal trends: establish a long position on the market during its seasonally strong period, establish a short position during its seasonally weak period, or create a spread trade to capture the superior gains of a sector over the market.

THACKRAY'S 2013 INVESTOR'S GUIDE

CONTENTS

JANUARY

MONDAY	TUESDAY	WEDNESDAY
31	**1** 30	**2** 29
WEEK 01	CAN Closed - New Year's Day USA Market Closed - New Year's Day	
7 24	**8** 23	**9** 22
WEEK 02		
14 17	**15** 16	**16** 15
WEEK 03		
21 10	**22** 9	**23** 8
WEEK 04 USA Market Closed- Martin Luther King Jr. Day		
28 3	**29** 2	**30** 1
WEEK 05		

THURSDAY	FRIDAY
3 28	**4** 27
10 21	**11** 20
17 14	**18** 13
24 7	**25** 6
31	1

FEBRUARY

M	T	W	T	F	S	S
				1	2	3
4	5	6	7	8	9	10
11	12	13	14	15	16	17
18	19	20	21	22	23	24
25	26	27	28			

MARCH

M	T	W	T	F	S	S
				1	2	3
4	5	6	7	8	9	10
11	12	13	14	15	16	17
18	19	20	21	22	23	24
25	26	27	28	29	30	31

APRIL

M	T	W	T	F	S	S
1	2	3	4	5	6	7
8	9	10	11	12	13	14
15	16	17	18	19	20	21
22	23	24	25	26	27	28
29	30					

MAY

M	T	W	T	F	S	S
		1	2	3	4	5
6	7	8	9	10	11	12
13	14	15	16	17	18	19
20	21	22	23	24	25	26
27	28	29	30	31		

JANUARY
S U M M A R Y

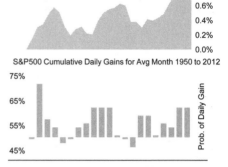

S&P500 Cumulative Daily Gains for Avg Month 1950 to 2012

	Dow Jones	S&P 500	Nasdaq	TSX Comp
Month Rank	6	5	1	4
# Up	40	38	26	16
# Down	22	24	14	11
% Pos	65	61	65	59
% Avg. Gain	1.0	1.1	2.6	1.0

Dow & S&P 1950-2011, Nasdaq 1972-2011, TSX 1985-2011

♦ Traditionally, January tends to be a positive month for the stock market and it often sets the sentiment for the rest of the year. January 2011 and 2012 produced gains of 2.3% and 4.4% respectively. ♦ The retail sector starts its seasonal trend in January- it has been positive over the last five years and performed strongly in 2012. ♦ Silver starts its seasonal trade in January and in January 2012 it strongly outperformed the S&P 500. ♦ Three defensive sectors, utilities, telecom and consumer staples tend to perform poorly in January.

BEST / WORST JANUARY BROAD MKTS. 2003-2012

BEST JANUARY MARKETS
- ♦ Russell 2000 (2006) 8.9%
- ♦ Nasdaq (2012) 8.0%
- ♦ Russell 2000 (2012) 7.0%

WORST JANUARY MARKETS
- ♦ Russell 3000 Value (2009) -11.9%
- ♦ Russell 2000 (2009) -11.2%
- ♦ Nasdaq (2008) -9.9%

Index Values End of Month

	2003	2004	2005	2006	2007	2008	2009	2010	2011	2012
Dow	8,054	10,488	10,490	10,865	12,622	12,650	8,001	10,067	11,892	12,633
S&P 500	856	1,131	1,181	1,280	1,438	1,379	826	1,074	1,286	1,312
Nasdaq	1,321	2,066	2,062	2,306	2,464	2,390	1,476	2,147	2,700	2,814
TSX	6,569	8,521	9,204	11,946	13,034	13,155	8,695	11,094	13,552	12,452
Russell 1000	873	1,163	1,219	1,341	1,507	1,444	860	1,133	1,371	726
Russell 2000	925	1,443	1,551	1,822	1,989	1,773	1,102	1,496	1,942	793
Russell 3000 Growth	1,378	1,872	1,871	2,066	2,238	2,214	1,386	1,879	2,330	2,433
Russell 3000 Value	1,668	2,229	2,450	2,717	3,151	2,883	1,638	2,100	2,507	2,490

Percent Gain for January

	2003	2004	2005	2006	2007	2008	2009	2010	2011	2012
Dow	-3.5	0.3	-2.7	1.4	1.3	-4.6	-8.8	-3.5	2.7	3.4
S&P 500	-2.7	1.7	-2.5	2.5	1.4	-6.1	-8.6	-3.7	2.3	4.4
Nasdaq	-1.1	3.1	-5.2	4.6	2.0	-9.9	-6.4	-5.4	1.8	8.0
TSX	-0.7	3.7	-0.5	6.0	1.0	-4.9	-3.3	-5.5	0.8	4.2
Russell 1000	-2.5	1.8	-2.6	2.7	1.8	-6.1	-8.3	-3.7	2.3	4.8
Russell 2000	-2.9	4.3	-4.2	8.9	1.6	-6.9	-11.2	-3.7	-0.3	7.0
Russell 3000 Growth	-2.5	2.2	-3.5	2.4	2.5	-8.0	-5.1	-4.4	2.2	6.0
Russell 3000 Value	-2.6	1.7	-2.1	4.1	1.1	-4.2	-11.9	-3.0	1.9	3.8

January Market Avg. Performance 2003 to 2012[1]

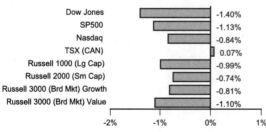

Dow Jones	-1.40%
SP500	-1.13%
Nasdaq	-0.84%
TSX (CAN)	0.07%
Russell 1000 (Lg Cap)	-0.99%
Russell 2000 (Sm Cap)	-0.74%
Russell 3000 (Brd Mkt) Growth	-0.81%
Russell 3000 (Brd Mkt) Value	-1.10%

Interest Corner Jan[2]

	Fed Funds %[3]	3 Mo. T-Bill %[4]	10 Yr %[5]	20 Yr %[6]
2012	0.25	0.06	1.83	2.59
2011	0.25	0.15	3.42	4.33
2010	0.25	0.08	3.63	4.38
2009	0.25	0.24	2.87	3.86
2008	3.00	1.96	3.67	4.35

(1) Russell Data provided by Russell (2) Federal Reserve Bank of St. Louis- end of month values (3) Target rate set by FOMC (4)(5)(6) Constant yield maturities.

THACKRAY SECTOR THERMOMETER

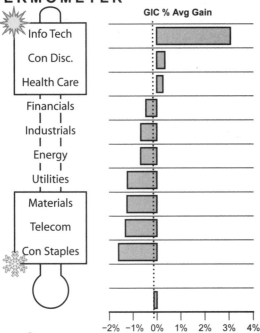

GIC[2] % Avg Gain	Fq % Gain >S&P 500	SP GIC SECTOR 1990-2011[1]
3.1 %	77 %	Information Technology
0.3	50	Consumer Discretionary
0.3	59	Health Care
-0.5	64	Financials
-0.7	32	Industrials
-0.7	41	Energy
-1.2	32	Utilities
-1.2	41	Materials
-1.3	45	Telecom
-1.6 %	27 %	Consumer Staples
-0.1 %	N/A %	S&P 500

Sector Commentary

♦ After underperforming in November and December, the materials sector took off with a vengeance in January 2012, producing a return of 11.1%. This is not typical for January and for the next five months the materials sector underperformed the S&P 500 to pay back for its short January burst. ♦ The financial sector was the second leading sector, producing a return of 8.0%. When the financial sector performs strongly, particularly when it is not seasonally one of the top sectors, it is a sign of a healthy stock market. ♦ In January 2012, the three defensive sectors, consumer staples, utilities and telecom, were at the bottom of the performance ranking, producing losses of 1.7%, 3.7% and 3.9% respectively. This is typical at this time of the year for these sectors. With a low frequency of outperforming the S&P 500, the consumer staples sector often makes a good choice to short sell.

Sub-Sector Commentary

♦ In January 2012, silver, gold and the metals and mining sector were the top three sub-sectors. They produced gains of 19.2%, 13.9% and 13.8%, respectively. January is often a strong month for silver in which it is one of the top performing sub-sectors. Its rise in 2012 was mainly the result of its sharp correction at the end of 2011.

		SELECTED SUB-SECTORS 1990-2011[3]
2.5 %	55 %	Homebuilders
2.3	68	Software & Services
2.2	64	Silver (London)
1.2	45	Biotech (93-2011)
1.1	55	Steel
1.0	55	Railroads
0.6	55	Gold (London PM)
0.1	44	Agriculture (94-2011)
-0.1	50	Banks
-0.2	55	Pharmaceuticals
-0.3	45	Transportation
-0.3	50	Retail
-1.1	45	Metals and Mining
-1.2	43	Chemicals

(1) Sector data provided by Standard and Poors (2) GIC is short form for Global Industry Classification (3) Sub Sector data provided by Standard and Poors, except where marked by symbol.

THACKRAY SECTOR THERMOMETER PORTFOLIO (TSTP) BEATS MARKET BY 13% per year (Avg.) (1990-2011)

The *Thackray Sector Thermometer* strategy is in the 2013 book as it shows the strength of seasonality on a monthly basis and the importance of asset allocation. Although it is best for investors to implement specific strategies based upon seasonal strength, many investors have successfully overweighted their portfolios based upon the top three sectors (S&P GIC) in the *Thackray Sector Thermometer Portfolio*.

From a portfolio perspective, funds are divided up evenly amongst the three top sectors at the beginning of each month. At the end of the month, the three sectors are sold and the proceeds are invested in the top three sectors for the next month. The process repeats itself with the accumulated funds being invested at the start of each month. Funds are accumulated month by month until the end of the time period.

For each month, the same sectors are used from year to year, over the study period. For example the same three sectors would be used every January.

TSTP Avg. Gain of 21% vs. 8% for S&P 500

Following the *Thackray Sector Thermometer Portfolio* (TSTP) strategy from 1990 to 2011 has produced an average return of 21%, compared with the S&P 500 which produced an average gain of 8% over the same period. To illustrate how much of an impact investing in different sectors of the market can have on a portfolio, the same sector selection process was used for the three worst performing sectors. Investing in the three worst sectors from 1990 to 2011 has produced an average loss of 3% per year.

Hot and Cold Box Sector Portfolios

The *Hot Box* refers to the top three sectors on the Thackray Sector Thermometer tagged with an image of the sun.

The *Cold Box* refers to the bottom three sectors tagged with an image of a snowflake.

Monthly results for each sector in the Hot and Cold Boxes are posted on the Monthly Sector Performance pages beside the Thackray Sector Thermometer (TST).

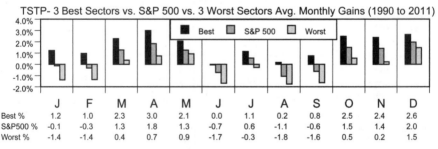

TSTP- 3 Best Sectors vs. S&P 500 vs. 3 Worst Sectors Avg. Monthly Gains (1990 to 2011)

	J	F	M	A	M	J	J	A	S	O	N	D	Avg. Year Gain
Best %	1.2	1.0	2.3	3.0	2.1	0.0	1.1	0.2	0.8	2.5	2.4	2.6	21.3%
S&P500 %	-0.1	-0.3	1.3	1.8	1.3	-0.7	0.6	-1.1	-0.6	1.5	1.4	2.0	7.6%
Worst %	-1.4	-1.4	0.4	0.7	0.9	-1.7	-0.3	-1.8	-1.6	0.5	0.2	1.5	-2.9%

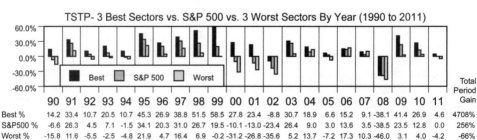

TSTP- 3 Best Sectors vs. S&P 500 vs. 3 Worst Sectors By Year (1990 to 2011)

	90	91	92	93	94	95	96	97	98	99	00	01	02	03	04	05	06	07	08	09	10	11	Total Period Gain
Best %	14.2	33.4	10.7	20.5	10.7	45.3	26.9	38.8	51.5	58.5	27.8	23.4	-8.8	30.7	18.9	6.6	15.2	9.1	-38.1	41.4	26.9	4.6	4708%
S&P500 %	-6.6	26.3	4.5	7.1	-1.5	34.1	20.3	31.0	26.7	19.5	-10.1	-13.0	-23.4	26.4	9.0	3.0	13.6	3.5	-38.5	23.5	12.8	0.0	256%
Worst %	-15.8	11.6	-5.5	-2.5	-4.8	21.9	4.7	16.4	6.9	-0.2	-31.2	-26.8	-35.6	5.2	13.7	-7.2	17.3	10.3	-46.0	3.1	4.0	-4.2	-66%

TSTP 2011 Best 3 Sectors vs. S&P 500 vs. Worst 3 Sectors

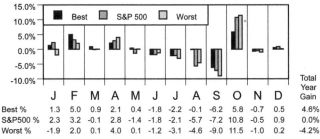

	J	F	M	A	M	J	J	A	S	O	N	D	Total Year Gain
Best %	1.3	5.0	0.9	2.1	0.4	-1.8	-2.2	-0.1	-6.2	5.8	-0.7	0.5	4.6%
S&P500 %	2.3	3.2	-0.1	2.8	-1.4	-1.8	-2.1	-5.7	-7.2	10.8	-0.5	0.9	0.0%
Worst %	-1.9	2.0	0.1	4.0	-1.1	-1.2	-3.1	-4.6	-9.0	11.5	-1.0	0.2	-4.2%

The year 2011 was anything but typical, as the defensive sectors outperformed the cyclical sectors in the spring and then the cyclical sectors took off early in October. Usually the defensive sectors outperform in the summer months and the cyclical sectors start their outperformance in late October. Despite this counter-trend, the TSTP managed to outperform the S&P 500.

% Monthly Gains Ranked by TSTP vs. S&P 500 (JAN-JUN 2011/12, JUL-DEC 2011)

2012	2011	JAN	2012	2011	FEB	2012	2011	MAR
4.4	2.3	S&P 500	4.1	3.2	S&P 500	3.1	-0.1	S&P 500
7.6	4.2	Info Tech	5.5	6.8	Energy	-3.4	1.5	Energy
5.9	-0.7	Cons. Disc.	-0.5	2.5	Materials	1.2	1.7	Industrials
3.0	0.4	Health Care	4.5	5.8	Cons. Disc.	4.4	-0.6	Cons. Disc.
8.0	2.8	Financials	3.4	2.4	Cons. Staples	0.1	1.7	Materials
6.9	4.2	Industrials	2.3	2.0	Industrials	7.3	-2.7	Financials
1.5	7.3	Energy	4.8	2.8	Financials	1.0	5.2	Telecom
-3.7	1.1	Utilities	7.2	1.8	Info Tech	1.0	-0.2	Utilities
11.1	-0.1	Materials	1.0	2.8	Health Care	5.0	-2.7	InfoTech
-3.9	-3.8	Telecom	0.0	0.8	Utilities	3.0	1.1	Cons. Staples
-1.7	-1.8	Cons. Staples	3.7	2.3	Telecom	4.3	1.7	Health Care

2012	2011	APR	2012	2011	MAY	2012	2011	JUN
-0.7	2.8	S&P 500	-6.3	-1.4	S&P 500	4.0	-1.8	S&P 500
-1.0	1.5	Energy	-1.3	2.4	Cons. Staples	5.6	-1.3	Health Care
-1.0	2.1	Materials	-9.3	-3.4	Financials	5.4	-1.5	Telecom
-1.1	2.7	Industrials	-3.9	2.2	Health Care	2.9	-2.6	Info Tech
-2.5	-0.1	Financials	-5.6	-0.5	Cons. Disc.	3.8	-0.5	Utilities
-1.9	2.9	Info Tech	-10.6	-4.6	Energy.	3.3	-2.9	Cons. Staples
1.2	3.9	Cons. Disc.	-7.8	-1.8	Info Tech	5.6	-1.9	Energy
1.8	3.8	Utilities	-8.0	-2.9	Materials	3.5	-0.8	Industrials
-0.3	6.4	Health Care	-6.4	-3.0	Industrials	1.8	-0.3	Cons. Disc.
0.1	5.1	Cons. Staples	-0.1	1.6	Utilities	4.9	-2.9	Financials
4.2	0.7	Telecom	2.6	1.6	Telecom	4.6	-0.5	Materials

2011	JUL	2011	AUG	2011	SEP
-2.1	S&P 500	-5.7	S&P 500	-7.2	S&P 500
-3.7	Financials	1.7	Utilities	-1.4	Telecom
-3.4	Materials	0.4	Cons. Staples	-4.6	Health Care
0.6	Energy	-2.4	Health Care	-12.6	Energy
1.6	Info Tech	-6.2	Info Tech	-0.1	Utilities
-1.6	Cons. Staples	-10.0	Energy	-3.7	Cons. Staples
-7.0	Industrials	-6.8	Industrials	-11.6	Financials
-3.9	Health Care	-9.7	Financials	-9.4	Industrials
-1.5	Cons. Disc.	-5.5	Cons. Disc.	-3.4	Info Tech
-1.1	Utilities	-6.9	Materials	-7.0	Cons. Disc.
-6.7	Telecom	-1.4	Telecom	-16.6	Materials

2011	OCT	2011	NOV	2011	DEC
10.8	S&P 500	-0.5	S&P 500	0.9	S&P 500
11.5	Info Tech	-1.9	Info Tech	0.9	Industrials
4.3	Cons. Staples	-0.9	Cons. Disc.	3.0	Utilities
1.8	Telecom	0.7	Health Care	-2.4	Materials
11.8	Cons. Disc.	-0.1	Materials	3.7	Telecom
5.6	Health Care	0.6	Industrials	1.6	Financials
17.6	Materials	2.4	Cons. Staples	1.0	Cons. Disc.
14.2	Financials	0.8	Telecom	2.8	Health Care
13.9	Industrials	-5.0	Financials	-1.1	Energy
17.0	Energy	1.7	Energy	2.4	Cons. Staples
3.5	Utilities	0.5	Utilities	-0.9	Info Tech

WEEK 01

Market Indices & Rates
Weekly Values**

Stock Markets	2011	2012
Dow	11,691	12,398
S&P500	1,273	1,278
Nasdaq	2,698	2,660
TSX	13,346	12,215
FTSE	6,015	5,661
DAX	6,967	6,102
Nikkei	10,462	8,480
Hang Seng	23,667	18,753

Commodities	2011	2012
Oil	89.53	102.39
Gold	1373.0	1606.6

Bond Yields	2011	2012
USA 5 Yr Treasury	2.04	0.88
USA 10 Yr T	3.40	1.99
USA 20 Yr T	4.26	2.71
Moody's Aaa	5.01	3.87
Moody's Baa	6.09	5.28
CAN 5 Yr T	2.48	1.29
CAN 10 Yr T	3.20	1.97

Money Market	2011	2012
USA Fed Funds	0.25	0.25
USA 3 Mo T-B	0.14	0.02
CAN tgt overnight rate	1.00	1.00
CAN 3 Mo T-B	0.98	0.81

Foreign Exchange	2011	2012
USD/EUR	1.31	1.29
USD/GBP	1.55	1.55
CAN/USD	1.00	1.02
JPY/USD	82.70	76.89

JANUARY

M	T	W	T	F	S	S
	1	2	3	4	5	6
7	8	9	10	11	12	13
14	15	16	17	18	19	20
21	22	23	24	25	26	27
28	29	30	31			

FEBRUARY

M	T	W	T	F	S	S
				1	2	3
4	5	6	7	8	9	10
11	12	13	14	15	16	17
18	19	20	21	22	23	24
25	26	27	28			

MARCH

M	T	W	T	F	S	S
				1	2	3
4	5	6	7	8	9	10
11	12	13	14	15	16	17
18	19	20	21	22	23	24
25	26	27	28	29	30	31

SILVER — THREE BEST PERIODS
JAN to MAR, & SEP, & NOV

The silver strategy has been moved to the beginning of the book for 2013, as the major seasonal period starts in January. If there is only one time of the year that investors should look at investing in silver, it is the period from January to March. That is not to say that September and November cannot be fruitful, but greater emphasis should be given to the beginning of the year.

The three periods of strength are the result of silver being both a precious metal and an industrial metal. With two strong influences affecting silver, opportunities are produced in its yearly trends. The rise from January 1st to March 31st is mainly the result of increased economic activity at the start of the new year. Generally, this is the time of the year when positive expectations are formed for the economy over the upcoming year and as a result investors focus on the industrial aspect of silver, pushing up its price.

10.7% and
positive 69% of the time

Silver often performs well in September because of its relationship with gold as a precious metal. Gold often rises at this time of year as the result of the large quantities of gold jewellery that gets consumed in the fourth quarter of the year (see *Gold Shines* strategy). As gold often has a weak month in October, so does silver. Both silver and gold tend to turnaround in November and produce an average gain. As investors adjust their year-end portfolios in December, both gold and silver generally put in mediocre performances and underperform the S&P 500. Once again silver tends to outperform at the beginning of the year. It is important to note that when silver is in a bull run with lots of momentum, it will bridge the gaps, performing well in both October and December. Investors can benefit from using technical analysis to fine tune strategies in choosing buy and sell dates.

Source: Bank of England
London pricing is recognized as the world benchmark for silver prices.

Silver Performance
Jan-Mar, Sep & Nov 1984-2011

	Jan1 to Mar31	Sep1 to Sep30	Nov1 to Nov30	Compound Growth
1984	8.3 %	-0.1 %	-2.0 %	6.0 %
1985	5.9	-3.1	0.1	2.7
1986	-3.2	6.8	-4.0	-0.7
1987	19.4	1.3	5.4	27.5
1988	0.8	-4.5	-3.8	-7.4
1989	-4.7	4.2	6.4	5.6
1990	-4.8	-0.7	-3.2	-8.5
1991	-8.5	8.4	-0.6	-1.4
1992	6.7	1.3	-0.8	7.2
1993	6.0	-16.8	1.5	-10.5
1994	12.1	4.9	-5.1	11.7
1995	6.4	3.9	-3.4	6.8
1996	7.3	-6.0	-1.7	-0.9
1997	6.9	9.4	10.0	28.7
1998	5.8	12.5	-2.6	16.1
1999	0.4	9.8	-2.1	7.9
2000	-7.4	-0.5	-2.3	-10.0
2001	-5.4	9.2	-3.2	0.1
2002	3.4	-0.7	-1.0	1.7
2003	-4.4	0.2	4.2	-0.2
2004	31.2	-1.1	8.3	40.5
2005	5.5	11.7	5.7	24.6
2006	33.1	-8.3	13.3	38.2
2007	3.5	14.2	-0.6	17.5
2008	21.9	-5.8	9.1	25.2
2009	21.5	13.1	9.5	50.5
2010	3.0	17.0	13.2	36.4
2011	23.6	-26.4	-8.4	-16.6
Avg	6.9 %	1.9 %	1.5 %	10.7 %
Fq>0	75 %	57 %	43 %	69 %

Silver (London) - Avg. Year 1984 to 2011

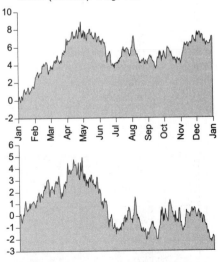

Silver / S&P 500 Rel. Strength- Avg Yr. 1984-2011

2011-12 Strategy Performance

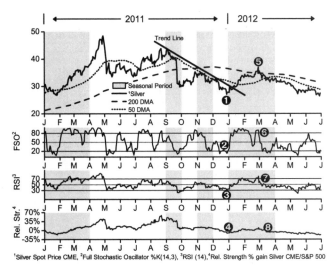

¹Silver Spot Price CME, ²Full Stochastic Oscillator %K(14,3), ³RSI (14),⁴Rel. Strength % gain Silver CME/S&P 500

Market Indices & Rates
Weekly Values**

Stock Markets	2011	2012
Dow	11,717	12,440
S&P500	1,281	1,290
Nasdaq	2,731	2,705
TSX	13,394	12,247
FTSE	6,009	5,656
DAX	7,004	6,131
Nikkei	10,528	8,439
Hang Seng	23,987	19,064

Commodities	2011	2012
Oil	91.03	100.44
Gold	1373.9	1636.6

Bond Yields	2011	2012
USA 5 Yr Treasury	1.96	0.83
USA 10 Yr T	3.36	1.95
USA 20 Yr T	4.26	2.66
Moody's Aaa	5.01	3.85
Moody's Baa	6.07	5.21
CAN 5 Yr T	2.52	1.28
CAN 10 Yr T	3.23	1.96

Money Market	2011	2012
USA Fed Funds	0.25	0.25
USA 3 Mo T-B	0.15	0.02
CAN tgt overnight rate	1.00	1.00
CAN 3 Mo T-B	0.96	0.78

Foreign Exchange	2011	2012
USD/EUR	1.32	1.27
USD/GBP	1.57	1.54
CAN/USD	0.99	1.02
JPY/USD	82.93	76.86

Silver (CME Spot Price) Performance

In 2011 and 2012, silver proved to be a volatile investment. As gold has become popular, interest in silver has increased. In 2011, during its best seasonal time, from January to March, silver produced a strong gain of 24%. During its next two seasonal periods in 2011, it produced losses. Right at the start of its strong seasonal period in January 2012, silver once again rose sharply. Overall, during the last year and a half, investing in silver during its strong seasonal periods has been positive and outperformed a buy and hold strategy.

Technical Conditions– January to March 2012

Entry Date January 1st, 2012 –Bullish– Although most investors would shy away from an investment that has corrected sharply, just before a seasonal period it often represents a very good buying opportunity, as was the case with silver at the beginning of 2012❶. The FSO turned up above 20❷, just before the entry date (bullish signal) the RSI bounced off 30❸ also just before the entry date (bullish signal). Shortly after entry, silver started to show signs of outperforming the S&P 500❹.

Entry Strategy –Buy Position on Entry Date– Positive price action accompanied by positive technical signals indicated a full allocation at the start of the seasonal trade. If investors did hold back part of their allocation, positive buying confirmation was given shortly after the entry date, as silver broke its trend line and then its 50 day moving average.

Exit Strategy– Sell Partial Position Early– Silver started to show weakness in early March turning down and crossing below its 50 day moving average. In the beginning of March, silver was trading below its 50 day moving average❺. Also in March, the FSO turned down below 80❻ and the RSI turned down below 70❼. Relative strength to the S&P 500 also started to deteriorate❽.

JANUARY

M	T	W	T	F	S	S
	1	2	3	4	5	6
7	8	9	10	11	12	13
14	15	16	17	18	19	20
21	22	23	24	25	26	27
28	29	30	31			

FEBRUARY

M	T	W	T	F	S	S
					1	2	3
4	5	6	7	8	9	10
11	12	13	14	15	16	17
18	19	20	21	22	23	24
25	26	27	28			

MARCH

M	T	W	T	F	S	S
				1	2	3
4	5	6	7	8	9	10
11	12	13	14	15	16	17
18	19	20	21	22	23	24
25	26	27	28	29	30	31

RETAIL – POST HOLIDAY BARGAIN
1st of II Retail Strategies for the Year
SHOP Jan 21st and RETURN Your Investment Apr 12th

Once again the retail sector outperformed the S&P 500 in 2012 during its seasonally strong period. This is the fifth straight year of outperformance and positive returns. The combination of strong returns and minimal drawdowns over the long-term make this one of the stronger seasonal trades.

A few weeks after the Christmas holidays, retail stocks go on sale, representing a good buying opportunity in mid to late January. The opportunity coincides with the earnings season.

Historically, the retail sector has outperformed from January 21st until April 12th - the start of the next earnings season. From 1990 to 2012, during its seasonally strong period, the retail sector has averaged 8.8%, compared with the S&P 500 which has averaged 2.2%. Not only has the retail sector had greater gains than the broad market, but it has also outperformed it on a fairly regular basis: 83% of the time.

6.6% extra & 83% of the time better than the S&P 500

Retail Sector vs. S&P 500 1990 to 2012			
Jan 21 to Apr 12	S&P 500	Positive Retail	Diff
1990	1.5 %	9.7 %	8.1 %
1991	14.5	29.9	15.4
1992	-2.9	-2.7	0.2
1993	3.5	-0.6	-4.0
1994	-5.8	2.0	7.8
1995	9.1	7.4	-1.8
1996	4.1	19.7	15.7
1997	-5.0	6.0	11.0
1998	13.5	20.1	6.6
1999	8.1	23.4	15.2
2000	1.5	5.8	4.3
2001	-11.8	-0.5	11.3
2002	-1.5	6.7	8.2
2003	-3.7	6.5	10.3
2004	0.6	6.7	6.1
2005	1.1	-1.6	-2.7
2006	2.1	3.4	1.3
2007	1.2	-0.7	-1.9
2008	0.6	3.5	3.0
2009	6.4	25.1	18.7
2010	5.1	15.5	10.4
2011	2.7	4.4	1.7
2012	5.5	12.1	6.6
Avg.	2.2 %	8.8 %	6.6 %
Fq > 0	74 %	78 %	83 %

Retail Sector - Avg. Year 1990 to 2011

Retail / S&P 500 Relative Strength - Avg Yr. 1990 - 2011

not nearly as strong as the cycle from January to April.

The January retail bounce coincides with the "rosy" stock market analysts' forecasts that tend to occur at the beginning of the year. These forecasts generally rely on healthy consumer spending as it makes up approximately 2/3 of the GDP. The retail sector benefits from the optimistic forecasts and tends to outperform the S&P 500.

From a seasonal basis, investors have been best served by exiting the retail sector in April and then returning to it later at the end of October (see *Retail Shop Early* strategy).

Most investors think the best time to invest in retail stocks is before Black Friday in November. Yes, there is a positive seasonal cycle at this time, but it is

(i) *Retail SP GIC Sector # 2550:*
An index designed to represent a cross section of retail companies
For more information on the retail sector, see www.standardandpoors.com.

2011-12 Strategy Performance

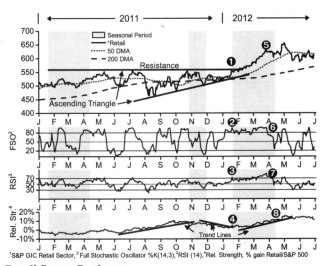

|←——— 2011 ———→ | 2012 ———→|

Seasonal Period
¹Retail
50 DMA
200 DMA
Resistance ❶
❺
Ascending Triangle
FSO² 80 50 20
RSI³ 70 50 30
Rel. Str.⁴ 20% 10% 0% -10%
❷
❻
❸
❼
❹
❽
Trend Lines
J F M A M J J A S O N D J F M A M J J

¹S&P GIC Retail Sector, ²Full Stochastic Oscillator %K(14,3),³RSI (14),⁴Rel. Strength, % gain Retail/S&P 500

Market Indices & Rates Weekly Values**

Stock Markets	2011	2012
Dow	11,839	12,601
S&P500	1,285	1,308
Nasdaq	2,721	2,768
TSX	13,406	12,319
FTSE	5,957	5,705
DAX	7,078	6,346
Nikkei	10,458	8,560
Hang Seng	24,122	19,676

Commodities	2011	2012
Oil	89.77	100.04
Gold	1358.2	1650.4

Bond Yields	2011	2012
USA 5 Yr Treasury	2.01	0.85
USA 10 Yr T	3.42	1.96
USA 20 Yr T	4.32	2.68
Moody's Aaa	5.07	3.83
Moody's Baa	6.12	5.20
CAN 5 Yr T	2.57	1.32
CAN 10 Yr T	3.28	1.98

Money Market	2011	2012
USA Fed Funds	0.25	0.25
USA 3 Mo T-B	0.16	0.04
CAN tgt overnight rate	1.00	1.00
CAN 3 Mo T-B	0.97	0.82

Foreign Exchange	2011	2012
USD/EUR	1.34	1.28
USD/GBP	1.59	1.54
CAN/USD	0.99	1.01
JPY/USD	82.57	76.91

Retail Sector Performance

Once again the retail sector performed very well during its seasonal period from January 21st to April 12th in 2012, producing a strong positive return and outperforming the S&P 500. The January to April seasonal period for the retail sector was the strongest period for the sector all year. The trade started right on time and finished up a bit past the seasonal exit date. With fairly strong economic numbers being printed at the beginning of January, the retail sector benefited from the expectation of strong sales. Even when investors started to doubt the economic growth later in the spring and deserted many of the cyclical sectors, the retail sector continued to perform well.

Technical Conditions – January 21st to April 12th, 2012
Entry Date Jan 21, 2012 – Bullish – A strong technical setup existed with the retail sector pushing up against resistance (favorable at the start of a seasonal trade)❶. The retail sector had just started to outperform the S&P 500❹, which trumps the negative indications of the FSO turning down below 80❷, and RSI turning below 70❸.

Entry Strategy – Buy Position on Entry Date– Conditions warranted a full allocation at the start of the seasonal period, as the retail sector had started to outperform the S&P 500 and was poised to break out of a bullish ascending triangle pattern.

Exit Strategy – Sell Partial Position Early– Technical indicators pointed to taking partial profits early. The retail sector started to turn down in late March❺, before the seasonal sell date in April. The FSO turned down below the 80❻ level in late March (bearish– signal to start exiting early). The RSI crossed below the 70❼ level in early April (bearish– signal to start exiting early). At exit date, the retail sector continued to outperform S&P 500 (bullish)❽.

JANUARY

M	T	W	T	F	S	S
	1	2	3	4	5	6
7	8	9	10	11	12	13
14	15	16	17	18	19	20
21	22	23	24	25	26	27
28	29	30	31			

FEBRUARY

M	T	W	T	F	S	S
				1	2	3
4	5	6	7	8	9	10
11	12	13	14	15	16	17
18	19	20	21	22	23	24
25	26	27	28			

MARCH

M	T	W	T	F	S	S
				1	2	3
4	5	6	7	8	9	10
11	12	13	14	15	16	17
18	19	20	21	22	23	24
25	26	27	28	29	30	31

TJX Companies Inc.
January 22nd to March 30th

In 2012, for the fifth straight year in a row, TJX during its seasonally strong period outperformed the S&P 500 and the retail sector. Over the long-term, this stock has typically outperformed the retail sector when the sector has been positive, making it an excellent complement to a retail sector investment at this time of the year.

TJX is an off-price apparel and home fashions retailer that typically reports its fourth quarter earnings approximately the third week of February. The company, like the retail sector, benefits from investors expecting positive results from the Christmas season.

TJX has a very similar period of seasonal strength as the retail sector. The best seasonal period for investing in TJX has been from January 22nd to March 30th. From 1990 to 2012, investing in this period has produced an average gain of 13.6%, which is substantially better than the 1.7% performance of the S&P 500. It is also important to note that the stock has been positive 74% of the time during this period.

13.6% & positive 74% of the time

Equally impressive is the amount of times TJX has produced a large gain, versus a large loss. In the last twenty-two years, TJX has only had one loss of 10% or greater. This compares to twelve times where the company had gains of 10% or greater.

TJX vs. Retail vs. S&P 500 1990 to 2012			
			Positive
Jan 22 to Mar 30	S&P 500	Retail	TJX
1990	0.2%	6.3%	6.7%
1991	13.3	21.7	61.9
1992	-2.3	1.7	17.0
1993	3.8	3.0	21.7
1994	-6.1	-0.1	-2.8
1995	8.1	9.7	-6.9
1996	5.5	19.7	43.6
1997	-1.1	10.4	-0.3
1998	12.6	19.7	25.4
1999	5.3	16.5	18.9
2000	3.2	5.1	35.4
2001	-13.6	1.7	16.4
2002	1.8	4.7	2.9
2003	-2.7	6.6	-6.7
2004	-1.8	5.4	3.5
2005	1.2	-0.6	-1.6
2006	3.1	4.5	3.8
2007	-0.7	-2.7	-10.2
2008	-0.8	1.4	13.1
2009	-6.3	8.1	29.0
2010	5.1	12.5	17.2
2011	3.5	3.5	6.1
2012	7.1	12.9	19.3
Avg	1.7%	14.4%	13.6%
Fq > 0	61%	87%	74%

It is interesting to note that the seasonally strong period for TJX ends before one of the strongest months of the year, April. It is possible that by the end of March, after a typically strong run for TJX that the full value of TJX's first quarter earnings report has already been priced into the stock and investors look to other companies in which to invest. This is particularly true if the economy and the stock market are in good shape.

On the other hand, in a soft economy, consumers favor off-price apparel companies such as TJX. In this scenario, TJX is more likely to perform strongly past the end of its seasonal period in March, allowing seasonal investors to continue to hold TJX until it shows signs of weakness.

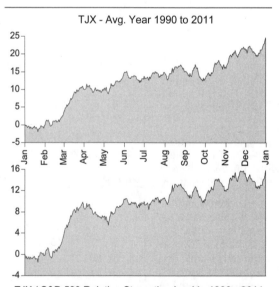

TJX - Avg. Year 1990 to 2011

TJX / S&P 500 Relative Strength - Avg Yr. 1990 - 2011

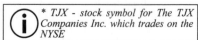

(i) *TJX - stock symbol for The TJX Companies Inc. which trades on the NYSE*

2011-12 Strategy Performance

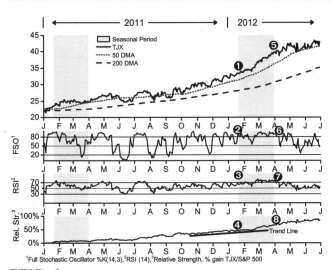

¹Full Stochastic Oscillator %K(14,3),²RSI (14),³Relative Strength, % gain TJX/S&P 500

Market Indices & Rates
Weekly Values**

Stock Markets	2011	2012
Dow	11,951	12,707
S&P500	1,291	1,318
Nasdaq	2,724	2,802
TSX	13,384	12,477
FTSE	5,935	5,757
DAX	7,103	6,466
Nikkei	10,410	8,825
Hang Seng	23,766	20,470

Commodities	2011	2012
Oil	86.82	99.31
Gold	1329.7	1688.8

Bond Yields	2011	2012
USA 5 Yr Treasury	1.98	0.84
USA 10 Yr T	3.40	2.01
USA 20 Yr T	4.29	2.77
Moody's Aaa	5.06	3.90
Moody's Baa	6.08	5.29
CAN 5 Yr T	2.55	1.37
CAN 10 Yr T	3.29	2.04

Money Market	2011	2012
USA Fed Funds	0.25	0.25
USA 3 Mo T-B	0.16	0.05
CAN tgt overnight rate	1.00	1.00
CAN 3 Mo T-B	0.96	0.85

Foreign Exchange	2011	2012
USD/EUR	1.37	1.31
USD/GBP	1.59	1.57
CAN/USD	1.00	1.01
JPY/USD	82.40	77.32

JANUARY

M	T	W	T	F	S	S
	1	2	3	4	5	6
7	8	9	10	11	12	13
14	15	16	17	18	19	20
21	22	23	24	25	26	27
28	29	30	31			

FEBRUARY

M	T	W	T	F	S	S
		1	2	3		
4	5	6	7	8	9	10
11	12	13	14	15	16	17
18	19	20	21	22	23	24
25	26	27	28			

MARCH

M	T	W	T	F	S	S
			1	2	3	
4	5	6	7	8	9	10
11	12	13	14	15	16	17
18	19	20	21	22	23	24
25	26	27	28	29	30	31

TJX Performance

TJX was a stellar performer throughout 2011 and the beginning of 2012. From October 2011 it remained solidly above its 50 day moving average. The stock benefited from being in the retail sector which was a stronger performer than the S&P 500, and it also benefited from being a defensive retailer, attracting investors that were taking a cautious stance in the market. As a result, it performed well in both stronger and weaker market conditions. During its seasonal period in 2012, TJX produced a gain of 19.3%, which compares to the S&P 500 which produced a respectable 7.1%.

Technical Conditions– January 22nd to March 30th, 2012
Entry Date January 22nd, 2012 –Bullish– Even before its seasonal start date, TJX was on a solid roll remaining above its 200 day moving average❶. Although on a technical basis TJX was overbought with the FSO above 80❷ and the RSI touching 70❸: TJX was continuing to outperform the S&P 500❹. This scenario is considered bullish until the price action of TJX shows signs of breaking down.

Entry Strategy –Buy Position on Entry Date– Although TJX was overbought according to the FSO and the RSI, it had a very positive price action and was outperforming the S&P 500.

Exit Strategy– Sell Partial Position on Exit Date– TJX had still not shown signs of rolling over on the exit date, as it remained above its 50 day moving average❺ and its FSO was still above 80❻ and its RSI still above 70❼. In addition TJX was still outperforming the S&P 500❽. Short-term sell signals from the FSO and RSI were triggered in early April as they both crossed below 80 and 70, respectively, confirming a full exit from TJX.

UNPLUG THE CHRISTMAS TREE
SHORT UTILITIES – Jan 1st to Mar 13th

At the beginning of the year, investors are more interested in growth investments rather than dividend investments. As a result, the utilities sector tends to underperform the S&P 500 up until mid-March.

If investors are looking for a strategy to reduce their portfolio risk at the beginning of the year, shorting the utilities sector should be a consideration.

3.6% extra and successful 61% of the time

Pairing up a short position in the utilities sector with a long position in the S&P 500 has performed well, regardless of the market direction. From 1990 to 2012, the utilities sector has only managed to beat the S&P 500 approximately one-quarter of the time. The largest loss shorting the utilities sector was 7.9% in 1993. The next largest loss was 4.0% in 2005. Overall, shorting the utilities sector has produced low drawdowns with a fairly strong positive upside.

Jan 1 to Mar 13	S&P 500	Negative Utilities	Diff
1990	-4.9 %	-7.6 %	-2.7 %
1991	13.4	0.8	-12.6
1992	-2.7	-9.1	-6.4
1993	3.2	7.9	4.6
1994	0.0	-7.6	-7.5
1995	6.7	3.2	-3.6
1996	3.7	-5.5	-9.2
1997	6.6	-3.3	-9.9
1998	10.1	0.3	-9.8
1999	5.3	-5.8	-11.1
2000	-5.8	-0.7	5.1
2001	-9.3	-9.1	0.2
2002	0.5	-1.8	-2.3
2003	-5.5	-8.4	-2.9
2004	0.8	2.4	1.6
2005	-1.0	4.0	5.0
2006	2.9	0.5	-2.3
2007	-2.8	3.0	5.9
2008	-10.4	-10.7	-0.3
2009	-16.2	-19.4	-3.2
2010	3.1	-4.8	-7.9
2011	3.7	2.9	-0.8
2012	11	-1.7	-12.7
Avg.	0.5 %	-3.1 %	-3.6 %
Fq > 0	57 %	39 %	26 %

S&P Utilities Sector vs. S&P 500 1990 to 2012

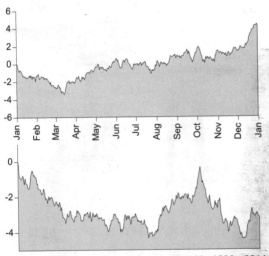

Utilities Sector - Avg. Year 1990 to 2011

Utilities / S&P 500 Relative Strength - Avg Yr. 1990 - 2011

formed the S&P 500, 26% of the time. In other words a pair trade with a long position in the S&P 500 and a short position in the utilities would have worked 74% of the time.

Very often the utilities sector puts in a strong run at the end of the year as investors sell their small-cap higher beta stocks for tax loss reasons and rotate into the more conservative utilities sector. When this phenomenon occurs and the utilities sector becomes overbought, this provides a very good opportunity to short the sector at the beginning of the year when the sector often corrects.

The average loss for the utilities sector has been 3.1% (gain for a short position) during its seasonal short period. This compares to a gain of 0.5% for the S&P 500. The real value for this trade is how often the utilities sector underperforms the S&P 500 during its seasonal period. Since 1990, the sector has underper-

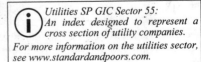

Utilities SP GIC Sector 55:
An index designed to represent a cross section of utility companies.
For more information on the utilities sector, see www.standardandpoors.com.

2011-12 Strategy Performance

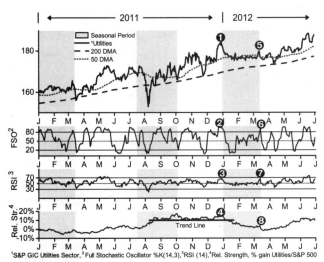

¹S&P GIC Utilities Sector, ²Full Stochastic Oscillator %K(14,3),³RSI (14),⁴Rel. Strength, % gain Utilities/S&P 500

Utilities Sector Performance

After a strong run at the end of 2011 and outperforming the S&P 500 in December, the utilities sector was primed for a correction at the beginning of the year. In 2012, the utilities sector started the year on a negative trend. Shorting the utilities sector played out very well as the sector put in a negative performance at the same time the broad market increased. The end result from shorting the utilities sector in 2012 during its seasonal period was a gain of 1.7%. During the same time period the S&P 500 produced a gain of 11%. If an investor took a short position in the utilities sector and a long position in the S&P 500, the total net gain from the pair trade would have been 12.7%.

Technical Conditions– January 1st to March 13th, 2012

Entry Date (SHORT) January 1st, 2012 –Bullish– The utilities sector was well above the 200 and 50 day moving averages❶. At the start of a negative seasonal trend, this is typically a good sign. In addition the FSO was overbought above 80❷ and the RSI was in the upper part of its band❸. Investors still had to be cautious, as the sector had not shown any signs of performing negatively relative to the S&P 500❹.

Entry Strategy –Sell Short Position on Entry Date– With the overbought condition occurring at the start of the seasonal trade, the probability of a successful trade was high, justifying a full entry on the strategy start date.

Exit Strategy –Cover Short Position on Exit Date– ❺The utilities sector had just started to show signs of outperformance at the end of its seasonal period with the FSO and RSI at the top of their ranges❻❼. The position should have been exited fully when the sector started to rise faster than the S&P 500 in late-March❽.

Market Indices & Rates Weekly Values**

Stock Markets	2011	2012
Dow	12,026	12,714
S&P500	1,303	1,324
Nasdaq	2,745	2,848
TSX	13,716	12,507
FTSE	5,960	5,768
DAX	7,171	6,588
Nikkei	10,389	8,823
Hang Seng	23,613	20,476

Commodities	2011	2012
Oil	90.68	97.81
Gold	1335.7	1739.6

Bond Yields	2011	2012
USA 5 Yr Treasury	2.10	0.73
USA 10 Yr T	3.54	1.88
USA 20 Yr T	4.41	2.66
Moody's Aaa	5.19	3.80
Moody's Baa	6.17	5.13
CAN 5 Yr T	2.62	1.29
CAN 10 Yr T	3.38	1.94

Money Market	2011	2012
USA Fed Funds	0.25	0.25
USA 3 Mo T-B	0.15	0.07
CAN tgt overnight rate	1.00	1.00
CAN 3 Mo T-B	0.95	0.88

Foreign Exchange	2011	2012
USD/EUR	1.37	1.31
USD/GBP	1.61	1.58
CAN/USD	0.99	1.00
JPY/USD	81.75	76.33

JANUARY

M	T	W	T	F	S	S
						1
1	2	3	4	5	6	
7	8	9	10	11	12	13
14	15	16	17	18	19	20
21	22	23	24	25	26	27
28	29	30	31			

FEBRUARY

M	T	W	T	F	S	S
					1	2	3
4	5	6	7	8	9	10
11	12	13	14	15	16	17
18	19	20	21	22	23	24
25	26	27	28			

MARCH

M	T	W	T	F	S	S
				1	2	3
4	5	6	7	8	9	10
11	12	13	14	15	16	17
18	19	20	21	22	23	24
25	26	27	28	29	30	31

FEBRUARY

	MONDAY	TUESDAY	WEDNESDAY
WEEK 05	28	29	30
WEEK 06	**4** 24	**5** 23	**6** 22
WEEK 07	**11** 17	**12** 16	**13** 15

WEEK 08	**18** 10
	
	CAN Market Closed -
	          Family Day
	
	USA Market Closed -
	          Presidents' Day
		19 9	**20** 8

WEEK 09	**25** 3	**26** 2	**27** 1

THURSDAY	FRIDAY
31	**1** 27
7 21	**8** 20
14 14	**15** 13
21 7	**22** 6
28	1

MARCH

M	T	W	T	F	S	S
				1	2	3
4	5	6	7	8	9	10
11	12	13	14	15	16	17
18	19	20	21	22	23	24
25	26	27	28	29	30	31

APRIL

M	T	W	T	F	S	S
1	2	3	4	5	6	7
8	9	10	11	12	13	14
15	16	17	18	19	20	21
22	23	24	25	26	27	28
29	30					

MAY

M	T	W	T	F	S	S
		1	2	3	4	5
6	7	8	9	10	11	12
13	14	15	16	17	18	19
20	21	22	23	24	25	26
27	28	29	30	31		

JUNE

M	T	W	T	F	S	S
					1	2
3	4	5	6	7	8	9
10	11	12	13	14	15	16
17	18	19	20	21	22	23
24	25	26	27	28	29	30

FEBRUARY
S U M M A R Y

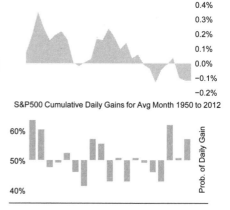

S&P500 Cumulative Daily Gains for Avg Month 1950 to 2012

	Dow Jones	S&P 500	Nasdaq	TSX Comp
Month Rank	9	11	9	5
# Up	35	33	20	15
# Down	27	29	20	12
% Pos	56	53	50	56
% Avg. Gain	0.0	-0.2	0.3	0.9

Dow & S&P 1950-2011, Nasdaq 1972-2011, TSX 1985-2011

♦ From 1950 to 2011, February has been the second worst month (S&P 500), producing an average loss of 0.2% and positive only 53% of the time ♦ In February 2012, the S&P 500 uncharacteristically performed extremely well producing a gain of 4.1% ♦ The oil sector tends to either do well in February or bottom towards the end of the month with a strong move into May, but this trade has not worked well in the last two years as investors became cautious early in the year and favored the defensive sectors. ♦

BEST / WORST FEBRUARY BROAD MKTS. 2003-2012

BEST FEBRUARY MARKETS
- Nasdaq (2012) 5.4%
- Russell 2000 (2011) 5.4%
- TSX Comp. (2005) 5.0%

WORST FEBRUARY MARKETS
- Russell 3000 Value (2009) -13.8%
- Russell 2000 (2009) -12.3%
- Dow (2009) -11.7%

Index Values End of Month

	2003	2004	2005	2006	2007	2008	2009	2010	2011	2012
Dow	7,891	10,584	10,766	10,993	12,269	12,266	7,063	10,325	12,226	12,952
S&P 500	841	1,145	1,204	1,281	1,407	1,331	735	1,104	1,327	1,366
Nasdaq	1,338	2,030	2,052	2,281	2,416	2,271	1,378	2,238	2,782	2,967
TSX	6,555	8,788	9,668	11,688	13,045	13,583	8,123	11,630	14,137	12,644
Russell 1000	858	1,178	1,244	1,341	1,478	1,396	768	1,168	1,415	756
Russell 2000	896	1,455	1,576	1,816	1,972	1,705	967	1,562	2,046	811
Russell 3000 Growth	1,367	1,880	1,889	2,059	2,195	2,165	1,276	1,942	2,407	2,542
Russell 3000 Value	1,619	2,272	2,522	2,725	3,094	2,755	1,412	2,164	2,596	2,577

Percent Gain for February

	2003	2004	2005	2006	2007	2008	2009	2010	2011	2012
Dow	-2.0	0.9	2.6	1.2	-2.8	-3.0	-11.7	2.6	2.8	2.5
S&P 500	-1.7	1.2	1.9	0.0	-2.2	-3.5	-11.0	2.9	3.2	4.1
Nasdaq	1.3	-1.8	-0.5	-1.1	-1.9	-5.0	-6.7	4.2	3.0	5.4
TSX	-0.2	3.1	5.0	-2.2	0.1	3.3	-6.6	4.8	4.3	1.5
Russell 1000	-1.7	1.2	2.0	0.0	-1.9	-3.3	-10.7	3.1	3.3	4.1
Russell 2000	-3.1	0.8	1.6	-0.3	-0.9	-3.8	-12.3	4.4	5.4	2.3
Russell 3000 Growth	-0.7	0.5	1.0	-0.3	-1.9	-2.2	-7.9	3.3	3.3	4.5
Russell 3000 Value	-3.0	1.9	2.9	0.3	-1.8	-4.5	-13.8	3.0	3.6	3.5

February Market Avg. Performance 2003 to 2012[1]

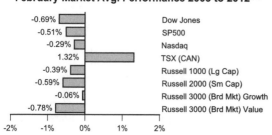

	-0.69%	Dow Jones
	-0.51%	SP500
	-0.29%	Nasdaq
	1.32%	TSX (CAN)
	-0.39%	Russell 1000 (Lg Cap)
	-0.59%	Russell 2000 (Sm Cap)
	-0.06%	Russell 3000 (Brd Mkt) Growth
	-0.78%	Russell 3000 (Brd Mkt) Value

Interest Corner Feb[2]

	Fed Funds % [3]	3 Mo. T-Bill % [4]	10 Yr % [5]	20 Yr % [6]
2012	0.25	0.08	1.98	2.73
2011	0.25	0.15	3.42	4.25
2010	0.25	0.13	3.61	4.40
2009	0.25	0.26	3.02	3.98
2008	3.00	1.85	3.53	4.37

(1) Russell Data provided by Russell (2) Federal Reserve Bank of St. Louis- end of month values (3) Target rate set by FOMC (4)(5)(6) Constant yield maturities.

THACKRAY SECTOR THERMOMETER

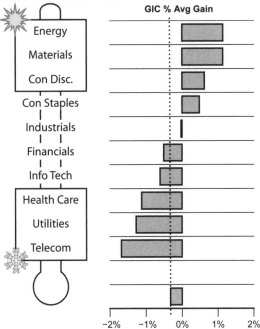

GIC[2] % Avg Gain	Fq % Gain >S&P 500	
SP GIC SECTOR 1990-2011[1]		
1.1 %	50 %	Energy
1.1	64	Materials
0.6	73	Consumer Discretionary
0.5	50	Consumer Staples
0.0	55	Industrials
-0.5	64	Financials
-0.6	50	Information Technology
-1.1	36	Health Care
-1.3	23	Utilities
-1.7 %	36 %	Telecom
-0.3 %	N/A %	S&P 500

Sector Commentary

♦ After coming off a strong month in January 2012, the technology sector continued to power ahead in the month of February, producing a gain of 7.2%. ♦ A lot of this gain was the result of Apple rising sharply and bringing the other technology stocks along for the ride. ♦ The energy sector produced a strong gain of 5.5% for the month, but this rise was in the first three-quarters of the month. In the last quarter of the month the sector started a multi-month decline. ♦ The financial sector continued to perform well, producing a gain of 4.8% and as a result indicated solid returns for the market in the near future.

Sub-Sector Commentary

♦ In February 2012, silver continued to power higher producing a gain of 10.8%. The two other sub-sectors at the top of the list were agriculture and homebuilders, both putting in strong out-of-season performances of 9.0%. The three worst sub-sectors in February 2012 were railroads, metals and mining and steel, producing losses of 4.5%, 5.6% and 6.4%, respectively.

SELECTED SUB-SECTORS 1990-2011[3]		
2.6 %	50 %	Silver (London)
1.7	59	Metals and Mining
1.6	71	Chemicals
1.4	73	Retail
1.0	50	Gold (London PM)
1.0	55	Steel
0.3	59	Transportation
0.0	50	Railroads
-0.3	59	Banks
-0.5	50	Agriculture (94-2011)
-0.6	59	Homebuilders
-0.6	45	Software & Services
-1.2	36	Pharmaceuticals
-2.0	50	Biotech (93-2011)

(1) Sector data provided by Standard and Poors (2) GIC is short form for Global Industry Classification (3) Sub Sector data provided by Standard and Poors, except where marked by symbol.

DuPont
January 28th to May 5th

Dupont has been positive for the last twelve years during its seasonally strong period, extending a record of being positive twenty-two times over the last twenty-three years. In 2012 and for the fifth year in a row, Dupont outperformed the S&P 500. The Dupont trade is considered a strong consistent performer at this time of the year.

DuPont is a diversified chemicals company that operates in seven segments: Agriculture & Nutrition, Electronics & Communications, Performance Chemicals, Performance Coatings, Performance Materials, Safety & Protection, and Pharmaceuticals.

The chemicals sector is a large part of the U.S. materials sector, which has a seasonally strong period from January 23rd to May 5th. DuPont has a similar seasonal trend that starts a few days later on January 28th. Investors can use technical analysis to determine if an earlier position in DuPont should be taken.

10.9% & positive 96% of the time

The DuPont seasonal trade has worked very well since 1990, producing an average gain of 10.9% with a very high 96% frequency rate of being positive.

DuPont vs. S&P 500
1990 to 2012

Jan 28 to May 5	S&P 500	DD	Diff
		Positive	
1990	3.9%	0.3%	-3.5%
1991	13.3	19.6	6.3
1992	0.5	11.7	11.3
1993	1.5	15.2	13.8
1994	-5.4	6.6	12.0
1995	10.6	21.6	11.0
1996	3.2	6.3	3.0
1997	8.5	4.6	-3.9
1998	15.1	34.9	19.7
1999	8.4	32.6	24.2
2000	2.4	-16.2	-18.6
2001	-6.5	12.8	19.3
2002	-5.3	3.2	8.4
2003	9.3	11.3	2.0
2004	-2.0	2.5	4.5
2005	-0.2	2.6	2.8
2006	3.3	13.4	10.1
2007	5.9	4.2	-1.7
2008	5.8	11.1	5.4
2009	6.9	24.9	18.1
2010	6.2	15.3	9.0
2011	2.7	7.2	4.4
2012	4.0	4.3	0.3
Avg	4.0%	10.9%	6.9%
Fq > 0	78%	96%	83%

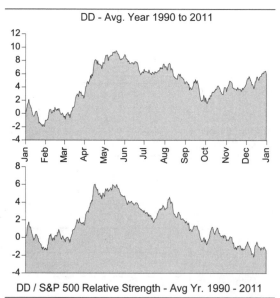

DD - Avg. Year 1990 to 2011

DD / S&P 500 Relative Strength - Avg Yr. 1990 - 2011

to 2011 Dupont has generated an average loss of 2.4% and was only positive 41% of the time. This compares to the S&P 500 which has produced an average gain of 3.7% and has been positive 68% of the time during the same time period.

If investors are interested in purchasing DuPont, on a seasonal basis it is clear that they should concentrate their efforts from the end of January to the beginning of May seasonal period.

Investors should be aware that DuPont does not perform as well as the broad market from May 6th to the end of the year. In fact, during this period, from 1990

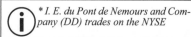

(i) * I. E. du Pont de Nemours and Company (DD) trades on the NYSE

2011-12 Strategy Performance

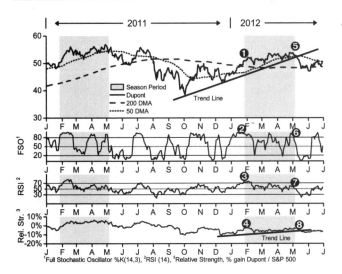

¹Full Stochastic Oscillator %K(14,3), ²RSI (14), ³Relative Strength, % gain Dupont / S&P 500

Market Indices & Rates Weekly Values**		
Stock Markets	**2011**	**2012**
Dow	12,227	12,860
S&P500	1,323	1,347
Nasdaq	2,794	2,911
TSX	13,819	12,496
FTSE	6,056	5,881
DAX	7,328	6,750
Nikkei	10,613	8,962
Hang Seng	23,148	20,844
Commodities	**2011**	**2012**
Oil	86.69	98.51
Gold	1358.7	1729.7
Bond Yields	**2011**	**2012**
USA 5 Yr Treasury	2.36	0.81
USA 10 Yr T	3.68	1.99
USA 20 Yr T	4.52	2.77
Moody's Aaa	5.28	3.89
Moody's Baa	6.22	5.17
CAN 5 Yr T	2.75	1.40
CAN 10 Yr T	3.46	2.04
Money Market	**2011**	**2012**
USA Fed Funds	0.25	0.25
USA 3 Mo T-B	0.14	0.09
CAN tgt overnight rate	1.00	1.00
CAN 3 Mo T-B	0.96	0.89
Foreign Exchange	**2011**	**2012**
USD/EUR	1.36	1.32
USD/GBP	1.61	1.58
CAN/USD	0.99	1.00
JPY/USD	82.74	77.13

Dupont Performance

In October 2011, Dupont started to steadily rise, performing approximately at market, which was increasing at the same time. Dupont continued to perform at market during its seasonal period and managed to only slightly outperform the S&P 500.

Dupont is a diversified chemical company that tends to benefit from stronger economic conditions. In the late spring, as economic expectations were reduced, Dupont started to underperform the S&P 500 (after the end of its seasonal period).

Technical Conditions– January 28th to May 5th, 2012

Entry Date January 28th, 2012 –Bullish– At the start of the seasonal trade Dupont was trading above its 50 and 200 day moving averages❶. Although the FSO and RSI were both in overbought territory❷❸, Dupont had already started to show some signs of outperforming the S&P 500❹. Overall, conditions were bullish for Dupont.

Entry Strategy –Buy Position on Entry Date– As a clear entry signal had not been given before the seasonal entry date, the first allocation to Dupont should have taken place at the entry date.

Exit Strategy – Sell Position on Exit Date– Dupont broke its upward trend line at the same time that it was ending its seasonal trade❺. The FSO at the beginning of May produced a sell signal as it crossed below 80❻. The RSI also indicated a weak trend as it crossed below 50❼. A confirming sell signal was made when Dupont started to underperform the S&P 500 shortly after the seasonal sell date❽.

FEBRUARY

M	T	W	T	F	S	S
				1	2	3
4	5	6	7	8	9	10
11	12	13	14	15	16	17
18	19	20	21	22	23	24
25	26	27	28			

MARCH

M	T	W	T	F	S	S
				1	2	3
4	5	6	7	8	9	10
11	12	13	14	15	16	17
18	19	20	21	22	23	24
25	26	27	28	29	30	31

APRIL

M	T	W	T	F	S	S
1	2	3	4	5	6	7
8	9	10	11	12	13	14
15	16	17	18	19	20	21
22	23	24	25	26	27	28
29	30					

** Weekly avg closing values- except Fed Funds & CAN overnight tgt rate weekly closing values.

OIL – WINTER/SPRING STRATEGY
1st of II Oil Stock Strategies for the Year
February 25th to May 9th

(Stocks)

For three years in a row, the energy sector has produced a loss and underperformed the S&P 500 during its winter-spring seasonal period. In 2012 the energy sector produced a loss of 13.4%, the worst performance over the last twenty-nine years. The losses over the last three years have all occurred before a large correction in the spring. Nevertheless, the *Oil-Winter/Spring Strategy* is still a strong seasonal performer over the long-term. From 1984 to 2012, for the two and half months starting on February 25th and ending May 9th, the energy sector (XOI) has outperformed the S&P 500 by an average 4.4%.

What is even more impressive are the positive returns 24 out of 29 times, and the outperformance of the S&P 500, 23 out of 29 times.

4.4% extra and 24 out of 29 times positive, in just over two months

XOI vs S&P 500 1984 to 2012			
Feb 25 to May 9	S&P 500	positive XOI	Diff
1984	1.7 %	5.6 %	3.9 %
1985	1.4	4.9	3.5
1986	6.0	7.7	1.7
1987	3.7	25.5	21.8
1988	-3.0	5.6	8.6
1989	6.3	8.1	1.8
1990	5.8	-0.6	-6.3
1991	4.8	6.8	2.0
1992	0.9	5.8	4.9
1993	0.3	6.3	6.0
1994	-4.7	3.2	7.9
1995	7.3	10.3	3.1
1996	-2.1	2.2	4.3
1997	1.8	4.7	2.9
1998	7.5	9.8	2.3
1999	7.3	35.4	28.1
2000	4.3	22.2	17.9
2001	0.8	10.2	9.4
2002	-1.5	5.3	6.9
2003	12.1	5.7	-6.4
2004	-3.5	4.0	7.5
2005	-1.8	-1.0	0.8
2006	2.8	9.4	6.6
2007	4.2	10.1	5.8
2008	2.6	7.6	5.0
2009	20.2	15.8	-4.4
2010	0.5	-2.3	-2.8
2011	3.1	-0.6	-3.7
2012	-0.8	-13.4	-12.5
Avg	3.0 %	7.4 %	4.4 %
Fq > 0	76 %	83 %	79 %

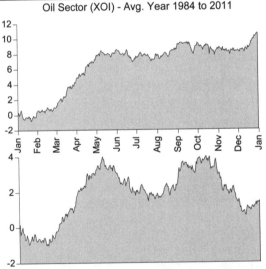

Oil Sector (XOI) - Avg. Year 1984 to 2011

Oil Sector / S&P 500 Relative Strength - Avg Yr. 1984 - 2011

A lot of investors assume that the time to buy oil stocks is just before the winter cold sets in. The rationale is that oil will climb in price as the temperature drops.

The results in the market have not supported this assumption. The dynamic of the price for a barrel of oil has more to do with oil inventory. Refineries have a choice: they can produce either gasoline or heating oil. As the winter progresses, refineries start to convert their operations from heating oil to gasoline.

During this switch-over time, low inventory levels of both heating oil and gasoline can drive up the price of a barrel of oil and oil stocks. In early May, before the kick-off of the driving season (Memorial Day in May), the refineries have finished their conversion to gasoline. The price of oil

(i) *Amex Oil Index (XOI):*
An index designed to represent a cross section of widely held oil corporations involved in various phases of the oil industry.
For more information on the XOI index, see www.cboe.com

2011-12 Strategy Performance

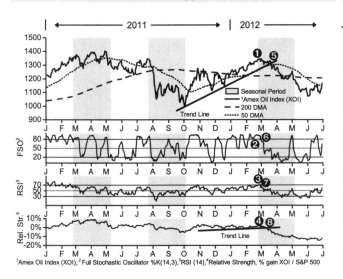

[1]Amex Oil Index (XOI), [2]Full Stochastic Oscillator %K(14,3), [3]RSI (14), [4]Relative Strength, % gain XOI / S&P 500

Market Indices & Rates
Weekly Values**

Stock Markets	2011	2012
Dow	12,298	12,877
S&P500	1,336	1,353
Nasdaq	2,823	2,938
TSX	14,032	12,412
FTSE	6,071	5,898
DAX	7,409	6,765
Nikkei	10,792	9,187
Hang Seng	23,215	21,188

Commodities	2011	2012
Oil	85.34	101.80
Gold	1374.3	1722.2

Bond Yields	2011	2012
USA 5 Yr Treasury	2.34	0.84
USA 10 Yr T	3.60	1.97
USA 20 Yr T	4.45	2.76
Moody's Aaa	5.26	3.84
Moody's Baa	6.15	5.15
CAN 5 Yr T	2.78	1.41
CAN 10 Yr T	3.48	2.04

Money Market	2011	2012
USA Fed Funds	0.25	0.25
USA 3 Mo T-B	0.11	0.11
CAN tgt overnight rate	1.00	1.00
CAN 3 Mo T-B	0.96	0.93

Foreign Exchange	2011	2012
USD/EUR	1.36	1.31
USD/GBP	1.61	1.58
CAN/USD	0.99	1.00
JPY/USD	83.45	78.59

Amex Oil Index (XOI) Performance

In 2011 and the beginning of 2012, the energy sector performed poorly relative to the S&P 500. Overall, the sector contracted because of the expectation of slower economic growth. To make matters worse, the sector underperformed during its seasonally strong period. Typically, the February to May seasonal period is a strong trade. In the last two years the energy sector has underperformed in this period, which indicated a weakness in the S&P 500 and ultimately pointed to its near term correction.

Technical Conditions– February 25th to May 9th, 2012
Entry Date February 25th, 2012 –Bullish– The energy sector was well above its 50 and 200 day moving averages and above its upward sloping trend line❶. The sector was initially overbought with the FSO above 80❷ and the RSI touching 70❸. With the energy sector performing at market❹, and strong price action above its trend line the initial setup was considered bullish.

Entry Strategy –Buy Position on Entry Date– Overall, justification to enter the trade existed, as there were no strong bearish signals.

Exit Strategy –Sell Position Early– Shortly after the seasonal buy date, the technical picture changed very fast. The sector broke its upward trend line❺. The FSO turned below 80❻ and the RSI turned back from 70❼. In addition, the energy sector started to underperform the S&P 500❽. With all of these negative technical signals, pulling back at least a partial position in the sector was warranted.

FEBRUARY
M	T	W	T	F	S	S
				1	2	3
4	5	6	7	8	9	10
11	12	13	14	15	16	17
18	19	20	21	22	23	24
25	26	27	28			

MARCH
M	T	W	T	F	S	S
				1	2	3
4	5	6	7	8	9	10
11	12	13	14	15	16	17
18	19	20	21	22	23	24
25	26	27	28	29	30	31

APRIL
M	T	W	T	F	S	S
1	2	3	4	5	6	7
8	9	10	11	12	13	14
15	16	17	18	19	20	21
22	23	24	25	26	27	28
29	30					

** Weekly avg closing values- except Fed Funds & CAN overnight tgt rate weekly closing values.

ROYAL BANK— A TRADE TO BANK ON
①Oct 10-Nov 28 ②Jan 23-Apr 13

Canadians love their banks and tend to hold large amounts of the banking sector in their portfolios. Their love for the sector has remained strong, as international accolades have supported a positive viewpoint of Canadian banks. In a 2012 Bloomberg report, the Canadian banks dominated the top ten strongest banks in the world, with four banks in the top ten.

For years, Royal Bank was considered one of the most conservative banks and often attracted investors during tough times. After a few mis-steps in their expansion into the U.S., Royal Bank seems to be getting back on track.

Through its ups and downs, Royal Bank has followed the same general pattern as the banking sector: rising in autumn and then once again in the new year.

12.6% gain & positive 74% of the time

In the period from October 10th to November 28th, from 1989 to 2011, Royal Bank has produced an average gain of 5.3% and has been positive 87% of the time. The bank tends to perform well at this time, as Canadians tend to increase their bank holdings before the year-end earnings reports are released in late November. It is not a coincidence that Royal Bank's seasonally strong period ends at approximately the same time as their year-end earnings announcements. Seasonal investors benefit from buying Royal Bank before the "masses," whom are also trying to take advantage of the possibility of positive earnings.

The second seasonal period from January 23rd to April 13 is also very positive. Canadian banks tend to outperform the TSX Composite, as they benefit from the typically strong economic forecasts at the beginning of the year. In addition, they "echo," or get a boost from the strong seasonal performance of the U.S banks at this time.

Royal Bank* vs. S&P/TSX Comp 1989/90 to 2011/12 Positive

Year	Oct 10 to Nov 28 TSX Comp	RY	Jan 23 to Apr 13 TSX Comp	RY	Compound Growth TSX Comp	RY
1989/90	-2.8 %	2.4 %	-6.3 %	-10.0 %	-8.9 %	-7.8 %
1990/91	0.2	3.5	9.8	11.6	10.0	15.5
1991/92	2.9	3.3	-6.8	-14.5	-4.1	-11.6
1992/93	1.8	5.0	10.7	17.6	12.6	23.4
1993/94	3.8	0.0	-5.6	-13.1	-2.1	-13.1
1994/95	-4.7	2.2	5.0	13.2	0.0	15.7
1995/96	4.0	3.3	3.6	0.0	7.7	3.3
1996/97	10.7	23.3	-6.2	1.3	3.9	24.9
1997/98	-8.7	7.6	19.9	24.0	9.4	33.4
1998/99	18.0	20.9	4.8	0.6	23.7	21.6
1999/00	10.9	8.6	3.8	34.5	15.1	46.0
2000/01	-14.5	5.1	-14.1	-12.0	-26.5	-7.5
2001/02	7.1	3.2	2.3	11.8	9.6	15.4
2002/03	16.4	18.1	-4.3	1.8	11.4	20.2
2003/04	3.4	0.3	2.0	1.8	5.4	2.1
2004/05	2.8	4.0	4.5	17.6	7.3	22.3
2005/06	3.1	7.3	5.5	7.0	8.8	14.8
2006/07	7.2	8.5	6.9	7.1	14.5	16.2
2007/08	-4.4	-5.1	8.2	-4.9	3.5	-9.8
2008/09	-3.4	4.3	9.4	35.0	5.7	40.8
2009/10	0.2	1.3	6.7	12.6	6.9	14.1
2010/11	2.9	0.4	4.3	12.4	7.3	12.8
2011/12	0.5	-6.3	-2.9	3.8	-2.4	-2.8
Avg.	2.5 %	5.3 %	2.7 %	6.9 %	5.2 %	12.6 %
Fq > 0	74 %	87 %	70 %	74 %	78 %	74 %

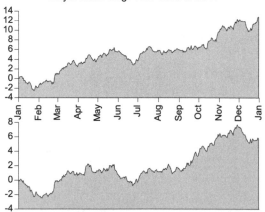

Royal Bank* Avg. Year 1990 to 2011

Royal Bank / TSX Comp. Rel. Str. - Avg Yr. 1990 - 2011

Ⓨ *Alternate Strategy—*
Investors can bridge the gap between the two positive seasonal trends for the bank sector by holding from October 10th to April 13th. Longer term investors may prefer this strategy, shorter term investors can use technical tools to determine the appropriate strategy.

ⓘ ** Royal Bank of Canada (RBC) is a diversified financial services company that trades on both the Toronto and NYSE exchanges under the symbol RY.*

2011-12 Strategy Performance

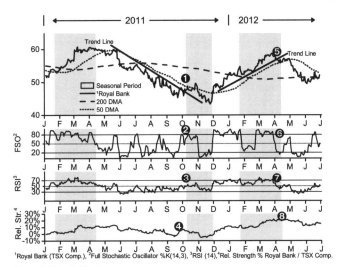

¹Royal Bank (TSX Comp.), ²Full Stochastic Oscillator %K(14,3), ³RSI (14),⁴Rel. Strength % Royal Bank / TSX Comp.

Royal Bank Performance

In 2011 and the first half of 2012, Royal Bank performed well relative to the TSX Composite. This is partly because the two other non-financial major sectors of the market, energy and materials performed poorly. Compared with the S&P 500, a much more diversified index, Royal Bank underperformed. Nevertheless, seasonal investors have benefited from being in the Royal Bank during periods of seasonal strength over the long-term.

Technical Conditions– October 10, 2011 to April 13, 2012

Entry Date October 10th, 2011 –Bullish– At the start of its seasonal cycle in October 2011, Royal Bank broke its downward trend line and was trading just below its 50 day moving average❶. A good start to the seasonal trade. The FSO was below 80 and rising❷ and the RSI was at a neutral 50❸. In the three weeks prior, Royal Bank had been outperforming the TSX Composite❹.

Entry Strategy –Buy Position on Entry Date– Initially the trade looked positive with the breakout of the down trend line and warranted a large allocation. The only drawback was that Royal Bank was just starting to underperform the TSX Composite. This trend persisted until the end of the first leg of the trade.

Exit Strategy – Sell Position on Exit Date– Assuming that investors hold Royal Bank during the time period between the end of its first seasonal period and the start of its second period, as most investors will hold their position during this time period, a full exit was warranted on April 13th. Just prior to its exit date, Royal Bank had crossed below its uptrend line and was at its 50 day moving average❺. The FSO had already traded below 80❻ in late March and the RSI had already come back from 70❼. On the exit date, Royal Bank was already showing signs of starting to underperform the market❽.

Market Indices & Rates
Weekly Values**

Stock Markets	2011	2012
Dow	12,129	12,968
S&P500	1,312	1,362
Nasdaq	2,750	2,951
TSX	13,960	12,695
FTSE	5,971	5,933
DAX	7,230	6,875
Nikkei	10,616	9,549
Hang Seng	22,999	21,448

Commodities	2011	2012
Oil	95.71	107.19
Gold	1405.5	1757.5

Bond Yields	2011	2012
USA 5 Yr Treasury	2.18	0.89
USA 10 Yr T	3.46	2.01
USA 20 Yr T	4.31	2.79
Moody's Aaa	5.17	3.85
Moody's Baa	6.06	5.15
CAN 5 Yr T	2.61	1.47
CAN 10 Yr T	3.32	2.05

Money Market	2011	2012
USA Fed Funds	0.25	0.25
USA 3 Mo T-B	0.13	0.09
CAN tgt overnight rate	1.00	1.00
CAN 3 Mo T-B	0.95	0.94

Foreign Exchange	2011	2012
USD/EUR	1.37	1.33
USD/GBP	1.62	1.58
CAN/USD	0.98	1.00
JPY/USD	82.40	80.17

FEBRUARY

M	T	W	T	F	S	S
				1	2	3
4	5	6	7	8	9	10
11	12	13	14	15	16	17
18	19	20	21	22	23	24
25	26	27	28			

MARCH

M	T	W	T	F	S	S
				1	2	3
4	5	6	7	8	9	10
11	12	13	14	15	16	17
18	19	20	21	22	23	24
25	26	27	28	29	30	31

APRIL

M	T	W	T	F	S	S
1	2	3	4	5	6	7
8	9	10	11	12	13	14
15	16	17	18	19	20	21
22	23	24	25	26	27	28
29	30					

Post-it Note– 3M Seasonal Outperforms
Feb 3rd to May 12th

In 2012, the 3M trade produced a slight loss and underperformed the S&P 500, but that does not invalidate the trade. Overall, in the spring time of 2012 the cyclical sectors which generally benefit from a rising economy, including the industrial sector, underperformed the market. 3M followed the industrial sector in its underperformance. The long-term trend of seasonal outperformance for 3M remains intact, as the stock was positive and outperformed the S&P 500 in the previous three years.

Many investors consider 3M to be a bellwether stock for the broad market. Although 3M can produce similar results as the market over the year, the stock still has a profitable seasonal pattern from February 3rd to May 12th.

7.2% & positive 70% of the time

The 3M seasonal pattern is very similar to the seasonal pattern for the industrial sector and provides an opportunity for investors looking to "juice" their returns in the spring.

3M vs. S&P 500 1990 to 2012			
			Positive
Feb 3 to May 12	S&P 500	3M	Diff
1990	6.4 %	6.2 %	-0.1 %
1991	9.5	6.2	-3.4
1992	1.8	6.5	4.6
1993	0.5	16.3	15.8
1994	-7.9	-6.8	1.1
1995	11.2	20.5	9.4
1996	2.6	-0.8	-3.3
1997	6.6	8.4	1.8
1998	11.4	7.1	-4.3
1999	8.1	24.1	16.0
2000	0.8	-8.2	-9.0
2001	-7.7	8.0	15.7
2002	-6.0	12.0	18.0
2003	10.5	-0.1	-10.5
2004	-3.4	9.4	12.8
2005	-2.8	-9.1	-6.2
2006	1.6	20.0	18.4
2007	4.0	15.8	11.8
2008	0.6	-4.4	-4.9
2009	10.0	17.6	7.6
2010	6.2	7.5	1.3
2011	3.4	10.1	6.7
2012	2.1	-0.8	-2.9
Avg	3.0 %	7.2 %	4.2 %
Fq > 0	78 %	70 %	61 %

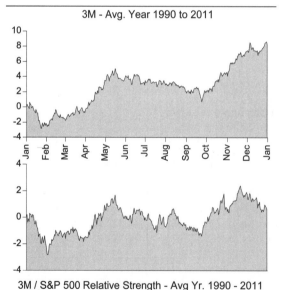

3M - Avg. Year 1990 to 2011

3M / S&P 500 Relative Strength - Avg Yr. 1990 - 2011

During its seasonal period from February 3rd to May 12th for the years 1990 to 2012, 3M has produced an average gain of 7.2% and has been positive 70% of the time.

Investors should note that most of the occurrences of 3M underperforming the S&P 500 have taken place when 3M has produced a loss during its seasonal period, and most of the occurrences of outperformance have taken place when 3M has produced a gain. In other words, 3M tends to perform better in positive market conditions. The good news is that the S&P 500 tends to be positive during 3M's seasonal period, which helps 3M outperform.

The sweet spot for the seasonal trade occurs in April when the industrial sector is typically one of the top performing sectors.

Investors will be wise to consider exiting their position at the beginning of May as 3M tends to underperform the market at this time until the end of September.

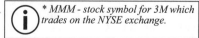

* MMM - stock symbol for 3M which trades on the NYSE exchange.

2011-12 Strategy Performance

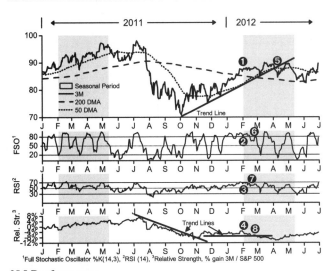

¹Full Stochastic Oscillator %K(14,3), ²RSI (14), ³Relative Strength, % gain 3M / S&P 500

Market Indices & Rates
Weekly Values**

Stock Markets	2011	2012
Dow	12,156	12,979
S&P500	1,319	1,370
Nasdaq	2,770	2,977
TSX	14,174	12,690
FTSE	5,968	5,911
DAX	7,216	6,891
Nikkei	10,630	9,713
Hang Seng	23,263	21,483

Commodities	2011	2012
Oil	101.03	107.54
Gold	1423.2	1748.8

Bond Yields	2011	2012
USA 5 Yr Treasury	2.17	0.86
USA 10 Yr T	3.47	1.97
USA 20 Yr T	4.31	2.74
Moody's Aaa	5.14	3.82
Moody's Baa	6.05	5.08
CAN 5 Yr T	2.69	1.43
CAN 10 Yr T	3.33	1.99

Money Market	2011	2012
USA Fed Funds	0.25	0.25
USA 3 Mo T-B	0.13	0.09
CAN tgt overnight rate	1.00	1.00
CAN 3 Mo T-B	0.95	0.93

Foreign Exchange	2011	2012
USD/EUR	1.39	1.33
USD/GBP	1.63	1.59
CAN/USD	0.97	0.99
JPY/USD	82.06	81.03

3M Performance

3M performed "at market," starting in November 2011 and continued this trend into the beginning of its seasonal period in February. On an absolute basis this trend was positive, but it put 3M into overbought territory when it was starting its seasonal period. 3M along with the industrial sector started to underperform the S&P 500 in March as investor interest in the cyclical sector waned.

Technical Conditions– February 3rd to May 12th, 2012

Entry Date February 3rd, 2012 –Bullish– On a positive note, 3M was still in an uptrend above its trend line at the start of its seasonal period❶. Nevertheless, it was in an overbought state as the FSO was above 80❷ and the RSI was touching 70❸, warranting caution. 3M was well positioned for its seasonal trade, as it was still performing at market with the S&P 500❹.

Entry Strategy –Buy Position on Entry Date– Overall, justification to enter the trade existed, but caution was warranted.

Exit Strategy –Sell Position Early– Shortly after the seasonal buy date the technical picture became negative in mid-February. The FSO turned below 80❺ and the RSI turned back from 70❼ and although the action of these two indicators were not causes to sell, they did raise concern. The technical picture deteriorated further as 3M started to underperform the S&P 500 towards the end of February❽, providing justification to sell a partial position early. In April 3M broke below its trend line and 50 day moving average, justifying a full exit from the trade❺.

FEBRUARY

M	T	W	T	F	S	S
				1	2	3
4	5	6	7	8	9	10
11	12	13	14	15	16	17
18	19	20	21	22	23	24
25	26	27	28			

MARCH

M	T	W	T	F	S	S
				1	2	3
4	5	6	7	8	9	10
11	12	13	14	15	16	17
18	19	20	21	22	23	24
25	26	27	28	29	30	31

APRIL

M	T	W	T	F	S	S
1	2	3	4	5	6	7
8	9	10	11	12	13	14
15	16	17	18	19	20	21
22	23	24	25	26	27	28
29	30					

** Weekly avg closing values- except Fed Funds & CAN overnight tgt rate weekly closing values.

MARCH

	MONDAY	TUESDAY	WEDNESDAY
WEEK 09	25	26	27
WEEK 10	4 27	5 26	6 25
WEEK 11	11 20	12 19	13 18
WEEK 12	18 13	19 12	20 11
WEEK 13	25 6	26 5	27 4

THURSDAY	FRIDAY
28	**1** 30
7 24	**8** 23
14 17	**15** 16
21 10	**22** 9
28 3	**29** 2

USA Market Closed- Good Friday
CAN Market Closed- Good Friday

APRIL

M	T	W	T	F	S	S
1	2	3	4	5	6	7
8	9	10	11	12	13	14
15	16	17	18	19	20	21
22	23	24	25	26	27	28
29	30					

MAY

M	T	W	T	F	S	S
		1	2	3	4	5
6	7	8	9	10	11	12
13	14	15	16	17	18	19
20	21	22	23	24	25	26
27	28	29	30	31		

JUNE

M	T	W	T	F	S	S
					1	2
3	4	5	6	7	8	9
10	11	12	13	14	15	16
17	18	19	20	21	22	23
24	25	26	27	28	29	30

JULY

M	T	W	T	F	S	S
1	2	3	4	5	6	7
8	9	10	11	12	13	14
15	16	17	18	19	20	21
22	23	24	25	26	27	28
29	30	31				

MARCH SUMMARY

	Dow Jones	S&P 500	Nasdaq	TSX Comp
Month Rank	5	4	8	3
# Up	40	40	25	17
# Down	22	22	15	10
% Pos	65	65	63	63
% Avg. Gain	1.1	1.1	0.6	1.3

Dow & S&P 1950-2011, Nasdaq 1972-2011, TSX 1985-2011

S&P500 Cumulative Daily Gains for Avg Month 1950 to 2012

Prob. of Daily Gain

♦ In March 2012, the S&P 500 produced a gain of 3.1%, ending a triple hitter with January, February and March putting in strong performances. ♦ The financial sector was the top performing sector, producing a return of 7.3%. The worst performing sector was the energy sector with a loss of 3.4% (energy is typically the best performing sector). ♦ Like 2011, once again, a sector shift took place in the market at this time, with the defensives starting to uncharacteristically perform strongly at this time of the year- foreshadowing a possible future correction.

BEST / WORST MARCH BROAD MKTS. 2003-2012

BEST MARCH MARKETS
- ♦ Nasdaq (2009) 10.9%
- ♦ Russell 3000 Gr (2009) 8.7%
- ♦ Russell 2000 (2009) 8.7%

WORST MARCH MARKETS
- ♦ TSX Comp (2003) -3.2%
- ♦ Russell 2000 (2005) -3.0%
- ♦ Nasdaq (2005) -2.6%

Index Values End of Month

	2003	2004	2005	2006	2007	2008	2009	2010	2011	2012
Dow	7,992	10,358	10,504	11,109	12,354	12,263	7,609	10,857	12,320	13,212
S&P 500	848	1,126	1,181	1,295	1,421	1,323	798	1,169	1,326	1,408
Nasdaq	1,341	1,994	1,999	2,340	2,422	2,279	1,529	2,398	2,781	3,092
TSX	6,343	8,586	9,612	12,111	13,166	13,350	8,720	12,038	14,116	12,392
Russell 1000	866	1,160	1,222	1,359	1,492	1,385	834	1,238	1,417	779
Russell 2000	906	1,467	1,529	1,902	1,990	1,710	1,051	1,687	2,096	830
Russell 3000 Growth	1,391	1,847	1,850	2,094	2,206	2,149	1,387	2,054	2,414	2,620
Russell 3000 Value	1,620	2,252	2,481	2,765	3,137	2,733	1,529	2,304	2,604	2,649

Percent Gain for March

	2003	2004	2005	2006	2007	2008	2009	2010	2011	2012
Dow	1.3	-2.1	-2.4	1.1	0.7	0.0	7.7	5.1	0.8	2.0
S&P 500	0.8	-1.6	-1.9	1.1	1.0	-0.6	8.5	5.9	-0.1	3.1
Nasdaq	0.3	-1.8	-2.6	2.6	0.2	0.3	10.9	7.1	0.0	4.2
TSX	-3.2	-2.3	-0.6	3.6	0.9	-1.7	7.4	3.5	-0.1	-2.0
Russell 1000	0.9	-1.5	-1.7	1.3	0.9	-0.8	8.5	6.0	0.1	3.0
Russell 2000	1.1	0.8	-3.0	4.7	0.9	0.3	8.7	8.0	2.4	2.4
Russell 3000 Growth	1.7	-1.8	-2.1	1.7	0.5	-0.7	8.7	5.8	0.3	3.1
Russell 3000 Value	0.0	-0.9	-1.6	1.5	1.4	-0.8	8.3	6.5	0.3	2.8

March Market Avg. Performance 2003 to 2012[1]

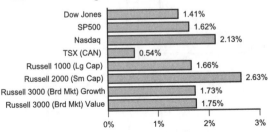

- Dow Jones 1.41%
- SP500 1.62%
- Nasdaq 2.13%
- TSX (CAN) 0.54%
- Russell 1000 (Lg Cap) 1.66%
- Russell 2000 (Sm Cap) 2.63%
- Russell 3000 (Brd Mkt) Growth 1.73%
- Russell 3000 (Brd Mkt) Value 1.75%

Interest Corner Mar[2]

	Fed Funds % [3]	3 Mo. T-Bill % [4]	10 Yr % [5]	20 Yr % [6]
2012	0.25	0.07	2.23	3.00
2011	0.25	0.09	3.47	4.29
2010	0.25	0.16	3.84	4.55
2009	0.25	0.21	2.71	3.61
2008	2.25	1.38	3.45	4.30

(1) Russell Data provided by Russell (2) Federal Reserve Bank of St. Louis- end of month values (3) Target rate set by FOMC (4)(5)(6) Constant yield maturities.

THACKRAY SECTOR THERMOMETER

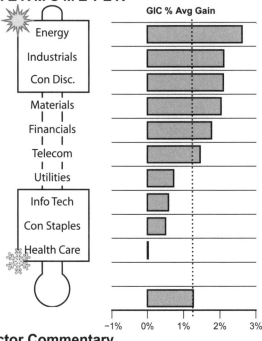

GIC(2) % Avg Gain	Fq % Gain >S&P 500	
SP GIC SECTOR 1990-2011(1)		
2.6 %	64 %	Energy
2.1	73	Industrials
2.1	73	Consumer Discretionary
2.0	55	Materials
1.8	55	Financials
1.5	59	Telecom
0.7	45	Utilities
0.6	41	Information Technology
0.5	50	Consumer Staples
0.0 %	27 %	Health Care
1.3 %	N/A %	S&P 500

Sector Commentary

♦ The top sector in March 2012 was the financial sector, indicating a healthy market, but there were signs that the market was weakening. The defensive sectors were starting to show strength: the health care and consumer staples sector, produced gains of 4.3% and 3.0%, respectively. ♦ In contrast the energy sector was the worst performing sector, producing a loss of 3.4%. ♦ The sector "world" was flipped upside down, as energy on average has been the best performing sector and health care, the worst performing sector. This "flipped" condition indicates a possible weak market ahead. When the defensive sectors outperform at a time in the year when they are typically weak, investors need to be cautious, as the market is susceptible to a correction.

Sub-Sector Commentary

In March 2012, the banking sector put in a solid performance of 8.3%, followed by the homebuilders with an 8.0% gain. The market was still rolling along, but it was showing signs that some of the speculative money was being removed. ♦ After two solid months of stellar performances, silver found itself at the bottom of the sub-sector list with a loss of 12.9%. The metals and mining sector was the second worst sector with a loss of 7.0%.

SELECTED SUB-SECTORS 1990-2011(3)		
3.7 %	77 %	Retail
2.9	55	Silver (London)
2.7	64	Steel
2.3	73	Transportation
2.3	59	Railroads
2.0	54	Chemicals
1.6	59	Software & Services
1.4	45	Metals and Mining
1.2	45	Banks
0.4	41	Homebuilders
0.1	27	Pharmaceuticals
0.0	28	Agriculture (94-2011)
-0.8	41	Gold (London PM)
-0.8	30	Biotech (93-2011)

(1) Sector data provided by Standard and Poors (2) GIC is short form for Global Industry Classification (3) Sub Sector data provided by Standard and Poors, except where marked by symbol.

AMD vs. INTC

AMD vs. Intel
①Feb 24-May 5 ②May 6-Jul 29

In 2012, the AMD-Intel trade worked very well mainly because AMD produced a substantial loss of 43% at the time it is best to short sell the stock.

The two heavy weight semiconductor fabricators, AMD and Intel (INTC), have benefited immensely from the proliferation of low cost computers, particularly in the 1990's. Since 2000, the stock price of both companies has lost ground. Despite the ups and downs of the semiconductor market, both Intel and AMD have still exhibited seasonal trends.

Generally, from the end of February to the beginning of May, AMD has shown a fairly strong positive seasonal trend. From February 24th to May 5th, for the time period 1990 to 2012, AMD has produced an average return of 19.5% and has been positive 61% of the time. The frequency level of positive returns is acceptable, but it is not extraordinarily high. Given that the size of the losses are relatively small compared to the gains during this time period, AMD is still a stock worth considering at this time.

46.9% average gain & 83% of the time positive

From May 6th to July 29th, AMD and Intel have very different seasonal patterns – AMD tends to decrease and INTC tends to increase. This is the makings of a great pair trade. On average AMD has produced a loss of 18.9% and INTC has produced a gain of 2.8%. Putting the two trades together during the years 1990 to 2012, February-May (long AMD) and May-July (long INTC and short AMD) has produced an average gain of 46.9% and has been positive 83% of the time.

Investors should also know that there are other profitable time periods to trade both INTC and AMD. Both stocks tend to have a weak September and a strong October and November.

(i) *Intel (INTC) trades on the Nasdaq. Advanced Micro Devices Inc. (AMD) trades on the NYSE.*

Long AMD & Short INTC - Feb 24 to May 5
Short AMD & Long INTC - May 6 to July 29

| | Pos. when Long | |
| | Neg. when Short | |

Year	Feb 24 to May 5 Pos. AMD	May 6 to Jul 29 Neg. AMD	May 6 to Jul 29 Pos. INTC	Compound Growth
1990	8.1 %	-14.9 %	3.0 %	27.4 %
1991	56.5	-15.5	-6.2	71.0
1992	-7.7	-52.1	8.0	47.8
1993	38.0	-19.1	4.4	70.4
1994	14.3	8.0	0.3	5.5
1995	17.4	-4.0	23.6	49.7
1996	-4.9	-37.8	6.1	36.9
1997	28.4	-22.7	8.5	68.4
1998	24.1	-39.1	3.4	76.8
1999	-7.7	1.1	8.6	-0.7
2000	124.1	-22.8	4.7	185.6
2001	40.2	-43.0	-5.4	92.9
2002	-14.0	-26.2	-28.9	-16.3
2003	40.5	-3.4	30.9	88.7
2004	2.6	-17.5	-7.5	12.8
2005	-11.2	36.2	11.9	-32.8
2006	-14.8	-44.5	-6.8	17.4
2007	-7.9	2.5	7.5	-3.3
2008	-2.7	-35.5	-4.4	27.6
2009	113.9	-14.1	20.1	186.9
2010	10.1	-9.3	-5.2	14.7
2011	3.7	-17.3	-5.4	16.0
2012	-1.5	-43.0	-6.7	34.0
Avg.	19.5 %	-18.9 %	2.8 %	46.9 %
Fq >0	61 %	17 %	61 %	83 %

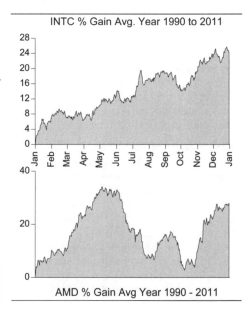

INTC % Gain Avg. Year 1990 to 2011

AMD % Gain Avg Year 1990 - 2011

2011-12 Strategy Performance

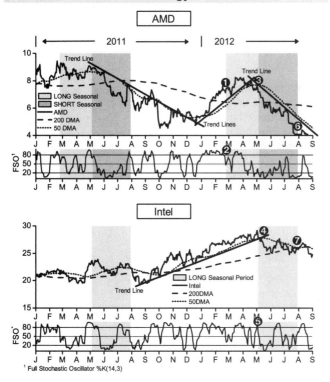

Market Indices & Rates
Weekly Values**

Stock Markets	2011	2012
Dow	12,109	12,878
S&P500	1,310	1,359
Nasdaq	2,736	2,951
TSX	13,861	12,428
FTSE	5,912	5,836
DAX	7,101	6,777
Nikkei	10,462	9,722
Hang Seng	23,540	20,937

Commodities	2011	2012
Oil	103.74	106.31
Gold	1423.9	1685.8

Bond Yields	2011	2012
USA 5 Yr Treasury	2.14	0.87
USA 10 Yr T	3.46	2.00
USA 20 Yr T	4.33	2.78
Moody's Aaa	5.17	3.88
Moody's Baa	6.08	5.11
CAN 5 Yr T	2.74	1.45
CAN 10 Yr T	3.33	1.98

Money Market	2011	2012
USA Fed Funds	0.25	0.25
USA 3 Mo T-B	0.10	0.08
CAN tgt overnight rate	1.00	1.00
CAN 3 Mo T-B	0.95	0.91

Foreign Exchange	2011	2012
USD/EUR	1.39	1.32
USD/GBP	1.61	1.58
CAN/USD	0.97	0.99
JPY/USD	82.49	81.51

¹ Full Stochastic Oscillator %K(14,3)

Intel & AMD Performance
February 24th to May 5th & May 6th to July 29th, 2012

AMD was on a continuous decline from May of 2011 and then managed to turn around at the beginning of 2012, rising above its 50 day moving average, starting a new uptrend. Coming into its seasonal long period, it was still above its trend line and its 50 day moving average❶ despite a short-term oversold reading from the FSO❷. Over the long part of the seasonal trade AMD, produced a loss of 1.5% and was showing strong negative tendencies as it had broken its up trend line and its 50 day moving average❸.

At the start of its seasonal long period, Intel was also showing similar negative tendencies, crossing over its trend line and trading below its 50 day moving average❹. The FSO had also previously turned below 80❺.

Despite Intel having a weak technical picture, AMD's picture was even worse (good for it seasonal short period). At this point an investor had the choice to either short AMD by itself, or pair it with a long position in Intel. Both strategies worked out very well as AMD produced a large loss (43.3%) during its seasonal short period❻, much bigger than Intel's loss❼.

MARCH

M	T	W	T	F	S	S
			1	2	3
4	5	6	7	8	9	10
11	12	13	14	15	16	17
18	19	20	21	22	23	24
25	26	27	28	29	30	31

APRIL

M	T	W	T	F	S	S
1	2	3	4	5	6	7
8	9	10	11	12	13	14
15	16	17	18	19	20	21
22	23	24	25	26	27	28
29	30					

MAY

M	T	W	T	F	S	S
	1	2	3	4	5
6	7	8	9	10	11	12
13	14	15	16	17	18	19
20	21	22	23	24	25	26
27	28	29	30	31		

** Weekly avg closing values- except Fed Funds & CAN overnight tgt rate weekly closing values.

POWER FOR YOUR PORTFOLIO
March 5th to April 6th

GE is considered a bellwether for the stock market, but investors should expect this stock to move more than the market, even if it closely follows the market's direction. At the time of writing this report, GE had a higher beta than the S&P 500.

Investors should note that GE tends to have a track record of outperforming the S&P 500 when the market is performing well and underperforming when the market is performing poorly. Despite this trend, overall GE is a strong seasonal stock from March 5th to April 6th. During this time period, from 1990 to 2012, GE has produced an average return of 6.6% and has been positive 70% of the time. This compares to an average return of 1.9% for the S&P 500 and a positive frequency rate of 65%.

6.6% & positive 70% of the time

Although the positive frequency rate is only marginally higher than the S&P 500, the value of the trade can be seen by the frequency that GE outperforms the S&P 500, 74% of the time.

GE vs. S&P 500 1990 to 2012

Mar 5 to Apr 6	S&P 500	3M	Positive Diff
1990	1.4%	3.2%	1.9%
1991	1.6	4.2	2.6
1992	-0.9	-2.6	-1.7
1993	-1.4	7.2	8.6
1994	-3.6	-6.9	-3.3
1995	4.3	4.5	0.2
1996	0.8	3.2	2.4
1997	-4.2	-0.5	3.7
1998	7.1	13.7	6.6
1999	5.7	12.8	7.0
2000	6.5	12.4	5.9
2001	-8.6	-7.6	1.0
2002	-2.7	-7.7	-5.0
2003	6.9	18.1	11.2
2004	-0.6	-4.2	-3.6
2005	-3.1	-1.7	1.4
2006	1.7	4.3	2.6
2007	4.1	0.4	-3.7
2008	3.3	12.1	8.8
2009	17.2	67.3	50.1
2010	5.9	15.5	9.5
2011	1.1	0.9	-0.2
2012	2.1	2.7	0.7
Avg	1.9%	6.6%	4.6%
Fq > 0	65%	70%	74%

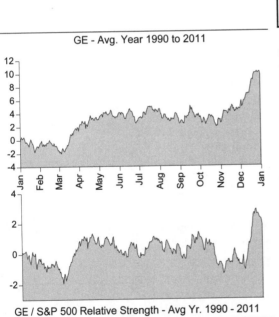

GE - Avg. Year 1990 to 2011

GE / S&P 500 Relative Strength - Avg Yr. 1990 - 2011

sell signals are triggered, or the stock starts to underperform the market.

Investors should also note that GE can perform well in the first half of December, particularly from December 5th to December 19th. In this time period, from 1990 to 2011, GE has produced an average gain of 3.3% and has been positive 82% of the time. It is possible that money managers are doing some year-end window dressing and adjusting their portfolios to include bellwether stocks such as GE.

Although GE still has a positive tendency after the beginning of April, on average it performs the same as the market. If GE is outperforming the market, investors can maintain their position until either technical

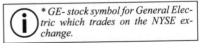

GE- stock symbol for General Electric which trades on the NYSE exchange.

2011-12 Strategy Performance

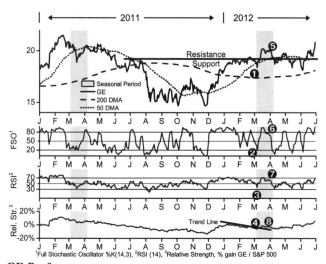

¹Full Stochastic Oscillator %K(14,3), ²RSI (14), ³Relative Strength, % gain GE / S&P 500

GE Performance

GE started to underperform the S&P 500 from February 2011 and continued this trend until November. In December this trend changed as GE started to outperform the S&P 500. When it came time to enter the seasonal trade for GE, it had a shallow pullback indicating possible further weakness. GE was only able to eke out a small outperformance compared to the S&P 500 over its seasonal period.

Technical Conditions–March 5th to April 6th, 2012
Entry Date March 5th, 2012 –Neutral– Just before the seasonal entry date, GE had turned down from its resistance level and by the start of the seasonal trade was trading at its 50 day moving average❶. The FSO was just above 20❷. The RSI was trading below 50❸ and GE was still underperforming the S&P 500❹.

Entry Strategy –Buy Partial Position on Entry Date– The technical picture for GE was not strong and although the historical track record of this seasonal trade is strong, investors would have been warranted in using a conservative strategy, of either waiting for an upturn above the resistance level, or a partial allocation on the entry date.

Exit Strategy –Sell Partial Position Early– Investors would have been warranted to sell a partial position in GE early as the stock had already turned down❺. The FSO had already crossed below 80❻ in mid-March, indicating a partial sell. Just previous to this event the RSI had turned back from 70❼ and GE was underperforming the market❽. By the time the exit date arrived, GE was at its resistance level and trading below its 50 day moving average. At this time, there was not a strong justification to remain in the trade.

Market Indices & Rates
Weekly Values**

Stock Markets	2011	2012
Dow	11,819	13,163
S&P500	1,278	1,394
Nasdaq	2,653	3,035
TSX	13,645	12,459
FTSE	5,697	5,940
DAX	6,670	7,056
Nikkei	9,098	10,019
Hang Seng	22,662	21,291

Commodities	2011	2012
Oil	99.77	106.13
Gold	1409.7	1667.6

Bond Yields	2011	2012
USA 5 Yr Treasury	1.95	1.06
USA 10 Yr T	3.29	2.21
USA 20 Yr T	4.18	3.00
Moody's Aaa	5.07	4.05
Moody's Baa	5.98	5.28
CAN 5 Yr T	2.52	1.61
CAN 10 Yr T	3.18	2.13

Money Market	2011	2012
USA Fed Funds	0.25	0.25
USA 3 Mo T-B	0.09	0.09
CAN tgt overnight rate	1.00	1.00
CAN 3 Mo T-B	0.91	0.91

Foreign Exchange	2011	2012
USD/EUR	1.40	1.31
USD/GBP	1.61	1.57
CAN/USD	0.98	0.99
JPY/USD	80.28	83.18

MARCH

M	T	W	T	F	S	S
			1	2	3
4	5	6	7	8	9	10
11	12	13	14	15	16	17
18	19	20	21	22	23	24
25	26	27	28	29	30	31

APRIL

M	T	W	T	F	S	S
1	2	3	4	5	6	7
8	9	10	11	12	13	14
15	16	17	18	19	20	21
22	23	24	25	26	27	28
29	30					

MAY

M	T	W	T	F	S	S
	1	2	3	4	5
6	7	8	9	10	11	12
13	14	15	16	17	18	19
20	21	22	23	24	25	26
27	28	29	30	31		

SUPER SEVEN DAYS
7 Best Days of the Month

The end of the month tends to be an excellent time to invest: portfolio managers "window dress" (adjust their portfolios to look good for month end reports), investors stop procrastinating and invest their extra cash, and brokers try to increase their commissions by investing their client's extra cash.

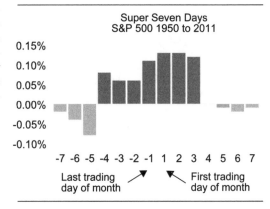

From 1950 to 2011
All 7 days better
than market average

All of these factors tend to produce above average returns in the market during the days around month end.

The above graph illustrates the strength of the Super Seven days. The Super Seven days are the last four trading days of the month and the first three trading days of the next month represented by the dark columns from day -4 to day 3. All of the Super Seven days have daily average gains above the daily market average gain of 0.03% (since 1950).

% Gain Super Seven Day Period From 2002 to 2011

	2002	2003	2004	2005	2006	2007	2008	2009	2010	2011	Avg.
Jan	-3.8 %	-1.1 %	-2.5 %	1.8 %	-0.1 %	1.6 %	-4.5 %	-0.5 %	0.0 %	1.2 %	-0.9 %
Feb	5.2	-0.3	0.9	2.2	-0.4	-5.6	-2.8	4.1	1.0	1.2	-0.5
Mar	-2.0	0.2	3.7	0.9	0.8	0.1	1.2	3.5	2.0	1.4	0.6
Apr	-1.8	1.7	-1.2	1.2	0.0	1.5	1.3	4.3	-3.8	0.9	0.6
May	-3.1	5.7	1.9	0.2	0.5	1.6	0.1	5.0	2.7	-1.2	1.4
Jun	-3.6	0.2	-2.1	0.3	1.9	1.8	-3.9	-0.2	-4.2	5.6	-1.0
Jul	-0.5	-3.3	1.3	1.3	0.9	-5.6	2.2	2.1	1.1	-5.8	0.1
Aug	-7.3	3.4	0.8	1.7	0.4	0.8	-2.4	-2.4	4.7	0.5	-0.6
Sep	0.0	2.0	2.9	-1.6	1.8	1.4	-7.3	-1.0	1.1	-1.6	0.6
Oct	2.0	2.0	4.4	2.0	-1.3	-0.8	12.2	-1.9	1.0	2.6	2.0
Nov	-2.6	2.8	1.2	-0.3	1.0	5.5	8.8	-0.6	3.7	8.2	2.1
Dec	4.1	2.7	-1.8	0.4	-0.1	-5.7	7.7	0.9	1.5	1.2	1.2
Avg.	-1.1 %	1.3 %	0.8 %	0.8 %	0.0 %	0.0 %	1.1 %	0.4 %	0.9 %	1.2 %	0.5 %

The Super Seven is back on track with the last four years producing fairly strong gains. The last year that produced an average negative result was 2002, which was a disastrous year for the market. The first major decline started on March 12 and pushed the market down more than 30%. The second major decline started on August 22 and pushed the market down more than 15%. Both of these declines had a large effect on the results of the Super Seven for the year.

⚠️ *Historically it has been best not to use the Super Seven for July and August. Both of these months have negative average performances and have been negative more often than positive over the last ten years.*

Despite these negative periods, the Super Seven has accounted for much of the total gain of the stock market. If there is one time of the month that investors should be concentrating on investing, it is the last four trading days of the current month and the first three of the next month.

2011-12 Strategy Performance

Market Indices & Rates
Weekly Values**

Stock Markets	2011	2012
Dow	12,106	13,132
S&P500	1,303	1,402
Nasdaq	2,711	3,072
TSX	14,034	12,435
FTSE	5,825	5,889
DAX	6,856	7,051
Nikkei	9,507	10,092
Hang Seng	22,888	20,886

Commodities	2011	2012
Oil	104.32	106.40
Gold	1436.1	1653.4

Bond Yields	2011	2012
USA 5 Yr Treasury	2.10	1.16
USA 10 Yr T	3.38	2.32
USA 20 Yr T	4.22	3.07
Moody's Aaa	5.10	4.09
Moody's Baa	6.00	5.34
CAN 5 Yr T	2.60	1.70
CAN 10 Yr T	3.21	2.24

Money Market	2011	2012
USA Fed Funds	0.25	0.25
USA 3 Mo T-B	0.09	0.09
CAN tgt overnight rate	1.00	1.00
CAN 3 Mo T-B	0.91	0.90

Foreign Exchange	2011	2012
USD/EUR	1.42	1.32
USD/GBP	1.62	1.59
CAN/USD	0.98	0.99
JPY/USD	81.05	83.07

2011 - S&P 500 - % Gains Last 4 Days of Month & First 3 Days of Next Month

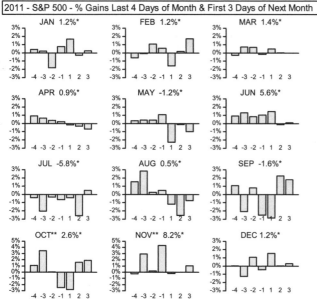

2012 - S&P 500 - % Gains Last 4 Days of Month & First 3 Days of Next Month

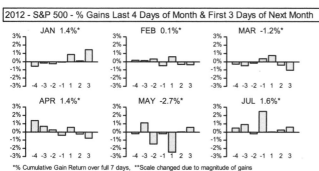

*% Cumulative Gain Return over full 7 days, **Scale changed due to magnitude of gains

Super Seven Performance

The Super Seven came to the rescue once again with very strong gains in 2011 and 2012. In 2011, the Super Seven days produced an average gain of 1.2% per month, or a compound gain of 14.5% for the year. This compares to the total return for the S&P 500 for the year of 0%.

In the first six months of 2012, the Super Seven strategy has produced an average gain of 0.60% per month and has accounted for almost one-half of the gains of the market.

Investors should note that the Super Seven days can have large gains and losses, much more than the average day during the year. The large price movements can be seen particularly in October and November of 2011.

MARCH

M	T	W	T	F	S	S
				1	2	3
4	5	6	7	8	9	10
11	12	13	14	15	16	17
18	19	20	21	22	23	24
25	26	27	28	29	30	31

APRIL

M	T	W	T	F	S	S
1	2	3	4	5	6	7
8	9	10	11	12	13	14
15	16	17	18	19	20	21
22	23	24	25	26	27	28
29	30					

MAY

M	T	W	T	F	S	S
		1	2	3	4	5
6	7	8	9	10	11	12
13	14	15	16	17	18	19
20	21	22	23	24	25	26
27	28	29	30	31		

** Weekly avg closing values- except Fed Funds & CAN overnight tgt rate weekly closing values.

CANADIANS GIVE 3 CHEERS FOR AMERICAN HOLIDAYS

When I used to work on the retail side of the investment business, I was always amazed at how often the Canadian market increased on American holidays, when the Canadian stock market was open and the American market was closed.

The holidays always had light volume, tended not to have large increases or decreases, but nevertheless usually ended the day with a gain.

1% average gain from 1977 to 2011 and 94% of the time positive

How the trade works

For the three big holidays in the United States that do not exist in Canada (Memorial, Independence and U.S. Thanksgiving Days), buy at the end of the market day before the holiday (TSX Composite) and sell at the end of the U.S. holiday when the U.S markets are closed.

For U.S. investors to take advantage of this trade they must have access to the TSX Composite. Unfortunately, as of the current time SEC regulations do not allow Americans to purchase foreign ETFs.

Generally, markets perform well around most major American holidays, hence the trading strategies for American holidays included in this book. The typical U.S. holiday trade is to get into the stock market the day before the holiday and then exit the day after the holiday.

The main reason for the strong performance around these holidays is a lack of institutional involvement in the markets, allowing bullish retail investors to push up the markets.

On the actual holidays, there are no economic news releases in America and very seldom is there anything released in Canada of significance. During market hours without any influences, the market tends to float, preferring to wait until the next day before making any significant moves.

Despite this laxidasical action during the day, the TSX Composite tends to end the day on a gain. This is true for the three major holidays that are covered in this book: Memorial, Independence and U.S. Thanksgiving Day.

From a theoretical perspective a lot of the gain that is captured on the U.S. holiday is realized on the next day when the markets are open in the United States. This does not invalidate the *Canadians Give 3 Cheers* trade – it presents more alternatives for the astute investor.

For example, an investor can allocate a portion of money to a standard American holiday trade and another portion to the *Canadian Give 3 Cheers* version. By spreading out the exit days, the overall risk in the trade is reduced.

S&P/TSX Comp
Gain 1977-2011   Positive ☐

	Memorial	Independence	Thanksgiving	Compound Growth
1977	0.10 %	-0.08 %	0.61 %	0.63 %
1978	-0.05	-0.16	0.57	0.36
1979	1.11	0.23	0.58	1.93
1980	1.64	0.76	0.89	3.32
1981	0.51	-0.15	1.03	1.40
1982	-0.18	-0.01	0.35	0.17
1983	0.29	0.53	0.15	0.97
1984	0.86	-0.11	0.73	1.48
1985	0.61	0.31	0.31	1.24
1986	0.23	-0.02	0.22	0.44
1987	-0.11	1.08	1.57	2.55
1988	0.44	0.08	0.58	1.11
1989	0.10	-0.12	-0.11	-0.13
1990	0.11	0.43	0.02	0.57
1991	0.02	0.18	-0.09	0.11
1992	-0.06	0.35	0.36	0.65
1993	0.42	-0.18	0.14	0.38
1994	-0.19	0.70	0.91	1.43
1995	0.14	0.25	0.29	0.68
1996	0.11	0.25	0.54	0.90
1997	1.08	-0.04	-0.85	0.18
1998	0.56	0.18	0.51	1.25
1999	0.57	1.63	1.14	3.39
2000	0.43	1.04	0.91	2.40
2001	-0.02	-0.23	0.70	0.45
2002	-0.01	0.08	0.38	0.45
2003	0.03	0.03	0.26	0.31
2004	0.84	-0.02	0.55	1.39
2005	0.56	0.39	1.48	2.45
2006	0.70	1.04	0.70	2.46
2007	0.35	-0.03	0.76	1.08
2008	0.24	-0.94	1.28	0.56
2009	0.76	0.36	-1.29	-0.18
2010	0.78	-0.92	0.34	0.19
2011	0.23	0.64	-0.75	0.12
Avg	0.38 %	0.22 %	0.45 %	1.05 %
Fq > 0	80 %	60 %	86 %	94 %

2011-12 Strategy Performance

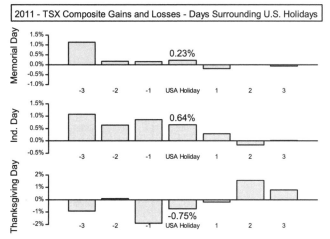

2011 - TSX Composite Gains and Losses - Days Surrounding U.S. Holidays

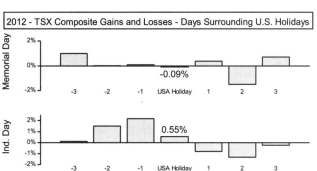

2012 - TSX Composite Gains and Losses - Days Surrounding U.S. Holidays

Market Indices & Rates
Weekly Values**

Stock Markets	2011	2012
Dow	12,305	13,185
S&P500	1,323	1,409
Nasdaq	2,767	3,107
TSX	14,031	12,446
FTSE	5,941	5,818
DAX	7,030	6,996
Nikkei	9,622	10,131
Hang Seng	23,382	20,753

Commodities	2011	2012
Oil	105.54	105.11
Gold	1423.4	1673.7

Bond Yields	2011	2012
USA 5 Yr Treasury	2.23	1.05
USA 10 Yr T	3.47	2.22
USA 20 Yr T	4.29	2.97
Moody's Aaa	5.15	4.00
Moody's Baa	6.05	5.25
CAN 5 Yr T	2.74	1.59
CAN 10 Yr T	3.32	2.13

Money Market	2011	2012
USA Fed Funds	0.25	0.25
USA 3 Mo T-B	0.09	0.08
CAN tgt overnight rate	1.00	1.00
CAN 3 Mo T-B	0.92	0.92

Foreign Exchange	2011	2012
USD/EUR	1.41	1.33
USD/GBP	1.60	1.60
CAN/USD	0.97	1.00
JPY/USD	82.85	82.84

MARCH

M	T	W	T	F	S	S
				1	2	3
4	5	6	7	8	9	10
11	12	13	14	15	16	17
18	19	20	21	22	23	24
25	26	27	28	29	30	31

APRIL

M	T	W	T	F	S	S
1	2	3	4	5	6	7
8	9	10	11	12	13	14
15	16	17	18	19	20	21
22	23	24	25	26	27	28
29	30					

MAY

M	T	W	T	F	S	S
	1	2	3	4	5
6	7	8	9	10	11	12
13	14	15	16	17	18	19
20	21	22	23	24	25	26
27	28	29	30	31		

Canadians Give 3 Cheers Performance

Overall, Canadians profited during U.S. holidays in 2011. Memorial Day and Independence Day were both winners. On the other hand, Thanksgiving was a loser. Typically, American Thanksgiving is a strong performer in the Canadian stock market, but in 2011 the stock markets around the world dropped on American Thanksgiving as Germany had a very poor bond auction. At the time, the sentiment was that if Germany could have a weak bond auction, what would the next Greek auction hold in store? Nevertheless, the weak Thanksgiving results did not totally negate the gains from the previous two holiday trades.

So far in 2012, Memorial Day has produced a nominal loss and Independence Day a much larger gain. Although no one knows what will happen on American Thanksgiving this year, investing for Thanksgiving day has a strong track record of being positive 86% of the time, making it a trade that short-term investors should consider.

** Weekly avg closing values- except Fed Funds & CAN overnight tgt rate weekly closing values.

APRIL

	MONDAY	TUESDAY	WEDNESDAY
WEEK 14	**1** 29	**2** 28	**3** 27
WEEK 15	**8** 22	**9** 21	**10** 20
WEEK 16	**15** 15	**16** 14	**17** 13
WEEK 17	**22** 8	**23** 7	**24** 6
WEEK 18	**29** 1	**30**	1

THURSDAY		FRIDAY	
4	26	**5**	25
11	19	**12**	18
18	12	**19**	11
25	5	**26**	4
2		3	

MAY

M	T	W	T	F	S	S
		1	2	3	4	5
6	7	8	9	10	11	12
13	14	15	16	17	18	19
20	21	22	23	24	25	26
27	28	29	30	31		

JUNE

M	T	W	T	F	S	S
					1	2
3	4	5	6	7	8	9
10	11	12	13	14	15	16
17	18	19	20	21	22	23
24	25	26	27	28	29	30

JULY

M	T	W	T	F	S	S
1	2	3	4	5	6	7
8	9	10	11	12	13	14
15	16	17	18	19	20	21
22	23	24	25	26	27	28
29	30	31				

AUGUST

M	T	W	T	F	S	S
			1	2	3	4
5	6	7	8	9	10	11
12	13	14	15	16	17	18
19	20	21	22	23	24	25
26	27	28	29	30	31	

APRIL
S U M M A R Y

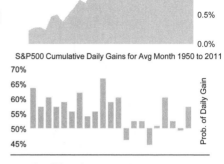

	Dow Jones	S&P 500	Nasdaq	TSX Comp
Month Rank	1	2	4	7
# Up	40	43	26	16
# Down	22	19	14	11
% Pos	65	69	65	59
% Avg. Gain	2.0	1.5	1.5	0.8

Dow & S&P 1950-2011, Nasdaq 1972-2011, TSX 1985-2011

S&P500 Cumulative Daily Gains for Avg Month 1950 to 2011

♦ April is typically one of the best months of the year. ♦ April has recently turned out to be a pivotal month, producing market peaks in 2011 and 2012. Investors should be watching for the same trend to take place in 2013. ♦ The energy and materials sectors tend to perform well in April, but these seasonal trades did not work in 2011 and 2012. If energy does not perform well in April when it is typically strong, investors should be cautious going forward. ♦ The Canadian dollar also has a strong track record of outperforming the U.S. dollar in April.

BEST / WORST APRIL BROAD MKTS. 2003-2012

BEST APRIL MARKETS
- ♦ Russell 2000 (2009) 15.3%
- ♦ Nasdaq (2009) 12.3%
- ♦ Russell 3000 Value (2009) 10.9%

WORST APRIL MARKETS
- ♦ Russell 2000 (2005) -5.8%
- ♦ Russell 2000 (2004) -5.2%
- ♦ TSX Comp. (2004) -4.0%

Index Values End of Month

	2003	2004	2005	2006	2007	2008	2009	2010	2011	2012
Dow	8,480	10,226	10,193	11,367	13,063	12,820	8,168	11,009	12,811	13,214
S&P 500	917	1,107	1,157	1,311	1,482	1,386	873	1,187	1,364	1,398
Nasdaq	1,464	1,920	1,922	2,323	2,525	2,413	1,717	2,461	2,874	3,046
TSX	6,586	8,244	9,369	12,204	13,417	13,937	9,325	12,211	13,945	12,293
Russell 1000	934	1,138	1,198	1,373	1,553	1,453	917	1,259	1,458	774
Russell 2000	991	1,391	1,440	1,900	2,024	1,780	1,212	1,781	2,150	817
Russell 3000 Growth	1,495	1,820	1,807	2,090	2,305	2,261	1,524	2,081	2,494	2,611
Russell 3000 Value	1,759	2,188	2,426	2,825	3,241	2,858	1,696	2,369	2,667	2,617

Percent Gain for April

	2003	2004	2005	2006	2007	2008	2009	2010	2011	2012
Dow	6.1	-1.3	-3.0	2.3	5.7	4.5	7.3	1.4	4.0	0.0
S&P 500	8.1	-1.7	-2.0	1.2	4.3	4.8	9.4	1.5	2.8	-0.7
Nasdaq	9.2	-3.7	-3.9	-0.7	4.3	5.9	12.3	2.6	3.3	-1.5
TSX	3.8	-4.0	-2.5	0.8	1.9	4.4	6.9	1.4	-1.2	-0.8
Russell 1000	7.9	-1.9	-2.0	1.1	4.1	5.0	10.0	1.8	2.9	-0.7
Russell 2000	9.4	-5.2	-5.8	-0.1	1.7	4.1	15.3	5.6	2.6	-1.6
Russell 3000 Growth	7.5	-1.5	-2.3	-0.2	4.5	5.2	9.9	1.3	3.3	-0.3
Russell 3000 Value	8.6	-2.8	-2.2	2.1	3.3	4.6	10.9	2.8	2.4	-1.2

April Market Avg. Performance 2003 to 2012[1]

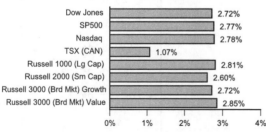

	Dow Jones	2.72%
	SP500	2.77%
	Nasdaq	2.78%
	TSX (CAN)	1.07%
	Russell 1000 (Lg Cap)	2.81%
	Russell 2000 (Sm Cap)	2.60%
	Russell 3000 (Brd Mkt) Growth	2.72%
	Russell 3000 (Brd Mkt) Value	2.85%

Interest Corner Apr[2]

	Fed Funds %[3]	3 Mo. T-Bill %[4]	10 Yr %[5]	20 Yr %[6]
2012	0.25	0.10	1.95	2.73
2011	0.25	0.04	3.32	4.15
2010	0.25	0.16	3.69	4.36
2009	0.25	0.14	3.16	4.10
2008	2.00	1.43	3.77	4.49

(1) Russell Data provided by Russell (2) Federal Reserve Bank of St. Louis- end of month values (3) Target rate set by FOMC (4)(5)(6) Constant yield maturities.

THACKRAY SECTOR THERMOMETER

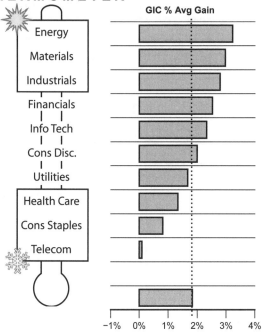

GIC[2] % Avg Gain	Fq % Gain >S&P 500	SP GIC SECTOR 1990-2011[1]
3.2 %	68 %	Energy
3.0	50	Materials
2.8	64	Industrials
2.5	55	Financials
2.3	55	Information Technology
2.0	55	Consumer Discretionary
1.7	45	Utilities
1.3	45	Health Care
0.8	41	Consumer Staples
0.1 %	27 %	Telecom
1.8 %	N/A %	S&P 500

Sector Commentary

♦ Three out of the top four sectors in April 2012 were defensive sectors (telecom, utilities and consumer staples, with returns of 4.2%, 1.8%, 0.1%, respectively). April is a cyclical month – if there is any month where the cyclicals typically outperform, it is April. Not so in 2012, as the cyclicals were all gathered at the bottom of the sector rankings. The energy, materials and industrials were three of the bottom sectors in the market.

Sub-Sector Commentary

♦ The railroad sub-sector is typically strong in April, and in 2012 it produced a very strong 5.8% gain, which compares to the S&P 500 which had a minor loss of 0.1%. The homebuilders were the top sub-sector, producing a gain of 6.5%. Consistent with the major sector trends, the commodities were the biggest losers. The worst performing of the group was the steel sub-sector with a loss of 6.7%.

		SELECTED SUB-SECTORS 1990-2011[3]
3.4 %	59 %	Railroads
3.1	68	Chemicals
3.0	55	Banks
2.7	59	Transportation
2.0	45	Steel
1.8	50	Pharmaceuticals
1.8	45	Homebuilders
1.7	41	Metals and Mining
1.7	45	Software & Services
0.7	41	Retail
0.7	45	Gold (London PM)
0.6	45	Silver (London)
-0.1	56	Agriculture (94-2011)
-0.6	35	Biotech (93-2011)

(1) Sector data provided by Standard and Poors (2) GIC is short form for Global Industry Classification (3) Sub Sector data provided by Standard and Poors, except where marked by symbol.

18 DAY EARNINGS MONTH EFFECT
Markets Outperform 1st 18 Calendar Days of Earnings Months

Earnings season occurs the first month of every quarter. At this time, public companies report their financials for the previous quarter and often give guidance on future expectations. As a result investors tend to bid up stocks, anticipating good earnings.

Earnings are a major driver of stock market prices as investors generally like to get in the stock market early in anticipation of favorable results, which helps to run up stock prices in the first half of the month.

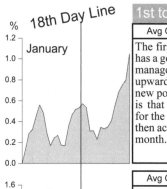

	1st to 18th Day Gain S&P500			
	JAN	APR	JUL	OCT
1950	0.54 %	4.28 %	-3.56 %	2.88 %
1951	4.85	3.41	4.39	1.76
1952	2.02	-3.57	-0.44	-1.39
1953	-2.07	-2.65	0.87	3.38
1954	2.50	3.71	2.91	-1.49
1955	-3.28	4.62	3.24	-4.63
1956	-2.88	-1.53	4.96	2.18
1957	-4.35	2.95	2.45	-4.93
1958	2.78	1.45	1.17	2.80
1959	1.09	4.47	1.23	0.79
1960	-3.34	2.26	-2.14	1.55
1961	2.70	1.75	-0.36	2.22
1962	-4.42	-1.84	2.65	0.12
1963	3.30	3.49	-1.27	2.26
1964	2.05	1.99	2.84	0.77
1965	2.05	2.31	1.87	1.91
1966	1.64	2.63	2.66	2.77
1967	6.80	1.84	3.16	-1.51
1968	-0.94	7.63	1.87	2.09
1969	-1.76	-0.27	-2.82	3.37
1970	-1.24	-4.42	6.83	-0.02
1971	1.37	3.17	0.42	-1.01
1972	1.92	2.40	-1.22	-2.13
1973	0.68	0.02	2.00	1.46
1974	-2.04	0.85	-2.58	13.76
1975	3.50	3.53	-2.09	5.95
1976	7.55	-2.04	0.38	-3.58
1977	-3.85	2.15	0.47	-3.18
1978	-4.77	4.73	1.40	-2.00
1979	3.76	0.11	-1.19	-5.22
1980	2.90	-1.51	6.83	4.83
1981	-0.73	-0.96	-0.34	2.59
1982	-4.35	4.33	1.33	13.54
1983	4.10	4.43	-2.20	1.05
1984	1.59	-0.80	-1.16	1.20
1985	2.44	0.10	1.32	2.72
1986	-1.35	1.46	-5.77	3.25
1987	9.96	-1.64	3.48	-12.16
1988	1.94	0.12	-1.09	2.75
1989	3.17	3.78	4.20	-2.12
1990	-4.30	0.23	1.73	-0.10
1991	0.61	3.53	3.83	1.20
1992	0.42	3.06	1.83	-1.45
1993	0.26	-0.60	-1.06	2.07
1994	1.67	-0.74	2.46	1.07
1995	2.27	0.93	2.52	0.52
1996	-1.25	-0.29	-4.04	3.42
1997	4.78	1.22	3.41	-0.33
1998	-0.92	1.90	4.67	3.88
1999	1.14	2.54	3.36	-2.23
2000	-0.96	-3.80	2.69	-6.57
2001	2.10	6.71	-1.36	2.66
2002	-1.79	-2.00	-10.94	8.48
2003	2.50	5.35	1.93	4.35
2004	2.51	0.75	-3.46	-0.05
2005	-1.32	-2.93	2.50	-4.12
2006	2.55	1.22	0.51	3.15
2007	1.41	4.33	-3.20	1.48
2008	-9.75	5.11	-1.51	19.36
2009	-5.88	8.99	2.29	2.89
2010	1.88	1.94	3.32	3.81
2011	2.97	-1.56	-1.15	8.30
Avg	0.59. %	1.50 %	0.76 %	0.83 %

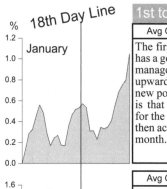

18th Day Line — 1st to 18th Day 1950-2011

January

Avg Gain 0.6%	Fq Pos 63%

The first month of the year generally has a good start. Investors and money managers generally push the market upward as they try to lock in their new positions for the year. The result is that the market tends to increase for the first eighteen days, pause, and then accelerate through the end of the month.

April

Avg Gain 1.5%	Fq Pos 71%

This month has a reputation of being a strong month. If you look at the graph you can see that almost all of the gains have come in the first half of the month. It is interesting to note that the month returns tend to peak just after the last day to file tax returns.

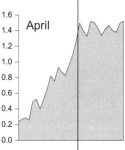

July

Avg Gain 0.8%	Fq Pos 63%

This is the month in which the market can peak in strong bull markets. The returns in the first half of the month can be positive, but investors should be cautious, as the time period following in August and September has a tendency towards negative returns.

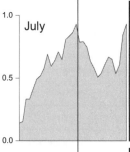

October

Avg Gain 0.8%	Fq Pos 65%

This is the month with a bad reputation. Once again, the first part of the month tends to do well. It is the middle segment, centered around the notorious Black Monday, that brings down the results. Toward the end of the month investors realize that the world has not ended and start to buy stocks again, providing a strong finish to the month.

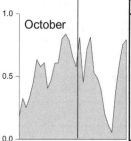

2011-12 Strategy Performance

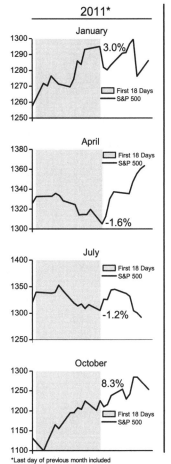

2011*

January — 3.0%

April — -1.6%

July — -1.2%

October — 8.3%

*Last day of previous month included

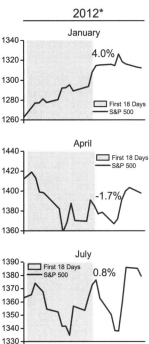

2012*

January — 4.0%

April — -1.7%

July — 0.8%

Legend: First 18 Days / S&P 500

WEEK 14

Market Indices & Rates
Weekly Values**

Stock Markets	2011	2012
Dow	12,402	13,150
S&P500	1,333	1,407
Nasdaq	2,791	3,095
TSX	14,202	12,278
FTSE	6,026	5,785
DAX	7,192	6,900
Nikkei	9,656	9,887
Hang Seng	24,278	20,635

Commodities	2011	2012
Oil	109.75	103.51
Gold	1451.9	1651.4

Bond Yields	2011	2012
USA 5 Yr Treasury	2.28	1.02
USA 10 Yr T	3.54	2.21
USA 20 Yr T	4.35	2.98
Moody's Aaa	5.19	4.03
Moody's Baa	6.10	5.29
CAN 5 Yr T	2.82	1.63
CAN 10 Yr T	3.41	2.14

Money Market	2011	2012
USA Fed Funds	0.25	0.25
USA 3 Mo T-B	0.05	0.08
CAN tgt overnight rate	1.00	1.00
CAN 3 Mo T-B	0.97	0.94

Foreign Exchange	2011	2012
USD/EUR	1.43	1.32
USD/GBP	1.63	1.59
CAN/USD	0.96	0.99
JPY/USD	84.82	82.27

APRIL

M	T	W	T	F	S	S
1	2	3	4	5	6	7
8	9	10	11	12	13	14
15	16	17	18	19	20	21
22	23	24	25	26	27	28
29	30					

Earnings Month Effect Performance

Despite weakening economic conditions, company earnings have held up relatively well in 2011 and the first half of 2012. As a result, the first eighteen calendar days in the earnings months have produced very respectable results. Although the frequency of losses and gains in 2011 and year-to-date for 2012 are approximately equal, the magnitude of the gains is much greater.

It is interesting to note that the first eighteen calendar days in April for 2011 and 2012 produced negative results. Historically the first part of April tends to be strong, even compared to the other earnings months. Although it is not a necessary condition, a weak first half of April should be a cautionary signal that the markets could be in for a "rough" patch.

MAY

M	T	W	T	F	S	S
		1	2	3	4	5
6	7	8	9	10	11	12
13	14	15	16	17	18	19
20	21	22	23	24	25	26
27	28	29	30	31		

JUNE

M	T	W	T	F	S	S
					1	2
3	4	5	6	7	8	9
10	11	12	13	14	15	16
17	18	19	20	21	22	23
24	25	26	27	28	29	30

** Weekly avg closing values- except Fed Funds & CAN overnight tgt rate weekly closing values.

CONSUMER SWITCH
SELL CONSUMER DISCRETIONARY
BUY CONSUMER STAPLES
Consumer Staples Outperform Apr 23 to Oct 27

The *Consumer Switch* strategy has allowed investors to use a set portion of their account to switch between the two related consumer sectors. To use this strategy, investors invest in the consumer discretionary sector from October 28th to April 22nd, and then use the proceeds to invest in the consumer staples sector from April 23rd to October 27th, and then repeat the cycle.

The end result has been outperformance compared with buying and holding both consumer sectors, or buying and holding the broad market.

> ## 2368% total aggregate gain compared with 313% for the S&P 500

The basic premise of the strategy is that the consumer discretionary sector tends to outperform during the favorable six months when more money flows into the market, pushing up stock prices. On the other hand, the consumer staples sector tends to outperform when investors are looking for safety and stability of earnings in the six months when the market tends to move into a defensive mode.

Consumer Staples & Discretionary Switch Strategy*			
Investment Period	Buy @ Beginning of Period	% Gain @ End of Period	% Gain Cumulative
90 Apr23 - 90 Oct29	Staples	7.7%	8%
90 Oct29 - 91 Apr23	Discretionary	41.7	53
91 Apr23 - 91 Oct28	Staples	2.1	56
91 Oct28 - 92 Apr23	Discretionary	15.9	81
92 Apr23 - 92 Oct27	Staples	6.3	92
92 Oct27 - 93 Apr23	Discretionary	6.3	104
93 Apr23 - 93 Oct27	Staples	5.8	116
93 Oct27 - 94 Apr25	Discretionary	-3.7	108
94 Apr25 - 94 Oct27	Staples	10.2	129
94 Oct27 - 95 Apr24	Discretionary	4.4	139
95 Apr24 - 95 Oct27	Staples	15.3	176
95 Oct27 - 96 Apr23	Discretionary	17.3	227
96 Apr23 - 96 Oct27	Staples	12.6	265
96 Oct27 - 97 Apr23	Discretionary	5.1	283
97 Apr23 - 97 Oct27	Staples	2.5	293
97 Oct27 - 98 Apr23	Discretionary	35.9	434
98 Apr23 - 98 Oct27	Staples	-0.7	423
98 Oct27 - 99 Apr23	Discretionary	41.8	651
99 Apr23 - 99 Oct27	Staples	-9.7	578
99 Oct27 - 00 Apr24	Discretionary	11.9	659
00 Apr24 - 00 Oct27	Staples	16.5	785
00 Oct27 - 01 Apr23	Discretionary	9.8	872
01 Apr23 - 01 Oct29	Staples	4.0	910
01 Oct29 - 02 Apr23	Discretionary	16.1	1073
02 Apr23 - 02 Oct28	Staples	-13.9	910
02 Oct28 - 03 Apr23	Discretionary	3.0	941
03 Apr23 - 03 Oct27	Staples	8.4	1028
03 Oct27 - 04 Apr23	Discretionary	9.6	1137
04 Apr23 - 04 Oct27	Staples	-7.4	1045
04 Oct27 - 05 Apr25	Discretionary	-2.0	1021
05 Apr25 - 05 Oct27	Staples	-0.5	1016
05 Oct27 - 06 Apr24	Discretionary	9.2	1119
06 Apr24 - 06 Oct27	Staples	10.6	1249
06 Oct27 - 07 Apr23	Discretionary	6.3	1334
07 Apr23 - 07 Oct29	Staples	4.6	1400
07 Oct29 - 08 Apr23	Discretionary	-13.7	1194
08 Apr23 - 08 Oct27	Staples	-21.5	916
08 Oct27 - 09 Apr23	Discretionary	17.7	1096
09 Apr23 - 09 Oct27	Staples	20.6	1342
09 Oct27 - 10 Apr23	Discretionary	29.7	1770
10 Apr23 - 10 Oct27	Staples	2.4	1815
10 Oct27 - 11 Apr25	Discretionary	13.7	2079
11 Apr25 - 11 Oct27	Staples	2.2	2126
11 Oct27 - 12 Apr 23	Discretionary	10.9	2368

* If buy date lands on weekend or holiday, then date used is next trading date

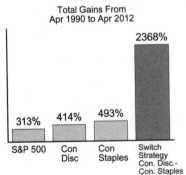

Total Gains From Apr 1990 to Apr 2012

- S&P 500: 313%
- Con Disc: 414%
- Con Staples: 493%
- Switch Strategy Con. Disc.- Con. Staples: 2368%

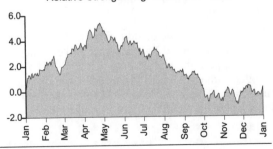

Consumer Discretionary / Consumer Staples Relative Strength Avg. Year 1990 - 2011

2011-12 Strategy Performance

Consumer Discretionary

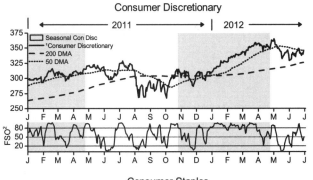

Consumer Staples

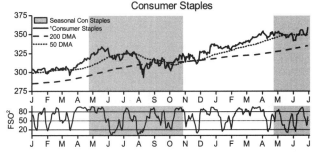

Consumer Discretionary / Consumer Staples[3]

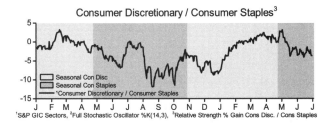

[1]S&P GIC Sectors, [2]Full Stochastic Oscillator %K(14,3), [3]Relative Strength % Gain Cons Disc. / Cons Staples

Market Indices & Rates Weekly Values**		
Stock Markets	2011	2012
Dow	12,309	12,857
S&P500	1,317	1,373
Nasdaq	2,761	3,024
TSX	13,851	12,047
FTSE	5,998	5,648
DAX	7,162	6,652
Nikkei	9,632	9,541
Hang Seng	24,087	20,381
Commodities	2011	2012
Oil	108.21	102.53
Gold	1463.7	1659.3
Bond Yields	2011	2012
USA 5 Yr Treasury	2.22	0.88
USA 10 Yr T	3.51	2.04
USA 20 Yr T	4.33	2.81
Moody's Aaa	5.16	3.94
Moody's Baa	6.07	5.19
CAN 5 Yr T	2.78	1.54
CAN 10 Yr T	3.39	2.02
Money Market	2011	2012
USA Fed Funds	0.25	0.25
USA 3 Mo T-B	0.06	0.09
CAN tgt overnight rate	1.00	1.00
CAN 3 Mo T-B	0.95	0.95
Foreign Exchange	2011	2012
USD/EUR	1.45	1.31
USD/GBP	1.63	1.59
CAN/USD	0.96	1.00
JPY/USD	83.73	80.97

APRIL

M	T	W	T	F	S	S
1	2	3	4	5	6	7
8	9	10	11	12	13	14
15	16	17	18	19	20	21
22	23	24	25	26	27	28
29	30					

MAY

M	T	W	T	F	S	S
	1	2	3	4	5	
6	7	8	9	10	11	12
13	14	15	16	17	18	19
20	21	22	23	24	25	26
27	28	29	30	31		

JUNE

M	T	W	T	F	S	S
					1	2
3	4	5	6	7	8	9
10	11	12	13	14	15	16
17	18	19	20	21	22	23
24	25	26	27	28	29	30

Consumer Switch Strategy Performance

The Consumer Switch strategy keeps turning out successful performances and the last couple of years has been no exception.

As can be seen from the above graphs, both the consumer discretionary sector and the consumer staples sector generally rose at the same time of the year. The success of the strategy has been in the relative performance of the two sectors. The consumer discretionary sector outperformed during the October to April time period and the consumer staples sector outperformed from the May to October time period. In other words, the strategy has continued to work as it should.

** Weekly avg closing values- except Fed Funds & CAN overnight tgt rate weekly closing values.

BIG BLUE – Makes Green
Positive Action During Earnings Season
①Apr14-May19 ②Jul7-Jul30 ③Oct28-Nov26

What do April, July and October have in common? They are all earnings months and IBM tends to perform well at some time in the month. January is also an earnings month, and IBM also outperforms the S&P 500 at this time, but the results are not as strong as the other three earnings months.

18.6% gain & positive 91% of time

In April, starting on the 14th, IBM tends to outperform the S&P 500 just after the earnings season gets underway.

In July, starting on July 7th, IBM tends to outperform the S&P 500 at the same time as the earnings seasons gets underway.

In October, starting on October 28th, IBM tends to outperform the S&P 500 after the earnings season is underway.

In all cases, the average seasonal trend lasts past the earnings season period.

It is possible that investors rotate into IBM, a blue chip company with a lower beta than the market, as the market starts to fade the earnings season.

> ⓘ *International Business Machines Corporation (IBM) is an information technology (IT) company that trades on NYSE.*

IBM vs. S&P 500 1990 to 2011   Positive

Year	Apr 14 to May 19 S&P 500	IBM	Jul 7 to Jul 30 S&P 500	IBM	Oct 28 to Nov 26 S&P 500	IBM	Compound Growth S&P 500	IBM
1990	3.0 %	7.7 %	-0.8 %	-4.8 %	3.9	6.8 %	6.1 %	9.5 %
1991	-2.1	-3.9	3.4	3.0	-1.6	-0.1	-0.5	-1.1
1992	2.5	5.9	2.4	-2.8	2.6	-0.8	7.7	2.1
1993	-0.4	0.3	1.5	-5.1	-0.3	21.7	0.8	15.9
1994	2.3	16.9	2.7	8.3	-2.9	-4.4	2.0	21.1
1995	2.0	8.0	1.6	11.9	3.5	-0.5	7.2	20.2
1996	5.1	-0.6	-3.4	9.7	7.9	24.9	9.5	36.3
1997	13.0	26.5	3.9	11.8	8.5	21.9	27.3	72.5
1998	0.0	19.9	-1.2	17.3	11.4	15.4	10.0	62.1
1999	-0.4	30.5	-4.3	-4.1	9.3	11.5	4.1	39.5
2000	-2.3	-3.3	-2.5	9.9	-2.7	6.7	-7.4	13.3
2001	9.2	22.1	1.2	-0.6	4.8	4.7	15.7	27.0
2002	-0.4	0.1	-8.7	-2.3	1.7	14.1	-7.5	11.5
2003	6.0	9.8	0.2	-3.6	2.7	1.6	9.0	7.5
2004	-3.6	-6.4	-1.3	1.6	5.1	5.2	0.0	0.0
2005	1.5	-8.8	3.3	10.1	7.6	7.9	12.7	8.4
2006	-1.7	-2.1	0.4	-1.5	1.7	2.9	0.3	-0.7
2007	4.8	13.8	-3.7	5.0	-8.3	-10.3	-7.5	7.1
2008	7.0	9.0	1.7	7.8	4.6	2.5	13.8	20.5
2009	5.8	5.6	9.8	16.0	4.4	5.5	21.3	29.1
2010	-6.9	-0.1	7.2	4.0	0.6	1.9	0.4	5.8
2011	2.2	4.1	-3.5	2.3	-9.8	-4.8	-11.0	1.4
Avg.	2.1 %	7.0 %	0.4 %	4.3 %	2.5 %	6.1 %	5.2 %	18.6 %
Fq>0	59 %	68 %	59	64 %	73 %	73 %	73 %	91 %

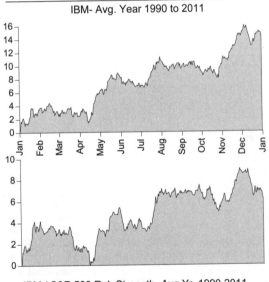

IBM- Avg. Year 1990 to 2011

IBM / S&P 500 Rel. Strength- Avg Yr. 1990-2011

2011-12 Strategy Performance

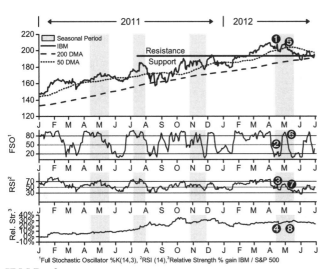

¹Full Stochastic Oscillator %K(14,3), ²RSI (14),³Relative Strength % gain IBM / S&P 500

Market Indices & Rates
Weekly Values**

Stock Markets	2011	2012
Dow	12,357	13,013
S&P500	1,321	1,380
Nasdaq	2,776	3,014
TSX	13,827	12,121
FTSE	5,952	5,739
DAX	7,153	6,716
Nikkei	9,594	9,550
Hang Seng	23,846	20,792

Commodities	2011	2012
Oil	109.46	103.02
Gold	1197.7	1644.8

Bond Yields	2011	2012
USA 5 Yr Treasury	2.12	0.86
USA 10 Yr T	3.41	2.00
USA 20 Yr T	4.23	2.76
Moody's Aaa	5.16	3.93
Moody's Baa	5.98	5.15
CAN 5 Yr T	2.68	1.61
CAN 10 Yr T	3.28	2.05

Money Market	2011	2012
USA Fed Funds	0.25	0.25
USA 3 Mo T-B	0.06	0.08
CAN tgt overnight rate	1.00	1.00
CAN 3 Mo T-B	0.96	0.98

Foreign Exchange	2011	2012
USD/EUR	1.44	1.31
USD/GBP	1.64	1.60
CAN/USD	0.96	0.99
JPY/USD	82.31	81.13

APRIL

M	T	W	T	F	S	S
1	2	3	4	5	6	7
8	9	10	11	12	13	14
15	16	17	18	19	20	21
22	23	24	25	26	27	28
29	30					

MAY

M	T	W	T	F	S	S
		1	2	3	4	5
6	7	8	9	10	11	12
13	14	15	16	17	18	19
20	21	22	23	24	25	26
27	28	29	30	31		

JUNE

M	T	W	T	F	S	S
					1	2
3	4	5	6	7	8	9
10	11	12	13	14	15	16
17	18	19	20	21	22	23
24	25	26	27	28	29	30

IBM Performance

In 2011, and up until June 2012, IBM performed very well and managed to generally stay above its 200 day moving average. Most of IBM's gains were made in 2011 and in 2012 generally performed at market. Investor's should be looking forward to the next seasonal trade as IBM offers a number of times where it tends to outperform the S&P 500.

Technical Conditions– April 12th to May 19th, 2012
Entry Date April 14th, 2012 –Bullish– Initially, the entry was set up very well for IBM as it was above its support level and its 50 day moving average❶. The FSO had just turned up above 20❷ and the RSI was bouncing off 50❸. In addition, IBM had turned down slightly, but it had not broken down relative to the S&P 500❹.

Entry Strategy –Buy Position on Entry Date– Although IBM was set up well at the beginning of its seasonal period in April, it faltered along with the market. Shortly after entry, it broke below its 50 day moving average.

Exit Strategy –Sell Partial Position Early & Remainder on Exit Date– At the beginning of May, IBM broke below its 50 day moving average for a second time (bearish signal)❺. At the same time, the FSO turned sharply below 80❻. The RSI also traded below 50❼. Although IBM was trading at approximately "market," the market was suffering in May and IBM suffered with it❽.

Overall, the technical signals justified selling a partial position early. On the exit date the situation had not improved and with IBM sitting on resistance, a prudent seasonal investor would consider exiting the rest of the position.

CANADIAN DOLLAR STRONG APRIL

Since the year 2000 when the price of oil started its ascent, the Canadian dollar has been labelled as a "petro" currency by foreign investors.

All other things being equal, if oil increases in price, investors favor the Canadian dollar over the U.S. dollar. They do so with good reason, as Canada is a net exporter of oil and benefits from its rising price.

Oil tends to do well in the month of April as this is the heart of one of the strongest seasonal strategies – oil and oil stocks outperform from February 25th to May 9th (see *Oil Winter/Spring Strategy*). With the rising price of oil in April the Canadian dollar gets a free ride upwards.

April has been a strong month for the Canadian dollar relative to the U.S. dollar. The largest losses have had a tendency to occur in years when the Fed Reserve has been aggressively hiking their target rate.

At some point during the years 1987, 2000, 2004 and 2005, the Fed increased their target rate by a total of at least 1% in each year. Since 1971 three of these years (1987, 2004 and 2005) were three of the biggest losers for the Canadian dollar in the month of April.

The Canadian dollar has been strong in April regardless of the long-term trend

CAD vs USD Avg. % Gain 1971 to 2011

of the dollar moving either up or down. The Canadian dollar started at approximately par in 1971 and reached a low in 2002 of $0.62 and then reached a recent high of $1.09 in 2007.

In both the ups and downs of the economy, the Canadian dollar has outperformed the U.S. dollar in April.

CAD vs USD Apr % Gain 1971-2012   Positive

		1980	0.44 %	1990	0.44 %	2000	-2.09%	2010	-0.26 %
1971	-0.10%	1981	-0.74	1991	0.65	2001	2.65	2011	2.70
1972	0.53	1982	0.89	1992	-0.48	2002	1.74	2012	1.16
1973	-0.41	1983	0.36	1993	-1.02	2003	2.60		
1974	1.08	1984	-0.62	1994	0.09	2004	-4.58		
1975	-1.56	1985	0.04	1995	3.17	2005	-3.81		
1976	0.55	1986	1.69	1996	-0.15	2006	4.62		
1977	0.91	1987	-2.38	1997	-0.97	2007	3.99		
1978	0.09	1988	0.41	1998	-0.78	2008	1.73		
1979	1.61	1989	0.60	1999	3.42	2009	5.68		
Avg.	0.30 %		-0.02%		0.44 %		1.25 %		1.20 %

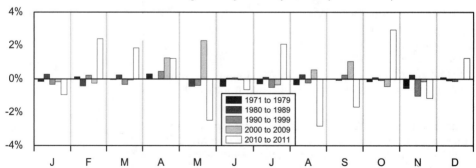

CAD vs. USD Avg. Year By Month By Decade (1971 to 2011)

Legend:
- 1971 to 1979
- 1980 to 1989
- 1990 to 1999
- 2000 to 2009
- 2010 to 2011

2011-12 Strategy Performance

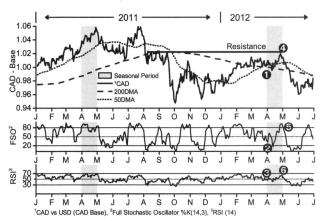

¹CAD vs USD (CAD Base), ²Full Stochastic Oscillator %K(14,3), ³RSI (14)

Market Indices & Rates
Weekly Values**

Stock Markets	2011	2012
Dow	12,668	13,090
S&P500	1,352	1,387
Nasdaq	2,858	3,016
TSX	13,910	12,093
FTSE	6,069	5,724
DAX	7,438	6,672
Nikkei	9,693	9,531
Hang Seng	23,857	20,700

Commodities	2011	2012
Oil	112.73	103.80
Gold	1514.7	1646.7

Bond Yields	2011	2012
USA 5 Yr Treasury	2.04	0.84
USA 10 Yr T	3.36	1.98
USA 20 Yr T	4.18	2.74
Moody's Aaa	5.13	3.95
Moody's Baa	5.93	5.15
CAN 5 Yr T	2.62	1.66
CAN 10 Yr T	3.23	2.07

Money Market	2011	2012
USA Fed Funds	0.25	0.25
USA 3 Mo T-B	0.06	0.09
CAN tgt overnight rate	1.00	1.00
CAN 3 Mo T-B	0.98	1.05

Foreign Exchange	2011	2012
USD/EUR	1.47	1.32
USD/GBP	1.66	1.62
CAN/USD	0.95	0.99
JPY/USD	81.65	81.02

Canadian Dollar Performance

In April 2011 and 2012, the Canadian dollar once again put in a positive performance. This is despite the Canadian dollar's overall decline for a year and a half, up until the middle of 2012. The Canadian dollar often benefits from a rising oil price as many investors refer to the Canadian currency as a "petro" currency. In 2011 and 2012, oil was very volatile but it still managed to increase in April (historically the strongest month for oil) for both years, helping to boost the Canadian dollar.

Technical Conditions– April 1st to April 30th, 2012
Entry Date April 1st, 2012 –Bullish– After a rise in value during January, the Canadian dollar consolidated for the next two months. Entering its seasonal phase, it was sitting at its 50 and 200 day moving averages❶. The FSO was sitting in its mid-range and not showing a trend❷. Similarly the RSI was also not showing a trend❸.

Entry Strategy –Buy Position on Entry Date– At the start of its seasonal trade, the Canadian dollar had not presented a strong bullish or bearish case. When this happens in a consolidation phase, it is best to err on the bullish side and wait to be proven wrong.

Exit Strategy –Sell Position on Exit Day– ❹ In the second half of April the Canadian dollar was rising sharply up to its resistance point, a level at which it often has trouble exceeding $1.02. On the exit date the Canadian dollar was just below resistance. At the end of a seasonal period, this is usually a good reason to exit. To support the exit case the FSO turned sharply down below 80❺ and the RSI turned down from a high level❻.

Right after the seasonal period for the Canadian dollar, the stock market started to correct and as a result the U.S. dollar increased relative to the Canadian dollar. The seasonal trade for the dollar ended perfectly.

** Weekly avg closing values- except Fed Funds & CAN overnight tgt rate weekly closing values.

APRIL

M	T	W	T	F	S	S
1	2	3	4	5	6	7
8	9	10	11	12	13	14
15	16	17	18	19	20	21
22	23	24	25	26	27	28
29	30					

MAY

M	T	W	T	F	S	S
		1	2	3	4	5
6	7	8	9	10	11	12
13	14	15	16	17	18	19
20	21	22	23	24	25	26
27	28	29	30	31		

JUNE

M	T	W	T	F	S	S
					1	2
3	4	5	6	7	8	9
10	11	12	13	14	15	16
17	18	19	20	21	22	23
24	25	26	27	28	29	30

MAY

	MONDAY	TUESDAY	WEDNESDAY
WEEK 18	29	30	**1** 30
WEEK 19	**6** 25	**7** 24	**8** 23
WEEK 20	**13** 18	**14** 17	**15** 16
WEEK 21	**20** 11 CAN Market Closed- Victoria Day	**21** 10	**22** 9
WEEK 22	**27** 4 USA Market Closed- Memorial Day	**28** 3	**29** 2

THURSDAY		FRIDAY	
2	29	**3**	28
9	22	**10**	21
16	15	**17**	14
23	8	**24**	7
30	1	**31**	

JUNE

M	T	W	T	F	S	S
					1	2
3	4	5	6	7	8	9
10	11	12	13	14	15	16
17	18	19	20	21	22	23
24	25	26	27	28	29	30

JULY

M	T	W	T	F	S	S
1	2	3	4	5	6	7
8	9	10	11	12	13	14
15	16	17	18	19	20	21
22	23	24	25	26	27	28
29	30	31				

AUGUST

M	T	W	T	F	S	S
			1	2	3	4
5	6	7	8	9	10	11
12	13	14	15	16	17	18
19	20	21	22	23	24	25
26	27	28	29	30	31	

SEPTEMBER

M	T	W	T	F	S	S
						1
2	3	4	5	6	7	8
9	10	11	12	13	14	15
16	17	18	19	20	21	22
23	24	25	26	27	28	29
30						

MAY
S U M M A R Y

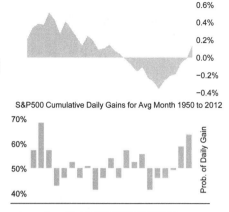

	Dow Jones	S&P 500	Nasdaq	TSX Comp
Month Rank	8	8	5	2
# Up	31	35	24	18
# Down	31	27	16	9
% Pos	50	56	60	67
% Avg. Gain	0.0	0.2	1.0	1.9

Dow & S&P 1950-2011, Nasdaq 1972-2011, TSX 1985-2011

S&P500 Cumulative Daily Gains for Avg Month 1950 to 2012

♦ The beginning of May is often the time that investors should start to become cautious and defensive. ♦ On average, at this time of the year the market peaks or at least flattens out. May has been a weak month for the last three years. In 2012, it produced a loss of 6.3% in the S&P 500. The telecom sector produced a gain of 2.6%, which was the only positive sector for the month. ♦ The defensive sectors dominated the sector ranks and although they produced losses, they performed much better than the cyclicals.

BEST / WORST MAY BROAD MKTS. 2003-2012

BEST MAY MARKETS
♦ TSX Comp. (2009) 11.2%
♦ Russell 2000 (2003) 10.6%
♦ Nasdaq (2003) 9.0%

WORST MAY MARKETS
♦ Russell 3000 Value (2010) -8.5%
♦ Nasdaq (2010) -8.3%
♦ S&P500 (2010) -8.2%

Index Values End of Month

	2003	2004	2005	2006	2007	2008	2009	2010	2011	2012
Dow	8,850	10,188	10,467	11,168	13,628	12,638	8,500	10,137	12,570	12,393
S&P 500	964	1,121	1,192	1,270	1,531	1,400	919	1,089	1,345	1,310
Nasdaq	1,596	1,987	2,068	2,179	2,605	2,523	1,774	2,257	2,835	2,827
TSX	6,860	8,417	9,607	11,745	14,057	14,715	10,370	11,763	13,803	11,513
Russell 1000	986	1,152	1,239	1,330	1,605	1,477	965	1,157	1,439	724
Russell 2000	1,096	1,412	1,533	1,792	2,105	1,860	1,247	1,644	2,108	762
Russell 3000 Growth	1,574	1,852	1,895	2,009	2,386	2,344	1,596	1,920	2,461	2,437
Russell 3000 Value	1,873	2,206	2,486	2,742	3,348	2,853	1,790	2,169	2,632	2,456

Percent Gain for May

	2003	2004	2005	2006	2007	2008	2009	2010	2011	2012
Dow	4.4	-0.4	2.7	-1.7	4.3	-1.4	4.1	-7.9	-1.9	-6.2
S&P 500	5.1	1.2	3.0	-3.1	3.3	1.1	5.3	-8.2	-1.4	-6.3
Nasdaq	9.0	3.5	7.6	-6.2	3.1	4.6	3.3	-8.3	-1.3	-7.2
TSX	4.2	2.1	2.5	-3.8	4.8	5.6	11.2	-3.7	-1.0	-6.3
Russell 1000	5.5	1.3	3.4	-3.2	3.4	1.6	5.3	-8.1	-1.3	-6.4
Russell 2000	10.6	1.5	6.4	-5.7	4.0	4.5	2.9	-7.7	-2.0	-6.7
Russell 3000 Growth	5.3	1.8	4.9	-3.9	3.5	3.7	4.7	-7.7	-1.3	-6.7
Russell 3000 Value	6.4	0.8	2.5	-2.9	3.3	-0.2	5.5	-8.5	-1.3	-6.1

May Market Avg. Performance 2003 to 2012[1]

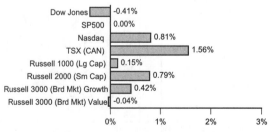

Dow Jones	-0.41%
SP500	0.00%
Nasdaq	0.81%
TSX (CAN)	1.56%
Russell 1000 (Lg Cap)	0.15%
Russell 2000 (Sm Cap)	0.79%
Russell 3000 (Brd Mkt) Growth	0.42%
Russell 3000 (Brd Mkt) Value	-0.04%

Interest Corner May[2]

	Fed Funds %[3]	3 Mo. T-Bill %[4]	10 Yr %[5]	20 Yr %[6]
2012	0.25	0.07	1.59	2.27
2011	0.25	0.06	3.05	3.91
2010	0.25	0.16	3.31	4.05
2009	0.25	0.14	3.47	4.34
2008	2.00	1.89	4.06	4.74

(1) Russell Data provided by Russell (2) Federal Reserve Bank of St. Louis- end of month values (3) Target rate set by FOMC (4)(5)(6) Constant yield maturities.

THACKRAY SECTOR THERMOMETER

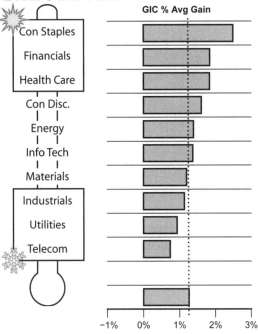

GIC[2] % Avg Gain	Fq % Gain >S&P 500	SP GIC SECTOR 1990-2011[1]
2.5 %	64 %	Consumer Staples
1.8	45	Financials
1.8	50	Health Care
1.6	55	Consumer Discretionary
1.4	36	Energy
1.4	55	Information Technology
1.2	36	Materials
1.1	36	Industrials
0.9	45	Utilities
0.7 %	50 %	Telecom
1.3 %	N/A %	S&P 500

Sector Commentary

♦ In May of 2012, the defensive sectors outperformed across the board. ♦ The telecom sector produced a gain of 2.6% ♦ The utilities, consumer staples and health care sectors were the next best performing sectors, and produced losses of 0.1%, 1.3% and 3.9% respectively. This compared to the S&P 500 which produced a loss of 6.3%. ♦ Although the consumer staples sector is typically one of the top sectors in May, the rest of the defensive sectors typically do not perform well. When the defensive sectors jump to the top of the pack, investors should be wary of a market correction.

Sub-Sector Commentary

♦ The agriculture sub-sector produced a gain of 3.4% in May 2012, which was the only positive performance amongst the sub-sectors tracked. ♦ Homebuilders were the next best performing sub-sector, but only managed to produce a loss of 1.3%. ♦ The three worst performing sub-sectors from the list were silver, metals and mining, and steel, with losses of 9.9%, 13.0% and 18.2%, respectively. The cyclical sub-sectors continued to get punished in May, as investors were concerned by slowing international growth.

SELECTED SUB-SECTORS 1990-2011[3]		
2.5 %	65 %	Biotech (93-2011)
2.5	50	Agriculture (94-2011)
2.3	45	Banks
2.1	43	Chemicals
2.1	59	Steel
2.0	59	Retail
2.0	55	Metals and Mining
1.9	55	Railroads
1.6	45	Pharmaceuticals
0.9	59	Gold (London PM)
0.9	32	Software & Services
0.7	45	Transportation
0.5	55	Silver (London)
-1.3	45	Homebuilders

(1) Sector data provided by Standard and Poors (2) GIC is short form for Global Industry Classification (3) Sub Sector data provided by Standard and Poors, except where marked by symbol.

U.S. GOVERNMENT BONDS (7-10YR.)
May 6th to October 3rd

Since 1982 interest rates have been on a long-term decline and as a result bonds have increased in value. Hidden in this trend is a strong seasonal tendency for U.S. government bonds (7-10 year maturities) to outperform from May 6th to October 3rd.

4.8% gain &
positive 77% of the time

Bonds outperform from the late spring into autumn for three reasons. First, governments and companies tend to raise more money through bond issuance at the beginning of the year to meet their needs for the rest of the year. With more bonds competing in the market for money, interest rates tend to increase.

Second, optimistic forecasts at the beginning of the year for stronger GDP growth tend to increase inflation expectations and as a result interest rates respond by increasing. As GDP expectations tend to decrease in the summer months, interest rates respond by retreating.

U.S. Gov. Bonds 7-10 yr. Total Return* vs. S&P 500 1999 to 2011			
			Positive
May 6 to Oct 3	S&P 500	Gov. Bonds	Diff
1999	-4.8%	-2.1%	2.7%
2000	-0.4	6.7	7.2
2001	-15.3	7.1	22.4
2002	-23.7	11.9	35.6
2003	11.2	0.0	-11.2
2004	0.9	4.4	3.5
2005	4.6	-0.2	-4.9
2006	0.6	5.3	4.7
2007	2.3	3.0	0.7
2008	-21.9	3.4	25.3
2009	13.4	1.1	-12.3
2010	-1.7	9.8	11.5
2011	-17.7	12.6	30.3
Avg	-4.0%	4.8%	8.9%
Fq > 0	46%	77%	77%

For seasonal investors looking to put their money to work in the unfavorable six months of the year, buying bonds in the summer months fits perfectly.

Although the beginning of May has been a good time to increase an allocation to bonds, when the stock market has continued higher into July, the bond market's entry point can be correspondingly delayed. Nevertheless, May has proven to be a good entry point for government bonds.

Investors should note that government bonds have a track record of appreciating in November and December, but despite their typical positive performance at this time, there are other investments, such as high yield bonds, corporate bonds and equities that have a better return profile.

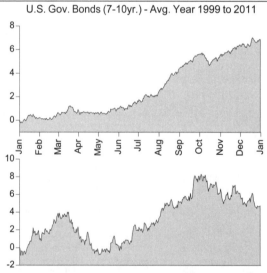

U.S. Gov. Bonds (7-10yr.) - Avg. Year 1999 to 2011

Gov. Bonds/S&P 500 Rel. Strength - Avg Yr. 1999 - 2011

Third, the stock market often peaks in May and investors rotate their money into bonds. As the demand for bonds increases, interest rates decrease and bonds increase in value.

* Source: Barclays Capital Inc.
The U.S. Treasury: 7-10 Year is a total return index, which includes both interest and capital appreciation.
For more information on fixed income indices, see www.barcap.com.

2011-12 Strategy Performance

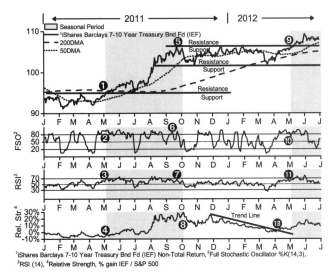

¹iShares Barclays 7-10 Year Treasury Bnd Fd (IEF) Non-Total Return, ²Full Stochastic Oscillator %K(14,3),
³RSI (14), ⁴Relative Strength, % gain IEF / S&P 500

Government Bonds (7-10yr) Performance

The seasonal trade for government bonds worked very well in 2011 and 2012. In both years, government bonds increased in value at the start of their seasonal periods, as money rotated out of the stock market and into the bond market. It is interesting to note that from the end of the government bond seasonal period in 2011 to the beginning of the government bond seasonal period in 2012, government bonds traded in a range and did not increase in value.

Technical Conditions– May 2011 to May 2012

Entry Date May 6th, 2011 –Bullish– In May 2011, government bonds had just completed a bullish "double bottom" pattern and were pushing up against resistance as well as just below the 200 day moving average (bullish for the start of a seasonally strong period)❶. The FSO was showing an overbought reading above 80❷ and the RSI was approaching 70❸. At the time government bonds were not yet outperforming the S&P 500❹.

Entry Strategy –Buy Partial Position Early– The FSO had turned up above 80 early April, justifying a partial early entry.

Exit Strategy –Sell Partial Position Early– Coming into the seasonal exit date government bonds maintained an upwards trend❺. Despite the positive trend, a few weeks prior to the end of the seasonal period, both the FSO and RSI turned below 80 and 70 respectively❻❼, justifying a partial early exit. On the seasonal exit date, government bonds started to underperform the S&P 500❽.

Entry Date May 6th, 2012 –Bullish– In May 2012, government bonds were pushing up against resistance❾. The FSO❿ and RSI⓫ were at the top of their ranges, but had not shown weakness. Most importantly, government bonds had already started to outperform the S&P 500 in early April⓬.

Market Indices & Rates
Weekly Values**

Stock Markets	2010	2011
Dow	12,712	13,201
S&P500	1,348	1,393
Nasdaq	2,835	3,027
TSX	13,652	12,148
FTSE	5,991	5,746
DAX	7,454	6,682
Nikkei	9,932	9,366
Hang Seng	23,342	21,185

Commodities	2010	2011
Oil	106.16	103.46
Gold	1519.7	1649.0

Bond Yields	2010	2011
USA 5 Yr Treasury	1.92	0.82
USA 10 Yr T	3.24	1.95
USA 20 Yr T	4.07	2.72
Moody's Aaa	5.00	3.95
Moody's Baa	5.82	5.15
CAN 5 Yr T	2.53	1.57
CAN 10 Yr T	3.17	2.02

Money Market	2010	2011
USA Fed Funds	0.25	0.25
USA 3 Mo T-B	0.03	0.09
CAN tgt overnight rate	1.00	1.00
CAN 3 Mo T-B	0.97	1.03

Foreign Exchange	2010	2011
USD/EUR	1.47	1.32
USD/GBP	1.65	1.62
CAN/USD	0.96	0.99
JPY/USD	80.70	80.02

MAY

M	T	W	T	F	S	S
	1	2	3	4	5	
6	7	8	9	10	11	12
13	14	15	16	17	18	19
20	21	22	23	24	25	26
27	28	29	30	31		

JUNE

M	T	W	T	F	S	S
					1	2
3	4	5	6	7	8	9
10	11	12	13	14	15	16
17	18	19	20	21	22	23
24	25	26	27	28	29	30

JULY

M	T	W	T	F	S	S
1	2	3	4	5	6	7
8	9	10	11	12	13	14
15	16	17	18	19	20	21
22	23	24	25	26	27	28
29	30	31				

** Weekly avg closing values- except Fed Funds & CAN overnight tgt rate weekly closing values.

Being out of the market feels good when it is going down. And the market has a habit of going down after the beginning of May. Although sometimes a strong market can continue into July and less frequently into autumn, it has historically made sense to reduce your equity exposure in May.

$1,128,103 gain on $10,000

The accompanying table uses the S&P 500 to compare the returns made from Oct 28th to May 5th (favorable six months), to the returns made during the remainder of the year (unfavorable six months). From 1950 to 2012, the October to May time period has produced stunning results.

Starting with $10,000 and investing from October 28th to May 5th every year (October 28th, 1950, to May 5th, 2012) has produced a gain of $1,128,103. On the flip side, being invested from May 6th to October 27th, has actually lost money. An initial investment of $10,000 has lost $3,398 over the same time period.

Investors often worry about being out of the market at a time when the market is rallying, and missing out on profits. Over the last sixty-two years, during the unfavorable six months, the S&P 500 has only had gains of greater than 10%, eight times. This compares with twenty-five times in the favorable six months. Being out of the markets during the unfavorable six months has proven to be a wiser strategy than being out of the markets during the other six months.

	S&P 500 % May 6 to Oct 27	$10,000 Start	S&P 500 % Oct 28 to May 5	$10,000 Start
1950/51	8.5%	10,851	15.2%	11,517
1951/52	0.2	10,870	3.7	11,947
1952/53	1.8	11,067	3.9	12,413
1953/54	-3.1	10,727	16.6	14,475
1954/55	13.2	12,141	18.1	17,097
1955/56	11.4	13,528	15.1	19,681
1956/57	-4.6	12,903	0.2	19,711
1957/58	-12.4	11,302	7.9	21,265
1958/59	15.1	13,013	14.5	24,356
1959/60	-0.6	12,939	-4.5	23,270
1960/61	-2.3	12,647	24.1	28,869
1961/62	2.7	12,993	-3.1	27,982
1962/63	-17.7	10,698	28.4	35,929
1963/64	5.7	11,306	9.3	39,264
1964/65	5.1	11,882	5.5	41,440
1965/66	3.1	12,253	-5.0	39,388
1966/67	-8.8	11,180	17.7	46,364
1967/68	0.6	11,241	3.9	48,171
1968/69	5.6	11,872	0.2	48,249
1969/70	-6.2	11,141	-19.7	38,722
1970/71	5.8	11,782	24.9	48,346
1971/72	-9.6	10,647	13.7	54,965
1972/73	3.7	11,046	0.3	55,154
1973/74	0.3	11,084	-18.0	45,205
1974/75	-23.2	8,513	28.5	58,073
1975/76	-0.4	8,480	12.4	65,290
1976/77	0.9	8,554	-1.6	64,231
1977/78	-7.8	7,890	4.5	67,146
1978/79	-2.0	7,732	6.4	71,476
1979/80	-0.1	7,723	5.8	75,605
1980/81	20.2	9,283	1.9	77,047
1981/82	-8.5	8,498	-1.4	76,001
1982/83	15.0	9,769	21.4	92,293
1983/84	0.3	9,803	-3.5	89,085
1984/85	3.9	10,183	8.9	97,057
1985/86	4.1	10,604	26.8	123,044
1986/87	0.4	10,651	23.7	152,196
1987/88	-21.0	8,409	11.0	168,904
1988/89	7.1	9,010	10.9	187,380
1989/90	8.9	9,814	1.0	189,242
1990/91	-10.0	8,837	25.0	236,498
1991/92	0.9	8,916	8.5	256,590
1992/93	0.4	8,952	6.2	272,550
1993/94	4.5	9,356	-2.8	264,789
1994/95	3.2	9,656	11.6	295,636
1995/96	11.5	10,762	10.7	327,219
1996/97	9.2	11,757	18.5	387,591
1997/98	5.6	12,419	27.2	493,003
1998/99	-4.5	11,860	26.5	623,489
1999/00	-3.8	11,415	10.5	688,842
2000/01	-3.7	10,992	-8.2	632,435
2001/02	-12.8	9,586	-2.8	614,583
2002/03	-16.4	8,016	3.2	634,369
2003/04	11.3	8,921	8.8	689,985
2004/05	0.3	8,952	4.2	718,942
2005/06	0.5	9,000	12.5	808,503
2006/07	3.9	9,350	9.3	883,804
2007/08	2.0	9,534	-8.3	810,240
2008/09	-39.7	5,750	6.5	862,619
2009/10	17.7	6,766	9.6	934,470
2010/11	1.4	6,862	12.9	1,067,851
2011/12	-3.8	6,602	6.6	1,138,103
Total Gain (Loss)		**($3,398)**		**$1,128,103**

S&P 500 Unfavorable 6 Month Avg. Gain vs Favorable 6 Month Avg. Gain (1950-2012)

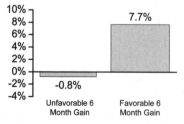

7.7%

-0.8%

Unfavorable 6 Month Gain — Favorable 6 Month Gain

(i) *The above growth rates are geometric averages in order to represent the cumulative growth of a dollar investment over time. These figures differ from the arithmetic mean calculations used in the Six 'N' Six Take a Break Strategy, which are used to represent an average year.*

2011-12 Strategy Performance

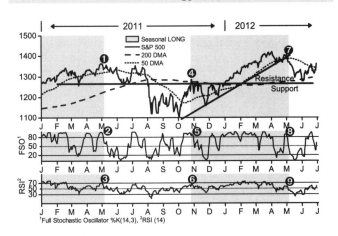

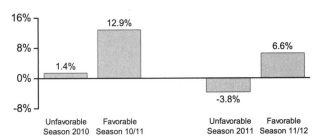

Favorable vs. Unfavorable Seasons 2010-2012 (S&P 500)

Market Indices & Rates
Weekly Values**

Stock Markets	2011	2012
Dow	12,673	12,890
S&P500	1,346	1,360
Nasdaq	2,850	2,941
TSX	13,501	11,734
FTSE	5,962	5,551
DAX	7,451	6,517
Nikkei	9,769	9,062
Hang Seng	23,244	20,309

Commodities	2011	2012
Oil	100.65	96.99
Gold	1503.8	1591.6

Bond Yields	2011	2012
USA 5 Yr Treasury	1.87	0.77
USA 10 Yr T	3.20	1.88
USA 20 Yr T	4.05	2.63
Moody's Aaa	4.98	3.87
Moody's Baa	5.83	5.08
CAN 5 Yr T	2.54	1.49
CAN 10 Yr T	3.22	1.99

Money Market	2011	2012
USA Fed Funds	0.25	0.25
USA 3 Mo T-B	0.03	0.10
CAN tgt overnight rate	1.00	1.00
CAN 3 Mo T-B	0.97	1.01

Foreign Exchange	2011	2012
USD/EUR	1.43	1.30
USD/GBP	1.63	1.61
CAN/USD	0.96	1.00
JPY/USD	80.81	79.86

MAY

M	T	W	T	F	S	S
	1	2	3	4	5	
6	7	8	9	10	11	12
13	14	15	16	17	18	19
20	21	22	23	24	25	26
27	28	29	30	31		

JUNE

M	T	W	T	F	S	S
					1	2
3	4	5	6	7	8	9
10	11	12	13	14	15	16
17	18	19	20	21	22	23
24	25	26	27	28	29	30

JULY

M	T	W	T	F	S	S
1	2	3	4	5	6	7
8	9	10	11	12	13	14
15	16	17	18	19	20	21
22	23	24	25	26	27	28
29	30	31				

Favorable / Unfavorable Season Performance Strategy–
May 6th to October 27th, 2011

In May of 2011, most stock markets around the world were well into correction phases. At that time, the S&P 500 was just starting to correct❶, and quickly fell below its 50 day moving average. Both the FSO and RSI turned down from neutral positions❷❸ and the stock market corrected for the next few months.

Technical Conditions– October 28th to May 5th, 2012
Entry Date October 28th, 2011 – <u>Bullish</u> – The S&P 500 had just completed a bottoming process in early October❹. Its breakout was confirmed when the S&P 500 breached the high levels set in August and September. On the entry date, the S&P 500 sat just above its support line, which is bullish, despite the fact that the FSO was above 80❺ and the RSI touching 70❻.

Entry Strategy – <u>Buy Partial Position Early</u>– Buying an early partial position was warranted as the FSO turned up above 20 at the beginning of October and the RSI turned up from a neutral status.

Exit Strategy – <u>Sell Partial Position Early</u>– The market turned down in early April 2012 and then shortly after broke its 50 day moving average and uptrend line❼. Both the FSO and the RSI turned down at the beginning of May❽❾. A full exit was warranted at this time.

In analysing long-term trends for the broad markets such as the S&P 500 or the TSX Composite, a large data set is preferable because it incorporates various economic cycles. The daily data set for the TSX Composite starts in 1977.

Over this time period, investors have been rewarded for following the six month cycle of investing from October 28th to May 5th, versus the other unfavorable six months, May 6th to October 27th.

Starting with an investment of $10,000 in 1977, investing in the unfavorable six months has produced a loss of $3,817, versus investing in the favorable six months which has produced a gain of $181,207.

$181,207 gain on $10,000 since 1977

The TSX Composite Average Year 1977 to 2011 (graph below) indicates that the market tended to peak in mid-July or the end of August. In our book *Time In Time Out, Outsmart the Stock Market Using Calendar Investment Strategies*, Bruce Lindsay and I analysed a number of market trends and peaks over different decades.

What we found was that the markets tend to peak at the beginning of May or mid-July. The mid-July peak was usually the result of a strong bull market in place that had a lot of momentum.

The main reason that the TSX Composite data shows a peak occurring in July-August is that the data is primarily from the biggest bull market in history, starting in 1982.

Does a later average peak in the stock market mean that the best six month cycle does not work? No. Dividing the year up into six month intervals, the period from October to May is far superior compared with the other half of the year.

The table below illustrates the superiority of the best six months over the worst six months. Going down the table year by year, the period from October 28 to May 5th outperforms the period from May 6th to October 27.

In a strong bull market investors always have the choice of using a stop loss or technical indicators to help extend the exit point past the May date.

	TSX Comp May 6 to Oct 27	$10,000 Start	TSX Comp Oct 28 to May 5	$10,000 Start
1977/78	-3.9 %	9,608	13.1 %	11,313
1978/79	12.1	10,775	21.3	13,728
1979/80	2.9	11,084	23.0	16,883
1980/81	22.5	13,579	-2.4	16,479
1981/82	-17.0	11,272	-18.2	13,488
1982/83	16.6	13,138	34.6	18,150
1983/84	-0.9	13,015	-1.9	17,811
1984/85	1.6	13,226	10.7	19,718
1985/86	0.5	13,299	16.5	22,978
1986/87	-1.9	13,045	24.8	28,666
1987/88	-23.4	9,992	15.3	33,050
1988/89	2.7	10,260	5.7	34,939
1989/90	7.9	11,072	-13.3	30,294
1990/91	-8.4	10,148	13.1	34,266
1991/92	-1.6	9,982	-2.0	33,571
1992/93	-2.3	9,750	15.3	38,704
1993/94	10.8	10,801	1.7	39,365
1994/95	-0.1	10,792	0.3	39,483
1995/96	1.3	10,936	18.2	46,671
1996/97	8.3	11,843	10.8	51,725
1997/98	7.3	12,707	17.0	60,510
1998/99	-22.3	9,870	17.1	70,871
1999/00	-0.2	9,853	36.9	97,009
2000/01	-2.9	9,570	-14.4	83,062
2001/02	-12.2	8,399	9.4	90,875
2002/03	-16.4	7,020	4.0	94,476
2003/04	15.1	8,079	10.3	104,252
2004/05	3.9	8,398	7.8	112,379
2005/06	8.1	9,080	19.8	134,587
2006/07	0.0	9,079	12.2	151,053
2007/08	3.8	9,426	-0.2	150,820
2008/09	-40.2	5,638	15.7	174,551
2009/10	11.9	6,307	7.4	187,526
2010/11	5.8	6,674	7.1	200,778
2011/12	-7.4	6,183	-4.8	191,207
Total Gain (Loss)	**($-3,817)**			**$181,207**

TSX Composite % Gain Avg. Year 1977 to 2011

2011-12 Strategy Performance

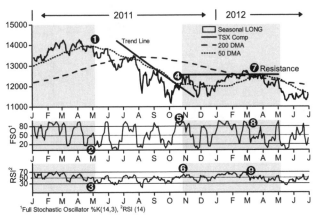

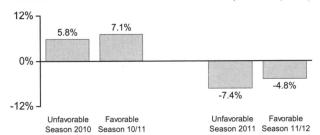

Favorable vs. Unfavorable Seasons 2010-2012 (TSX Composite)

5.8%	7.1%	-7.4%	-4.8%
Unfavorable Season 2010	Favorable Season 10/11	Unfavorable Season 2011	Favorable Season 11/12

Market Indices & Rates
Weekly Values**

Stock Markets	2011	2012
Dow	12,541	12,548
S&P500	1,335	1,319
Nasdaq	2,801	2,853
TSX	13,543	11,354
FTSE	5,923	5,383
DAX	7,315	6,363
Nikkei	9,603	8,833
Hang Seng	23,047	19,408

Commodities	2011	2012
Oil	98.46	93.12
Gold	1491.9	1561.4

Bond Yields	2011	2012
USA 5 Yr Treasury	1.83	0.74
USA 10 Yr T	3.15	1.74
USA 20 Yr T	3.99	2.46
Moody's Aaa	4.93	3.72
Moody's Baa	5.76	4.98
CAN 5 Yr T	2.50	1.44
CAN 10 Yr T	3.19	1.91

Money Market	2011	2012
USA Fed Funds	0.25	0.25
USA 3 Mo T-B	0.05	0.09
CAN tgt overnight rate	1.00	1.00
CAN 3 Mo T-B	0.96	1.00

Foreign Exchange	2011	2012
USD/EUR	1.42	1.27
USD/GBP	1.62	1.59
CAN/USD	0.97	1.01
JPY/USD	81.44	79.73

MAY

M	T	W	T	F	S	S
	1	2	3	4	5	
6	7	8	9	10	11	12
13	14	15	16	17	18	19
20	21	22	23	24	25	26
27	28	29	30	31		

JUNE

M	T	W	T	F	S	S
					1	2
3	4	5	6	7	8	9
10	11	12	13	14	15	16
17	18	19	20	21	22	23
24	25	26	27	28	29	30

JULY

M	T	W	T	F	S	S
1	2	3	4	5	6	7
8	9	10	11	12	13	14
15	16	17	18	19	20	21
22	23	24	25	26	27	28
29	30	31				

TSX Composite Performance– May 6th to October 27, 2012
From 2010 to 2012 the favorable seasons have together produced a bigger net gain than the unfavorable seasons. This is despite the fact that both the favorable and unfavorable seasons had one loss and gain period each. This illustrates that although the favorable period may have a loss, or the unfavorable period may have a gain, overall the favorable six months is a much better time to be invested. On the exit date in 2011, the market was already showing signs of weakness as it had traded below its 50 day moving average❶ and the FSO and the RSI were at the bottom of their ranges❷❸. Overall there was no indication that the position should be held past the exit date.

Technical Conditions– October 28th to May 5th, 2012
Entry Date October 28th, 2012 –Bullish– The TSX Composite had just broken above its downward trend line and was trading above its 50 day moving average❹. The FSO was above 80❺ and the RSI was close to 70❻, indicating that it was possible that the market may become overbought shortly.

Entry Strategy –Buy Position On Entry Date– Although this proved to be a high point and set up resistance for later times, initially the technical picture was strong.

Exit Strategy –Sell Partial Position Early– In March, the TSX Composite turned down early, below resistance and below its 50 and 200 day moving averages❼, justifying a partial exit. In support, the FSO had crossed below 80 a few days earlier❽ and the RSI had started to turn down from 50❾.

COSTCO– BUY AT A DISCOUNT
①May26 to Jun30 ②Oct4 to Dec1

Shoppers are attracted to Costco because of their consistently low prices. They take comfort in the fact that although the prices may not always be the lowest, they are consistently in the lower range.

Many investors see Costco as a bargain stock, but there are two times when it is a seasonal bargain: May 26th to June 30th and October 4th to December 1st. From 1990 to 2011, during the period of May 26th to June 30th, Costco has averaged a gain of 5.9% and has been positive 68% of the time. From October 4th to December 1st, Costco has averaged a gain of 10.1% and has been positive 77% of the time.

Although Costco has averaged a larger gain than the S&P 500 during its second seasonal period, they both have the same frequency rating of positive occurrences, 77%.

17% gain & positive 91% of the time

Putting both seasonal periods together has produced a 91% positive success rate and an average gain of 17.0%. Although the earlier strong years in the 1990's skews that data to the high-side, Costco has still maintained its strong seasonal performances in both the May to June and the October to December time frames.

When investors go shopping for stocks, Costco is one consumer staples company that should be on their list. They should also remember not to bulk up with too much, even if it is selling at a discount.

Costco vs. S&P 500 1990 to 2011   Positive ☐

Year	May 26 to Jun 30 S&P 500	May 26 to Jun 30 COST	Oct 4 to Dec 1 S&P 500	Oct 4 to Dec 1 COST	Compound Growth S&P 500	Compound Growth COST
1990	1.0	16.5 %	3.5	26.5 %	4.5	47.4 %
1991	-1.7	-2.1	-2.4	-3.7	-4.0	-5.7
1992	-1.4	-2.2	5.0	22.7	3.5	20.1
1993	0.4	17.2	0.1	13.4	0.5	32.9
1994	-2.6	10.7	-2.8	-6.3	-5.3	3.7
1995	3.1	19.2	4.2	-2.1	7.4	16.7
1996	-1.2	9.4	9.3	15.5	8.0	26.4
1997	4.5	3.1	1.0	16.6	5.6	20.2
1998	2.1	17.6	17.2	41.1	19.7	65.9
1999	6.9	8.1	9.0	30.7	16.5	41.2
2000	5.3	10.0	-7.8	-3.6	-2.9	6.1
2001	-4.2	9.3	6.3	12.3	1.8	22.6
2002	-8.7	-0.8	14.3	4.6	4.4	3.8
2003	4.4	5.3	3.9	13.5	8.5	19.4
2004	2.5	10.3	5.3	17.3	7.9	29.4
2005	0.1	-1.5	3.1	13.9	3.2	12.2
2006	-0.2	5.0	4.7	6.0	4.5	11.3
2007	-0.2	3.8	-3.8	8.9	-4.6	12.9
2008	-7.0	-1.7	-25.8	-23.5	-30.9	-24.7
2009	3.6	-5.2	8.2	7.5	12.1	1.9
2010	-4.0	-3.0	5.2	5.0	1.0	1.9
2011	0.0	1.2	13.2	6.7	13.2	7.9
Avg.	0.1 %	5.9 %	3.2 %	10.1 %	3.4 %	17.0 %
Fq>0	55 %	68 %	77 %	77 %	77 %	91 %

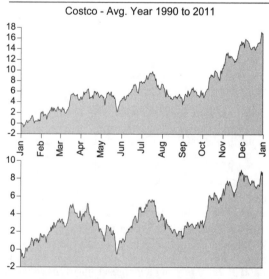

Costco - Avg. Year 1990 to 2011

Costco / S&P 500 Rel. Strength- Avg Yr. 1990-2011

ⓘ *COST - stock symbol for Costco which trades on the Nasdaq exchange.*

2011-12 Strategy Performance

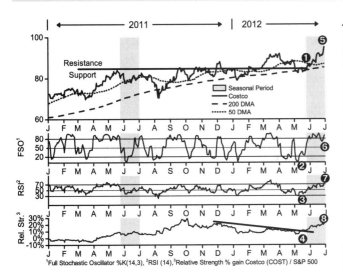

[1] Full Stochastic Oscillator %K(14,3), [2] RSI (14), [3] Relative Strength % gain Costco (COST) / S&P 500

Market Indices & Rates
Weekly Values**

Stock Markets	2011	2012
Dow	12,395	12,498
S&P500	1,322	1,318
Nasdaq	2,769	2,843
TSX	13,730	11,540
FTSE	5,877	5,335
DAX	7,144	6,342
Nikkei	9,489	8,613
Hang Seng	22,842	18,825

Commodities	2011	2012
Oil	99.58	90.98
Gold	1523.1	1572.4

Bond Yields	2011	2012
USA 5 Yr Treasury	1.77	0.76
USA 10 Yr T	3.10	1.76
USA 20 Yr T	3.96	2.44
Moody's Aaa	4.95	3.76
Moody's Baa	5.74	5.09
CAN 5 Yr T	2.38	1.39
CAN 10 Yr T	3.08	1.87

Money Market	2011	2012
USA Fed Funds	0.25	0.25
USA 3 Mo T-B	0.06	0.09
CAN tgt overnight rate	1.00	1.00
CAN 3 Mo T-B	0.95	0.97

Foreign Exchange	2011	2012
USD/EUR	1.41	1.26
USD/GBP	1.63	1.57
CAN/USD	0.98	1.02
JPY/USD	81.60	79.60

Costco Performance

Costco spent a lot of its time in 2011 and 2012 battling the resistance level in the low to mid-80s. When it came time to enter the seasonal period in late May, it was ready to outperform. During its seasonal period Costco went on to perform extremely well.

Technical Conditions– May 26th to June 30th, 2012

Entry Date May 26th, 2012 –Bullish– On the entry date, Costco was just at its resistance level (bullish sign at the beginning of a seasonal period)❶. The FSO in early May crossed back above 20❷ and the RSI bounced off 30❸. The real setup for this trade and the indication that the stock was ready to move higher was its outperformance over the S&P 500 that started in mid-May❹.

Entry Strategy –Buy Partial Position Early– With positive indications from the FSO and the RSI a few weeks prior to Costco's buy date and a position just below the resistance level, a partial allocation earlier in May was justified with a full allocation on the entry date.

Exit Strategy– Sell Partial Position on Exit Date– Before the exit date there was no indication that selling was the right strategy as the stock was not showing any signs of stopping its upwards progress❺. The FSO had turned down earlier in the month❻, but the RSI was continuing higher❼ and Costco was still outperforming the S&P 500❽. The best strategy on the exit date was to sell a partial position and sell the remainder when the stock started to deteriorate technically.

MAY

M	T	W	T	F	S	S
	1	2	3	4	5	
6	7	8	9	10	11	12
13	14	15	16	17	18	19
20	21	22	23	24	25	26
27	28	29	30	31		

JUNE

M	T	W	T	F	S	S
					1	2
3	4	5	6	7	8	9
10	11	12	13	14	15	16
17	18	19	20	21	22	23
24	25	26	27	28	29	30

JULY

M	T	W	T	F	S	S
1	2	3	4	5	6	7
8	9	10	11	12	13	14
15	16	17	18	19	20	21
22	23	24	25	26	27	28
29	30	31				

** Weekly avg closing values- except Fed Funds & CAN overnight tgt rate weekly closing values.

MEMORIAL DAY – BE EARLY & STAY LATE
Positive 2 Market Days Before Memorial Day to 5 Market Days into June

A lot of strategies that focus on investing around holidays concentrate on the market performance the day before and the day after a holiday.

Not all holidays were created equal. The typical Memorial Day trade is to invest the day before the holiday and sell the day after. If you invested in the stock market just for these two days you would be missing out on a lot of gains.

1.1% average gain and positive 64% of the time

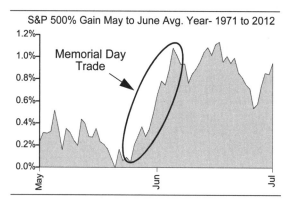

S&P 500% Gain May to June Avg. Year- 1971 to 2012

Memorial Day Trade

Historically, the best strategy has been to invest two market days before Memorial Day and hold until five market days into June. Extending the investment into June makes sense. The first few days in June tend to be positive– so why sell early?

The graph shows the performance of the S&P 500 on a calendar basis for the months of May and June from 1971 to 2012.

The increase from the end of May into June represents the opportunity with the *"Memorial Day - Be Early & Stay Late"* trade. The graph clearly shows a spike in the market that occurs at the end of the month and carries on into June.

Investors using the typical Memorial Day trade, miss out on the majority of the gain. The *Memorial Day - Be Early & Stay Late* strategy has produced an average gain of 1.1% and has been positive 64% of the time (S&P 500, 1971 to 2012). Not a bad gain for being invested an average of ten market days.

The *Memorial Day - Be Early & Stay Late* trade can be extended into June primarily because the first market days of the month tend to be positive. These days are part of the end of the month effect. (see *Super Seven* strategy).

2 Market Days Before Memorial Day to 5 Market Days Into June - S&P 500 — Positive ☐

1971	1.5 %	1980	5.1 %	1990	1.1 %	2000	5.2 %	2010	-1.6 %
1972	-2.4	1981	0.2	1991	0.9	2001	-0.9	2011	-2.7
1973	1.7	1982	-2.6	1992	-0.5	2002	-5.4	2012	-0.3
1974	6.3	1983	-2.1	1993	-1.3	2003	7.0		
1975	3.8	1984	1.2	1994	0.4	2004	2.3		
1976	-0.7	1985	4.3	1995	0.9	2005	0.6		
1977	1.0	1986	4.3	1996	0.0	2006	-0.2		
1978	3.1	1987	5.5	1997	2.2	2007	-2.1		
1979	1.9	1988	4.5	1998	-0.5	2008	-2.2		
		1989	2.4	1999	2.3	2009	4.1		
Avg.	1.8 %		2.3 %		0.6 %		0.8 %		-1.5 %

2012 Strategy Performance

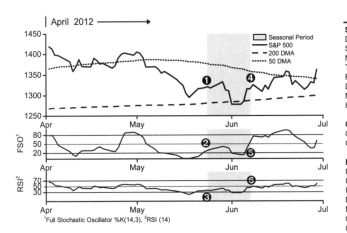

¹Full Stochastic Oscillator %K(14,3), ²RSI (14)

Market Indices & Rates
Weekly Values**

Stock Markets	2011	2012
Dow	12,315	12,378
S&P500	1,318	1,309
Nasdaq	2,778	2,821
TSX	13,640	11,497
FTSE	5,905	5,325
DAX	7,171	6,263
Nikkei	9,593	8,573
Hang Seng	23,340	18,747

Commodities	2011	2012
Oil	100.99	87.09
Gold	1537.4	1571.6

Bond Yields	2011	2012
USA 5 Yr Treasury	1.63	0.69
USA 10 Yr T	3.01	1.61
USA 20 Yr T	3.89	2.29
Moody's Aaa	4.95	3.65
Moody's Baa	5.70	5.01
CAN 5 Yr T	2.28	1.27
CAN 10 Yr T	3.03	1.78

Money Market	2011	2012
USA Fed Funds	0.25	0.25
USA 3 Mo T-B	0.05	0.08
CAN tgt overnight rate	1.00	1.00
CAN 3 Mo T-B	0.96	0.93

Foreign Exchange	2011	2012
USD/EUR	1.44	1.24
USD/GBP	1.64	1.55
CAN/USD	0.98	1.03
JPY/USD	80.93	78.87

Memorial Day Performance

The Memorial Day trade has historically been a good trade, but in recent years it has not paid off. Investors should be cautious with this trade as the market is often volatile at this time of the year.

Technical Conditions– 2 Market Days Before Memorial Day to 5 Market Days into June, 2012

Entry Date May 24th, 2012 –Bullish– The setup for the Memorial Day trade was positive as the market had corrected sharply from the beginning of April and had just started to rebound into the Memorial Day seasonal period❶. The FSO had crossed above 20❷ a few days earlier and the RSI had likewise crossed back up and over 30❸.

Entry Strategy –Buy Partial Position Early– With the FSO and the RSI showing a positive bias, a partial early entry was justified a few days before the start of the trade.

Exit Strategy –Sell Position on Exit Date– The Memorial Day trade is a short-term trade making it difficult to use longer term trends to make technical decisions. On the exit date, the S&P 500 had moved above its 200 day moving average❹. The FSO was just below 80❺ and the RSI was at 50❻.

MAY

M	T	W	T	F	S	S
	1	2	3	4	5
6	7	8	9	10	11	12
13	14	15	16	17	18	19
20	21	22	23	24	25	26
27	28	29	30	31		

JUNE

M	T	W	T	F	S	S
					1	2
3	4	5	6	7	8	9
10	11	12	13	14	15	16
17	18	19	20	21	22	23
24	25	26	27	28	29	30

JULY

M	T	W	T	F	S	S
1	2	3	4	5	6	7
8	9	10	11	12	13	14
15	16	17	18	19	20	21
22	23	24	25	26	27	28
29	30	31				

** Weekly avg closing values- except Fed Funds & CAN overnight tgt rate weekly closing values.

- 64 -

JUNE

	MONDAY	TUESDAY	WEDNESDAY
WEEK 23	**3** 27	**4** 26	**5** 25
WEEK 24	**10** 20	**11** 19	**12** 18
WEEK 25	**17** 13	**18** 12	**19** 11
WEEK 26	**24** 6	**25** 5	**26** 4
WEEK 27	1	2	3

THURSDAY	FRIDAY
6 24	**7** 23
13 17	**14** 16
20 10	**21** 9
27 3	**28** 2
4	5

JULY

M	T	W	T	F	S	S
1	2	3	4	5	6	7
8	9	10	11	12	13	14
15	16	17	18	19	20	21
22	23	24	25	26	27	28
29	30	31				

AUGUST

M	T	W	T	F	S	S
			1	2	3	4
5	6	7	8	9	10	11
12	13	14	15	16	17	18
19	20	21	22	23	24	25
26	27	28	29	30	31	

SEPTEMBER

M	T	W	T	F	S	S
						1
2	3	4	5	6	7	8
9	10	11	12	13	14	15
16	17	18	19	20	21	22
23	24	25	26	27	28	29
30						

OCTOBER

M	T	W	T	F	S	S
	1	2	3	4	5	6
7	8	9	10	11	12	13
14	15	16	17	18	19	20
21	22	23	24	25	26	27
28	29	30	31			

JUNE SUMMARY

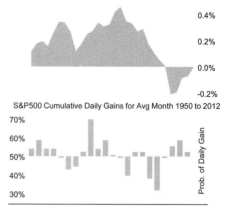

	Dow Jones	S&P 500	Nasdaq	TSX Comp
Month Rank	11	10	6	11
# Up	28	31	23	12
# Down	34	31	17	15
% Pos	45	50	58	44
% Avg. Gain	-0.4	-0.1	0.7	-0.3

Dow & S&P 1950-2011, Nasdaq 1972-2011, TSX 1985-2011

S&P500 Cumulative Daily Gains for Avg Month 1950 to 2012

♦ On average, June is not a strong month. From 1950 to 2011, June has been the third worst month of the year, producing an average loss of 0.1%. ♦ In 2012, the May correction continued into the first few days of June, but the market bounced sharply, producing a gain in June of 4.0%, in the S&P 500. ♦ Despite the strong rally in the S&P 500, the TSX Composite produced a modest gain of only 0.7% as the cyclicals continued to underperform. ♦ Investors should be watching for the biotech sector to start its seasonal trend in late June.

BEST / WORST JUNE BROAD MKTS. 2003-2012

BEST JUNE MARKETS
- ♦ Russell 2000 (2012) 4.8%
- ♦ Russell 3000 Value (2012) 4.7%
- ♦ Russell 2000 (2004) 4.1%

WORST JUNE MARKETS
- ♦ Dow (2008) -10.2%
- ♦ Russell 3000 Value (2008) -9.8%
- ♦ Nasdaq (2008) -9.1%

Index Values End of Month

	2003	2004	2005	2006	2007	2008	2009	2010	2011	2012
Dow	8,985	10,435	10,275	11,150	13,409	11,350	8,447	9,774	12,414	12,880
S&P 500	975	1,141	1,191	1,270	1,503	1,280	919	1,031	1,321	1,362
Nasdaq	1,623	2,048	2,057	2,172	2,603	2,293	1,835	2,109	2,774	2,935
TSX	6,983	8,546	9,903	11,613	13,907	14,467	10,375	11,294	13,301	11,597
Russell 1000	998	1,171	1,242	1,330	1,573	1,352	966	1,091	1,412	751
Russell 2000	1,114	1,470	1,590	1,801	2,072	1,714	1,263	1,515	2,056	798
Russell 3000 Growth	1,595	1,876	1,892	2,000	2,350	2,175	1,613	1,810	2,421	2,505
Russell 3000 Value	1,894	2,258	2,515	2,757	3,265	2,574	1,773	2,037	2,572	2,572

Percent Gain for June

	2003	2004	2005	2006	2007	2008	2009	2010	2011	2012
Dow	1.5	2.4	-1.8	-0.2	-1.6	-10.2	-0.6	-3.6	-1.2	3.9
S&P 500	1.1	1.8	0.0	0.0	-1.8	-8.6	0.0	-5.4	-1.8	4.0
Nasdaq	1.7	3.1	-0.5	-0.3	0.0	-9.1	3.4	-6.5	-2.2	3.8
TSX	1.8	1.5	3.1	-1.1	-1.1	-1.7	0.0	-4.0	-3.6	0.7
Russell 1000	1.2	1.7	0.3	0.0	-2.0	-8.5	0.1	-5.7	-1.9	3.7
Russell 2000	1.7	4.1	3.7	0.5	-1.6	-7.8	1.3	-7.9	-2.5	4.8
Russell 3000 Growth	1.3	1.3	-0.1	-0.5	-1.5	-7.2	1.1	-5.7	-1.6	2.8
Russell 3000 Value	1.1	2.4	1.2	0.5	-2.5	-9.8	-0.9	-6.1	-2.3	4.7

June Market Avg. Performance 2003 to 2012[1]

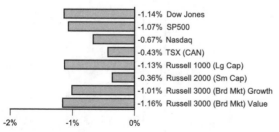

- -1.14% Dow Jones
- -1.07% SP500
- -0.67% Nasdaq
- -0.43% TSX (CAN)
- -1.13% Russell 1000 (Lg Cap)
- -0.36% Russell 2000 (Sm Cap)
- -1.01% Russell 3000 (Brd Mkt) Growth
- -1.16% Russell 3000 (Brd Mkt) Value

Interest Corner Jun[2]

	Fed Funds %[3]	3 Mo. T-Bill %[4]	10 Yr %[5]	20 Yr %[6]
2012	0.25	0.09	1.67	2.38
2011	0.25	0.03	3.18	4.09
2010	0.25	0.18	2.97	3.74
2009	0.25	0.19	3.53	4.30
2008	2.00	1.90	3.99	4.59

(1) Russell Data provided by Russell (2) Federal Reserve Bank of St. Louis- end of month values (3) Target rate set by FOMC (4)(5)(6) Constant yield maturities.

THACKRAY SECTOR THERMOMETER

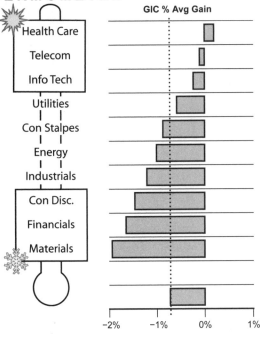

GIC[2] % Avg Gain	Fq % Gain >S&P 500	
SP GIC SECTOR 1990-2011[1]		
0.2 %	59 %	Health Care
-0.1	64	Telecom
-0.2	41	Information Technology
-0.6	50	Utilities
-0.9	36	Consumer Staples
-1.0	36	Energy
-1.2	41	Industrials
-1.5	45	Consumer Discretionary
-1.6	36	Financials
-1.9 %	32 %	Materials
-0.7 %	N/A %	S&P 500

Sector Commentary

♦ In June 2012, all of the major sectors in the market produced positive results. Two of the top three sectors were the same as the long-term average best sectors: health care and telecom. ♦ It is interesting that despite the strong market performance that these top two sectors were defensive sectors. Both of these sectors have a fairly high frequency rate of beating the S&P 500. ♦ Typically the next best sector is information technology, but its success rate of beating the S&P 500 is less than 50%, leaving it susceptible to underperformance. In 2012, it was the second worst sector. ♦ Energy is usually a mediocre sector, but in 2012 it was the top sector, forecasting a positive performance for the sector for its seasonal period starting in July.

Sub-Sector Commentary

♦ After a weak May 2012, the market performance in June pumped hope back into the markets and the homebuilders sub-sector jumped right back up to the top of the sub-sector list, producing a 12.6% gain. It is unusual for the homebuilders sub-sector to perform so well in June and as a result, its strength indicated the possibility of strong markets ahead.

		SELECTED SUB-SECTORS 1990-2011[3]
2.4 %	77 %	Software & Services
0.3	64	Pharmaceuticals
-0.2	50	Gold (London PM)
-0.8	59	Retail
-1.1	55	Metals and Mining
-1.1	45	Biotech (93-2011)
-1.3	50	Steel
-1.4	41	Railroads
-1.4	33	Agriculture (94-2011)
-1.6	32	Transportation
-2.1	41	Silver (London)
-2.1	36	Homebuilders
-2.4	32	Chemicals
-3.0	23	Banks

(1) Sector data provided by Standard and Poors (2) GIC is short form for Global Industry Classification (3) Sub Sector data provided by Standard and Poors, except where marked by symbol.

BIOTECH SUMMER SOLSTICE
June 23rd to Sep 13th

The *Biotech Summer Solstice* trade starts on June 23rd and lasts until September 13th. The trade is aptly named as its outperformance starts approximately on the day summer solstice starts– the longest day of the year.

There are two main drivers of the trade: biotech is a good substitute for technology stocks in the summer, and investors want to take a position in the biotech sector before the autumn conferences.

11.4% extra & 85% of the time better than the S&P 500

Biotech vs. S&P 500 1992 to 2011

Jun 23 to Sep 13	S&P 500	Biotech (Positive)	Diff
1992	4.0 %	17.9 %	13.8 %
1993	3.6	3.6	0.0
1994	3.2	24.2	21.0
1995	5.0	31.5	26.5
1996	2.1	7.0	4.9
1997	2.8	-18.9	-21.7
1998	-8.5	20.6	29.1
1999	0.6	64.3	63.7
2000	2.3	7.6	5.4
2001	-10.8	-3.6	7.2
2002	-10.0	8.1	18.2
2003	2.3	6.4	4.1
2004	-0.8	8.9	9.6
2005	1.4	26.0	24.5
2006	5.8	7.4	1.6
2007	-1.2	6.0	7.2
2008	-5.0	11.4	16.5
2009	16.8	7.7	-9.1
2010	2.4	2.8	0.4
2011	-8.9	-3.7	5.2
Avg	0.4 %	11.7 %	11.4 %
Fq>0	65 %	85 %	85 %

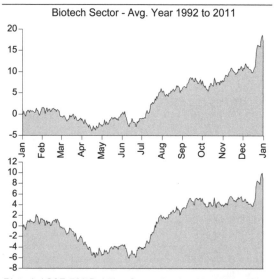

Biotech Sector - Avg. Year 1992 to 2011

Biotech / S&P 500 Relative Strength - Avg Yr. 1992 - 2011

The biotechnology sector is often considered the cousin of the technology sector, a good place for speculative investments. The sectors are similar as both include concept companies (companies without a product but with good potential).

Despite their similarity, investors view the sectors differently. The technology sector is viewed as being largely dependent on the economy and conversely the biotech sector as being much less dependent on the economy. The end product of biotechnology companies is mainly medicine, which is not economically sensitive.

As a result, in the softer summer months, investors are more willing to commit speculative money into the biotech sector, compared with the technology sector.

The biotech sector is one of the few sectors that starts its outperformance in June. This is in part because of the biotech conferences that occur in autumn. With positive announcements in autumn, the price of biotech companies on the stock market can increase dramatically. As a result, investors try to lock in positions early.

> (i) *Biotech SP GIC Sector # 352010: Companies primarily engaged in the research, development, manufacturing and/or marketing of products based on genetic analysis and genetic engineering. This includes companies specializing in protein-based therapeutics to treat human diseases.*

2011-12 Strategy Performance

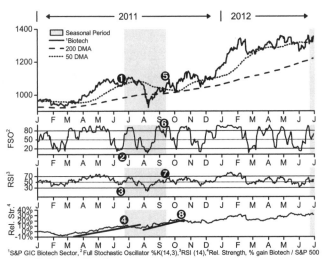

[1]S&P GIC Biotech Sector, [2]Full Stochastic Oscillator %K(14,3),[3]RSI (14),[4]Rel. Strength, % gain Biotech / S&P 500

Market Indices & Rates
Weekly Values**

Stock Markets	2011	2012
Dow	12,057	12,332
S&P500	1,282	1,304
Nasdaq	2,682	2,814
TSX	13,225	11,514
FTSE	5,832	5,422
DAX	7,096	6,063
Nikkei	9,451	8,462
Hang Seng	22,640	18,429

Commodities	2011	2012
Oil	100.01	84.44
Gold	1539.8	1605.8

Bond Yields	2011	2012
USA 5 Yr Treasury	1.58	0.70
USA 10 Yr T	3.00	1.61
USA 20 Yr T	3.90	2.29
Moody's Aaa	4.97	3.67
Moody's Baa	5.73	5.03
CAN 5 Yr T	2.24	1.24
CAN 10 Yr T	3.01	1.77

Money Market	2011	2012
USA Fed Funds	0.25	0.25
USA 3 Mo T-B	0.05	0.09
CAN tgt overnight rate	1.00	1.00
CAN 3 Mo T-B	0.94	0.89

Foreign Exchange	2011	2012
USD/EUR	1.45	1.25
USD/GBP	1.64	1.55
CAN/USD	0.98	1.03
JPY/USD	80.15	79.08

JUNE

M	T	W	T	F	S	S
					1	2
3	4	5	6	7	8	9
10	11	12	13	14	15	16
17	18	19	20	21	22	23
24	25	26	27	28	29	30

JULY

M	T	W	T	F	S	S
						1
2	3	4	5	6	7	8
9	10	11	12	13	14	15
16	17	18	19	20	21	22
23	24	25	26	27	28	29
30	31					

AUGUST

M	T	W	T	F	S	S
		1	2	3	4	
5	6	7	8	9	10	11
12	13	14	15	16	17	18
19	20	21	22	23	24	25
26	27	28	29	30	31	

Biotech Sector Performance

In 2011, the biotech sector started its outperformance in February, as the stock market was rotating out of the cyclicals that typically do well at this time of the year. As a result, the biotech sector was a recipient of the funds. Although the sector produced a loss during its seasonal time of 3.7% (June 23rd to September 13th), it fared much better than the S&P 500 which lost 8.9% over the same time period.

Technical Conditions– June 23rd to September 13th, 2011
Entry Date June 23rd, 2011 –Bullish– Just before the start of its seasonal period, the biotech sector was trading above its 50 day moving average❶, and the FSO had just turned up above 20❷ and at the same time the RSI was trending upwards❸. The sector was also outperforming the S&P 500❹. Unfortunately the market corrected strongly in July, bringing down the biotech sector.

Entry Strategy –Buy Partial Position Early– With the FSO turning up above the 20 and the RSI trending upwards, an early partial allocation was justified. The net gain from the early allocation was small, but still positive.

Exit Strategy – Sell Partial Position Early and Remainder Past Exit Date– The FSO turned below 80 at the beginning of September❺, justifying a partial early exit. The other technical signals were neutral or positive at the time, allowing the remainder of the position to be held until the technicals showed weakness. The RSI remained flat for the last few weeks of the trade❼. The biotech sector traded above its 50 and 200 day moving averages at the end of its seasonal period (bullish)❺. Biotech's performance relative to the S&P 500, gave further justification to hold the remainder of the trade past its seasonal date, up until mid-October when the sector started to underperform❽.

PotashCorp
Fertilize Your Profits - June 23rd to Jan 11th

Fertilizer stocks have displayed a strong seasonal trend from the end of June to the beginning of January. The stock prices of fertilizer companies are highly correlated to grain prices which often rise in the second half of the year (the main harvest season for the northern hemisphere).

In addition, fertilizer companies benefit from the spending patterns of farmers. In order to reduce taxes at the end of the year, farmers will often make large purchases, including fertilizer. This helps to drive up the price of fertilizer stocks.

21% & positive & 82% of the time

PotashCorp, the world's largest fertilizer company by capacity, has a profitable seasonal trend from June 23rd to January 11th. During this time period, from 1990/91 to 2011/12, it has produced an average return of 21.1% and has been positive 82% of the time. These results far exceed the S&P TSX Composite which has produced an average return of 3.2% and has only been positive 55% of the time during the same period.

Potash Corp vs. S&P/TSX Composite 1990/91 to 2010/11			
			Positive
June 23 to Jan 11	TSX Comp	POT	Diff
1990/91	-8.8%	6.9%	15.7%
1991/92	2.2	19.3	17.2
1992/93	-0.9	4.6	5.5
1993/94	13.0	31.6	18.6
1994/95	3.3	43.2	39.8
1995/96	5.2	35.7	30.5
1996/97	18.6	35.8	17.3
1997/98	-3.7	8.3	12.0
1998/99	-4.1	-4.5	-0.4
1999/00	21.4	9.1	-12.3
2000/01	-12.5	41.4	53.9
2001/02	-0.5	11.7	12.2
2002/03	-4.7	6.8	11.5
2003/04	18.1	29.3	11.2
2004/05	5.9	44.9	39.0
2005/06	15.6	-16.2	-31.8
2006/07	12.5	72.1	59.6
2007/08	-2.5	72.2	74.7
2008/09	-37.7	-56.9	-19.2
2009/10	21.5	25.9	4.4
2010/11	13.6	63.0	49.4
2011/12	-6.1	-12.9	-6.8
Avg	3.2%	21.1%	18.3%
Fq > 0	55%	82%	77%

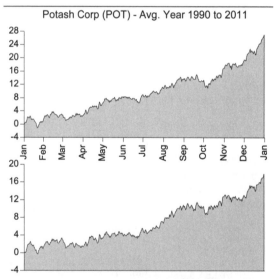

Potash Corp (POT) - Avg. Year 1990 to 2011

POT / TSX Comp Relative Strength - Avg Yr. 1990 - 2011

to a very impressive increase in price during 2004 and 2005. The correction in 2008 was the result of the world suffering an economic slowdown, and farmers around the world reduced their fertilizer application. The correction in 2011/12, was largely the result of a sharp commodity correction in the markets.

Up until recently, it has not been possible to invest directly in the fertilizer company sector via an ETF. That changed with the launch of the Global X Fertilizers/Potash ETF (SOIL), trading in the U.S. It is expected that SOIL will have a similar seasonal trend to the fertilizer stocks.

Since 1990, there have only been three seasonally strong periods that have produced a loss of greater than 10%; 2005/06, 2008/09 and 2011/12. The negative performance in 2005/06 was largely a correction

ⓘ *PotashCorp (POT) trades on both the S&P TSX Composite and NYSE. It is the world's largest fertilizer company by capacity.*

2011-12 Strategy Performance

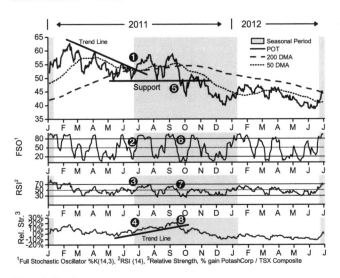

^{1}Full Stochastic Oscillator %K(14,3), ^{2}RSI (14), ^{3}Relative Strength, % gain PotashCorp / TSX Composite

Potash Performance

Overall, PotashCorp performed poorly in 2011 and the first half of 2012. Although investing in Potash just during its seasonal period would have lost money, staying out of Potash-Corp during its non-favorable time would have saved money as the stock continued on a downward trend.

Technical Conditions– June 23rd to January 11th, 2012

Entry Date June 23rd, 2011 –Bullish– At the start of the seasonal period, PotashCorp broke upwards through its down trend line and was trading at its 50 and 200 day moving averages❶. The FSO had just turned upwards above 20❷ and the RSI had just crossed 50❸. In addition, PotashCorp had been outperforming the market over the last four weeks❹. All of these indicators pointed to a bullish scenario, but as the market fell in June, so did Potash.

Entry Strategy –Buy Position on Entry Date– All of the technical signals lined up for a buy at the beginning of the seasonal period. The only concerning trend was one of lower highs and lower lows, indicating caution.

Exit Strategy– Sell Position Early– This trade failed in September as PotashCorp crossed below its 50 and 200 day moving averages❺. The FSO and RSI turned sharply down❻❼ and then PotashCorp broke support and started to underperform the TSX Composite❽.

WEEK 24

Market Indices & Rates
Weekly Values**

Stock Markets	2011	2012
Dow	11,978	12,580
S&P500	1,273	1,324
Nasdaq	2,638	2,836
TSX	12,931	11,478
FTSE	5,747	5,467
DAX	7,136	6,165
Nikkei	9,467	8,578
Hang Seng	22,199	18,979

Commodities	2011	2012
Oil	95.89	83.32
Gold	1526.6	1609.6

Bond Yields	2011	2012
USA 5 Yr Treasury	1.58	0.71
USA 10 Yr T	2.99	1.62
USA 20 Yr T	3.90	2.32
Moody's Aaa	4.98	3.67
Moody's Baa	5.73	5.05
CAN 5 Yr T	2.22	1.25
CAN 10 Yr T	2.98	1.77

Money Market	2011	2012
USA Fed Funds	0.25	0.25
USA 3 Mo T-B	0.05	0.10
CAN tgt overnight rate	1.00	1.00
CAN 3 Mo T-B	0.94	0.88

Foreign Exchange	2011	2012
USD/EUR	1.43	1.26
USD/GBP	1.63	1.56
CAN/USD	0.98	1.03
JPY/USD	80.47	79.31

JUNE

M	T	W	T	F	S	S
					1	2
3	4	5	6	7	8	9
10	11	12	13	14	15	16
17	18	19	20	21	22	23
24	25	26	27	28	29	30

JULY

M	T	W	T	F	S	S
1	2	3	4	5	6	7
8	9	10	11	12	13	14
15	16	17	18	19	20	21
22	23	24	25	26	27	28
29	30	31				

AUGUST

M	T	W	T	F	S	S
		1	2	3	4
5	6	7	8	9	10	11
12	13	14	15	16	17	18
19	20	21	22	23	24	25
26	27	28	29	30	31	

** Weekly avg closing values- except Fed Funds & CAN overnight tgt rate weekly closing values.

INDEPENDENCE DAY – THE FULL TRADE
PROFIT BEFORE & AFTER FIREWORKS
Two Market Days Before June Month End
To 5 Market Days After Independence Day

The beginning of July is a time for celebration and the markets tend to agree.

Based on previous market data, the best way to take advantage of this trend is to be invested for the two market days prior to the June month end and hold until five market days after Independence Day. This time period has produced above average returns on a fairly consistent basis.

0.8% avg. gain & 71% of the time positive

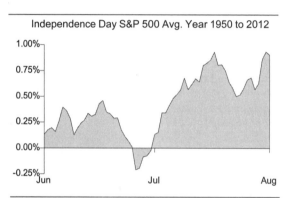

Independence Day S&P 500 Avg. Year 1950 to 2012

The typical Independence Day trade put forward by quite a few pundits has been to invest one or two days before the holiday and take profits one or two days after the holiday.

Although this strategy has produced profits, it has left a lot of money on the table. This strategy misses out on the positive days at the end of June and on the full slate of positive days after Independence Day.

The beginning part of the *Independence Day* positive trend is driven by two combining factors.

First, portfolio managers "window dress" (buying stocks that have a favorable perception in the market); thereby pushing stock prices up at the end of the month.

Second, investors have become "wise" to the *Independence Day Trade* and try to jump in before everyone else.

Depending on market conditions at the time, investors should consider extending the exit date until eighteen calendar days in July. With July being an earnings month, the market can continue to rally until mid-month (see *18 Day Earnings Month Strategy*).

(i) *History of Independence Day:*
Independence Day is celebrated on July 4th because that is the day when the Continental Congress adopted the final draft of the Declaration of Independence in 1776. Independence Day was made an official holiday at the end of the War of Independence in 1783. In 1941 Congress declared the 4th of July a federal holiday.

S&P 500, 2 Market Days Before June Month End To 5 Market Days after Independence Day % Gain 1950 to 2012   Positive [   ]

1950	-4.4 %	1960	-0.1 %	1970	1.5 %	1980	1.4 %	1990	1.7 %	2000	1.8 %	2010	0.4 %
1951	1.5	1961	1.7	1971	3.2	1981	-2.4	1991	1.4	2001	-2.6	2011	1.8
1952	0.9	1962	9.8	1972	0.3	1982	-0.6	1992	2.8	2002	-4.7	2012	0.7
1953	0.8	1963	0.5	1973	2.1	1983	1.5	1993	-0.6	2003	1.2		
1954	2.9	1964	2.3	1974	-8.8	1984	-0.7	1994	0.4	2004	-1.7		
1955	4.9	1965	5.0	1975	-0.2	1985	1.5	1995	1.8	2005	1.5		
1956	3.4	1966	2.1	1976	2.4	1986	-2.6	1996	-2.8	2006	2.1		
1957	3.8	1967	1.3	1977	-0.6	1987	0.4	1997	3.7	2007	0.8		
1958	2.0	1968	2.3	1978	0.6	1988	-0.6	1998	2.7	2008	-3.4		
1959	3.3	1969	-1.5	1979	1.3	1989	0.9	1999	5.1	2009	-4.3		
Avg.	1.9 %		2.3 %		0.2 %		-0.1 %		1.8 %		-0.9 %		1.0 %

2012 Strategy Performance

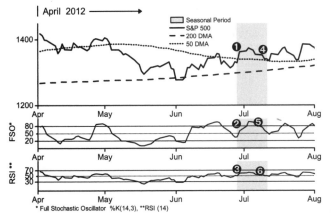

* Full Stochastic Oscillator %K(14,3), **RSI (14)

Market Indices & Rates
Weekly Values**

Stock Markets	2011	2012
Dow	12,073	12,724
S&P500	1,283	1,344
Nasdaq	2,665	2,901
TSX	12,974	11,599
FTSE	5,723	5,556
DAX	7,197	6,322
Nikkei	9,544	8,750
Hang Seng	21,848	19,325

Commodities	2011	2012
Oil	92.63	81.26
Gold	1535.8	1597.9

Bond Yields	2011	2012
USA 5 Yr Treasury	1.52	0.73
USA 10 Yr T	2.96	1.64
USA 20 Yr T	3.87	2.32
Moody's Aaa	4.95	3.64
Moody's Baa	5.72	5.02
CAN 5 Yr T	2.15	1.26
CAN 10 Yr T	2.94	1.76

Money Market	2011	2012
USA Fed Funds	0.25	0.25
USA 3 Mo T-B	0.02	0.09
CAN tgt overnight rate	1.00	1.00
CAN 3 Mo T-B	0.89	0.88

Foreign Exchange	2011	2012
USD/EUR	1.43	1.26
USD/GBP	1.61	1.57
CAN/USD	0.98	1.02
JPY/USD	80.34	79.66

Independence Day Performance

The *Independence Day* trade setup well in 2012, as the market had corrected slightly in mid-June. Although the *Independence Day* trade gave back some of its gains halfway through the trade, it still had a profitable outcome.

When making a short-term trade, it is preferable to have a back-drop of positive seasonality either at the same time as the trade or right after it. If the trade does not work, at least you have comfort knowing that there is support from another positive seasonal trend. The *18 Day Earnings Effect* strategy provides a seasonal safety net for the *Independence Day* trade. The *Independence Day* trade lasts five trading days into July, while the *18 Day Earnings Effect* lasts eighteen calendar days into July. In 2012, the *Independence Day* trade and the *18 Day Earnings Effect* Strategy were both positive.

Technical Conditions– Two Market Days Before June Month End to Five Market Days After Independence Day, 2012

Entry Date June 28th, 2012 –Bullish– The temporary dip in late June provided an opportunity to enter the *Independence Day* trade in a "cheaper" market. On the entry date, the S&P 500 traded up through its 50 day moving average❶ and the FSO crossed back over 50❷. The RSI was also increasing and crossed back over 50❸.

Entry Strategy –Buy Position on Entry Date– On the entry date, the conditions were favorable to buy into the market.

Exit Strategy– Sell Partial Position Early– Sell partial position early as the S&P 500 was weakening❹ and the FSO crossed back below 80❺. Sell remaining allocation on exit date as the RSI crossed back below 50❻ and the S&P 500 traded to its 50 day moving average.

JUNE

M	T	W	T	F	S	S
					1	2
3	4	5	6	7	8	9
10	11	12	13	14	15	16
17	18	19	20	21	22	23
24	25	26	27	28	29	30

JULY

M	T	W	T	F	S	S
1	2	3	4	5	6	7
8	9	10	11	12	13	14
15	16	17	18	19	20	21
22	23	24	25	26	27	28
29	30	31				

AUGUST

M	T	W	T	F	S	S
		1	2	3	4
5	6	7	8	9	10	11
12	13	14	15	16	17	18
19	20	21	22	23	24	25
26	27	28	29	30	31	

** Weekly avg closing values- except Fed Funds & CAN overnight tgt rate weekly closing values.

Johnson & Johnson
July 14th to October 21st

The health care sector by nature is defensive and attracts investors when they become concerned with stock market valuations or an economic slowdown. The advantage of investing in Johnson and Johnson during its strong seasonal period is that this period coincides with the weak period of the broad stock market.

The stock market often peaks mid-month July, just as the earnings season is getting underway– the same time as JNJ's seasonal period starts.

JNJ is not only attractive because of its lack of sensitivity to discretionary spending, but also because it has a higher than average dividend yield.

6.4% & positive 73% of the time

JNJ - Avg. Year 1990 to 2011

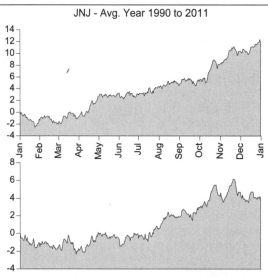

JNJ / S&P 500 Relative Strength - Avg Yr. 1990 - 2011

JNJ vs. S&P 500 1990 to 2011			
			Positive
Jul 14 to Oct 21	S&P 500	JNJ	Diff
1990	-14.9%	-4.1%	10.9%
1991	2.6	1.9	-0.7
1992	0.2	7.5	7.3
1993	3.9	4.9	1.1
1994	3.6	28.9	25.3
1995	4.7	19.7	15.0
1996	9.9	7.4	-2.4
1997	6.1	-5.5	-11.6
1998	-8.2	12.5	20.7
1999	-7.9	8.2	16.1
2000	-6.6	-3.5	3.1
2001	-11.7	10.1	21.8
2002	-2.4	21.0	23.4
2003	4.8	-2.0	-6.8
2004	-0.8	4.3	5.1
2005	-3.6	-0.5	3.0
2006	10.2	13.9	3.7
2007	-3.3	1.3	4.6
2008	-23.0	-3.9	19.0
2009	20.0	4.5	-15.5
2010	7.8	5.8	-2.0
2011	-6.0	-5.7	0.3
Avg	-0.7%	5.8%	6.4%
Fq > 0	50%	68%	73%

positive return, typically over 4%. Large returns for the S&P 500 are not typical during this time of the year, making JNJ an attractive holding in a seasonal portfolio.

◉ Seasonal Hotspot

JNJ typically releases its Q3 earnings mid-October and as a result, on average the company performs particularly well from October 11th to the 21st. October tends to be a volatile month and investors focus on stable companies that have the potential to report solid earnings. During the seasonal Hotspot, from 1990 to 2011, JNJ produced an average gain of 3.8% and was positive 73% of the time. It outperformed the S&P 500 by 2.0% and 64% of the time.

JNJ has a strong track record of performing well from July 14th to October 21st. During this time period, from 1990 to 2011, JNJ produced an average gain of 5.8% and was positive 68% of the time. It also outperformed the S&P 500, 73% of the time. The maximum drawdown for JNJ during this time period was 5.7%. This compares to the S&P 500 which had seven periods with greater losses than 5.7%.

It is also important to note that all of the times when JNJ, in its seasonally strong period, underperformed the S&P 500 occurred when the S&P 500 produced a

ⓘ *Johnson and Johnson (JNJ) is a diversified health care company that operates in three segments: Consumer, Pharmaceutical, and Medical Devices and Diagnostics. JNJ trades on the NYSE.*

2011-12 Strategy Performance

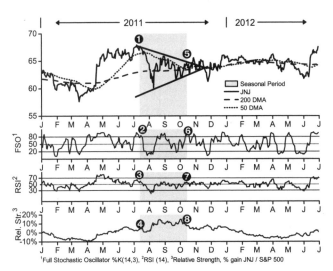

[1]Full Stochastic Oscillator %K(14,3), [2]RSI (14), [3]Relative Strength, % gain JNJ / S&P 500

	WEEK 26
Market Indices & Rates	
Weekly Values**	

Stock Markets	2011	2012
Dow	12,298	12,629
S&P500	1,309	1,331
Nasdaq	2,750	2,870
TSX	13,140	11,419
FTSE	5,856	5,497
DAX	7,274	6,213
Nikkei	9,742	8,802
Hang Seng	22,141	19,105

Commodities	2011	2012
Oil	93.73	80.25
Gold	1498.0	1575.3

Bond Yields	2011	2012
USA 5 Yr Treasury	1.67	0.72
USA 10 Yr T	3.11	1.64
USA 20 Yr T	4.05	2.33
Moody's Aaa	5.11	3.60
Moody's Baa	5.88	5.00
CAN 5 Yr T	2.24	1.22
CAN 10 Yr T	3.04	1.72

Money Market	2011	2012
USA Fed Funds	0.25	0.25
USA 3 Mo T-B	0.02	0.09
CAN tgt overnight rate	1.00	1.00
CAN 3 Mo T-B	0.92	0.87

Foreign Exchange	2011	2012
USD/EUR	1.44	1.25
USD/GBP	1.60	1.56
CAN/USD	0.97	1.03
JPY/USD	80.84	79.63

JUNE

M	T	W	T	F	S	S
					1	2
3	4	5	6	7	8	9
10	11	12	13	14	15	16
17	18	19	20	21	22	23
24	25	26	27	28	29	30

JULY

M	T	W	T	F	S	S
1	2	3	4	5	6	7
8	9	10	11	12	13	14
15	16	17	18	19	20	21
22	23	24	25	26	27	28
29	30	31				

AUGUST

M	T	W	T	F	S	S
		1	2	3	4
5	6	7	8	9	10	11
12	13	14	15	16	17	18
19	20	21	22	23	24	25
26	27	28	29	30	31	

Johnson and Johnson Performance

In April 2011, JNJ started to outperform the S&P 500. This was a direct result of investors being concerned with the markets and rotating out of the cyclicals into defensive stocks. Cyclicals typically perform well in April and when they underperform and defensive stocks outperform, it is a signal that the market is susceptible to a correction. Unfortunately, the early run-up took the steam out of JNJ excelling during its typically strong seasonal period. Although JNJ produced a loss during this period in 2011, it managed to outperform the S&P 500.

Technical Conditions– July 14th to October 21st, 2011

Entry Date July 14th, 2011 – <u>Mildly Bullish</u>– After a strong run in April, JNJ started to consolidate in May and June❶. The FSO was above 80❷ and rolling down. Also, the RSI had turned down from the high 60❸. In mid-June JNJ started to underperform the S&P 500❹.

Entry Strategy – <u>Buy Position on Entry Date</u>– Although JNJ had not broken down at the start of its seasonal trade, the technical signals were not strong, giving justification for only a partial buy on the entry date. Soon after, JNJ broke through its 50 day moving average before it started to consolidate over the next few months.

Exit Strategy – <u>Sell Position on Exit Date</u>– On the exit date, JNJ was at its 50 day moving average❺.The FSO turned down below 80❻ and the RSI was neutral❼. In addition, JNJ had just started to underperform the S&P 500❽. There was not a good reason to stay in this stock past its exit date.

** Weekly avg closing values- except Fed Funds & CAN overnight tgt rate weekly closing values.

JULY

	MONDAY	TUESDAY	WEDNESDAY
WEEK 27	**1** 30 CAN Market Closed- Canada Day	**2** 29	**3** 28
WEEK 28	**8** 23	**9** 22	**10** 21
WEEK 29	**15** 16	**16** 15	**17** 14
WEEK 30	**22** 9	**23** 8	**24** 7
WEEK 31	**29** 2	**30** 1	**31**

THURSDAY		FRIDAY	
4	27	**5**	26
USA Market Closed - Independence Day			
11	20	**12**	19
18	13	**19**	12
25	6	**26**	5
1		2	

AUGUST

M	T	W	T	F	S	S
			1	2	3	4
5	6	7	8	9	10	11
12	13	14	15	16	17	18
19	20	21	22	23	24	25
26	27	28	29	30	31	

SEPTEMBER

M	T	W	T	F	S	S
						1
2	3	4	5	6	7	8
9	10	11	12	13	14	15
16	17	18	19	20	21	22
23	24	25	26	27	28	29
30						

OCTOBER

M	T	W	T	F	S	S
	1	2	3	4	5	6
7	8	9	10	11	12	13
14	15	16	17	18	19	20
21	22	23	24	25	26	27
28	29	30	31			

NOVEMBER

M	T	W	T	F	S	S
				1	2	3
4	5	6	7	8	9	10
11	12	13	14	15	16	17
18	19	20	21	22	23	24
25	26	27	28	29	30	

JULY
SUMMARY

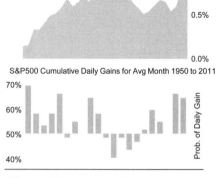

	Dow Jones	S&P 500	Nasdaq	TSX Comp
Month Rank	4	6	10	6
# Up	38	33	20	17
# Down	24	29	20	10
% Pos	61	53	50	63
% Avg. Gain	1.2	1.0	0.1	0.8

Dow & S&P 1950-2011, Nasdaq 1972-2011, TSX 1985-2011

S&P500 Cumulative Daily Gains for Avg Month 1950 to 2011

♦ When a summer rally occurs, the gains are usually made in July. ♦ Typically, it is the first part of the July that produces the gains as the market rallies around Independence Day and into the earnings season. ♦ In 2012, July was a volatile month and the market rallied into mid-month, corrected and rallied again towards the end of the month. Overall, July was positive. ♦ The two major sector opportunities in July are gold and energy. Gold has started its summer rally in early July for the last two years. Investors should be watching for the same trend in 2013.

BEST / WORST JULY BROAD MKTS. 2002-2011

BEST JULY MARKETS
- ♦ Russell 2000 (2009) 9.5%
- ♦ Dow (2009) 8.6%
- ♦ Russell 3000 Value (2009) 8.2%

WORST JULY MARKETS
- ♦ Russell 2000 (2002) -15.2%
- ♦ Russell 3000 Value (2002) -9.9%
- ♦ Nasdaq (2002) -9.2%

Index Values End of Month

	2002	2003	2004	2005	2006	2007	2008	2009	2010	2011
Dow	8,737	9,234	10,140	10,641	11,186	13,212	11,378	9,172	10,466	12,143
S&P 500	912	990	1,102	1,234	1,277	1,455	1,267	987	1,102	1,292
Nasdaq	1,328	1,735	1,887	2,185	2,091	2,546	2,326	1,979	2,255	2,756
TSX	6,605	7,258	8,458	10,423	11,831	13,869	13,593	10,787	11,713	12,946
Russell 1000	931	1,016	1,129	1,288	1,331	1,523	1,334	1,038	1,165	718
Russell 2000	975	1,183	1,370	1,689	1,741	1,929	1,776	1,384	1,618	797
Russell 3000 Growth	1,471	1,639	1,764	1,988	1,955	2,305	2,139	1,727	1,937	2,390
Russell 3000 Value	1,773	1,922	2,216	2,589	2,809	3,099	2,570	1,920	2,172	2,483

Percent Gain for July

	2002	2003	2004	2005	2006	2007	2008	2009	2010	2011
Dow	-5.5	2.8	-2.8	3.6	0.3	-1.5	0.2	8.6	7.1	-2.2
S&P 500	-7.9	1.6	-3.4	3.6	0.5	-3.2	-1.0	7.4	6.9	-2.1
Nasdaq	-9.2	6.9	-7.8	6.2	-3.7	-2.2	1.4	7.8	6.9	-0.6
TSX	-7.6	3.9	-1.0	5.3	1.9	-0.3	-6.0	4.0	3.7	-2.7
Russell 1000	-7.5	1.8	-3.6	3.8	0.1	-3.2	-1.3	7.5	6.8	-2.3
Russell 2000	-15.2	6.2	-6.8	6.3	-3.3	-6.9	3.6	9.5	6.8	-3.7
Russell 3000 Growth	-6.2	2.8	-6.0	5.0	-2.2	-1.9	-1.6	7.1	7.0	-1.3
Russell 3000 Value	-9.9	1.5	-1.9	2.9	1.9	-5.1	-0.2	8.2	6.6	-3.5

July Market Avg. Performance 2002 to 2011[1]

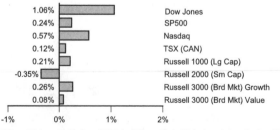

	Dow Jones	1.06%
	SP500	0.24%
	Nasdaq	0.57%
	TSX (CAN)	0.12%
	Russell 1000 (Lg Cap)	0.21%
	Russell 2000 (Sm Cap)	-0.35%
	Russell 3000 (Brd Mkt) Growth	0.26%
	Russell 3000 (Brd Mkt) Value	0.08%

Interest Corner Jul[2]

	Fed Funds %[3]	3 Mo. T-Bill %[4]	10 Yr %[5]	20 Yr %[6]
2011	0.25	0.10	2.82	3.77
2010	0.25	0.15	2.94	3.74
2009	0.25	0.18	3.52	4.29
2008	2.00	1.68	3.99	4.63
2007	5.25	4.96	4.78	5.00

(1) Russell Data provided by Russell (2) Federal Reserve Bank of St. Louis- end of month values (3) Target rate set by FOMC (4)(5)(6) Constant yield maturities.

THACKRAY SECTOR THERMOMETER

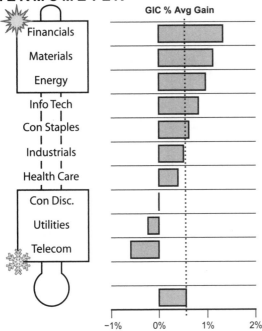

GIC[2] % Avg Gain	Fq % Gain >S&P 500	
SP GIC SECTOR 1990-2011[1]		
1.3 %	50 %	Financials
1.1	64	Materials
1.0	64	Energy
0.8	50	Information Technology
0.6	59	Consumer Staples
0.5	50	Industrials
0.4	41	Health Care
0.0	50	Consumer Discretionary
-0.2	45	Utilities
-0.6 %	45 %	Telecom
0.6 %	N/A %	S&P 500

Sector Commentary

♦ The first half of July tends to be positive as the broad market benefits from a run-up to earnings season. During this time period, the defensive sectors tend to lag behind the rest of the sectors. ♦ In the second half of the month, the S&P 500 tends to be weaker and as a result the defensive sectors lead at this time. Despite defensives benefiting in the second half of the month, on average, they tend to be the underperforming sectors over the whole month. ♦ When the S&P 500 produces a large loss in July, such as in 2011 when it lost 2.1%, investors should expect the defensive sectors to outperform the S&P 500.

Sub-Sector Commentary

♦ Biotech has the distinction of being one of the top sub-sectors in the month of July with a high 80% frequency of outperforming the S&P 500. ♦ Some of the non-mining cyclicals move to the top of the list. ♦ After being one of the top performing sub-sectors in June, software and services tends to put in a poor performance in July, with an average loss of 2.1% and a low frequency of beating the S&P 500 only 27%. ♦ It doesn't show up as a top sector, but on a seasonal basis gold enters its period of strength in July and starts to pick up its rate of performance versus the S&P 500.

SELECTED SUB-SECTORS 1990-2011[3]		
6.4 %	80 %	Biotech (93-2011)
2.5	64	Railroads
1.8	64	Chemicals
1.7	50	Homebuilders
1.5	59	Silver (London)
1.3	64	Banks
1.2	50	Transportation
0.5	55	Retail
0.4	50	Metals and Mining
0.1	50	Gold (London PM)
-0.2	45	Pharmaceuticals
-0.7	50	Steel
-1.3	44	Agriculture (94-2011)
-2.1	27	Software & Services

(1) Sector data provided by Standard and Poors (2) GIC is short form for Global Industry Classification (3) Sub Sector data provided by Standard and Poors, except where marked by symbol.

Altria Group, Inc., through its subsidiaries, engages in the manufacture and sale of cigarettes, smokeless products, and wine in the United States and internationally.

You may not think that smoking is good for you, but investing in tobacco stocks has been good for profits, especially from July 19th to December 19th of each year.

It makes sense that Altria starts to outperform in mid-July as this is when the broad stock market often peaks. At this time, investors still wanting to invest, rotate some of their available capital into defensive stocks, such as Altria.

11.4% & positive 82% of the time

Although the sweet spot of the seasonal trade is from mid-July into the beginning of September, Altria still manages to outperform until mid-December. The sweet spot period, from the beginning of September to mid-December has produced greater gains for Altria than the S&P 500, but its positive frequency is approximately equal. The value of this trade is not just the superior gains, but also the diversification that is added to the portfolio.

Altria vs. S&P 500 1990 to 2011			
			Positive
Jul 19 to Dec 19	S&P 500	MO	Diff
1990	-9.3%	2.0%	11.3%
1991	-0.7	8.6	9.3
1992	6.2	-2.4	-8.6
1993	4.6	15.4	10.8
1994	0.6	5.5	4.9
1995	9.6	19.0	9.5
1996	15.9	12.6	-3.3
1997	3.4	9.3	5.9
1998	0.1	31.6	31.4
1999	0.2	-40.6	-40.8
2000	-12.6	79.2	91.8
2001	-4.8	2.4	7.2
2002	0.3	-4.0	-4.3
2003	9.6	36.4	26.8
2004	8.4	23.2	14.8
2005	3.2	16.2	13.0
2006	15.3	10.8	-4.5
2007	-6.0	9.1	15.1
2008	-29.6	-25.3	4.3
2009	17.2	13.3	-3.9
2010	16.8	17.5	0.7
2011	-7.7	10.3	18.0
Avg	1.9%	11.4%	9.5%
Fq > 0	68%	82%	73%

gain of 11.4% and has been positive 82% of the time. This compares to the S&P 500 which has produced an average gain of 1.9% and has only been positive 68% of the time.

Investors should start to follow the performance of Altria in March, well before the start of its strong seasonal period. Very often, if Altria starts to outperform much earlier in the spring, this is an indication that investors are concerned about the "health" of the market and as a result are starting to favor defensive stocks. If Altria starts to send up this "smoke" signal in the spring, investors should invest cautiously in the market.

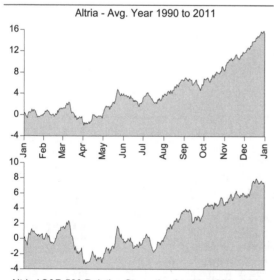

Altria - Avg. Year 1990 to 2011

Altria / S&P 500 Relative Strength - Avg Yr. 1990 - 2011

During the period of July 19th to December 19th, from 1990 to 2011, Altria has produced an average

(i) * MO - stock symbol for Altria which trades on the NYSE.

2011-12 Strategy Performance

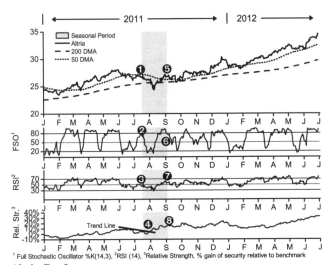

^{1} Full Stochastic Oscillator %K(14,3), ^{2}RSI (14), ^{3}Relative Strength, % gain of security relative to benchmark

Altria Performance

During 2011 and the first half of 2012, Altria strongly outperformed the S&P 500. This was mainly the result of investors seeking the safety of high dividend paying stocks, such as Altria. Investing during Altria's strong seasonal period was profitable and outperformed the S&P 500.

Technical Conditions

Entry Date July 19th, 2011 –Mildly Bullish– At the time of entry, Altria had been trading down from its high in May and was below its 50 day moving average ❶. The FSO had bounced downwards off 80❷ and the RSI was trading below 50❸. Also, at the time Altria was underperforming the S&P 500❹. This is hardly a very bullish scenario. It also must be remembered that the market was correcting strongly at the time and it was just a matter of time before investors would run to the defensive stocks again.

Entry Strategy –Buy Partial Position on Entry Date– Given that the technicals were not strong on the entry date, only a partial allocation was justified. The remaining allocation would have been made later in September when Altria crossed above its down trend line and starting trading above its 50 day moving average.

Exit Strategy – Sell Position on Exit Date– Altria put in a good performance in the last stages of its seasonal period❺. The FSO was above 80 and had just turned down❻. The RSI was also just below its overbought level❼. Altria had just started to perform at market❽. A full sell on the exit date was the best strategy as Altria started to turn down right on its exit date.

** Weekly avg closing values- except Fed Funds & CAN overnight tgt rate weekly closing values.

WEEK 27

Market Indices & Rates Weekly Values**

Stock Markets	2010	2011
Dow	10,025	12,643
S&P500	1,059	1,344
Nasdaq	2,156	2,848
TSX	11,339	13,399
FTSE	5,008	6,018
DAX	5,970	7,438
Nikkei	9,401	10,046
Hang Seng	20,043	22,659

Commodities	2010	2011
Oil	74.40	97.10
Gold	1199.7	1520.3

Bond Yields	2010	2011
USA 5 Yr Treasury	1.80	1.67
USA 10 Yr T	3.02	3.12
USA 20 Yr T	3.79	4.05
Moody's Aaa	4.72	5.07
Moody's Baa	6.08	5.84
CAN 5 Yr T	2.42	2.29
CAN 10 Yr T	3.15	3.04

Money Market	2010	2011
USA Fed Funds	0.25	0.25
USA 3 Mo T-B	0.16	0.02
CAN tgt overnight rate	0.50	1.00
CAN 3 Mo T-B	0.50	0.93

Foreign Exchange	2010	2011
USD/EUR	1.26	1.44
USD/GBP	1.51	1.60
CAN/USD	1.05	0.96
JPY/USD	87.99	80.93

JULY

M	T	W	T	F	S	S
1	2	3	4	5	6	7
8	9	10	11	12	13	14
15	16	17	18	19	20	21
22	23	24	25	26	27	28
29	30	31				

AUGUST

M	T	W	T	F	S	S
			1	2	3	4
5	6	7	8	9	10	11
12	13	14	15	16	17	18
19	20	21	22	23	24	25
26	27	28	29	30	31	

SEPTEMBER

M	T	W	T	F	S	S
						1
2	3	4	5	6	7	8
9	10	11	12	13	14	15
16	17	18	19	20	21	22
23	24	25	26	27	28	29
30						

GOLD SHINES
(Metal) Gold (Metal) Outperforms – July 12th to October 9th

"Foul cankering rust the hidden treasure frets, but gold that's put to use more gold begets."

(William Shakespeare, *Venus and Adonis*)

For many years, gold was thought to be a dead investment. It was only the "gold bugs" that espoused the virtues of investing in the precious metal. Investors were mesmerized with technology stocks and central bankers, confident of their currencies, were selling gold, "left, right and center."

4.3% gain & positive 68% of the time

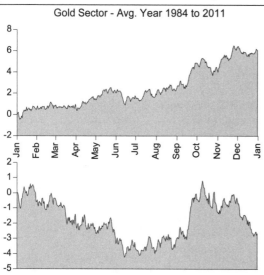

Gold Sector - Avg. Year 1984 to 2011

Gold / S&P 500 Relative Strength - Avg Yr. 1984 - 2011

Gold (Metal) London PM vs S&P 500 1984 to 2011			
Jul 12 to Oct 9th	S&P 500	Positive Gold	Diff
1984	7.4 %	0.5 %	-6.9 %
1985	-5.4	4.1	9.5
1986	-2.6	25.2	27.8
1987	0.9	3.9	3.0
1988	2.8	-7.5	-10.3
1989	9.4	-4.2	-13.6
1990	-15.5	12.1	27.6
1991	0.0	-2.9	-2.8
1992	-2.9	0.4	3.3
1993	2.7	-8.8	-11.5
1994	1.6	1.6	0.0
1995	4.3	-0.1	-4.3
1996	7.9	-0.4	-8.3
1997	5.9	4.4	-1.5
1998	-15.5	2.8	18.2
1999	-4.8	25.6	30.4
2000	-5.3	-4.5	0.8
2001	-10.5	8.4	18.8
2002	-16.2	1.7	17.9
2003	4.1	7.8	3.8
2004	0.8	3.8	2.9
2005	-1.9	11.4	13.4
2006	6.1	-8.8	-14.9
2007	3.1	11.0	8.0
2008	-26.6	-8.2	18.4
2009	21.9	15.2	- 6.7
2010	8.1	11.0	2.9
2011	-12.4	6.2	18.6
Avg.	-1.17 %	4.3 %	5.4 %
Fq > 0	54 %	68 %	64 %

Times have changed and investors have taken a shine to gold. In the last few years, gold has substantially outperformed the stock market. On a seasonal basis, on average from 1984 to 2011, gold has done well relative to the stock market from July 12th to October 9th. The reasons for gold's seasonal changes in price, are related to jewellery production and European Central banks selling cycles (see *Golden Times* strategy page).

The movement of gold stock prices, represented by the index (XAU) on the Philadelphia Exchange, coincides closely with the price of gold. Although there is a strong correlation between gold and gold stocks, there are other factors, such as company operations and hedging policies which determine each company's price in the market. Gold has typically started its seasonal strong period a few weeks earlier than gold stocks and finished just after gold stocks have turned down.

Investors should know that gold can have a run from November 1st to the end of the year. Although this is a positive time for gold, on average it does not perform as well as the S&P 500. From November 1st to Dec. 31st (1984 to 2011), gold has an average return of 1.8% and has been positive 79% of the time. In this time period, it has only outperformed the S&P 500 39% of the time, which has averaged a return of 3.1%. Investors should use technical analysis to determine the relative strength of gold at this time.

> Source: Bank of England
> London PM is recognized as the world benchmark for gold prices.
> London PM represents the close value of gold in afternoon trading in London.

2011-12 Strategy Performance

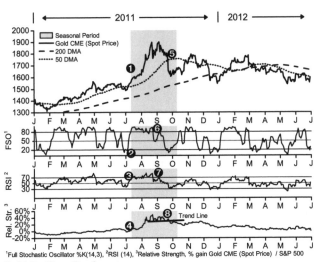

¹Full Stochastic Oscillator %K(14,3), ²RSI (14), ³Relative Strength, % gain Gold CME (Spot Price) / S&P 500

Market Indices & Rates Weekly Values**

Stock Markets	2010	2011
Dow	10,281	12,472
S&P500	1,086	1,315
Nasdaq	2,224	2,787
TSX	11,634	13,258
FTSE	5,212	5,879
DAX	6,134	7,221
Nikkei	9,595	9,974
Hang Seng	20,393	21,951

Commodities	2010	2011
Oil	76.38	96.71
Gold	1205.2	1572.5

Bond Yields	2010	2011
USA 5 Yr Treasury	1.81	1.48
USA 10 Yr T	3.05	2.94
USA 20 Yr T	3.83	3.89
Moody's Aaa	4.75	4.89
Moody's Baa	6.08	5.71
CAN 5 Yr T	2.51	2.16
CAN 10 Yr T	3.23	2.91

Money Market	2010	2011
USA Fed Funds	0.25	0.25
USA 3 Mo T-B	0.15	0.02
CAN tgt overnight rate	0.50	1.00
CAN 3 Mo T-B	0.53	0.92

Foreign Exchange	2010	2011
USD/EUR	1.28	1.41
USD/GBP	1.52	1.60
CAN/USD	1.04	0.96
JPY/USD	87.95	79.35

JULY

M	T	W	T	F	S	S
1	2	3	4	5	6	7
8	9	10	11	12	13	14
15	16	17	18	19	20	21
22	23	24	25	26	27	28
29	30	31				

AUGUST

M	T	W	T	F	S	S
		1	2	3	4
5	6	7	8	9	10	11
12	13	14	15	16	17	18
19	20	21	22	23	24	25
26	27	28	29	30	31	

SEPTEMBER

M	T	W	T	F	S	S
						1
2	3	4	5	6	7	8
9	10	11	12	13	14	15
16	17	18	19	20	21	22
23	24	25	26	27	28	29
30						

Gold Bullion Performance

In 2011, gold bullion came back into the spotlight as it once again made rapid gains over a short period of time. In early July, it started its rapid rise just as its seasonal period of strength was beginning. Towards the end of August it corrected sharply, giving up most of its gains. The stock markets around the world were also falling in September, but gold corrected even faster as many speculative investors had to cover their margin calls. For the rest of 201,1 and the first half of 2012, gold traded in a range, but generally underperformed the S&P 500.

Technical Conditions

Entry Date July 12th, 2011 –Bullish– Gold was technically well set up at the beginning of its seasonal period. It had just started a rising trend❶. The FSO had started to rise in early July and was just above 80❷ on the entry date and the RSI had just gone above 70❸, but had not shown signs of rolling over. In addition, gold had just started to outperform the S&P 500❹.

Entry Strategy –Buy Partial Position Early– With strong technicals, the entry scenario was bullish. The technicals turned positive at the beginning of July. If a full allocation was not made early, then the rest of the allocation was justified on the seasonal entry date.

Exit Strategy – Sell Partial Position Early– At the end of August, the price of gold started to become volatile. The FSO crossed below 80❺ and the RSI turned down from 70❼. Shortly afterwards, gold fell through its 50 day moving average❺ and gold started to show a continued trend of underperforming the S&P 500❽. Based upon the weakening technicals in early September, an early partial exit of the gold position was justified.

GOLDEN TIMES

(Stocks) Gold Stocks Outperform – July 27th to September 25th

Gold stocks were shunned for many years. It is only recently that interest has sparked again. What few investors know is that even during the twenty year bear market in gold that started in 1981, it was possible to make money in gold stocks.

6.3% when the S&P 500 has been negative

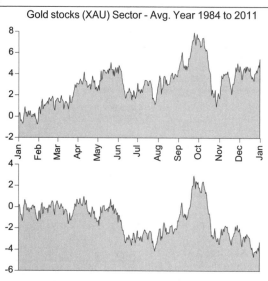

Gold stocks (XAU) Sector - Avg. Year 1984 to 2011

XAU / S&P 500 Relative Strength - Avg Yr. 1984-2011

XAU (Gold Stocks) vs S&P 500 1984 to 2011			
Jul 27 to		Positive	
Sep 25	S&P 500	XAU	Diff
1984	10.4 %	20.8 %	10.4 %
1985	-6.1	-5.5	0.6
1986	-3.5	36.9	40.4
1987	3.5	23.0	19.5
1988	1.7	-11.9	-13.7
1989	1.8	10.5	8.7
1990	-13.4	3.8	17.2
1991	1.6	-11.9	-13.5
1992	0.7	-3.8	-4.5
1993	1.9	-7.3	-9.2
1994	1.4	18.2	16.8
1995	3.6	-1.0	-4.6
1996	7.9	-1.0	-8.9
1997	-0.1	8.7	8.8
1998	-8.4	12.0	20.5
1999	-5.2	16.9	22.1
2000	-0.9	-2.8	-1.9
2001	-15.8	3.2	19.0
2002	-1.5	29.8	31.4
2003	0.5	11.0	10.5
2004	2.4	16.5	14.1
2005	-1.3	20.5	21.8
2006	4.6	-11.9	-16.8
2007	2.3	14.0	11.7
2008	-3.9	-18.5	-14.6
2009	6.7	6.0	-0.6
2010	3.0	14.7	11.7
2011	-14.7	-13.7	1.0
Avg.	-0.8 %	6.3 %	7.1 %
Fq > 0	57 %	61 %	64 %

On average from 1984 (start of the XAU index) to 2011, gold stocks as represented by the XAU index, have outperformed the S&P 500 from July 27th to September 25th. One factor that has led to a rise in the price of gold stocks in August and September is the Indian festival and wedding season that starts in October and finishes in November during Diwali. The Asian culture places a great emphasis on gold as a store of value and a lot of it is "consumed" as jewellery during the festival and wedding season. The price of gold tends to increase in the months preceding this season as the jewellery fabricators purchase gold to make their final product.

The August-September increase in gold stocks coincides with the time that a lot of investors are pulling their money out of the broad market and are looking for a place to invest. This makes gold a very attractive investment at this time of the year.

Be careful. Just as the gold stocks tend to go up in August-September, they also tend to go down in October. Historically, this negative trend has been caused by European Central banks selling some of their gold holdings in autumn when their annual allotment of possible sales is renewed yearly. In recent years, European Central banks have reduced gold sales. This has muted gold's negative trend in October.

In addition, investors can take advantage of the positive trend in gold from November 1st to December 31st. In this time period, gold stocks (XAU) have produced an average return of 3.8% and have been positive 50% of the time, beating the S&P 500, 39% of the time (1984-2011). Seasonal investors should consider this trade if the fundamentals warrant it and gold has strong momentum at the time.

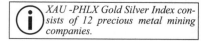

(i) *XAU -PHLX Gold Silver Index consists of 12 precious metal mining companies.*

2011-12 Strategy Performance

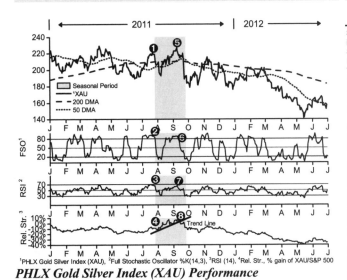

¹PHLX Gold Silver Index (XAU), ²Full Stochastic Oscillator %K(14,3), ³RSI (14), ⁴Rel. Str., % gain of XAU/S&P 500

PHLX Gold Silver Index (XAU) Performance

Gold stocks started out their seasonal period with a strong performance. Later in September, the sector fell dramatically, much more than the market, when investors became concerned with the European outlook and the health of the U.S. market. The reason that gold and gold stocks performed worse than the market in the sell-off is that a lot of investors buy gold and gold stocks on margin, and when margin calls were made in the sell-off, investors sold their gold holdings without respite. For investors fine tuning their buy and hold decisions, there were some early signals at the beginning of June that a partial position should be sold.

Technical Conditions

Entry Date July 27th, 2011 –Mildly Bullish– At the start of the seasonal period, gold stocks had just started to turn down ❶. The FSO had just crossed below 80❷ and the RSI had just bounced off 70❸. On a more positive note, gold stocks were performing at market❹. Shortly after in August, gold stocks started to outperform the S&P 500.

Entry Strategy –Buy Partial Position Early– A few weeks before the seasonal entry date, the FSO turned up above 20 and the RSI bounced off 30. Both of these conditions supported entering the sector early.

Exit Strategy– Sell Partial Position Early– In early September, gold stocks started to sell off aggressively, and at that point the XAU crossed below the 50 and 200 day moving averages (bearish)❺. The FSO also turned down from 80❻ at the same time, justifying a partial exit. Similarly, the RSI bounced off 70❼. Serious concern was raised when gold stocks started to underperform the S&P 500 in the first week of September, justifying a partial to full early exit❽.

Market Indices & Rates
Weekly Values**

Stock Markets	2010	2011
Dow	10,250	12,590
S&P500	1,084	1,329
Nasdaq	2,225	2,820
TSX	11,614	13,371
FTSE	5,226	5,846
DAX	6,055	7,228
Nikkei	9,308	10,010
Hang Seng	20,450	22,029

Commodities	2010	2011
Oil	77.60	98.02
Gold	1189.1	1597.8

Bond Yields	2010	2011
USA 5 Yr Treasury	1.71	1.50
USA 10 Yr T	2.97	2.97
USA 20 Yr T	3.76	3.93
Moody's Aaa	4.69	4.91
Moody's Baa	5.96	5.75
CAN 5 Yr T	2.39	2.21
CAN 10 Yr T	3.19	2.93

Money Market	2010	2011
USA Fed Funds	0.25	0.25
USA 3 Mo T-B	0.16	0.03
CAN tgt overnight rate	0.75	1.00
CAN 3 Mo T-B	0.61	0.92

Foreign Exchange	2010	2011
USD/EUR	1.29	1.43
USD/GBP	1.53	1.62
CAN/USD	1.04	0.95
JPY/USD	87.13	78.77

JULY

M	T	W	T	F	S	S
1	2	3	4	5	6	7
8	9	10	11	12	13	14
15	16	17	18	19	20	21
22	23	24	25	26	27	28
29	30	31				

AUGUST

M	T	W	T	F	S	S
			1	2	3	4
5	6	7	8	9	10	11
12	13	14	15	16	17	18
19	20	21	22	23	24	25
26	27	28	29	30	31	

SEPTEMBER

M	T	W	T	F	S	S
						1
2	3	4	5	6	7	8
9	10	11	12	13	14	15
16	17	18	19	20	21	22
23	24	25	26	27	28	29
30						

Oil stocks tend to outperform the market from July 24th to October 3rd. Earlier in the year, there is a first wave of outperformance from late February to early May. Although the first wave has had an incredible record of outperformance, the second wave in July is still noteworthy.

While the first wave has more to do with inventories during the switch from producing heating oil to gasoline, the second wave is more related to the conversion of production from gasoline to heating oil and the effects of the hurricane season.

Extra 2.1% &
57% of the time better than S&P 500

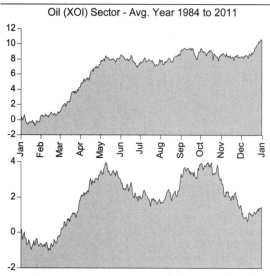

Oil (XOI) Sector - Avg. Year 1984 to 2011

Oil (XOI) / S&P 500 Relative Strength - Avg Yr. 1984 - 2011

XOI vs. S&P 500 1984 to 2011			
Jul 24 to Oct 3	S&P 500	Positive XOI	Diff
1984	9.1 %	9.0 %	-0.1 %
1985	-4.3	6.7	11.0
1986	-2.1	15.7	17.7
1987	6.6	-1.2	-7.8
1988	3.0	-3.6	-6.6
1989	5.6	5.7	0.1
1990	-12.4	-0.5	11.8
1991	1.3	0.7	-0.7
1992	-0.4	2.9	3.3
1993	3.2	7.8	4.6
1994	1.9	-3.6	-5.5
1995	5.2	-2.2	-7.4
1996	10.5	7.7	-2.8
1997	3.0	8.9	5.9
1998	-12.0	1.4	13.5
1999	-5.5	-2.1	3.3
2000	-3.6	12.2	15.8
2001	-10.0	-5.1	4.8
2002	2.7	7.3	4.6
2003	4.2	5.5	1.4
2004	4.2	10.9	6.7
2005	-0.6	14.3	14.9
2006	7.6	-8.5	-16.9
2007	-0.1	-4.2	-4.1
2008	-14.3	-18.1	-3.8
2009	5.0	3.0	-2.0
2010	4.0	8.5	4.5
2011	-18.3	-26	-7.7
Avg	-0.2 %	1.9 %	2.1 %
Fq > 0	57 %	61 %	57 %

Second, the hurricane season can play havoc with the production of oil and drive up prices substantially. The official duration of the hurricane season in the Gulf of Mexico is from June 1st to November 30th, but most major hurricanes occur in September and early October.

The threat of a strong hurricane can shut down the oil platforms temporarily, interrupting production. If a strong hurricane strikes the platforms, it can do significant damage and put the them out of commission for an extended period of time.

First, there is a large difference between how heating oil and gasoline are stored and consumed. For individuals and businesses, gasoline is consumed in an immediate fashion. It is stored by the local distributor and the supplies are drawn upon as needed. Heating oil, on the other hand, is largely inventoried by individuals, farms and business operations in rural areas.

The inventory process starts before the cold weather arrives. The production facilities have to start switching from gasoline to heating oil, dropping their inventory levels and boosting prices.

> (i) *Amex Oil Index (XOI):*
> *An index designed to represent a cross section of widely held oil corporations involved in various phases of the oil industry.*
> *For more information on the XOI index, see www.cboe.com*

2010-11-12 Sector Performance

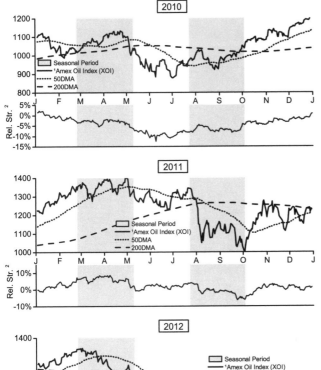

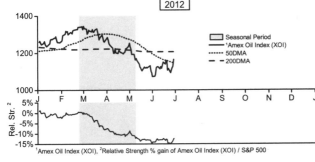

[1]Amex Oil Index (XOI), [2]Relative Strength % gain of Amex Oil Index (XOI) / S&P 500

Market Indices & Rates
Weekly Values**

Stock Markets	2010	2011
Dow	10,499	12,356
S&P500	1,108	1,313
Nasdaq	2,271	2,794
TSX	11,720	13,153
FTSE	5,322	5,880
DAX	6,173	7,259
Nikkei	9,597	9,986
Hang Seng	21,006	22,484

Commodities	2010	2011
Oil	78.16	97.82
Gold	1168.0	1618.7

Bond Yields	2010	2011
USA 5 Yr Treasury	1.73	1.50
USA 10 Yr T	3.02	2.97
USA 20 Yr T	3.83	3.91
Moody's Aaa	4.76	4.84
Moody's Baa	5.94	5.72
CAN 5 Yr T	2.41	2.14
CAN 10 Yr T	3.20	2.87

Money Market	2010	2011
USA Fed Funds	0.25	0.25
USA 3 Mo T-B	0.15	0.07
CAN tgt overnight rate	0.75	1.00
CAN 3 Mo T-B	0.64	0.92

Foreign Exchange	2010	2011
USD/EUR	1.30	1.44
USD/GBP	1.56	1.64
CAN/USD	1.03	0.95
JPY/USD	87.10	77.72

JULY

M	T	W	T	F	S	S
1	2	3	4	5	6	7
8	9	10	11	12	13	14
15	16	17	18	19	20	21
22	23	24	25	26	27	28
29	30	31				

AUGUST

M	T	W	T	F	S	S
			1	2	3	4
5	6	7	8	9	10	11
12	13	14	15	16	17	18
19	20	21	22	23	24	25
26	27	28	29	30	31	

SEPTEMBER

M	T	W	T	F	S	S
						1
2	3	4	5	6	7	8
9	10	11	12	13	14	15
16	17	18	19	20	21	22
23	24	25	26	27	28	29
30						

Amex Oil Index (XOI) Performance

Sometimes when a sector underperforms during its first of two seasonal periods, if its second seasonal period occurs shortly after the first, the sector will often outperform in the second period. This was not the case for XOI in 2011 as it underperformed in its first seasonal period from February to May and later underperformed in its second seasonal period from late July to early October. It also went on to underperform in its next seasonal period from the end of February to the beginning of May in 2012.

As the energy sector goes through a cyclical adjustment, it is especially wise to use technical indicators in making decisions to enter and exit trades.

** Weekly avg closing values- except Fed Funds & CAN overnight tgt rate weekly closing values.

Seasonal Investment Time Line[1]

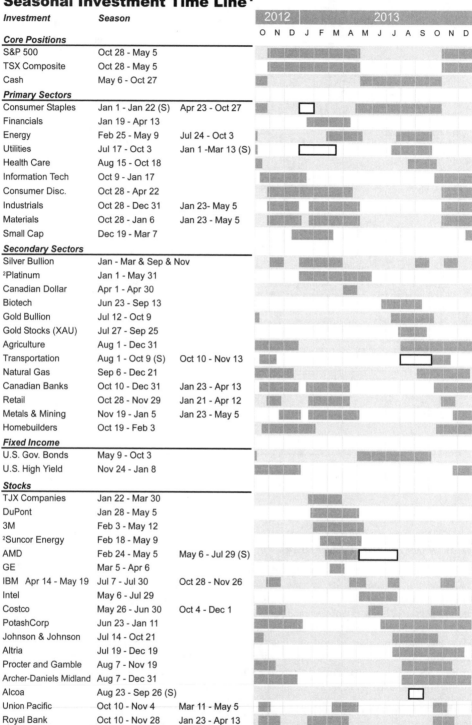

Investment	Season		2012	2013
			O N D J F M A M J J A S O N D	
Core Positions				
S&P 500	Oct 28 - May 5			
TSX Composite	Oct 28 - May 5			
Cash	May 6 - Oct 27			
Primary Sectors				
Consumer Staples	Jan 1 - Jan 22 (S)	Apr 23 - Oct 27		
Financials	Jan 19 - Apr 13			
Energy	Feb 25 - May 9	Jul 24 - Oct 3		
Utilities	Jul 17 - Oct 3	Jan 1 -Mar 13 (S)		
Health Care	Aug 15 - Oct 18			
Information Tech	Oct 9 - Jan 17			
Consumer Disc.	Oct 28 - Apr 22			
Industrials	Oct 28 - Dec 31	Jan 23- May 5		
Materials	Oct 28 - Jan 6	Jan 23 - May 5		
Small Cap	Dec 19 - Mar 7			
Secondary Sectors				
Silver Bullion	Jan - Mar & Sep & Nov			
[2]Platinum	Jan 1 - May 31			
Canadian Dollar	Apr 1 - Apr 30			
Biotech	Jun 23 - Sep 13			
Gold Bullion	Jul 12 - Oct 9			
Gold Stocks (XAU)	Jul 27 - Sep 25			
Agriculture	Aug 1 - Dec 31			
Transportation	Aug 1 - Oct 9 (S)	Oct 10 - Nov 13		
Natural Gas	Sep 6 - Dec 21			
Canadian Banks	Oct 10 - Dec 31	Jan 23 - Apr 13		
Retail	Oct 28 - Nov 29	Jan 21 - Apr 12		
Metals & Mining	Nov 19 - Jan 5	Jan 23 - May 5		
Homebuilders	Oct 19 - Feb 3			
Fixed Income				
U.S. Gov. Bonds	May 9 - Oct 3			
U.S. High Yield	Nov 24 - Jan 8			
Stocks				
TJX Companies	Jan 22 - Mar 30			
DuPont	Jan 28 - May 5			
3M	Feb 3 - May 12			
[2]Suncor Energy	Feb 18 - May 9			
AMD	Feb 24 - May 5	May 6 - Jul 29 (S)		
GE	Mar 5 - Apr 6			
IBM Apr 14 - May 19	Jul 7 - Jul 30	Oct 28 - Nov 26		
Intel	May 6 - Jul 29			
Costco	May 26 - Jun 30	Oct 4 - Dec 1		
PotashCorp	Jun 23 - Jan 11			
Johnson & Johnson	Jul 14 - Oct 21			
Altria	Jul 19 - Dec 19			
Procter and Gamble	Aug 7 - Nov 19			
Archer-Daniels Midland	Aug 7 - Dec 31			
Alcoa	Aug 23 - Sep 26 (S)			
Union Pacific	Oct 10 - Nov 4	Mar 11 - May 5		
Royal Bank	Oct 10 - Nov 28	Jan 23 - Apr 13		

Long Investment ▓▓▓▓▓▓▓   Short Investment (S) ☐

[1] Holiday, End of Month, Witches' Hangover, - et al not included. [2] Strategies from Thackray's 2012 Investor's Guide

AUGUST

	MONDAY	TUESDAY	WEDNESDAY
WEEK 31	29	30	31
WEEK 32	**5** 26 CAN Market Closed- Civic Day	**6** 25	**7** 24
WEEK 33	**12** 19	**13** 18	**14** 17
WEEK 34	**19** 12	**20** 11	**21** 10
WEEK 35	**26** 5	**27** 4	**28** 3

THURSDAY	FRIDAY
1 30	**2** 29
8 23	**9** 22
15 16	**16** 15
22 9	**23** 8
29 2	**30** 1

SEPTEMBER

M	T	W	T	F	S	S
						1
2	3	4	5	6	7	8
9	10	11	12	13	14	15
16	17	18	19	20	21	22
23	24	25	26	27	28	29
30						

OCTOBER

M	T	W	T	F	S	S
	1	2	3	4	5	6
7	8	9	10	11	12	13
14	15	16	17	18	19	20
21	22	23	24	25	26	27
28	29	30	31			

NOVEMBER

M	T	W	T	F	S	S
				1	2	3
4	5	6	7	8	9	10
11	12	13	14	15	16	17
18	19	20	21	22	23	24
25	26	27	28	29	30	

DECEMBER

M	T	W	T	F	S	S
						1
2	3	4	5	6	7	8
9	10	11	12	13	14	15
16	17	18	19	20	21	22
23	24	25	26	27	28	29
30	31					

AUGUST
S U M M A R Y

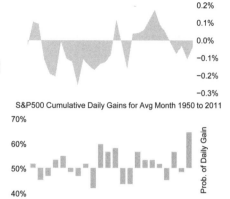

S&P500 Cumulative Daily Gains for Avg Month 1950 to 2011

	Dow Jones	S&P 500	Nasdaq	TSX Comp
Month Rank	10	9	11	10
# Up	35	34	21	14
# Down	27	28	19	13
% Pos	56	55	53	52
% Avg. Gain	-0.1	0.0	0.0	-0.3

Dow & S&P 1950-2011, Nasdaq 1972-2011, TSX 1985-2011

August is typically a marginal month and has been the fourth worst month from 1950 to 2011, and has been "flat" with an average gain of 0%. ♦ If there is a summer rally, it is often in jeopardy in August. ♦ In August 2011, the S&P 500 lost 5.7%, but in 2012 investors became optimistic that Europe was on the mend and the S&P 500 rallied 2.0%. ♦ There are a lot of sector opportunities in August, with new major seasonal trends starting in the agriculture, health care and transportation sectors.

BEST / WORST AUGUST BROAD MKTS. 2002-2011

BEST AUGUST MARKETS
- ♦ Russell 3000 Value (2009) 4.9%
- ♦ Russell 2000 (2003) 4.5%
- ♦ Nasdaq (2006) 4.4%

WORST AUGUST MARKETS
- ♦ Russell 2000 (2011) -8.8%
- ♦ Russell 2000 (2010) -7.5%
- ♦ Russell 3000 Value (2011) -6.7%

Index Values End of Month

	2002	2003	2004	2005	2006	2007	2008	2009	2010	2011
Dow	8,664	9,416	10,174	10,482	11,381	13,358	11,544	9,496	10,015	11,614
S&P 500	916	1,008	1,104	1,220	1,304	1,474	1,283	1,021	1,049	1,219
Nasdaq	1,315	1,810	1,838	2,152	2,184	2,596	2,368	2,009	2,114	2,579
TSX	6,612	7,510	8,377	10,669	12,074	13,660	13,771	10,868	11,914	12,769
Russell 1000	934	1,035	1,132	1,275	1,360	1,540	1,350	1,073	1,110	675
Russell 2000	972	1,236	1,362	1,656	1,791	1,970	1,838	1,422	1,496	727
Russell 3000 Growth	1,474	1,682	1,751	1,959	2,013	2,341	2,162	1,758	1,839	2,252
Russell 3000 Value	1,780	1,951	2,242	2,567	2,851	3,127	2,613	2,014	2,069	2,316

Percent Gain for August

	2002	2003	2004	2005	2006	2007	2008	2009	2010	2011
Dow	-0.8	2.0	0.3	-1.5	1.7	1.1	1.5	3.5	-4.3	-4.4
S&P 500	0.5	1.8	0.2	-1.1	2.1	1.3	1.2	3.4	-4.7	-5.7
Nasdaq	-1.0	4.3	-2.6	-1.5	4.4	2.0	1.8	1.5	-6.2	-6.4
TSX	0.1	3.5	-1.0	2.4	2.1	-1.5	1.3	0.8	1.7	-1.4
Russell 1000	0.3	1.9	0.3	-1.1	2.2	1.2	1.2	3.4	-4.7	-6.0
Russell 2000	-0.4	4.5	-0.6	-1.9	2.9	2.2	3.5	2.8	-7.5	-8.8
Russell 3000 Growth	0.2	2.6	-0.8	-1.4	3.0	1.5	1.0	1.8	-5.1	-5.7
Russell 3000 Value	0.4	1.5	1.2	-0.9	1.5	0.9	1.7	4.9	-4.8	-6.7

August Market Avg. Performance 2002 to 2011[1]

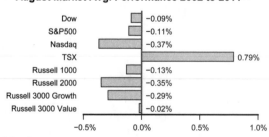

Dow	-0.09%
S&P500	-0.11%
Nasdaq	-0.37%
TSX	0.79%
Russell 1000	-0.13%
Russell 2000	-0.35%
Russell 3000 Growth	-0.29%
Russell 3000 Value	-0.02%

Interest Corner Aug[2]

	Fed Funds % [3]	3 Mo. T-Bill % [4]	10 Yr % [5]	20 Yr % [6]
2011	0.25	0.02	2.23	3.19
2010	0.25	0.14	2.47	3.23
2009	0.25	0.15	3.40	4.14
2008	2.00	1.72	3.83	4.47
2007	5.25	4.01	4.54	4.87

(1) Russell Data provided by Russell (2) Federal Reserve Bank of St. Louis- end of month values (3) Target rate set by FOMC (4)(5)(6) Constant yield maturities.

THACKRAY SECTOR THERMOMETER

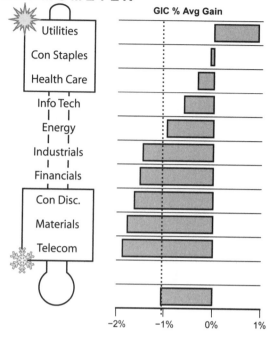

GIC[2] % Avg Gain	Fq % Gain >S&P 500	
SP GIC SECTOR 1990-2011[1]		
0.9 %	68 %	Utilities
-0.1	68	Consumer Staples
-0.3	73	Health Care
-0.6	50	Information Technology
-1.0	45	Energy
-1.5	32	Industrials
-1.5	36	Financials
-1.6	36	Consumer Discretionary
-1.8	41	Materials
-1.9 %	45 %	Telecom
-1.1 %	N/A %	S&P 500

Sector Commentary

♦ In August 2011, the S&P was down 5.7%, and only two sectors produced positive gains: the utilities sector with a gain of 1.6% and the consumer staples sector with a gain of 0.4%. ♦ The financial services sector and the energy sector were at the bottom of the list with losses of 9.7% and 10.0% respectively. The financial services sector was suffering the side-effects of the U.S. debt ceiling crisis that unfolded in early August.

Sub-Sector Commentary

♦ Historically, on average the biotech sub-sector continues to be at the top of the list with gold and agriculture. ♦ Although the pharmaceuticals sub-sector has an average negative performance, it has a high frequency rate of beating the S&P 500. ♦ Historically, the four worst sub-sectors are chemicals, railroads, transportation and steel. ♦ In August 2011, gold was the best performer with an 11.4% return. It was followed by silver with a return of 4.3% and pharmaceuticals with a loss of 0.2%, and the biotech sub-sector with a loss of 2.1%. In the very negative August of 2011, the sub-sectors generally ended up ranking relative to each other according to their historical average rankings.

SELECTED SUB-SECTORS 1990-2011[3]		
0.4 %	55 %	Biotech (93-2011)
0.4	50	Gold (London PM)
0.3	50	Agriculture (94-2011)
-0.3	68	Pharmaceuticals
-0.4	55	Homebuilders
-0.9	55	Software & Services
-0.9	59	Retail
-1.3	41	Banks
-1.4	45	Silver (London)
-1.7	45	Metals and Mining
-2.6	32	Chemicals
-2.6	41	Railroads
-3.1	27	Transportation
-4.0	45	Steel

(1) Sector data provided by Standard and Poors (2) GIC is short form for Global Industry Classification (3) Sub Sector data provided by Standard and Poors, except where marked by symbol.

Archer-Daniels Midland–
Plant Your Seeds For Growth
Aug 7th to Dec 31st

The agriculture sector generally performs well in the last five months of the year and ADM is no exception. If you had to choose just one part of the year in which to invest in ADM, it would have to be the last five months. From August 7th to December 31st, for the years 1990 to 2011, ADM produced an average gain of 14.3% and was positive 82% of the time.

The business of "growing" really takes place in the last part of the year. This is the harvest season for the northern hemisphere and when the cash flows. It is the period when expenditures are made and investors are much more interested in committing money to the agriculture sector.

14.3% & positive 82% of the time positive

Aug 7 to Dec 31	S&P 500	ADM	Diff
1990	-1.3%	0.1%	1.3%
1991	6.8	41.1	34.3
1992	3.6	3.1	-0.5
1993	4.0	1.7	-2.3
1994	0.5	31.9	31.4
1995	10.2	17.2	7.0
1996	11.8	27.5	15.6
1997	1.1	1.2	0.2
1998	12.8	9.4	-3.4
1999	13.0	-9.8	-22.8
2000	-9.8	58.5	68.2
2001	-4.4	14.6	19.0
2002	2.4	13.6	11.2
2003	15.0	16.7	1.7
2004	13.9	42.9	29.0
2005	1.8	18.7	16.9
2006	10.9	-21.9	-32.7
2007	0.1	34.5	34.5
2008	-29.9	5.4	35.3
2009	11.8	9.3	-2.6
2010	12.1	-0.3	-12.5
2011	4.9	-0.1	-5.0
Avg	4.1%	14.3%	10.2%
Fq > 0	82%	82%	64%

ADM vs. S&P 500 1990 to 2011 — Positive

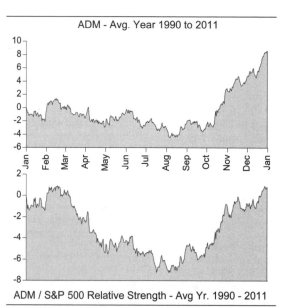

ADM - Avg. Year 1990 to 2011

ADM / S&P 500 Relative Strength - Avg Yr. 1990 - 2011

Investing in ADM for the last five months of the year has produced very good results over the long-term. On the other hand, the first seven months leading up to the favorable season has produced an average loss of 4.7% and has only been positive 41% of the time.

In other words, investors should avoid investing in ADM for the first seven months of the year. In fact, shorting ADM during the first seven months of the year and then switching to a long position for the last five months has proven to be a profitable strategy.

Seasonal investors can take advantage of the growing interest in the agriculture sector in the second half of the year by investing at the beginning of August. The idea is to get in before everyone else and get out when interest in the sector is at a maximum, towards the end of the year.

(i) * ADM - stock symbol for Archer-Daniels-Midland which trades on the NYSE. Archer-Daniels-Midland Company engages in the manufacture and sale of protein meal, vegetable oil, corn sweeteners, flour, biodiesel, ethanol, and other value-added food and feed ingredients.

2011-12 Strategy Performance

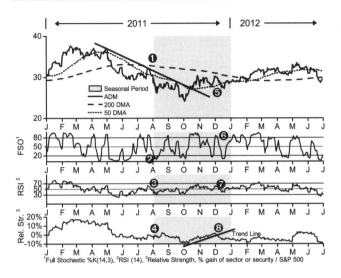

¹Full Stochastic %K(14,3), ²RSI (14), ³Relative Strength, % gain of sector or security / S&P 500

Market Indices & Rates
Weekly Values**

Stock Markets	2010	2011
Dow	10,664	11,745
S&P500	1,124	1,240
Nasdaq	2,293	2,639
TSX	11,801	12,528
FTSE	5,376	5,543
DAX	6,305	6,608
Nikkei	9,610	9,681
Hang Seng	21,530	21,982

Commodities	2010	2011
Oil	81.81	90.82
Gold	1195.2	1653.7

Bond Yields	2010	2011
USA 5 Yr Treasury	1.58	1.23
USA 10 Yr T	2.94	2.62
USA 20 Yr T	3.78	3.54
Moody's Aaa	4.73	4.43
Moody's Baa	5.86	5.38
CAN 5 Yr T	2.29	1.85
CAN 10 Yr T	3.11	2.64

Money Market	2010	2011
USA Fed Funds	0.25	0.25
USA 3 Mo T-B	0.16	0.04
CAN tgt overnight rate	0.75	1.00
CAN 3 Mo T-B	0.68	0.89

Foreign Exchange	2010	2011
USD/EUR	1.32	1.42
USD/GBP	1.59	1.63
CAN/USD	1.02	0.97
JPY/USD	85.98	77.74

ADM Performance

During its seasonal time in 2011, ADM was pulled down with the broad markets as investors fretted over economic problems in the U.S. and Europe. During its decline from August to September, ADM underperformed the S&P 500. When the market started to rally strongly in the beginning of October, ADM rallied and started to outperform the S&P 500. In the end, ADM produced a fractional loss over its entire seasonal period and underperformed the S&P 500.

Technical Conditions

Entry Date August 7th, 2011 –Neutral– On the seasonal entry date for ADM, positive technical signals did not exist. The stock was in a downtrend trading below its 50 and 200 day moving averages❶. The FSO was below 20 and had not turned up❷. The RSI was in its lower range❸ and ADM was "flat" against the markets for the previous two and a half months❹. The only factor going for ADM was that it was entering its seasonal period.

Entry Strategy –Buy Partial Position on Entry Date– Without a strong market and supporting technicals, only a small allocation was justified for ADM on its buy date.

Exit Strategy – Sell Partial Position Early– ADM had been consolidating over the two months before its exit date and traded below its 50 day moving average in early December❺. The FSO also turned below 80 at the beginning of December ❻ and at the time the RSI was neutral❼. Most importantly, ADM started to underperform the S&P 500 at the beginning of December, justifying a partial early exit❽.

AUGUST

M	T	W	T	F	S	S
			1	2	3	4
5	6	7	8	9	10	11
12	13	14	15	16	17	18
19	20	21	22	23	24	25
26	27	28	29	30	31	

SEPTEMBER

M	T	W	T	F	S	S
						1
2	3	4	5	6	7	8
9	10	11	12	13	14	15
16	17	18	19	20	21	22
23	24	25	26	27	28	29
30	31					

OCTOBER

M	T	W	T	F	S	S
	1	2	3	4	5	6
7	8	9	10	11	12	13
14	15	16	17	18	19	20
21	22	23	24	25	26	27
28	29	30	31			

** Weekly avg closing values- except Fed Funds & CAN overnight tgt rate weekly closing values.

TRANSPORTATION— ON A ROLL
①SELL SHORT (Aug1-Oct9) ②LONG (Oct10-Nov13)

In the past, my writings on the transportation sector have focused on the positive seasonal period. This is only half the story. Preceding transportation's positive seasonal period is a weak period, giving investors an opportunity to sell short the sector and profit from its decline. This weak period from August 1st to October 9 is followed by the strong period from October 10th to November 13th.

5.2% extra & positive 17 times out of 22

The transportation sector is very sensitive to economic expectations. Typically, when the economy is showing signs of improving, the transportation sector outperforms. When it is showing signs of deteriorating, the sector tends to underperform.

In the late summer months, investors tend to question the strength of an economic run which in turn puts pressure on the transportation sector. On average since 1990, the transportation sector has lost 4.6% from August 1st to October 9th.

In autumn, the market generally becomes positive about the expectations for the stock market's final months of the year which helps propel the transportation sector into positive territory. In addition, the price of oil tends to retreat in autumn. Since oil is one of the primary input costs for transportation, the sector benefits. From October 10th to November 13th, during the years 1990 to 2011, the transportation sector has gained an average of 6.5%.

ⓘ *The SP GICS Transportation Sector encompasses a wide range transportation based companies.*
For more information on the information technology sector, see www.standardandpoors.com

Transportation Sector vs. S&P 500 1990 to 2011
Negative Short ☐   Positive Long ☐

Year	SHORT Aug 1 to Oct 9		LONG Oct 10 to Nov 13		Compound Growth	
	S&P 500	Trans port	S&P 500	Trans port	S&P 500	Trans port
1990	-14.3 %	-19.2 %	4.1 %	3.3 %	19.0 %	23.1 %
1991	-2.8	0.5	5.5	9.6	8.5	9.1
1992	-5.1	-9.1	4.9	14.1	10.2	24.5
1993	2.7	-0.3	1.1	6.4	-1.6	6.8
1994	-0.7	-9.3	1.6	0.8	2.3	10.2
1995	2.9	-1.3	2.4	5.0	-0.6	6.4
1996	8.9	4.9	4.9	6.1	-4.4	0.9
1997	1.7	0.9	-5.6	-5.4	-7.2	-6.3
1998	-12.2	-16.5	14.4	12.5	28.3	31.0
1999	0.6	-11.0	4.5	4.0	3.9	15.4
2000	-2.0	-6.0	-3.6	13.0	-1.7	19.7
2001	-12.8	-20.0	7.8	14.1	21.5	36.9
2002	-14.8	-11.2	13.6	8.2	30.4	20.3
2003	4.9	4.9	1.9	8.0	-3.1	2.7
2004	1.9	6.6	5.5	11.1	3.6	3.7
2005	-3.1	-0.5	3.3	9.0	6.5	9.5
2006	5.8	6.4	2.5	3.8	-3.4	-2.9
2007	7.6	-0.2	-5.4	-2.9	-12.5	-2.7
2008	-28.2	-23.5	0.2	4.0	28.4	28.4
2009	8.5	6.7	2.1	5.9	-6.6	-1.2
2010	5.8	7.9	2.9	2.5	-3.0	-5.6
2011	-10.6	-11.8	9.4	11.4	21.0	24.2
Avg.	-2.5 %	-4.6 %	3.5 %	6.5 %	6.3 %	11.5 %
Fq>0	50	36	86	91	55	77

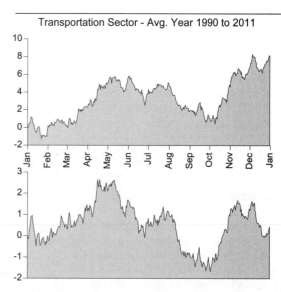

Transportation Sector - Avg. Year 1990 to 2011

Transportation / S&P 500 Rel. Strength- Avg Yr. 1990-2011

2011-12 Strategy Performance

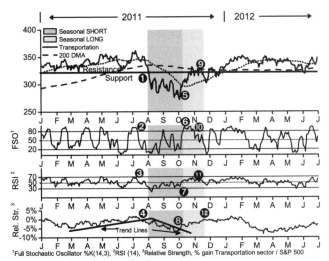

¹Full Stochastic Oscillator %K(14,3), ²RSI (14), ³Relative Strength, % gain Transportation sector / S&P 500

Market Indices & Rates
Weekly Values**

Stock Markets	2010	2011
Dow	10,469	11,036
S&P500	1,100	1,153
Nasdaq	2,231	2,444
TSX	11,667	12,212
FTSE	5,315	5,145
DAX	6,208	5,850
Nikkei	9,376	9,005
Hang Seng	21,349	19,764

Commodities	2010	2011
Oil	78.18	82.92
Gold	1205.7	1739.4

Bond Yields	2010	2011
USA 5 Yr Treasury	1.48	0.99
USA 10 Yr T	2.76	2.27
USA 20 Yr T	3.65	3.23
Moody's Aaa	4.60	4.32
Moody's Baa	5.78	5.31
CAN 5 Yr T	2.19	1.49
CAN 10 Yr T	3.02	2.43

Money Market	2010	2011
USA Fed Funds	0.25	0.25
USA 3 Mo T-B	0.15	0.03
CAN tgt overnight rate	0.75	1.00
CAN 3 Mo T-B	0.67	0.80

Foreign Exchange	2010	2011
USD/EUR	1.30	1.42
USD/GBP	1.57	1.63
CAN/USD	1.04	0.99
JPY/USD	85.76	77.03

Transportation Sector Performance

In 2011, the transportation sector acted according to its seasonal trends, almost to the day. The sector corrected sharply in August only to rebound in early October. Although a lot of this movement was the result of the general market movement, being in the right sector at the right time paid off. The transportation sector lost more than the S&P 500 (during its SHORT seasonal period) and made more than the S&P 500 (during its LONG seasonal period).

Technical Conditions– August 1st to November 13th, 2011
SHORT - Entry Date August 1st, 2011 –Bullish– Bullish SHORT position (expecting the market to decline). Just before the start of its seasonal period (short), the transportation sector dropped sharply through its 200 and 50 day moving averages. It also broke a support line❶. The FSO turned below 80 in early July❷. and the RSI turned below 70 at approximately at the same time❸. The transportation sector started to underperform the market in mid-July❹.

SHORT - Entry Strategy –Sell Short Partial Position Early– Technicals strongly supported entering a partial position early and the rest on the entry date.

LONG - Entry Date October 10th, 2011 –Bullish– The transportation sector rose sharply before the entry date and crossed its 50 day moving average❺. The FSO and RSI turned up in late September❻ ❼ and the transportation sector followed by starting to outperform in early October❽.

Exit Strategy – Sell Partial Position Early– The transportation sector turned down early and crossed back over its support level❾. The FSO crossed back below 80❿ in late October.   The RSI also turned down at the same time⓫. The transportation sector was still outperforming the S&P 500⓬. Overall, crossing back below the support level warranted a partial early exit.

AUGUST

M	T	W	T	F	S	S
			1	2	3	4
5	6	7	8	9	10	11
12	13	14	15	16	17	18
19	20	21	22	23	24	25
26	27	28	29	30	31	

SEPTEMBER

M	T	W	T	F	S	S
						1
2	3	4	5	6	7	8
9	10	11	12	13	14	15
16	17	18	19	20	21	22
23	24	25	26	27	28	29
30	31					

OCTOBER

M	T	W	T	F	S	S
	1	2	3	4	5	6
7	8	9	10	11	12	13
14	15	16	17	18	19	20
21	22	23	24	25	26	27
28	29	30	31			

AGRICULTURE MOOOVES
LAST 5 MONTHS OF THE YEAR – Aug to Dec

Agriculture, one of the hot sectors in recent years, has typically been hot during the last five months of the year (August to December).

This is the result of the major summer growing season in the northern hemisphere producing cash for the growers and subsequently increasing sales for the farming suppliers.

67% of the time
better than the S&P 500

Although this sector can represent a good opportunity, investors should be wary of the wide performance swings. Out of the seventeen cycles from 1994 to 2011, during August to December, there have been six years with absolute returns greater than +25% or less than -25%, and nine years of returns greater than +10% or less than -10%. In other words, this sector is very volatile.

Agriculture vs. S&P 500 1994 to 2011

Aug 1 to Dec 31	S&P 500	Positive Agri	Diff
1994	0.2 %	8.0 %	7.8 %
1995	9.6	31.7	22.1
1996	15.8	30.2	14.5
1997	1.7	14.7	13.0
1998	9.7	-3.4	-13.1
1999	10.6	-2.6	-13.2
2000	-7.7	68.0	75.7
2001	-5.2	12.5	17.7
2002	-3.5	6.0	9.5
2003	12.3	15.8	3.6
2004	10.0	44.6	34.6
2005	1.1	7.5	6.4
2006	11.1	-27.4	-38.5
2007	0.9	38.2	37.3
2008	-28.7	0.7	29.4
2009	12.9	4.0	-9.0
2010	14.2	9.9	-4.2
2011	-2.7	-5.9	-3.2
Avg.	3.5 %	14.0 %	10.6 %
Fq > 0	72 %	78 %	67 %

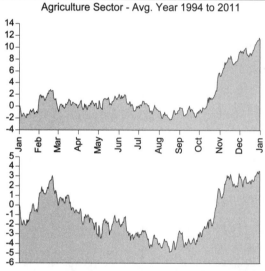

Agriculture Sector - Avg. Year 1994 to 2011

Agriculture / S&P 500 Relative Strength - Avg Yr. 1994-2011

On a year by year basis, the agriculture sector produced its biggest gain during its seasonally strong period in 2000, producing a gain of 68%. It is interesting to note that this is the same year that the technology sector's bubble burst. The agriculture sector benefited from the market correction because investors were looking for a safe haven to invest in – people need to eat, regardless of the performance of worldwide stock markets.

After realizing that technology stocks were not going to grow to the sky, investors started to have an epiphany–that the world might be running out of food and as a result, interest in the agriculture sector started to pick up.

In the second half of 2006, the agriculture sector corrected after a strong run in the first half of the year. In 2007 and the first half of 2008, the agriculture sector once again rocketed upwards due to the increase in prices of agricultural products.

Although food prices have had some reprieve with the global slowdown, the world population is still increasing and imbalances in food supply and demand will continue to exist in the future.

Investors should consider "moooving" into the agriculture sector for the last five months of the year.

ⓘ The SP GICS Agriculture Sector # 30202010
For more information on the agriculture sector, see www.standardandpoors.com

2011-12 Strategy Performance

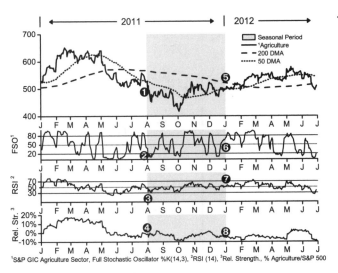

¹S&P GIC Agriculture Sector, Full Stochastic Oscillator %K(14,3), ²RSI (14), ³Rel. Strength., % Agriculture/S&P 500

Market Indices & Rates
Weekly Values**

Stock Markets	2010	2011
Dow	10,322	11,221
S&P500	1,083	1,171
Nasdaq	2,193	2,462
TSX	11,699	12,398
FTSE	5,267	5,235
DAX	6,117	5,810
Nikkei	9,228	8,983
Hang Seng	21,065	20,035

Commodities	2010	2011
Oil	74.86	85.35
Gold	1224.9	1796.7

Bond Yields	2010	2011
USA 5 Yr Treasury	1.44	0.93
USA 10 Yr T	2.61	2.17
USA 20 Yr T	3.42	3.13
Moody's Aaa	4.40	4.31
Moody's Baa	5.56	5.29
CAN 5 Yr T	2.16	1.51
CAN 10 Yr T	2.94	2.39

Money Market	2010	2011
USA Fed Funds	0.25	0.25
USA 3 Mo T-B	0.16	0.02
CAN tgt overnight rate	0.75	1.00
CAN 3 Mo T-B	0.66	0.85

Foreign Exchange	2010	2011
USD/EUR	1.28	1.44
USD/GBP	1.56	1.65
CAN/USD	1.04	0.98
JPY/USD	85.47	76.67

Agriculture Sector Performance

The agriculture sector started a steady decline at the end of February 2011, underperforming the market. Although the agriculture sector does not perform well until August, it was largely being brought down by the market's preference for defensive stocks at this time. At the time of entry for the seasonal period in August, the sector was still in decline and not showing any signs of abating its decline.

Technical Conditions

Entry Date August 1st, 2011 –Negative– On the entry date, the agriculture sector just started trading below its 50 day moving average❶. The FSO was still heading down and had not crossed below 20❷. Likewise the RSI was heading down and had not reached 30❸. The sector was basically performing at market ❹ as the market was heading "south" in August, as is often the case.

Entry Strategy –Buy Partial Position Late– It is rare that a sector should be entered into past its seasonal entry date, but all technical signs pointed to a delay for entry. Signals changed in the second week of August as the FSO and RSI bounced off their oversold levels. Entering at this time only helped a bit as the sector corrected strongly in August. Nevertheless, this delayed entry would have given the sector a profitable seasonal trade.

Exit Strategy – Sell Position On Exit Date– For the last part of December the agriculture sector was consolidating❺. The FSO was still rising❻, which is bullish and the RSI was neutral❼. The agriculture sector was underperforming the S&P 500❽. There was not a strong reason to stay in the market past the exit date.

AUGUST

M	T	W	T	F	S	S
			1	2	3	4
5	6	7	8	9	10	11
12	13	14	15	16	17	18
19	20	21	22	23	24	25
26	27	28	29	30	31	

SEPTEMBER

M	T	W	T	F	S	S
						1
2	3	4	5	6	7	8
9	10	11	12	13	14	15
16	17	18	19	20	21	22
23	24	25	26	27	28	29
30	31					

OCTOBER

M	T	W	T	F	S	S
	1	2	3	4	5	6
7	8	9	10	11	12	13
14	15	16	17	18	19	20
21	22	23	24	25	26	27
28	29	30	31			

Procter and Gamble– Something for Everyone
August 7th to November 19th

In investor's eyes, Procter and Gamble is a relatively defensive investment, as the company is in the consumer packaged goods business and its revenues are generated in over 180 countries. Defensive stocks have a reputation of producing sub-par performance compared with the broad market. This is not the case with PG, as on average it has outperformed the S&P 500 over the last twenty-two years.

10.7% & positive 86% of the time

Interestingly, on average, the gains have been produced largely in the second half of the year. In the first half of the year, PG has been relatively flat and has underperformed the S&P 500.

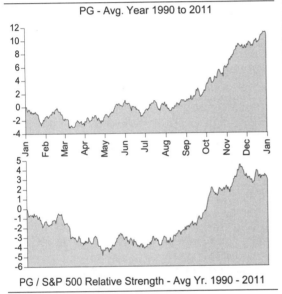

PG - Avg. Year 1990 to 2011

PG / S&P 500 Relative Strength - Avg Yr. 1990 - 2011

PG vs. S&P 500 - 1990 to 2011			
			Positive
Aug 7 to Nov19	S&P 500	PG	Diff
1990	-4.5%	8.4%	13.0%
1991	-2.9	-2.1	0.8
1992	0.7	10.1	9.4
1993	3.1	17.7	14.6
1994	1.0	19.5	18.6
1995	7.4	27.8	20.5
1996	12.0	18.4	6.3
1997	-1.6	0.3	1.9
1998	5.8	14.0	8.2
1999	9.4	18.9	9.5
2000	-6.5	32.0	38.5
2001	-4.1	11.2	15.3
2002	4.3	-0.7	-5.0
2003	7.8	8.2	0.4
2004	10.0	2.5	-7.5
2005	1.8	6.2	4.4
2006	9.5	7.4	-2.1
2007	-2.3	12.0	14.4
2008	-37.4	-8.1	29.3
2009	9.8	20.8	11.0
2010	7.0	6.7	-0.3
2011	1.4	4.4	3.0
Avg	1.4%	10.7%	9.3%
Fq > 0	68%	86%	82%

From a seasonal perspective, the best time to invest in PG has been from August 7th to November 19th. During this period, from 1990 to 2011, PG on average produced a gain of 10.7% and was positive 86% of the time. In addition it substantially outperformed the S&P 500, generating an extra profit of 9.3% and beating its performance 82% of the time.

Investors will often seek sanctuary in defensive stocks in late summer and early autumn. Although August is not typically the worst month of the year, it does have a weak risk reward profile. With the dreaded month of September falling right after August, investors become "gun shy" and start to become more conservative in August.

This trend benefits PG as more investors switch over to defensive companies. PG's outperformance on average starts to occur just after it releases its fourth quarter earnings in the beginning of August.

PG continues to outperform the S&P 500 through September and October. For the S&P 500, September on average is the worst month of the year and October is the most volatile month. The outperformance of PG continues into mid-November.

It is interesting to note that PG's seasonally strong period extends past the seasonal period for the consumer staples sector. It is possible that investors wait until after PG's first quarter results are released in the beginning of November before adjusting their portfolios.

ⓘ *The Procter and Gamble Company is a consumer packaged goods company. Its products are sold in more than 180 countries.*

2011-12 Strategy Performance

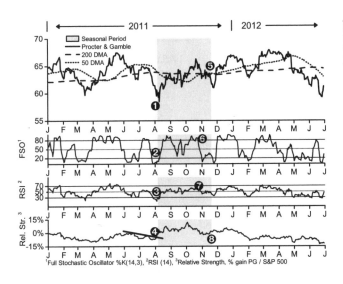

¹Full Stochastic Oscillator %K(14,3), ²RSI (14), ³Relative Strength, % gain PG / S&P 500

WEEK 34

Market Indices & Rates
Weekly Values**

Stock Markets	2010	2011
Dow	10,082	11,157
S&P500	1,057	1,160
Nasdaq	2,139	2,432
TSX	11,691	12,272
FTSE	5,172	5,138
DAX	5,942	5,562
Nikkei	8,971	8,714
Hang Seng	20,678	19,633

Commodities	2010	2011
Oil	72.87	84.99
Gold	1231.5	1808.1

Bond Yields	2010	2011
USA 5 Yr Treasury	1.41	0.97
USA 10 Yr T	2.56	2.19
USA 20 Yr T	3.32	3.12
Moody's Aaa	4.31	4.37
Moody's Baa	5.51	5.40
CAN 5 Yr T	2.10	1.54
CAN 10 Yr T	2.84	2.39

Money Market	2010	2011
USA Fed Funds	0.25	0.25
USA 3 Mo T-B	0.16	0.01
CAN tgt overnight rate	0.75	1.00
CAN 3 Mo T-B	0.64	0.87

Foreign Exchange	2010	2011
USD/EUR	1.27	1.44
USD/GBP	1.55	1.64
CAN/USD	1.06	0.99
JPY/USD	84.66	76.91

Procter and Gamble (PG) Performance

In 2011, the return profile for Procter and Gamble over its seasonal period was divided into two halves. In the first half, PG was rising when the market was falling, and in the second half, PG was falling when the market was rising. The overall net effect was that PG produced a positive return and outperformed the S&P 500 over its seasonal period.

Technical Conditions

Entry Date August 7th, 2011 –Bullish– Although PG was still in a downtrend at the start of its seasonal period (bearish)**❶**, the weight of technical evidence leaned to the bullish side. The FSO had just turned up and was about to cross 20**❷** and the RSI had just crossed above 30**❸**. Most importantly, PG had just started to outperform the S&P 500**❹**.

Entry Strategy –Buy Position on Entry Date– Technical signals indicated a positive outlook.

Exit Strategy – Sell Partial Position Early and Remainder Late– At the time of exit, PG had been consolidating at its 50 and 200 day moving averages and then turned below the averages**❺**. The FSO was neutral as was the RSI on the exit date as both indicators had turned below their overbought levels, 80 and 70, respectively, in the third week of October**❻❼**. This would have justified selling a partial position earlier. At the exit date, PG was outperforming the S&P 500, which helped the case for holding the remainder of the position**❽**. PG started to underperform mid-December.

** Weekly avg closing values- except Fed Funds & CAN overnight tgt rate weekly closing values.

AUGUST

M	T	W	T	F	S	S
			1	2	3	4
5	6	7	8	9	10	11
12	13	14	15	16	17	18
19	20	21	22	23	24	25
26	27	28	29	30	31	

SEPTEMBER

M	T	W	T	F	S	S
						1
2	3	4	5	6	7	8
9	10	11	12	13	14	15
16	17	18	19	20	21	22
23	24	25	26	27	28	29
30	31					

OCTOBER

M	T	W	T	F	S	S
	1	2	3	4	5	6
7	8	9	10	11	12	13
14	15	16	17	18	19	20
21	22	23	24	25	26	27
28	29	30	31			

HEALTH CARE
AUGUST PRESCRIPTION RENEWAL
August 15th to October 18th

Health care stocks have traditionally been classified as defensive stocks because of the stability of their earnings. Pharmaceutical and other health care companies typically still do well in an economic downturn.

Even in tough times, people still need to take their medication. As a result, investors have typically found comfort in this sector starting in the late summer doldrums and riding the momentum into early December.

2.7% more & 14 out of 22 times better than the S&P 500

Aug 15 to Oct 18	S&P 500	Positive Health Care	Diff
1990	-9.9 %	-1.3 %	8.6 %
1991	0.7	1.3	0.6
1992	-1.9	-9.0	-7.1
1993	4.1	13.5	9.5
1994	1.2	7.2	6.0
1995	4.9	11.7	6.7
1996	7.4	9.4	2.1
1997	2.1	5.8	3.7
1998	-0.6	3.0	3.6
1999	-5.5	-0.5	5.0
2000	-10.0	6.9	16.9
2001	-10.0	-0.4	9.6
2002	-3.8	2.4	6.2
2003	4.9	-0.5	-5.4
2004	4.6	-0.8	-5.4
2005	-4.2	-3.1	1.2
2006	7.7	6.4	-1.3
2007	8.0	6.0	-2.0
2008	-27.3	-20.4	6.8
2009	8.3	5.1	-3.3
2010	9.8	8.2	-1.6
2011	4.0	3.2	-0.8
Avg	-0.3 %	2.5 %	2.7 %
Fq > 0	59 %	64 %	64 %

Health Care vs. S&P 500 Performance 1990 to 2011

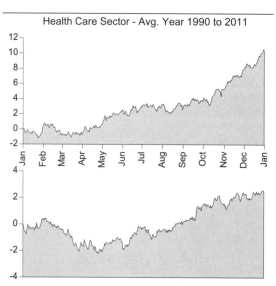

Health Care Sector - Avg. Year 1990 to 2011

Health Care / S&P 500 - Avg Yr. 1990 - 2011

From August 15th to October 18th (1990 to 2011), health care stocks have had a tendency to outperform the S&P 500 on a yearly basis.

During this time period, the broad market (S&P 500) produced an average loss of 0.3%, compared with the health care stocks that produced a gain of 2.5%.

Despite competing with a runaway market in 2003 and legal problems which required drugs to be withdrawn from the market in 2004, the sector has beaten the S&P 500 fourteen out of twenty-two times from 1990 to 2011.

The real benefit of investing in the health care sector has been the positive returns that have been generated when the market has typically been negative.

Since 1950, August and September have been the worst two-month combination for gains in the broad stock market.

Having an alternative sector to invest in during the summer and early autumn is a valuable asset.

Alternate Strategy—As the health care sector has had a tendency to perform at par with the broad market from late October to early December, an alternative strategy is to continue holding the health care sector during this time period if the fundamentals or technicals are favorable.

Health Care SP GIC Sector# 35: An index designed to represent a cross section of utility companies.
For more information on the materials sector, see www.standardandpoors.com.

2011-12 Strategy Performance

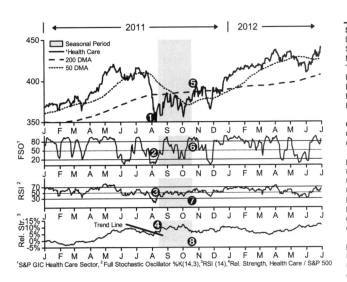

[1]S&P GIC Health Care Sector, [2]Full Stochastic Oscillator %K(14,3), [3]RSI (14), [4]Rel. Strength, Health Care / S&P 500

Stock Markets	2010	2011
Dow	10,212	11,489
S&P500	1,075	1,204
Nasdaq	2,169	2,549
TSX	12,014	12,642
FTSE	5,348	5,343
DAX	6,028	5,674
Nikkei	9,015	8,954
Hang Seng	20,748	20,280

Commodities	2010	2011
Oil	74.03	88.07
Gold	1245.4	1833.7

Bond Yields	2010	2011
USA 5 Yr Treasury	1.41	0.93
USA 10 Yr T	2.59	2.17
USA 20 Yr T	3.36	3.11
Moody's Aaa	4.39	4.34
Moody's Baa	5.59	5.40
CAN 5 Yr T	2.11	1.60
CAN 10 Yr T	2.85	2.41

Money Market	2010	2011
USA Fed Funds	0.25	0.25
USA 3 Mo T-B	0.14	0.02
CAN tgt overnight rate	0.75	1.00
CAN 3 Mo T-B	0.71	0.93

Foreign Exchange	2010	2011
USD/EUR	1.28	1.44
USD/GBP	1.54	1.63
CAN/USD	1.05	0.98
JPY/USD	84.37	76.79

Health Care Sector Performance

The health care sector strongly outperformed the S&P in March, April and May of 2011. This is not supposed to happen as this is not typically a strong period for health care stocks. During this time period, investors wanting to be in the market, but concerned about the economic outlook, favored the defensive sectors, such as health care, and shunned the cyclicals sectors. The problem was that on a relative basis, health care stocks became "bid up" before their seasonal period started, decreasing the potential for large returns in the health care sector.

Technical Conditions
***Entry Date August 15th, 2011*–<u>Bullish</u>–** The sector had already started to bounce at the beginning of August ❶. The FSO at the beginning of August had also bullishly turned up above 20❷ and the RSI had bullishly turned above 30❸. In addition, the health care sector had also started to outperform the S&P 500 at the beginning of the month❹.

Entry Strategy –<u>Buy Partial Position Early</u>– All signals pointed to an entry one week before the seasonal entry date. It does not seem to be much, but in a rapidly moving market it pays off, as it did in the case of the health care sector.

***Exit Strategy*–** <u>Sell Position on Exit Date</u>– Although the health care sector was rising on its seasonal exit date, there was little justification to hold on to the position❺. The FSO was overbought❻ and the RSI was neutral❼. The health care sector had not shown any signs of outperforming the S&P 500❽.

AUGUST

M	T	W	T	F	S	S
			1	2	3	4
5	6	7	8	9	10	11
12	13	14	15	16	17	18
19	20	21	22	23	24	25
26	27	28	29	30	31	

SEPTEMBER

M	T	W	T	F	S	S
						1
2	3	4	5	6	7	8
9	10	11	12	13	14	15
16	17	18	19	20	21	22
23	24	25	26	27	28	29
30	31					

OCTOBER

M	T	W	T	F	S	S
	1	2	3	4	5	6
7	8	9	10	11	12	13
14	15	16	17	18	19	20
21	22	23	24	25	26	27
28	29	30	31			

** Weekly avg closing values- except Fed Funds & CAN overnight tgt rate weekly closing values.

SEPTEMBER

	MONDAY	TUESDAY	WEDNESDAY
WEEK 36	**2** 28 USA Market Closed- Labour Day CAN Market Closed- Labour Day	**3** 27	**4** 26
WEEK 37	**9** 21	**10** 20	**11** 19
WEEK 38	**16** 14	**17** 13	**18** 12
WEEK 39	**23** 7	**24** 6	**25** 5
WEEK 40	**30**	1	2

SEPTEMBER

THURSDAY		FRIDAY	
5	25	**6**	24
12	18	**13**	17
19	11	**20**	10
26	4	**27**	3
3		4	

OCTOBER

M	T	W	T	F	S	S
	1	2	3	4	5	6
7	8	9	10	11	12	13
14	15	16	17	18	19	20
21	22	23	24	25	26	27
28	29	30	31			

NOVEMBER

M	T	W	T	F	S	S
				1	2	3
4	5	6	7	8	9	10
11	12	13	14	15	16	17
18	19	20	21	22	23	24
25	26	27	28	29	30	

DECEMBER

M	T	W	T	F	S	S
						1
2	3	4	5	6	7	8
9	10	11	12	13	14	15
16	17	18	19	20	21	22
23	24	25	26	27	28	29
30	31					

JANUARY

M	T	W	T	F	S	S
		1	2	3	4	5
6	7	8	9	10	11	12
13	14	15	16	17	18	19
20	21	22	23	24	25	26
27	28	29	30	31		

SEPTEMBER
S U M M A R Y

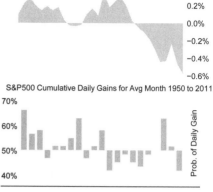

	Dow Jones	S&P 500	Nasdaq	TSX Comp
Month Rank	12	12	12	12
# Up	24	27	21	10
# Down	38	35	19	17
% Pos	39	44	53	37
% Avg. Gain	-0.9	-0.6	-0.7	-1.8

Dow & S&P 1950-2011, Nasdaq 1972-2011, TSX 1985-2011

S&P500 Cumulative Daily Gains for Avg Month 1950 to 2011

♦ From 1950 to 2011 on average, September was the weakest month of the year with a loss of 0.6% and a positive frequency of 39%. ♦ September 2011, produced a loss of 7.2% in the S&P 500. This is in contrast to the 8.8% gain in 2010 that was the result of Bernanke hinting strongly at increasing monetary liquidity with QE 2. ♦ Although September can produce positive results, seasonal investors should be cautious and take advantage of sectors that have relative outperformance, such as gold, health care and consumer staples.

BEST / WORST SEPTEMBER BROAD MKTS. 2002-2011

BEST SEPTEMBER MARKETS
- ♦ Russell 2000 (2010) 12.3%
- ♦ Nasdaq (2010) 12.0%
- ♦ Russell 3000 Gr (2010) 10.8%

WORST SEPTEMBER MARKETS
- ♦ TSX Comp. (2008) -14.7%
- ♦ Dow (2002) -12.4%
- ♦ Russell 3000 Gr (2008) -11.7%

Index Values End of Month

	2002	2003	2004	2005	2006	2007	2008	2009	2010	2011
Dow	7,592	9,275	10,080	10,569	11,679	13,896	10,851	9,712	10,788	10,913
S&P 500	815	996	1,115	1,229	1,336	1,527	1,166	1,057	1,141	1,131
Nasdaq	1,172	1,787	1,897	2,152	2,258	2,702	2,092	2,122	2,369	2,415
TSX	6,180	7,421	8,668	11,012	11,761	14,099	11,753	11,395	12,369	11,624
Russell 1000	833	1,023	1,145	1,285	1,391	1,597	1,219	1,115	1,211	623
Russell 2000	900	1,212	1,424	1,660	1,803	2,002	1,689	1,502	1,680	644
Russell 3000 Growth	1,322	1,660	1,772	1,967	2,063	2,434	1,910	1,834	2,037	2,077
Russell 3000 Value	1,584	1,928	2,277	2,595	2,901	3,220	2,420	2,090	2,230	2,131

Percent Gain for September

	2002	2003	2004	2005	2006	2007	2008	2009	2010	2011
Dow	-12.4	-1.5	-0.9	0.8	2.6	4.0	-6.0	2.3	7.7	-6.0
S&P 500	-11.0	-1.2	0.9	0.7	2.5	3.6	-9.1	3.6	8.8	-7.2
Nasdaq	-10.9	-1.3	3.2	0.0	3.4	4.0	-11.6	5.6	12.0	-6.4
TSX	-6.5	-1.2	3.5	3.2	-2.6	3.2	-14.7	4.8	3.8	-9.0
Russell 1000	-10.9	-1.2	1.1	0.8	2.3	3.7	-9.7	3.9	9.0	-7.6
Russell 2000	-7.3	-2.0	4.6	0.2	0.7	1.6	-8.1	5.6	12.3	-11.4
Russell 3000 Growth	-10.3	-1.3	1.2	0.4	2.5	4.0	-11.7	4.3	10.8	-7.8
Russell 3000 Value	-11.0	-1.2	1.5	1.1	1.7	3.0	-7.4	3.8	7.8	-8.0

September Market Avg. Performance 2002 to 2011[1]

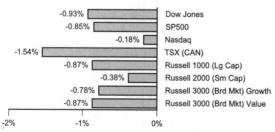

-0.93%	Dow Jones
-0.85%	SP500
-0.18%	Nasdaq
-1.54%	TSX (CAN)
-0.87%	Russell 1000 (Lg Cap)
-0.38%	Russell 2000 (Sm Cap)
-0.78%	Russell 3000 (Brd Mkt) Growth
-0.87%	Russell 3000 (Brd Mkt) Value

Interest Corner Sep[2]

	Fed Funds %[3]	3 Mo. T-Bill %[4]	10 Yr %[5]	20 Yr %[6]
2011	0.25	0.02	1.92	2.66
2010	0.25	0.16	2.53	3.38
2009	0.25	0.14	3.31	4.02
2008	2.00	0.92	3.85	4.43
2007	4.75	3.82	4.59	4.89

(1) Russell Data provided by Russell (2) Federal Reserve Bank of St. Louis- end of month values (3) Target rate set by FOMC (4)(5)(6) Constant yield maturities.

THACKRAY SECTOR THERMOMETER

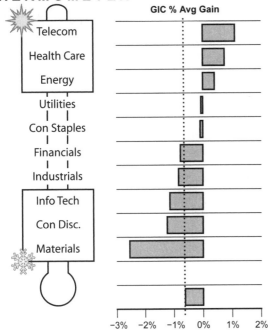

GIC[2] % Avg Gain	Fq % Gain >S&P 500	SP GIC SECTOR 1990-2011[1]
1.1 %	64 %	Telecom
0.7	64	Health Care
0.4	59	Energy
-0.1	36	Utilities
-0.1	59	Consumer Staples
-0.8	55	Financials
-0.8	45	Industrials
-1.1	68	Information Technology
-1.2	50	Consumer Discretionary
-2.5 %	18 %	Materials
-0.6 %	N/A %	S&P 500

Sector Commentary

♦ In September 2011, the defensive sectors were at the top of the list of performers, as would be expected when the S&P 500 loses 7.1%. ♦ The top sectors, in order were utilities, telecom, information technology, consumer staples and health care. All of the sectors are classified as defensive sectors, except one: technology, which often leads the market. ♦ The technology sector typically starts its strong seasonal performance in October and by performing relatively well compared with the other sectors of the market, a month early, the technology sector was hinting that better times might be just around the corner.

Sub-Sector Commentary

♦ Biotech is often one of the best performing sub-sectors in September, however, in 2011 it produced a minor loss of 0.2%. ♦ The biotech sub-sector's strong seasonal performance ends mid-September and exiting at this time in September 2011 would have been beneficial. ♦ Gold and silver are usually at the top of the rank of sub-sectors, but in September 2011, they both performed very poorly as speculative investors were being forced to sell their positions to meet their margin calls.

SELECTED SUB-SECTORS 1990-2011[3]		
3.1 %	68 %	Gold (London PM)
2.2	73	Silver (London)
1.4	60	Biotech (93-2011)
0.8	64	Pharmaceuticals
0.6	68	Software & Services
-0.4	56	Agriculture (94-2011)
-0.8	45	Retail
-1.0	32	Railroads
-1.0	50	Transportation
-1.1	55	Banks
-1.4	59	Homebuilders
-2.3	41	Metals and Mining
-2.7	21	Chemicals
-4.3	41	Steel

(1) Sector data provided by Standard and Poors (2) GIC is short form for Global Industry Classification (3) Sub Sector data provided by Standard and Poors, except where marked by symbol.

GAS FIRES UP IN SEPTEMBER
Natural Gas (Commodity) – Outperforms
Cash price increases from Sep 5th to Dec 21st

Most investors have stayed away from natural gas investments as the price of natural gas has had a multi-year decline due to the increasing supply of natural gas. The increase has been the result of new drilling techniques, specifically "fracking," a procedure of creating fractures in rock formations by injecting liquids into them, in order to let oil and natural gas flow more freely.

Fracking has brought the price of natural gas so low that in 2011 many producers started to shut-in their wells, and the trend has continued in 2012. Investors keep asking the question: can the price of natural gas go any lower? It is difficult to tell when natural gas will reach its base price, but as it gets closer and closer to this point, stabilizing more and more, the seasonal trends will have more of an impact.

If there is one time of the year that investors should consider investing in natural gas, it is from September 5th to December 21st.

48.7% & positive 82% of the time

We may not use natural gas ourselves, but most of us depend on it in one way or another. It is used for furnaces and hot water tanks and is usually responsible for producing some portion of the electrical power that we consume.

Natural Gas (Cash) Henry Hub LA
Seasonal Gains 1995 to 2011

	Negative	Positive	Negative
	Jan 1 to Sep 4	Sep 5 to Dec 21	Dec 22 to Dec 31
1995	-2.9 %	103.0 %	1.2 %
1996	-50.2	170.4	-46.2
1997	11.4	-13.1	-6.3
1998	-22.9	20.9	-6.7
1999	26.8	5.3	-11.2
2000	104.4	121.9	0.7
2001	-79.1	21.5	1.5
2002	15.9	61.3	-9.1
2003	2.6	47.1	-16.3
2004	-24.1	54.6	-11.6
2005	96.5	14.5	-29.6
2006	-45.6	17.4	-9.5
2007	-3.8	32.7	2.0
2008	1.0	-21.4	-0.9
2009	-66.6	208.0	0.7
2010	-35.9	10.4	2.4
2011	-3.1	-26.1	-1.7
Avg.	-4.5 %	48.7 %	-8.3 %

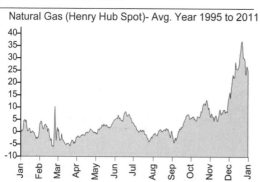

Natural Gas (Henry Hub Spot)- Avg. Year 1995 to 2011

As a result, there are two high consumption times for natural gas: winter and summer. The colder it gets in winter, the more natural gas is consumed to keep the furnaces going. The warmer it gets in the summer, the more natural gas is used to produce power for air conditioners. On the supply side, weather also plays a large factor in determining price. During the hurricane season in the Gulf of Mexico, the price of natural gas is affected by the forecast of the number, severity and impact of hurricanes.

The tail end of the hurricane season occurs in late autumn and early winter, at the same time distributors are accumulating natural gas inventories for the winter heating season. As a result, the price of natural gas tends to rise from the beginning of September. As the price is very dependent on the weather, it is also extremely volatile. Large percentage moves are not uncommon.

As a result of the hurricane season ending and the slowdown in accumulating natural gas inventories for winter heating, the price of natural gas frequently decreases during the last part of December.

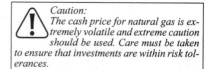

Caution:
The cash price for natural gas is extremely volatile and extreme caution should be used. Care must be taken to ensure that investments are within risk tolerances.

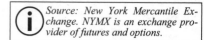

Source: New York Mercantile Exchange. NYMX is an exchange provider of futures and options.

2011-12 Strategy Performance

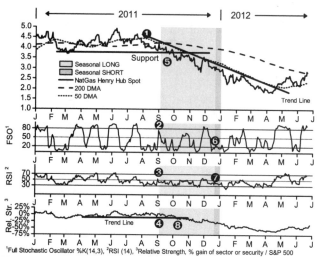

¹Full Stochastic Oscillator %K(14,3), ²RSI (14), ³Relative Strength, % gain of sector or security / S&P 500

Market Indices & Rates
Weekly Values

Stock Markets	2010	2011
Dow	10,401	11,211
S&P500	1,101	1,176
Nasdaq	2,229	2,505
TSX	12,069	12,578
FTSE	5,455	5,227
DAX	6,175	5,289
Nikkei	9,178	8,734
Hang Seng	21,254	19,831

Commodities	2010	2011
Oil	74.87	87.91
Gold	1252.5	1861.2

Bond Yields	2010	2011
USA 5 Yr Treasury	1.51	0.87
USA 10 Yr T	2.71	1.99
USA 20 Yr T	3.48	2.90
Moody's Aaa	4.50	4.11
Moody's Baa	5.67	5.24
CAN 5 Yr T	2.19	1.40
CAN 10 Yr T	2.93	2.23

Money Market	2010	2011
USA Fed Funds	0.25	0.25
USA 3 Mo T-B	0.14	0.02
CAN tgt overnight rate	1.00	1.00
CAN 3 Mo T-B	0.86	0.91

Foreign Exchange	2010	2011
USD/EUR	1.27	1.39
USD/GBP	1.54	1.60
CAN/USD	1.04	0.99
JPY/USD	83.97	77.39

Natural Gas Performance

In 2011, there was a lot of talk about how the future uses of natural gas would help to bolster the prices. T. Boone Pickens, a business magnate who runs a large hedge fund and is well respected in the finance and business world, was advocating the use of natural gas for many new uses such as fuel for truck fleets. There is no question that with low prices, new uses will be found– it is just a matter of time. In 2011, many investors were speculating that the bottom had finally been seen in natural gas as the price traded in the $3.50 to $5.00 range. In August, natural gas fell through its 200 day moving average and started its decline until it turned around in April 2012.

Technical Conditions
Entry Date September 5th, 2011 –Neutral– Natural gas had been consolidating for the first part of 2011. In August, natural gas broke its 200 day moving average to the downside❶ and in September continued to decline, but was still in a trading range above the low set in early March. On the entry date the FSO had risen but was not overbought❷. The RSI had risen but was still below 50❸. On a relative basis, natural gas was performing at market ❹.

Entry Strategy –Buy Partial Position on Entry Date– The
technical conditions for natural gas were not strong on the entry date, but a fundamental breakdown had not occurred.

Exit Strategy– Sell Position Early– After the entry date, natural gas continued its decline and broke its support level in September❺. The FSO❻ and the RSI❼ provided little support with making a technical decision for natural gas. Natural gas continued to underperform and a sell signal was confirmed when it started to underperform the S&P 500 in October❽.

SEPTEMBER

M	T	W	T	F	S	S
						1
2	3	4	5	6	7	8
9	10	11	12	13	14	15
16	17	18	19	20	21	22
23	24	25	26	27	28	29
30	31					

OCTOBER

M	T	W	T	F	S	S
	1	2	3	4	5	6
7	8	9	10	11	12	13
14	15	16	17	18	19	20
21	22	23	24	25	26	27
28	29	30	31			

NOVEMBER

M	T	W	T	F	S	S
				1	2	3
4	5	6	7	8	9	10
11	12	13	14	15	16	17
18	19	20	21	22	23	24
25	26	27	28	29	30	

Alcoa Inc. – SHORT SELL
August 23rd to September 26th

Alcoa has the distinction of "kicking off" the earnings season each quarter as it is the first large company to report. It typically reports in the second week of earnings months and the media covers its results with much fanfare.

Alcoa has a weak September trend, the same as the metals and mining sector. Alcoa's weak period from August 23rd to September 26th has provided investor's with a good opportunity to profit by taking a short position in the stock. From 1990 to 2011, shorting Alcoa during this time has produced an average gain of 6.4% (negative numbers in table represent a gain when shorting). The trade has also been both profitable 68% of the time and outperformed the S&P 500, 68% of the time.

6.4% gain & profitable 68% of the time

Although Alcoa can continue its negative performance until late October, it is generally prudent to exit the trade before Alcoa's Q4 earnings in early October.

Alcoa vs. S&P 500 Performance 1990 to 2011			
			Negative
Aug 23 to Sep 26	S&P 500	AA	Diff
1990	-3.6%	2.7%	6.3%
1991	-1.2	-3.2	-2.0
1992	-0.1	2.5	2.6
1993	0.3	-8.6	-8.9
1994	-0.3	10.5	10.8
1995	3.9	-14.3	-18.2
1996	2.3	-6.5	-8.8
1997	2.4	-5.3	-7.7
1998	-3.4	8.0	11.4
1999	-4.4	-11.5	-7.1
2000	-4.7	-27.5	-22.8
2001	-13.6	-23.9	-10.3
2002	-11.2	-27.4	-16.2
2003	0.4	-5.2	-5.5
2004	1.1	-3.2	-4.3
2005	-0.5	-14.7	-14.2
2006	2.9	-4.8	-7.7
2007	4.2	6.2	2.0
2008	-6.1	-27.1	-21.0
2009	1.8	4.1	2.4
2010	7.2	15.4	8.2
2011	3.5	-7.0	-10.4
Avg	-0.9%	-6.4%	-5.5%
Fq > 0	50%	32%	32%

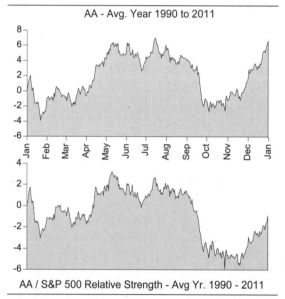

AA - Avg. Year 1990 to 2011

AA / S&P 500 Relative Strength - Avg Yr. 1990 - 2011

take on more stock market risk and pushed the market higher.

Despite the seasonal opportunity to profit from Alcoa's declining price, it has produced positive returns of 5% or greater four times since 1990. Investors should consider the magnitude of the potential loss before making a portfolio allocation decision.

Investors should also consider the current economic climate at the time and how cyclical stocks are responding. If the economy is showing signs of strong growth and the cyclical stocks are responding with strong momentum, investors should be extra cautious with this trade.

Generally the trade has not worked when the market has uncharacteristically rallied during the late summer and early autumn time period. More recently, the trade did not work in 2009 and 2010 when the Fed's quantitative easing programs motivated investors to

ⓘ * Alcoa (AA) is engaged in the production and management of aluminium, fabricated aluminium, and alumina combined. Alcoa trades on the NYSE.

2011-12 Strategy Performance

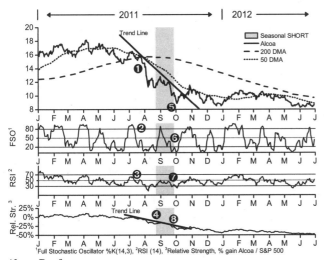

¹Full Stochastic Oscillator %K(14,3), ²RSI (14), ³Relative Strength, % gain Alcoa / S&P 500

Market Indices & Rates
Weekly Values**

Stock Markets	2010	2011
Dow	10,569	11,271
S&P500	1,124	1,190
Nasdaq	2,299	2,566
TSX	12,165	12,267
FTSE	5,547	5,247
DAX	6,252	5,332
Nikkei	9,455	8,641
Hang Seng	21,748	19,178

Commodities	2010	2011
Oil	75.65	88.93
Gold	1264.6	1809.7

Bond Yields	2010	2011
USA 5 Yr Treasury	1.47	0.91
USA 10 Yr T	2.74	2.03
USA 20 Yr T	3.55	2.92
Moody's Aaa	4.59	4.14
Moody's Baa	5.73	5.33
CAN 5 Yr T	2.24	1.47
CAN 10 Yr T	2.96	2.23

Money Market	2010	2011
USA Fed Funds	0.25	0.25
USA 3 Mo T-B	0.15	0.01
CAN tgt overnight rate	1.00	1.00
CAN 3 Mo T-B	0.91	0.88

Foreign Exchange	2010	2011
USD/EUR	1.30	1.38
USD/GBP	1.56	1.58
CAN/USD	1.03	0.99
JPY/USD	84.83	76.86

SEPTEMBER

M	T	W	T	F	S	S
						1
2	3	4	5	6	7	8
9	10	11	12	13	14	15
16	17	18	19	20	21	22
23	24	25	26	27	28	29
30	31					

OCTOBER

M	T	W	T	F	S	S
	1	2	3	4	5	6
7	8	9	10	11	12	13
14	15	16	17	18	19	20
21	22	23	24	25	26	27
28	29	30	31			

NOVEMBER

M	T	W	T	F	S	S
				1	2	3
4	5	6	7	8	9	10
11	12	13	14	15	16	17
18	19	20	21	22	23	24
25	26	27	28	29	30	

Alcoa Performance

Like many other metals and mining stocks in the beginning part of 2011, Alcoa underperformed the S&P 500. After earnings season in July, Alcoa's price fell precipitously. In August the stock consolidated, but underperformed the S&P 500. Alcoa maintained its underperformance even as the S&P 500 rallied in late 2011 and the beginning of 2012. From the beginning of 2011 to half way through 2012, Alcoa lost half of its value. Shorting Alcoa during its period of weak performance was profitable as Alcoa lost value and underperformed the market.

Technical Conditions

Entry Date August 23rd, 2011 –Bearish (Bullish for Short Position) – Alcoa crossed below its 50 and 200 day moving averages in late July❶, following behind the FSO which had just turned below 80❷ and the RSI which had started to trend downwards❸. At the entry date for the short position, Alcoa had established a trend of underperforming the S&P 500❹.

Entry Strategy –Sell Short Partial Position Early– Alcoa showed weak tendencies in early July with the FSO turning below 80, and breaking its 50 and 200 day moving averages. Although this date is well before the seasonal entry date, shorting at this time is justified because on an absolute average basis, the peak for Alcoa occurs in mid-July. It is just that the sweet spot for a short position occurs later.

Exit Strategy – Cover Partial Position On Exit Date– On the exit date, Alcoa was still trading down and was below its 50 and 200 day moving averages❺. The FSO had just turned upwards❻, but the RSI had yet to confirm a positive trend❼. Alcoa continued to underperform the S&P 500❽. Conditions changed abruptly at the beginning of October, justifying an exit of the full position.

SEPTEMBER PAIR TRADE
Long Gold – Short Sell Metals and Mining in September

Most retail investors shy away from taking a short position because of the perceived risk. But selling a position short can help reduce risk, especially when it is used in a pair trade.

Taking a long position in gold (expecting the price of gold to increase), and taking a short position in the metals and mining sector (expecting a decrease in price), has paid handsome rewards in the month of September from 1990 to 2011. This trade has netted an average return of 5.4% and has been positive 73% of the time.

The pair trade results have been better than if you just entered a long position for gold or a short position for the metals and mining sector.

There is a good reason that this pair trade makes sense. The metals and mining and the gold sector have a lot of the same factors driving their performance, at least on the supply side of the equation. If it costs more to get "stuff" out of the ground, then both sectors are effected.

Where the metals and mining sector and gold differ is in their demand cycle. Demand in the metals and mining sector slows down in the summer months as industrial production decreases during the holiday months. Gold, on the other hand, has a large spike in demand in the late summer from the gold fabricators having to buy enough gold for the Indian wedding and festival season.

Over the long-term, gold and the metals and mining sector, have monthly averages that generally move together.

September presents an exception to this trend and a profitable opportunity for a pair trade.

Gold vs. Metals and Mining Performance 1990 to 2011

| | Positive Long | | |
| | Negative Short | | |
Sept	Gold	M&M	Diff
1990	5.3 %	-4.0 %	9.3 %
1991	2.2	-2.9	5.0
1992	2.6	-1.2	3.9
1993	-4.3	-8.0	3.6
1994	2.4	3.7	-1.4
1995	0.4	-1.7	2.1
1996	-1.9	-2.1	0.2
1997	2.1	1.3	0.8
1998	7.5	26.8	-19.3
1999	17.3	3.0	14.3
2000	-1.2	-15.3	14.1
2001	7.4	-13.0	20.4
2002	3.5	-16.7	20.1
2003	3.3	-4.2	7.5
2004	2.1	5.5	-3.4
2005	9.2	7.3	1.9
2006	-3.9	-5.4	1.5
2007	10.6	11.9	-1.3
2008	6.2	-31.1	37.3
2009	4.2	7.9	-3.7
2010	4.9	10.1	-5.2
2011	-10.7	-22.5	11.8
Avg	3.1 %	-2.3 %	5.4 %
Fq > 0	77 %	41 %	73 %

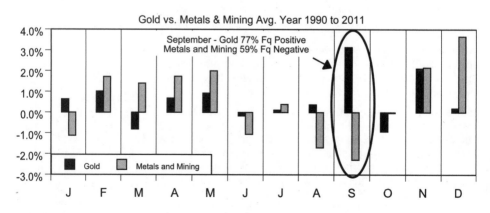

Gold vs. Metals & Mining Avg. Year 1990 to 2011

September - Gold 77% Fq Positive
Metals and Mining 59% Fq Negative

Gold   Metals and Mining

2011-12 Strategy Performance

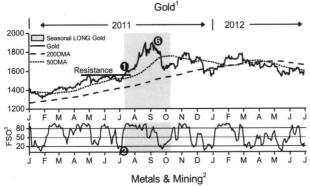

Gold[1]

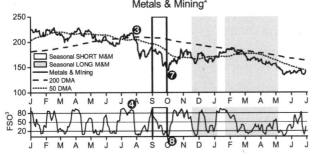

Metals & Mining[2]

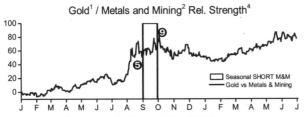

Gold[1] / Metals and Mining[2] Rel. Strength[4]

[1]Gold CME contract, [2]S&P GIC Sector, [3]Full Stochastic Oscillator %K(14,3),
[4]Relative Strength % Gain Gold* / Metals & Mining

Market Indices & Rates Weekly Values**

Stock Markets	2010	2011
Dow	10,755	11,088
S&P500	1,138	1,168
Nasdaq	2,350	2,536
TSX	12,172	11,872
FTSE	5,575	5,204
DAX	6,252	5,356
Nikkei	9,547	8,674
Hang Seng	22,037	18,468

Commodities	2010	2011
Oil	73.87	83.64
Gold	1287.1	1759.4

Bond Yields	2010	2011
USA 5 Yr Treasury	1.36	0.85
USA 10 Yr T	2.61	1.87
USA 20 Yr T	3.48	2.68
Moody's Aaa	4.55	3.98
Moody's Baa	5.66	5.18
CAN 5 Yr T	2.17	1.38
CAN 10 Yr T	2.88	2.12

Money Market	2010	2011
USA Fed Funds	0.25	0.25
USA 3 Mo T-B	0.16	0.01
CAN tgt overnight rate	1.00	1.00
CAN 3 Mo T-B	0.91	0.85

Foreign Exchange	2010	2011
USD/EUR	1.33	1.36
USD/GBP	1.57	1.55
CAN/USD	1.03	1.01
JPY/USD	84.77	76.47

SEPTEMBER

M	T	W	T	F	S	S
						1
2	3	4	5	6	7	8
9	10	11	12	13	14	15
16	17	18	19	20	21	22
23	24	25	26	27	28	29
30	31					

OCTOBER

M	T	W	T	F	S	S
1	2	3	4	5	6
7	8	9	10	11	12	13
14	15	16	17	18	19	20
21	22	23	24	25	26	27
28	29	30	31			

NOVEMBER

M	T	W	T	F	S	S
				1	2	3
4	5	6	7	8	9	10
11	12	13	14	15	16	17
18	19	20	21	22	23	24
25	26	27	28	29	30	

LONG Gold – SHORT Metals & Mining Performance

Gold had been consolidating from late April into the beginning of July. A partial early entry into a gold position was justified by the FSO turning up above 20❷ just before the start of its seasonal period. Gold then crossed above its 50 day moving average and resistance level❶.Technical conditions were lining up to short the metals and mining sector in July, when the sector turned below its 50 and 200 day moving averages❸ and the FSO crossed back below 80❹. At the beginning of September the pair trade was neutral❺. At the beginning of September, gold corrected sharply❻. The pair trade was successful because the metals and mining sector lost more than gold in September. Exiting from the short position in metals and mining at the end of September was very timely, as the sector started to perform well in October❼, supported by the FSO bouncing off 20❽, making this an ideal time "close" the pair trade❾.

CANADIAN BANKS — IN-OUT-IN AGAIN
①Oct 10-Dec 31   ②Jan 23-Apr 13

During the financial crisis of 2007/08, the Canadian banks were touted as being the best in the world. Canadians love to invest in their banks because the banks operate in a regulated environment and for long periods of time have grown their earnings and dividends. Although a lot of sectors in the Canadian market have very similar seasonally strong periods compared with the US, the seasonality for Canadian banks starts earlier than the US banks.

The difference in seasonally strong periods is driven by the difference in fiscal year-ends. The US banks have their year-end on December 31st and the Canadian banks on October 31st. Why does this make a difference? Typically, banks clean up their "books" at their year-end, by announcing any bad news. In addition, this is often the time period when the banks announce their positive news, including increases in dividends.

12% gain & and positive 78% of the time

The Canadian bank sector, from October 10th to December 31st for the years 1989 to 2011, has been positive 83% of the time and has produced an average gain of 5.5%. From January 23rd to April 13th, the sector has been positive 74% of the time and has produced an average gain of 6.2%. On a compounded basis, the strategy has been positive 78% of the time and produced an average gain of 12.0%.

Investors have a choice to either invest in each seasonal strategy separately and avoid the short time period between the strategies, or to hold the Canadian banking sector from October 10th to April 13th. Investors should consider that from January 1st to the 22nd, from 1990 to 2011, the sector has produced an average loss of 1.9% and has only been positive 43% of the time.

CDN Banks* vs. S&P/TSX Comp 1989/90 to 2011/12   Positive [ ]

Year	Oct 10 to Dec 31 TSX Comp	Oct 10 to Dec 31 CDN Banks	Jan 23 to Apr 13 TSX Comp	Jan 23 to Apr 13 CDN Banks	Compound Growth TSX Comp	Compound Growth CDN Banks
1989/90	-1.7%	-1.8%	-6.3%	-9.1%	-7.9%	-10.8%
1990/91	3.7	8.9	9.8	14.6	13.9	24.8
1991/92	5.2	10.2	-6.8	-11.6	-2.0	-2.6
1992/93	4.1	2.5	10.7	14.4	15.2	17.3
1993/94	6.3	6.8	-5.6	-13.3	0.3	-7.4
1994/95	-1.8	3.4	5.0	10.0	3.1	13.8
1995/96	4.9	3.5	3.6	-3.2	8.6	0.1
1996/97	9.0	15.1	-6.2	0.7	2.3	15.9
1997/98	-6.1	7.6	19.9	38.8	12.6	49.4
1998/99	18.3	28.0	4.8	13.0	24.0	44.6
1999/00	18.2	5.1	3.8	22.1	22.8	28.3
2000/01	-14.4	1.7	-14.1	-6.7	-26.4	-5.1
2001/02	11.9	6.5	2.3	8.2	14.5	15.1
2002/03	16.1	21.3	-4.3	2.6	11.1	24.4
2003/04	8.1	5.1	2.0	2.1	10.3	7.4
2004/05	4.9	6.2	4.5	6.9	9.6	13.5
2005/06	6.2	8.4	5.5	2.7	12.1	11.3
2006/07	10.4	8.4	6.9	3.2	18.0	11.8
2007/08	-3.0	-10.4	8.2	-3.5	5.0	-13.5
2008/09	-6.4	-14.8	9.4	24.4	2.4	6.1
2009/10	2.7	2.4	6.7	15.2	9.6	18.0
2010/11	7.2	-0.2	4.3	9.1	11.9	8.9
2011/12	3.2	3.1	-2.9	1.1	0.2	4.2
Avg.	4.7%	5.5%	2.7%	6.2%	7.4%	12.0%
Fq > 0	74%	83%	70%	74%	87%	78%

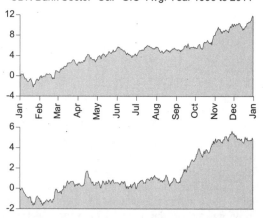

CDN Bank Sector* S&P GIC- Avg. Year 1990 to 2011

CDN Banks/S&P/TSX Rel. Strength - Avg Yr. 1990 - 2011

> **(Y) Alternate Strategy—**
> Investors can bridge the gap between the two positive seasonal trends for the bank sector by holding from October 10th to April 13th. Longer term investors may prefer this strategy, shorter term investors can use technical tools to determine the appropriate strategy.

> **(i)** * Banks SP GIC Canadian Sector Level 2
> An index designed to represent a cross section of banking companies. For more information on the bank sector, see www.standardandpoors.com.

2011-12 Strategy Performance

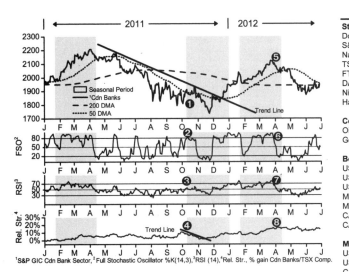

¹S&P GIC Cdn Bank Sector, ²Full Stochastic Oscillator %K(14,3),³RSI (14),⁴Rel. Str., % gain Cdn Banks/TSX Comp.

Market Indices & Rates
Weekly Values**

Stock Markets	2010	2011
Dow	10,825	11,063
S&P500	1,144	1,156
Nasdaq	2,373	2,490
TSX	12,317	11,685
FTSE	5,573	5,185
DAX	6,248	5,539
Nikkei	9,486	8,600
Hang Seng	22,297	17,785

Commodities	2010	2011
Oil	78.42	81.45
Gold	1304.4	1626.6

Bond Yields	2010	2011
USA 5 Yr Treasury	1.27	0.96
USA 10 Yr T	2.52	1.97
USA 20 Yr T	3.38	2.74
Moody's Aaa	4.52	4.06
Moody's Baa	5.58	5.31
CAN 5 Yr T	2.04	1.44
CAN 10 Yr T	2.77	2.18

Money Market	2010	2011
USA Fed Funds	0.25	0.25
USA 3 Mo T-B	0.16	0.02
CAN tgt overnight rate	1.00	1.00
CAN 3 Mo T-B	0.88	0.83

Foreign Exchange	2010	2011
USD/EUR	1.36	1.35
USD/GBP	1.58	1.56
CAN/USD	1.03	1.03
JPY/USD	83.72	76.73

Canadian Bank Sector Performance

The Canadian bank sector started to correct at the end of its seasonal period in April 2011. Later, at the beginning of October when it was to start its next seasonal period, the banking sector was showing a mildly positive technical setup, but the banking sector failed to outperform the TSX Composite for the next month. This was mainly the result of the cyclical sectors performing well at the same time that the bank sector was faltering. In mid-November, the Canadian banks started to pick up steam and outperform the TSX Composite. The exit date in April 2012 proved to be fairly timely as the banking sector and the broad market started to correct at the same time.

Technical Conditions– October 10th to April 13th, 2012
Entry Date October 10th, 2011 –Mildly Bullish– The Canadian banking sector had favorably just crossed its 50 day moving average, but it had not broken above its downward trend line❶. The FSO was at 80❷ and the RSI was a neutral 50❸. The sector had just recently turned down compared to the TSX❹.

Entry Strategy –Buy Partial Position Early– Although the sector was still trading below its 50 day moving average, the FSO crossed back over the 20 level in late September, justifying a partial early entry.

Exit Strategy – Sell Partial Position Early– In the second leg of the trade (January 23rd to April 13th), the Canadian banking sector was performing very well and outperforming the TSX Composite. The sector then turned down early in late March❺ and the FSO turned below 80❻ and the RSI dropped below 70❼, justifying a partial exit early. In addition the sector had recently moved from outperforming the TSX Composite to performing at market❽.

** Weekly avg closing values- except Fed Funds & CAN overnight tgt rate weekly closing values.

SEPTEMBER

M	T	W	T	F	S	S
						1
2	3	4	5	6	7	8
9	10	11	12	13	14	15
16	17	18	19	20	21	22
23	24	25	26	27	28	29
30	31					

OCTOBER

M	T	W	T	F	S	S
	1	2	3	4	5	6
7	8	9	10	11	12	13
14	15	16	17	18	19	20
21	22	23	24	25	26	27
28	29	30	31			

NOVEMBER

M	T	W	T	F	S	S
				1	2	3
4	5	6	7	8	9	10
11	12	13	14	15	16	17
18	19	20	21	22	23	24
25	26	27	28	29	30	

OCTOBER

	MONDAY	TUESDAY	WEDNESDAY
WEEK 40	30	**1** 30	**2** 29
WEEK 41	**7** 24	**8** 23	**9** 22

WEEK 42	**14** 17
	
	 USA Bond Market Closed-
	       Columbus Day
	
	 CAN Market Closed-
	       Thanksgiving Day
		15 16	**16** 15

WEEK 43	**21** 10	**22** 9	**23** 8
WEEK 44	**28** 3	**29** 2	**30** 1

THURSDAY	FRIDAY
3 28	**4** 27
10 21	**11** 20
17 14	**18** 13
24 7	**25** 6
31	1

NOVEMBER

M	T	W	T	F	S	S
				1	2	3
4	5	6	7	8	9	10
11	12	13	14	15	16	17
18	19	20	21	22	23	24
25	26	27	28	29	30	

DECEMBER

M	T	W	T	F	S	S
						1
2	3	4	5	6	7	8
9	10	11	12	13	14	15
16	17	18	19	20	21	22
23	24	25	26	27	28	29
30	31					

JANUARY

M	T	W	T	F	S	S
		1	2	3	4	5
6	7	8	9	10	11	12
13	14	15	16	17	18	19
20	21	22	23	24	25	26
27	28	29	30	31		

FEBRUARY

M	T	W	T	F	S	S
					1	2
3	4	5	6	7	8	9
10	11	12	13	14	15	16
17	18	19	20	21	22	23
24	25	26	27	28		

OCTOBER
S U M M A R Y

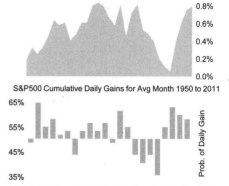

	Dow Jones	S&P 500	Nasdaq	TSX Comp
Month Rank	7	7	7	9
# Up	37	37	22	17
# Down	25	25	18	10
% Pos	60	60	55	63
% Avg. Gain	0.5	0.8	0.7	0.0

Dow & S&P 1950-2011, Nasdaq 1972-2011, TSX 1985-2011

S&P500 Cumulative Daily Gains for Avg Month 1950 to 2011

♦ October is very often a turnaround month. It is the most volatile month of the year and often provides opportunities for short-term traders. ♦ In 2011, the major correction in September setup the month of October for positive results. The S&P rallied strongly starting in the beginning of the month. ♦ Opportunities for October include: technology, Canadian banks, consumer discretionary, homebuilders, retail and industrials sectors. ♦ Investors have a lot of opportunities to choose from in October, and should stay attentive for the best entry dates.

BEST / WORST OCTOBER BROAD MKTS. 2002-2011

BEST OCTOBER MARKETS
♦ Russell 2000 (2011) 15.0%
♦ Nasdaq (2002) 13.5%
♦ Russell 3000 Value (2011) 11.5%

WORST OCTOBER MARKETS
♦ Russell 2000 (2008) -20.9%
♦ Russell 3000 Gr (2008) -18.0%
♦ Russell 3000 Value (2008) -17.8%

Index Values End of Month

	2002	2003	2004	2005	2006	2007	2008	2009	2010	2011
Dow	8,397	9,801	10,027	10,440	12,081	13,930	9,325	9,713	11,118	11,955
S&P 500	886	1,051	1,130	1,207	1,378	1,549	969	1,036	1,183	1,253
Nasdaq	1,330	1,932	1,975	2,120	2,367	2,859	1,721	2,045	2,507	2,684
TSX	6,249	7,773	8,871	10,383	12,345	14,625	9,763	10,911	12,676	12,252
Russell 1000	900	1,081	1,162	1,261	1,437	1,623	1,004	1,089	1,256	692
Russell 2000	928	1,313	1,451	1,607	1,906	2,058	1,336	1,399	1,748	741
Russell 3000 Growth	1,439	1,756	1,800	1,942	2,140	2,518	1,566	1,800	2,132	2,311
Russell 3000 Value	1,691	2,045	2,310	2,526	2,996	3,219	1,991	2,017	2,295	2,375

Percent Gain for October

	2002	2003	2004	2005	2006	2007	2008	2009	2010	2011
Dow	10.6	5.7	-0.5	-1.2	3.4	0.2	-14.1	0.0	3.1	9.5
S&P 500	8.6	5.5	1.4	-1.8	3.2	1.5	-16.9	-2.0	3.7	10.8
Nasdaq	13.5	8.1	4.1	-1.5	4.8	5.8	-17.7	-3.6	5.9	11.1
TSX	1.1	4.7	2.3	-5.7	5.0	3.7	-16.9	-4.2	2.5	5.4
Russell 1000	8.1	5.7	1.5	-1.9	3.3	1.6	-17.6	-2.3	3.8	11.1
Russell 2000	3.1	8.3	1.9	-3.2	5.7	2.8	-20.9	-6.9	4.0	15.0
Russell 3000 Growth	8.8	5.8	1.6	-1.3	3.7	3.4	-18.0	-1.9	4.7	11.3
Russell 3000 Value	6.7	6.1	1.5	-2.7	3.3	-0.1	-17.8	-3.5	2.9	11.5

October Market Avg. Performance 2002 to 2011[1]

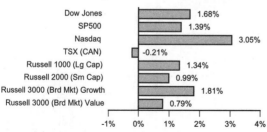

Dow Jones	1.68%
SP500	1.39%
Nasdaq	3.05%
TSX (CAN)	-0.21%
Russell 1000 (Lg Cap)	1.34%
Russell 2000 (Sm Cap)	0.99%
Russell 3000 (Brd Mkt) Growth	1.81%
Russell 3000 (Brd Mkt) Value	0.79%

Interest Corner Oct[2]

	Fed Funds % [3]	3 Mo. T-Bill % [4]	10 Yr % [5]	20 Yr % [6]
2011	0.25	0.01	2.17	2.89
2010	0.25	0.12	2.63	3.64
2009	0.25	0.05	3.41	4.19
2008	1.00	0.46	4.01	4.74
2007	4.50	3.94	4.48	4.79

(1) Russell Data provided by Russell (2) Federal Reserve Bank of St. Louis- end of month values (3) Target rate set by FOMC (4)(5)(6) Constant yield maturities.

THACKRAY SECTOR THERMOMETER

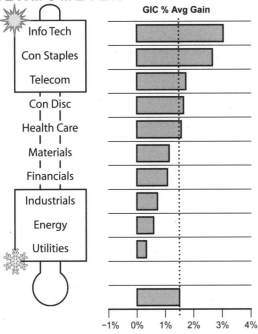

GIC[2] % Avg Gain	Fq % Gain >S&P 500	SP GIC SECTOR 1990-2011[1]
3.0 %	55 %	Information Technology
2.7	55	Consumer Staples
1.7	41	Telecom
1.7	50	Consumer Discretionary
1.6	45	Health Care
1.1	50	Materials
1.1	41	Financials
0.7	32	Industrials
0.6	45	Energy
0.3 %	36 %	Utilities
1.5 %	N/A %	S&P 500

Sector Commentary

♦ In October 2011, with the S&P 500 producing a gain of 10.7%, all of the defensive sectors were at the bottom of the performance list. ♦ When very large gains are made in a month, it would be expected that the defensives would underperform. ♦ October is typically one of the most volatile months of the year, but nevertheless it still, on average, has produced a positive return since 1950. ♦ Usually the performance of the defensives and the cyclicals is mixed in October, but in a really strong month, expect a reshuffle.

Sub-Sector Commentary

♦ Homebuilders, producing a gain of 24.5% in October 2011 was the top sub-sector from the selected list. Usually, the homebuilders sector is much further down the list, but its position on a monthly basis is deceiving. Homebuilders are a top performer in the second half of the month. When the market rallies early in October, homebuilders can perform well relative to the other sectors. ♦ The three bottom sectors were biotech, gold and pharmaceuticals all producing losses for the month. ♦ Investors should note that biotech finishes its seasonal period in mid-September, gold at the beginning of October and pharmaceuticals underperforms in the second half of October.

		SELECTED SUB-SECTORS 1990-2011[3]
6.3 %	74 %	Agriculture (94-2011)
4.7	68	Software & Services
4.6	73	Railroads
4.0	73	Transportation
2.2	55	Pharmaceuticals
2.1	36	Steel
2.0	67	Chemicals
1.8	50	Biotech (93-2011)
1.7	50	Retail
0.9	41	Banks
0.4	36	Homebuilders
0.0	36	Metals and Mining
-0.9	27	Gold (London PM)
-1.3	36	Silver (London)

(1) Sector data provided by Standard and Poors (2) GIC is short form for Global Industry Classification (3) Sub Sector data provided by Standard and Poors, except

UNION PACIFIC – JUMP ON BOARD
①Oct10-Nov4 ②Mar11-May5

Union Pacific follows the general seasonal pattern of the transportation sector: a strong spring, weak summer and a strong autumn.

The success of this trade can be seen in the frequency of how often the compound gains of Union Pacific, across both of its seasonal periods, outperforms the S&P 500. The seasonal period from October 10th to November 4th, for the years 1989 to 2011, has the same positive success rate of 78%, as the S&P 500, but it has produced more than double the average gain (6.6% vs. 2.9%). The period from March 11th to May 5th, for the years 1990 to 2012, also has the same positive success rate of 74%, as the S&P 500, but with almost triple the average gain (9.1% vs. 3.4%).

16.5% gain

Both of these seasonal trades are strong trades by themselves, as the average gain for Union Pacific is more than double the S&P 500 for each trade.

In addition, Union Pacific's frequency of positive performance over both seasonal periods is a very strong 96%, which is better than the S&P 500's success rate of 83%. It should also be noted that the only losing compound trade took place twenty-three years ago. Not only has this trade produced large returns, with a high frequency, but the drawdowns have also been small.

Investors should note that Union Pacific typically has a weak summer period and if it is held past the end of its seasonal period in May, a sell criteria should be established for when the stock starts to weaken.

(i) *UNP - stock symbol for Union Pacific which trades on the NYSE exchange.*

Union Pacific vs. S&P 500 1989/90 to 2011/12   Positive ▢

Year	Oct10 to Nov4 S&P 500	UNP	Mar11 to May5 S&P 500	UNP	Compound Growth S&P 500	UNP
1989/90	-6.2	-7.0 %	0.1	-5.1 %	-6.0	-11.8 %
1990/91	2.2	-3.4	1.6	9.3	3.8	5.6
1991/92	3.6	7.9	2.5	14.0	6.1	23.1
1992/93	3.6	9.6	-2.6	6.3	0.9	16.5
1993/94	-0.6	2.1	-2.7	-0.4	-3.3	1.6
1994/95	1.6	0.5	6.2	7.6	7.9	8.1
1995/96	2.1	4.0	1.3	1.1	3.4	5.1
1996/97	1.4	13.3	2.1	5.9	3.5	19.9
1997/98	-3.1	-3.8	4.8	9.1	1.6	4.9
1998/99	13.6	10.8	4.7	26.6	19.0	40.3
1999/00	2.0	6.8	2.7	20.7	4.7	28.9
2000/01	1.8	19.7	2.7	-1.6	4.5	17.8
2001/02	2.9	16.5	-7.8	-4.4	-5.2	11.3
2002/03	16.9	9.9	14.8	13.9	34.2	25.2
2003/04	1.4	8.6	-0.2	-4.5	1.2	3.7
2004/05	3.5	5.8	-3.0	-2.5	0.4	3.2
2005/06	2.0	-0.9	3.5	8.7	5.6	7.7
2006/07	1.0	1.0	7.3	18.1	8.4	19.3
2007/08	-3.6	6.7	10.5	23.6	6.6	31.9
2008/09	10.5	22.1	25.6	45.5	38.8	77.6
2009/10	-2.3	-1.1	1.8	3.8	-0.6	2.6
2010/11	4.8	8.1	3.1	8.1	8.0	16.9
2011/12	8.5	14.0	-0.1	5.5	8.3	20.3
Avg.	2.9 %	6.6 %	3.4 %	9.1 %	6.6 %	16.5 %
Fq>0	78 %	78 %	74 %	74 %	83 %	96 %

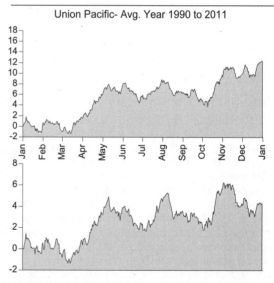

Union Pacific- Avg. Year 1990 to 2011

Union Pacific / S&P 500 Rel. Strength- Avg Yr. 1990-2011

2011-12 Strategy Performance

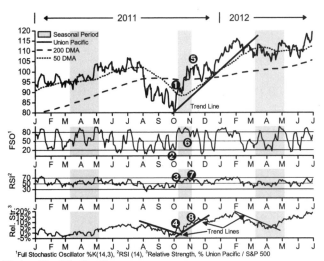

¹Full Stochastic Oscillator %K(14,3), ²RSI (14), ³Relative Strength, % Union Pacific / S&P 500

Union Pacific Performance

After bottoming below $35 in 2009, Union Pacific (UNP) performed extremely well and has traded above $120 in 2012. In 2009 and 2010, UNP appreciated in price regardless of season. More recently, the stock has settled back into its seasonal rhythm. In the last three seasonal cycles in 2011 and 2012, UNP has produced gains and outperformed the S&P 500. In the time between UNP's seasonal periods in 2011 and 2012, UNP either underperformed the market, or produced a loss.

Technical Conditions– October 10th to November 4th, 2011
Entry Date October 10th, 2011 –Bullish– Approaching the entry date, UNP had developed a bearish pattern of lower highs and lower lows and was trading below it 50 day moving average. A few days before the beginning of UNP's seasonal period, the situation changed– UNP "shot up," broke its negative price pattern and crossed above its 50 day moving average❶. Although the FSO gave an early entry signal in September❷, generally it is prudent to be cautious entering the market in the highest risk month of the year. The RSI crossed above 50 a few days before the start of the trade, creating a positive backdrop for an entry into the position❸. The "big buy signal" came just before the start of the seasonal period when UNP started to outperform the S&P 500❹.

Entry Strategy –Buy Position on Entry Date– Although the price action of UNP leading into the trade was negative, the few days before the trade created a bullish situation.

Exit Strategy– Sell Partial Position Early– Although UNP's price action was still bullish towards the end of the trade❺, both the FSO and the RSI, turned down from their upper levels before the trade had finished, justifying an early exit❻❼. A full exit was justified in mid-November when UNP started to underperform the S&P 500❽.

Market Indices & Rates
Weekly Values**

Stock Markets	2010	2011
Dow	10,924	10,926
S&P500	1,156	1,138
Nasdaq	2,382	2,437
TSX	12,461	11,451
FTSE	5,639	5,143
DAX	6,238	5,477
Nikkei	9,573	8,502
Hang Seng	22,793	16,988

Commodities	2010	2011
Oil	82.37	79.71
Gold	1335.4	1639.5

Bond Yields	2010	2011
USA 5 Yr Treasury	1.17	0.96
USA 10 Yr T	2.45	1.93
USA 20 Yr T	3.38	2.63
Moody's Aaa	4.56	3.91
Moody's Baa	5.59	5.26
CAN 5 Yr T	1.96	1.40
CAN 10 Yr T	2.74	2.15

Money Market	2010	2011
USA Fed Funds	0.25	0.25
USA 3 Mo T-B	0.13	0.01
CAN tgt overnight rate	1.00	1.00
CAN 3 Mo T-B	0.87	0.82

Foreign Exchange	2010	2011
USD/EUR	1.39	1.33
USD/GBP	1.59	1.55
CAN/USD	1.02	1.04
JPY/USD	82.77	76.74

OCTOBER
M	T	W	T	F	S	S
	1	2	3	4	5	6
7	8	9	10	11	12	13
14	15	16	17	18	19	20
21	22	23	24	25	26	27
28	29	30	31			

NOVEMBER
M	T	W	T	F	S	S
				1	2	3
4	5	6	7	8	9	10
11	12	13	14	15	16	17
18	19	20	21	22	23	24
25	26	27	28	29	30	

DECEMBER
M	T	W	T	F	S	S
						1
2	3	4	5	6	7	8
9	10	11	12	13	14	15
16	17	18	19	20	21	22
23	24	25	26	27	28	29
30	31					

INFORMATION TECHNOLOGY
USE IT OR LOSE IT
October 9th to January 17th

Information technology– the sector that investors love to love and love to hate. In recent years, most investors have made and lost money in this sector. When the sector is performing well, it can perform really well. When it is performing poorly, it can perform really poorly.

5.2% extra compared with the S&P 500

Technology stocks get bid up at the end of the year for three reasons.

First, a lot of companies operate with year end budgets and if they do not spend the money in their budget, they lose it.

In the last few months of the year, whatever money they have, they spend. Hence, the saying "use it or lose it."

The number one purchase item for this budget flush is technology equipment. An upgrade in technology equipment is something which a large number of employees in the company can benefit from and is easy to justify.

Second, consumers indirectly help push up technology stocks by purchasing electronic items during the holiday season.

Retail sales ramp up significantly on Black Friday, the Friday after Thanksgiving. Investors anticipate the upswing in sales and buy technology stocks.

Third, the "Conference Effect" helps maintain the momentum in January. This phenomenon is the result of investors increasing positions ahead of major conferences in order to benefit from positive announcements.

In the case of Information Technology, investors increase their holdings ahead of the Las Vegas Consumer Electronics Conference that typically occurs in the second week of January.

Info Tech & Nasdaq vs S&P 500
Oct 9 to Jan 17, 1989/90-2011/12

	S&P 500	Info Tech	Nas daq	Diff IT to S&P	Diff Nas to S&P
				Positive	
1989/90	-6.0 %	-6.9 %	-9.3 %	-1.0 %	-3.3 %
1990/91	4.6	13.4	8.0	8.8	3.3
1991/92	10.0	16.4	21.2	6.4	11.2
1992/93	7.2	11.2	21.5	4.0	14.3
1993/94	2.8	12.5	3.7	9.7	0.8
1994/95	3.3	16.0	3.0	12.7	-0.3
1995/96	4.1	-8.9	-1.4	-13.0	-5.5
1996/97	10.8	21.2	8.8	10.4	-2.0
1997/98	-1.3	-14.2	-10.3	-12.9	-9.0
1998/99	29.6	71.8	65.5	42.2	35.9
1999/00	9.7	29.2	40.8	19.5	31.1
2001/01	-5.6	-21.7	-20.2	-16.1	-14.5
2001/02	7.2	26.8	23.7	19.6	16.5
2002/03	12.9	30.0	21.9	17.0	8.9
2003/04	10.3	14.2	13.0	4.0	2.8
2004/05	5.6	6.8	8.7	1.2	3.2
2005/06	7.3	9.7	10.2	2.4	2.9
2006/07	6.0	7.1	7.8	1.1	1.8
2007/08	-14.1	-14.9	-15.8	-0.7	-1.7
2008/09	-13.7	-12.0	-12.1	1.6	1.6
2009/10	6.6	9.9	7.7	3.3	1.1
2010/11	11.0	13.6	14.7	2.6	3.7
2011/12	12.0	8.4	10.3	-3.6	-1.6
Avg	5.2 %	10.4 %	9.6 %	5.2 %	4.4 %
Fq > 0	78 %	74 %	74 %	74 %	65 %

InfoTech Sector % Gain Avg. Year 1990 to 2011

Info Tech / S&P 500 - Avg Yr. 1990 - 2011

> (i) *Information Technology SP GIC Sector 45: An index designed to represent a cross section of information technology companies.*
>
> *For more information on the information technology sector, see www.standardandpoors.com.*

2011-12 Strategy Performance

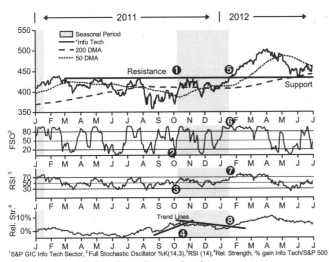

¹S&P GIC Info Tech Sector, ²Full Stochastic Oscillator %K(14,3),³RSI (14),⁴Rel. Strength, % gain Info Tech/S&P 500

Information Technology Sector Performance

The information technology sector lagged behind the S&P 500 for the first half of 2011 and only started to outperform in July. At the beginning of October the technology sector was outperforming, and was technically setup to perform well. Unfortunately, even though it produced a positive return, it put in a disappointing performance relative to the S&P 500. It was only after the end of the seasonal period that the technology sector managed to outperform the S&P 500.

Technical Conditions
Entry Date October 9th, 2011 –<u>Bullish</u>– Just prior to the entry date, the technology sector crossed above its 50 day moving average and then shortly after crossed its 200 day moving average. It was poised just below its resistance level, which is typically a good start to a seasonal trade❶. The FSO had already turned up and was still below 80❷ and the RSI had risen above 50❸. Initially, it looked like the information technology sector was continuing to outperform the S&P 500, but that changed shortly after the entry date❹.

Entry Strategy –<u>Buy Partial Position Early</u>– A few days before the official entry date, the information technology sector shot upwards and produced a short-term buy signal as the FSO crossed above 20.

Exit Strategy –<u>Sell Partial Position on Exit Date and Remainder Later</u>– The information technology sector was showing a lot of strength, rising into its exit date, as it had just traded through its 50 and 200 day moving averages, and was pushing right up against resistance on the exit date❺. The FSO was in an overbought state, but had not crossed back below 80❻ and the RSI was still moving higher❼. Most importantly, the sector was just starting to show signs of outperforming the S&P 500, justifying holding a partial position past the exit date❽.

Market Indices & Rates
Weekly Values**

Stock Markets	2010	2011
Dow	11,057	11,498
S&P500	1,173	1,205
Nasdaq	2,433	2,608
TSX	12,619	11,975
FTSE	5,702	5,421
DAX	6,399	5,918
Nikkei	9,469	8,771
Hang Seng	23,479	18,288

Commodities	2010	2011
Oil	82.17	85.56
Gold	1361.3	1668.0

Bond Yields	2010	2011
USA 5 Yr Treasury	1.16	1.14
USA 10 Yr T	2.50	2.22
USA 20 Yr T	3.52	2.92
Moody's Aaa	4.71	4.10
Moody's Baa	5.74	5.52
CAN 5 Yr T	1.93	1.55
CAN 10 Yr T	2.74	2.32

Money Market	2010	2011
USA Fed Funds	0.25	0.25
USA 3 Mo T-B	0.14	0.02
CAN tgt overnight rate	1.00	1.00
CAN 3 Mo T-B	0.89	0.87

Foreign Exchange	2010	2011
USD/EUR	1.40	1.37
USD/GBP	1.59	1.57
CAN/USD	1.01	1.02
JPY/USD	81.71	76.94

OCTOBER
M	T	W	T	F	S	S
	1	2	3	4	5	6
7	8	9	10	11	12	13
14	15	16	17	18	19	20
21	22	23	24	25	26	27
28	29	30	31			

NOVEMBER
M	T	W	T	F	S	S
				1	2	3
4	5	6	7	8	9	10
11	12	13	14	15	16	17
18	19	20	21	22	23	24
25	26	27	28	29	30	

DECEMBER
M	T	W	T	F	S	S
						1
2	3	4	5	6	7	8
9	10	11	12	13	14	15
16	17	18	19	20	21	22
23	24	25	26	27	28	29
30	31					

CONSUMER SWITCH
SELL CONSUMER STAPLES
BUY CONSUMER DISCRETIONARY
Con. Discretionary Outperforms From Oct 28 to Apr 22

This is the time to sell the sector of "need" and buy the sector of "want."

Companies that are classified as consumer staples sell products to the consumer that they need for their everyday life.

Consumers will generally still buy products from a consumer staples company, such as a drugstore, even if the economy and the stock market turns down.

On the other hand, consumer discretionary companies sell products that consumers do not necessarily need, such as furniture.

Why is this important? Consumer discretionary companies tend to outperform in the six favorable months of the market.

The discretionary sector benefits from the positive market forces and positive market forecasts that tend to take place in this period.

The consumer staples and discretionary sectors average year graphs illustrate the individual trends of the sectors.

The discretionary sector tends to outperform strongly from the end of October to April. Although the staples sector in the summer months has a slightly average negative performance, it still outperforms the discretionary sector.

At the end of the year, both sectors do well, but investing in the right sector at the right time can make a substantial difference in an investor's profits.

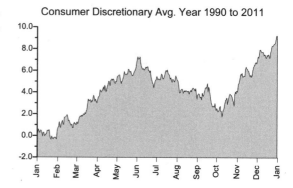

Consumer Discretionary Avg. Year 1990 to 2011

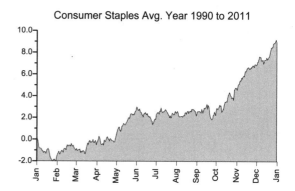

Consumer Staples Avg. Year 1990 to 2011

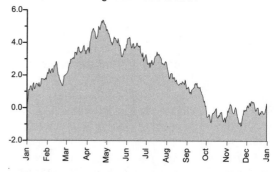

Con. Discretionary / Staples - Relative Strength Avg. Year 1990 to 2011

Alternate Strategy — The consumer discretionary stocks have dramatically outperformed the consumer staples stocks from December 27th to April 22nd. With both the discretionary and staples sectors performing well in November and December, depending on market conditions, investors can delay some or all of their allocation to the discretionary sector until the end of December.

2010-11-12 Consumer Disc. Performance

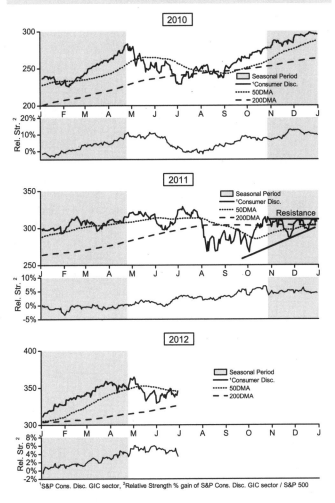

¹S&P Cons. Disc. GIC sector, ²Relative Strength % gain of S&P Cons. Disc. GIC sector / S&P 500

Market Indices & Rates Weekly Values**

Stock Markets	2010	2011
Dow	11,102	11,566
S&P500	1,178	1,218
Nasdaq	2,463	2,622
TSX	12,618	11,921
FTSE	5,735	5,434
DAX	6,550	5,878
Nikkei	9,445	8,751
Hang Seng	23,591	18,254

Commodities	2010	2011
Oil	81.11	86.67
Gold	1342.3	1645.6

Bond Yields	2010	2011
USA 5 Yr Treasury	1.14	1.07
USA 10 Yr T	2.54	2.20
USA 20 Yr T	3.56	2.92
Moody's Aaa	4.71	3.98
Moody's Baa	5.76	5.41
CAN 5 Yr T	1.91	1.56
CAN 10 Yr T	2.74	2.32

Money Market	2010	2011
USA Fed Funds	0.25	0.25
USA 3 Mo T-B	0.14	0.03
CAN tgt overnight rate	1.00	1.00
CAN 3 Mo T-B	0.89	0.87

Foreign Exchange	2010	2011
USD/EUR	1.39	1.38
USD/GBP	1.58	1.58
CAN/USD	1.02	1.02
JPY/USD	81.33	76.71

OCTOBER

M	T	W	T	F	S	S
	1	2	3	4	5	6
7	8	9	10	11	12	13
14	15	16	17	18	19	20
21	22	23	24	25	26	27
28	29	30	31			

NOVEMBER

M	T	W	T	F	S	S
				1	2	3
4	5	6	7	8	9	10
11	12	13	14	15	16	17
18	19	20	21	22	23	24
25	26	27	28	29	30	

DECEMBER

M	T	W	T	F	S	S
						1
2	3	4	5	6	7	8
9	10	11	12	13	14	15
16	17	18	19	20	21	22
23	24	25	26	27	28	29
30	31					

Consumer Discretionary Sector Performance– 2011 to 2012

In the first half of the 2011-12 seasonal trade, the consumer discretionary sector was consolidating in a bullish ascending triangle pattern. The pay-off came in the 2012 when the consumer discretionary sector broke resistance and performed strongly against the S&P 500. On the exit date, the trade was showing signs of tiring as the consumer discretionary sector came down to the 50 day moving average. The ideal exit point was a few weeks later in May.

** Weekly avg closing values- except Fed Funds & CAN overnight tgt rate weekly closing values.

The *Retail – Shop Early* strategy is the second retail sector strategy of the year and it occurs before the biggest shopping season of the year – the Christmas holiday season.

2.9% extra & 77% of the time better than S&P 500

The time to go shopping for retail stocks is at the end of October, which is about one month before Thanksgiving. It is the time when two favorable influences happen at the same time.

Retail Sector - Avg. Year 1990 to 2011

Retail / S&P 500 Relative Strength - Avg Yr. 1990 - 2011

First, historically the three best months in a row for the stock market have been November, December and January. The end of October usually represents an excellent buying opportunity, not only for the next three months, but the next six months.

Second, investors tend to buy retail stocks in anticipation of a strong holiday sales season. At the same time that the market tends to increase, investors are attracted back into the retail sector.

Retail sales tend to be lower in the summer and a lot of investors view investing in retail stocks at this time as dead money. During the summertime, investors prefer not to invest in this sector until it comes back into favor towards the end of October.

The trick to investing is not to be too early, but early. If an investor gets into a sector too early, they can suffer from the frustration of having dead money– having an investment that goes nowhere, while the rest of the market increases.

If an investor moves into a sector too late, there is very little upside potential. In fact, this can be a dangerous strategy because if the sales or earnings numbers disappoint the analysts, the sector can severely correct.

For the *Retail – Shop Early* strategy the time to enter is approximately one month before Black Friday.

Coincidentally, the end of October is also typically a good time to enter the broad market.

Oct 28 to Nov 29	Positive		
	S&P 500	Retail	Diff
1990	3.8 %	9.9 %	6.0 %
1991	-2.3	2.7	5.0
1992	2.8	5.5	2.8
1993	-0.6	6.3	6.9
1994	-2.3	0.4	2.7
1995	4.8	9.5	4.7
1996	8.0	0.4	-7.6
1997	8.9	16.9	7.9
1998	11.9	20.4	8.4
1999	8.6	14.1	5.5
2000	-2.7	9.9	12.6
2001	3.2	7.9	4.7
2002	4.3	-1.7	-6.0
2003	2.6	2.5	-0.1
2004	4.7	7.0	2.3
2005	6.7	9.9	3.2
2006	1.6	0.2	-1.4
2007	-4.3	-7.5	-3.2
2008	5.6	7.5	1.9
2009	2.6	3.6	1.0
2010	0.5	5.2	4.7
2011	-7.0	-4.5	2.5
Avg.	2.8 %	5.7 %	2.9 %
Fq > 0	73 %	86 %	77 %

Retail Sector vs. S&P 500 1990 to 2011

2010-11-12 Strategy Performance

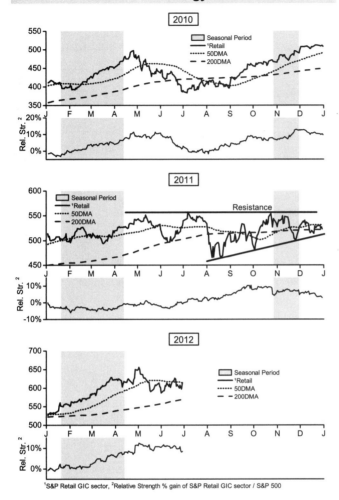

¹S&P Retail GIC sector, ²Relative Strength % gain of S&P Retail GIC sector / S&P 500

Market Indices & Rates
Weekly Values**

Stock Markets	2010	2011
Dow	11,138	11,986
S&P500	1,184	1,259
Nasdaq	2,501	2,693
TSX	12,631	12,289
FTSE	5,692	5,609
DAX	6,604	6,160
Nikkei	9,347	8,866
Hang Seng	23,340	19,303

Commodities	2010	2011
Oil	82.01	92.33
Gold	1334.4	1696.4

Bond Yields	2010	2011
USA 5 Yr Treasury	1.24	1.11
USA 10 Yr T	2.67	2.28
USA 20 Yr T	3.66	3.02
Moody's Aaa	4.77	3.97
Moody's Baa	5.80	5.36
CAN 5 Yr T	1.99	1.62
CAN 10 Yr T	2.83	2.38

Money Market	2010	2011
USA Fed Funds	0.25	0.25
USA 3 Mo T-B	0.13	0.02
CAN tgt overnight rate	1.00	1.00
CAN 3 Mo T-B	0.91	0.89

Foreign Exchange	2010	2011
USD/EUR	1.39	1.40
USD/GBP	1.59	1.60
CAN/USD	1.02	1.00
JPY/USD	81.08	76.03

OCTOBER

M	T	W	T	F	S	S
	1	2	3	4	5	6
7	8	9	10	11	12	13
14	15	16	17	18	19	20
21	22	23	24	25	26	27
28	29	30	31			

NOVEMBER

M	T	W	T	F	S	S
				1	2	3
4	5	6	7	8	9	10
11	12	13	14	15	16	17
18	19	20	21	22	23	24
25	26	27	28	29	30	

DECEMBER

M	T	W	T	F	S	S
						1
2	3	4	5	6	7	8
9	10	11	12	13	14	15
16	17	18	19	20	21	22
23	24	25	26	27	28	29
30	31					

Retail Sector Performance– October to November 2011

The retail sector in the autumn leg of its seasonal performance in 2011 was fairly well setup, as it was trading above its 50 and 200 day moving averages and pushing up against resistance. The broad stock market corrected at the end of October and brought the retail sector down with it. The retail sector was able to keep a pattern of rising lows and then in the new year, during its second leg, outperform the S&P 500 and produce strong results.

The retail sector continued to outperform the S&P 500 past its exit date and into the beginning of May when it peaked and then started to underperform.

** Weekly avg closing values- except Fed Funds & CAN overnight tgt rate weekly closing values.

HOMEBUILDERS
Oct 19th to February 3rd

The homebuilders sector has been in the spotlight for the last few years: first when the mortgage meltdown occurred in 2007 and 2008, and more recently as the housing market has bounced back giving the homebuilders sector a boost in 2012.

20% & positive 86% of the time

Historically, the best time to be in the homebuilders sector has been from October 19th to February 3rd. In this time period, during the years 1990/91 to 2011/12, the homebuilders sector has produced an average gain of 20% and have been positive 86% of the time. In the three years where losses occurred, the drawdowns were relatively small, at least compared to the large gains that the homebuilders sector has produced during its strong seasonal time period.

Home builders vs. S&P 500
1990-91 to 2011-12

Oct 19 to Feb 3	S&P 500	Home Builders	Diff (Positive)
1990-91	12.2%	54.0%	41.8%
1991-92	4.3	35.0	30.7
1992-93	8.6	31.2	22.5
1993-94	2.6	8.9	6.3
1994-95	2.4	-7.8	-10.2
1995-96	8.2	16.0	7.8
1996-97	10.7	5.5	-5.2
1997-98	6.6	19.5	12.9
1998-99	20.4	23.5	3.1
1999-00	13.6	-9.9	-23.5
2000-01	0.6	28.9	28.4
2001-02	5.0	54.3	49.2
2002-03	-2.7	7.8	10.5
2003-04	9.3	16.6	7.3
2004-05	6.8	35.9	29.1
2005-06	7.3	13.4	6.1
2006-07	6.1	19.2	13.1
2007-08	-9.4	17.5	26.9
2008-09	-10.9	-0.5	10.3
2009-10	0.9	7.9	7.0
2010-11	10.3	10.8	0.5
2011-12	9.8	51.6	41.9
Avg	5.6%	20.0%	14.4%
Fq > 0	86%	86%	86%

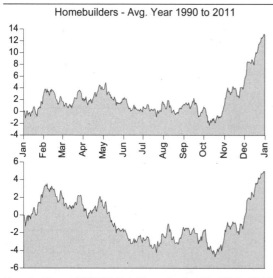

Homebuilders - Avg. Year 1990 to 2011

Homebuilders / S&P 500 Rel. Strength - Avg Yr. 1990 - 2011

This compares to the performance of the homebuilders during its favorable period, over the same number of years, where it has only had one major loss of 9.9% in 1999-2000.

The homebuilders sector by nature is very volatile and as a result, there will be large gains that will occasionally be made in the unfavorable season. However, from a risk-reward basis seasonal investors should favor the time period from October 19th to February 3rd.

Generally the rest of the year, other than the strong seasonal period, is a time that seasonal investors should avoid, as not only has the average performance relative to the S&P 500 been negative, but the homebuilders sector has produced both large gains and losses. In other words, the risk is substantially higher that a large drawdown will occur. For example, from 1990 to 2012, during the period of May 6th to October 18th, the homebuilders sector has lost 10% or more, ten times.

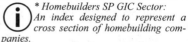

Homebuilders SP GIC Sector:
An index designed to represent a cross section of homebuilding companies.
For more information on the homebuilding sector, see www.standardandpoors.com.

2011-12 Strategy Performance

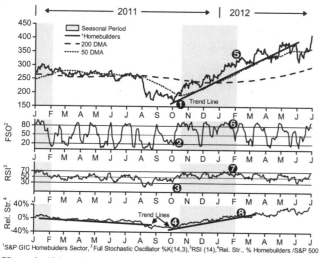

¹S&P GIC Homebuilders Sector, ²Full Stochastic Oscillator %K(14,3),³RSI (14),⁴Rel. Str., % Homebuilders /S&P 500

Homebuilders Sector Performance

The homebuilders sector consolidated for the first half of 2011 as it steadily underperformed a rising S&P 500. In late July, it dropped below its 50 day moving average and declined until the beginning of October. At this time, the S&P 500 started to perform strongly and the homebuilders sector also responded with very strong gains.

Technical Conditions– October 19th to February 3rd, 2012
Entry Date October 19th, 2011 –<u>Bullish</u>–The homebuilders sector bottomed in early October and then proceeded to break above its 50 day moving average, and a bit later its 200 day moving average. ❶   The FSO turned up above 20 in early October❷, confirming the rising RSI❸. The homebuilders sector was performing at market from late August to the mid-October, at which time it started to show signs of outperformance❹.

Entry Strategy –<u>Buy Partial Position Early</u>– The homebuilders sector turned up at the beginning of October and both the FSO and the RSI triggered early entry signals. At the time, the outperformance relative to the S&P 500 had not been strongly established and as a result, only an early partial allocation was justified.

Exit Strategy – <u>Sell Partial Position Early & Remainder Late</u> – The FSO turned down below 80❻ towards the end of January, following a weakening RSI❼. The action of both indicators justified a partial early exit at this time.   The homebuilders sector was still trading above the upward sloping trend line and was still outperforming the S&P 500❺. The exit point for the remainder of the allocation occurred in mid-February as the sector started to underperform the S&P 500❽.

** Weekly avg closing values- except Fed Funds & CAN overnight tgt rate weekly closing values.

WEEK 44

Market Indices & Rates
Weekly Values**

Stock Markets	2010	2011
Dow	11,281	11,895
S&P500	1,205	1,245
Nasdaq	2,547	2,663
TSX	12,764	12,297
FTSE	5,788	5,505
DAX	6,673	6,008
Nikkei	9,325	8,816
Hang Seng	24,176	19,611

Commodities	2010	2011
Oil	84.98	93.24
Gold	1365.5	1734.2

Bond Yields	2010	2011
USA 5 Yr Treasury	1.11	0.91
USA 10 Yr T	2.61	2.07
USA 20 Yr T	3.65	2.80
Moody's Aaa	4.75	3.84
Moody's Baa	5.79	5.11
CAN 5 Yr T	2.02	1.45
CAN 10 Yr T	2.85	2.20

Money Market	2010	2011
USA Fed Funds	0.25	0.25
USA 3 Mo T-B	0.13	0.01
CAN tgt overnight rate	1.00	1.00
CAN 3 Mo T-B	0.92	0.89

Foreign Exchange	2010	2011
USD/EUR	1.41	1.38
USD/GBP	1.61	1.60
CAN/USD	1.01	1.01
JPY/USD	80.84	78.18

OCTOBER

M	T	W	T	F	S	S
	1	2	3	4	5	6
7	8	9	10	11	12	13
14	15	16	17	18	19	20
21	22	23	24	25	26	27
28	29	30	31			

NOVEMBER

M	T	W	T	F	S	S
				1	2	3
4	5	6	7	8	9	10
11	12	13	14	15	16	17
18	19	20	21	22	23	24
25	26	27	28	29	30	

DECEMBER

M	T	W	T	F	S	S
						1
2	3	4	5	6	7	8
9	10	11	12	13	14	15
16	17	18	19	20	21	22
23	24	25	26	27	28	29
30	31					

NOVEMBER

	MONDAY	TUESDAY	WEDNESDAY
WEEK 44	28	29	30
WEEK 45	**4** 26	**5** 25	**6** 24
WEEK 46	**11** 19	**12** 18	**13** 17
WEEK 47	**18** 12	**19** 11	**20** 10
WEEK 48	**25** 5	**26** 4	**27** 3

THURSDAY	FRIDAY
31	**1** 29
7 23	**8** 22
14 16	**15** 15
21 9	**22** 8
28 2 USA Market Closed- Thanksgiving Day	**29** 1 USA Early Market Close Thanksgiving

DECEMBER

M	T	W	T	F	S	S
						1
2	3	4	5	6	7	8
9	10	11	12	13	14	15
16	17	18	19	20	21	22
23	24	25	26	27	28	29
30	31					

JANUARY

M	T	W	T	F	S	S
		1	2	3	4	5
6	7	8	9	10	11	12
13	14	15	16	17	18	19
20	21	22	23	24	25	26
27	28	29	30	31		

FEBRUARY

M	T	W	T	F	S	S
					1	2
3	4	5	6	7	8	9
10	11	12	13	14	15	16
17	18	19	20	21	22	23
24	25	26	27	28		

MARCH

M	T	W	T	F	S	S
					1	2
3	4	5	6	7	8	9
10	11	12	13	14	15	16
17	18	19	20	21	22	23
24	25	26	27	28	29	30

NOVEMBER SUMMARY

S&P500 Cumulative Daily Gains for Avg Month 1950 to 2011

	Dow Jones	S&P 500	Nasdaq	TSX Comp
Month Rank	3	3	3	8
# Up	41	40	26	16
# Down	21	22	14	11
% Pos	66	65	65	59
% Avg. Gain	1.5	1.5	1.6	0.7

Dow & S&P 1950-2011, Nasdaq 1972-2011, TSX 1985-2011

♦ The stock market in November typically performs well, but in 2011, the S&P 500 lost a modest 0.5%. ♦ The small loss does not convey the angst that investors suffered as the S&P 500 plummeted for most of November, only to skyrocket upwards at the end of the month. ♦ November is the time when the cyclical sectors usually start getting underway with their seasonal performances. ♦ In November 2011, extreme volatility caused investor concern and as a result, the best performing sector was consumer staples, with a gain of 2.4%.

BEST / WORST NOVEMBER BROAD MKTS. 2002-2011

BEST NOVEMBER MARKETS
- ♦ Nasdaq (2002) 11.2%
- ♦ Russell 2000 (2002) 8.8%
- ♦ Russell 2000 (2004) 8.6%

WORST NOVEMBER MARKETS
- ♦ Russell 2000 (2008) -12.0%
- ♦ Nasdaq (2008) -10.8%
- ♦ Russell 3000 Gr (2008) -8.5%

Index Values End of Month

	2002	2003	2004	2005	2006	2007	2008	2009	2010	2011
Dow	8,896	9,782	10,428	10,806	12,222	13,372	8,829	10,345	11,006	12,046
S&P 500	936	1,058	1,174	1,249	1,401	1,481	896	1,096	1,181	1,247
Nasdaq	1,479	1,960	2,097	2,233	2,432	2,661	1,536	2,145	2,498	2,620
TSX	6,570	7,859	9,030	10,824	12,752	13,689	9,271	11,447	12,953	12,204
Russell 1000	952	1,093	1,210	1,306	1,464	1,550	925	1,150	1,258	689
Russell 2000	1,010	1,358	1,575	1,683	1,954	1,908	1,176	1,441	1,807	737
Russell 3000 Growth	1,520	1,776	1,868	2,026	2,180	2,415	1,433	1,903	2,158	2,304
Russell 3000 Value	1,795	2,072	2,429	2,601	3,057	3,046	1,834	2,121	2,283	2,356

Percent Gain for November

	2002	2003	2004	2005	2006	2007	2008	2009	2010	2011
Dow	5.9	-0.2	4.0	3.5	1.2	-4.0	-5.3	6.5	-1.0	0.8
S&P 500	5.7	0.7	3.9	3.5	1.6	-4.4	-7.5	5.7	-0.2	-0.5
Nasdaq	11.2	1.5	6.2	5.3	2.7	-6.9	-10.8	4.9	-0.4	-2.4
TSX	5.1	1.1	1.8	4.2	3.3	-6.4	-5.0	4.9	2.2	-0.4
Russell 1000	5.7	1.0	4.1	3.5	1.9	-4.5	-7.9	5.6	0.1	-0.5
Russell 2000	8.8	3.5	8.6	4.7	2.5	-7.3	-12.0	3.0	3.4	-0.5
Russell 3000 Growth	5.6	1.1	3.7	4.3	1.9	-4.1	-8.5	5.7	1.2	-0.3
Russell 3000 Value	6.1	1.3	5.1	3.0	2.0	-5.4	-7.9	5.2	-0.5	-0.8

November Market Avg. Performance 2002 to 2011[1]

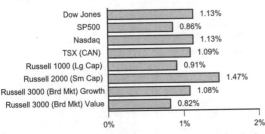

- Dow Jones 1.13%
- SP500 0.86%
- Nasdaq 1.13%
- TSX (CAN) 1.09%
- Russell 1000 (Lg Cap) 0.91%
- Russell 2000 (Sm Cap) 1.47%
- Russell 3000 (Brd Mkt) Growth 1.08%
- Russell 3000 (Brd Mkt) Value 0.82%

Interest Corner Nov[2]

	Fed Funds % [3]	3 Mo. T-Bill % [4]	10 Yr % [5]	20 Yr % [6]
2011	0.25	0.01	2.08	2.77
2010	0.25	0.17	2.81	3.80
2009	0.25	0.06	3.21	4.07
2008	1.00	0.01	2.93	3.71
2007	4.50	3.15	3.97	4.44

(1) Russell Data provided by Russell (2) Federal Reserve Bank of St. Louis- end of month values (3) Target rate set by FOMC (4)(5)(6) Constant yield maturities.

THACKRAY SECTOR THERMOMETER

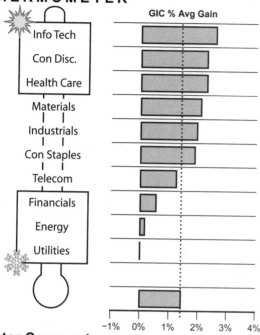

GIC[2] % Avg Gain	Fq % Gain >S&P 500	SP GIC SECTOR 1990-2011[1]
2.6 %	59 %	Information Technology
2.3	64	Consumer Discretionary
2.3	59	Health Care
2.1	59	Materials
1.9	68	Industrials
1.9	45	Consumer Staples
1.2	41	Telecom
0.5	32	Financials
0.2	32	Energy
0.0 %	36 %	Utilities
1.4 %	N/A %	S&P 500

Sector Commentary

♦ In November 2011, the market was volatile to say the least, correcting all the way to just after Thanksgiving and then shooting upwards at month end. ♦ The top two winners in this environment were consumer staples and energy. ♦ The bottom two sectors were information technology and the financial sectors, producing losses of 1.9% and 5% respectively. These two sectors often lead the market and when they are not performing well, it often spells disappointment or mediocre performance in the markets ahead. ♦ The market balanced itself in December with the S&P 500 producing a gain of 0.9%.

Sub-Sector Commentary

♦ In November 2011, the top performing sub-sectors from the list were homebuilders, agriculture, steel and pharmaceuticals, producing gains of 11.1%, 4.1%, 3.7% and 2.0% respectively. ♦ Historically, these sub-sectors are ranked at the top of the list. The pharmaceutical sub-sector's stronger performance in 2011 was the result of a bounce from very poor performance in October.

		SELECTED SUB-SECTORS 1990-2011[3]
4.2 %	53 %	Agriculture (94-2011)
3.5	59	Steel
3.2	64	Retail
2.5	50	Homebuilders
2.3	64	Software & Services
2.2	45	Biotech (93-2011)
2.2	59	Pharmaceuticals
2.2	59	Metals and Mining
2.1	59	Gold (London PM)
2.0	45	Transportation
1.8	55	Silver (London)
1.7	48	Chemicals
0.9	55	Railroads
0.7	45	Banks

(1) Sector data provided by Standard and Poors (2) GIC is short form for Global Industry Classification (3) Sub Sector data provided by Standard and Poors, except where marked by symbol.

MATERIAL STOCKS — MATERIAL GAINS
①Oct 28-Jan 6   ②Jan 23-May 5

Materials Composition – CAUTION

The U.S. materials sector is substantially different from the Canadian materials sector. The U.S. sector has over a 60% weight in chemical companies, versus the Canadian sector which has over a 60% weight in gold companies.

The materials sector (U.S.) generally does well during the favorable six months of the year, from the end of October to the beginning of May. The sector is economically sensitive and is leveraged to the economic forecasts. Generally, if the economy is expected to slow, the materials sector tends to decline and vice versa.

In the past, I have focused my writings on the seasonal strength of the materials sector in the time period between the latter days of January to the first few days of May. Although the materials sector has done very well at this time of year, there is also another time period when the materials sector has outperformed the broad markets – from October 28th to January 6th. During this time period, the sector has produced an average gain of 7.5% in the years from 1990 to 2011 and has been positive 87% of the time.

The second seasonal period from January 23rd to May 5th has produced an average gain of 7.9% (almost double the S&P 500) and has been positive 78% of the time.

Positive 96% of the time

The time period from January 7th to January 22nd has had an average loss of 3.2% and only been positive 30% of the time (1989/90 to 2011/12).

The complete materials strategy is in the market from October 28th to January 6th, out of the market from January 7th to the 22nd, and back in on January 23rd to May 5th. This strategy has produced an average gain of 15.9% and has been positive 96% of the time.

Materials vs. S&P 500 1989/90 to 2011/12   Positive ☐

Year	Oct 28 to Jan 6 S&P 500	Mat.	Jan 23 to May 5 S&P 500	Mat.	Compound Growth S&P 500	Mat.
1989/90	5.1 %	9.1 %	2.4 %	-3.1 %	7.7 %	5.7 %
1990/91	5.4	9.2	16.0	15.3	22.2	26.0
1991/92	8.8	1.5	-0.3	5.5	8.5	7.1
1992/93	3.8	5.6	1.9	4.3	5.8	10.2
1993/94	0.5	9.4	-4.9	-5.3	-4.4	3.6
1994/95	-1.1	-3.5	11.9	6.1	10.7	2.4
1995/96	6.4	7.6	4.6	11.1	11.3	19.5
1996/97	6.7	2.3	5.6	2.3	12.6	4.6
1997/98	10.2	1.4	15.8	20.9	27.7	22.6
1998/99	19.4	6.1	10.0	31.5	31.3	39.6
1999/00	8.2	15.7	-0.6	-7.1	7.6	7.5
2000/01	-5.9	19.2	-5.7	15.1	-11.2	37.2
2001/02	6.2	8.5	-4.1	14.9	1.8	24.7
2002/03	3.5	9.2	5.5	2.7	9.2	12.1
2003/04	9.0	16.6	-2.0	-3.0	6.8	13.1
2004/05	5.6	5.4	0.4	0.3	6.0	5.8
2005/06	9.0	16.3	5.1	14.7	14.6	33.5
2006/07	2.4	3.2	5.8	10.7	8.3	14.2
2007/08	-8.1	-5.1	7.4	16.7	-1.2	10.8
2008/09	10.1	12.0	9.2	23.3	20.3	38.1
2009/10	6.9	13.8	6.8	3.0	14.2	17.2
2010/11	7.7	11.7	4.0	4.2	12.1	16.4
2011/12	-0.5	-2.3	4.1	-2.7	3.5	-4.9
Avg.	5.2 %	7.5 %	4.3 %	7.9 %	9.8 %	15.9 %
Fq > 0	83 %	87 %	74 %	78 %	87 %	96 %

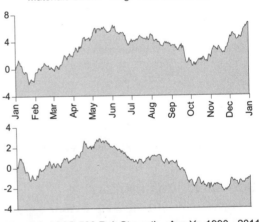

Materials Sector - Avg. Year 1990 to 2011

Materials / S&P 500 Rel. Strength - Avg Yr. 1990 - 2011

> Ⓨ *Alternate Strategy—*
> *Investors can bridge the gap between the two positive seasonal trends for the materials sector by holding from October 28th to May 5th. Longer term investors may prefer this strategy, shorter term investors can use technical tools to determine the appropriate strategy.*

> ⓘ *The SP GICS Materials Sector encompasses a wide range materials based companies.*
> *For more information on the information technology sector, see www.standardandpoors.com*

2011-12 Strategy Performance

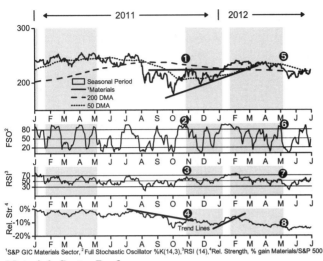

¹S&P GIC Materials Sector, ²Full Stochastic Oscillator %K(14,3), ³RSI (14), ⁴Rel. Strength, % gain Materials/S&P 500

Materials Sector Performance

When the S&P 500 started a strong advance at the beginning of October 2011, the materials sector benefited, breaking its downward trend and outperforming the S&P 500. After being beaten down in the summer of 2011, it would be expected that the materials sector would perform well when the market turned upwards. Unfortunately, a short time later, on the seasonal entry date for the materials sector, the S&P 500 corrected strongly and brought the materials sector down with it.

Technical Conditions– October 28th to May 5th, 2012

Entry Date October 28th, 2011 –Mildly Bullish– On the seasonal entry date, the materials sector was pushing up against resistance and had just crossed its 50 day moving average❶. The FSO was above 80❷ but had not turned down and the RSI had a neutral reading❸. The sector was just about to challenge its down trend of performance against the S&P 500❹. Overall, there was an absence of bearish indications, which translates to a mildly bullish condition.

Entry Strategy –Buy Partial Position Early– In early October, the FSO turned up above 20 and the RSI crossed back over 30. These conditions justified a partial early entry.

Exit Strategy –Sell Partial Position Early– From an absolute return basis, the trade did not fail until the end of the seasonal period in May❺. The problem was that it did not participate in the strong performance of the market. The material sector started to underperform at the beginning of February just after the second leg of the trade started. Although this action would justify a partial exit of the position, it was very early in the trade. The FSO did provide a sell signal a week before the end of the seasonal period❻, at the same time the RSI was turning down❼, but most of the damage was already done❽.

Market Indices & Rates Weekly Values**

Stock Markets	2010	2011
Dow	11,317	12,013
S&P500	1,214	1,254
Nasdaq	2,559	2,670
TSX	12,919	12,299
FTSE	5,831	5,506
DAX	6,743	5,929
Nikkei	9,769	8,639
Hang Seng	24,620	19,494

Commodities	2010	2011
Oil	86.86	96.97
Gold	1397.4	1778.0

Bond Yields	2010	2011
USA 5 Yr Treasury	1.25	0.90
USA 10 Yr T	2.68	2.05
USA 20 Yr T	3.81	2.79
Moody's Aaa	4.90	3.88
Moody's Baa	5.95	5.12
CAN 5 Yr T	2.19	1.39
CAN 10 Yr T	2.96	2.14

Money Market	2010	2011
USA Fed Funds	0.25	0.25
USA 3 Mo T-B	0.13	0.01
CAN tgt overnight rate	1.00	1.00
CAN 3 Mo T-B	0.94	0.89

Foreign Exchange	2010	2011
USD/EUR	1.38	1.37
USD/GBP	1.61	1.60
CAN/USD	1.01	1.01
JPY/USD	82.03	77.69

NOVEMBER

M	T	W	T	F	S	S
				1	2	3
4	5	6	7	8	9	10
11	12	13	14	15	16	17
18	19	20	21	22	23	24
25	26	27	28	29	30	

DECEMBER

M	T	W	T	F	S	S
						1
2	3	4	5	6	7	8
9	10	11	12	13	14	15
16	17	18	19	20	21	22
23	24	25	26	27	28	29
30	31					

JANUARY

M	T	W	T	F	S	S
		1	2	3	4	5
6	7	8	9	10	11	12
13	14	15	16	17	18	19
20	21	22	23	24	25	26
27	28	29	30	31		

INDUSTRIAL STRENGTH
①Oct 28-Dec 31   ②Jan 23-May 5

The industrial sector's seasonal trends are largely the same as the broad market, such as the S&P 500. Although the trends are similar, there still exists an opportunity to take advantage of the time period when the industrials tend to outperform.

12.5% gain & and positive 91% of the time

Industrials tend to outperform in the favorable six months, but there is an opportunity to temporarily get out of the sector to avoid a time period when the sector has, on average, decreased before turning positive again.

The overall strategy is to be invested in the industrial sector from October 28th to December 31st, sell at the end of the day on the 31st and re-enter the sector to be invested from January 23rd to May 5th.

Using the complete *Industrial Strength* strategy; from 1989/90 to 2011/12 the industrial sector has produced a total compounded average annual gain of 12.5%.

In addition, it has been positive 91% of the time and has outperformed the S&P 500, 81% of the time.

During the time period from January 1st to January 22nd, the industrial sector has on average lost 1.0% and has only been positive 50% of the time.

It should be noted that longer term investors may decide to be invested during the whole time period from October 28th to May 5th.

Shorter term investors may decide to use technical analysis to determine if and when they should temporarily sell the industrials sector during its weak period from January 1st to January 22nd.

Industrials vs. S&P 500 1989/90 to 2011/12   Positive ▢

Year	Oct 28 to Dec 31 S&P 500	Ind.	Jan 23 to May 5 S&P 500	Ind.	Compound Growth S&P 500	Ind.
1989/90	5.5 %	6.9 %	2.4 %	5.5 %	8.0 %	12.7 %
1990/91	8.4	10.7	16.0	15.2	25.7	27.5
1991/92	8.6	7.2	-0.3	-1.0	8.2	6.1
1992/93	4.1	6.3	1.9	5.4	6.1	12.0
1993/94	0.4	5.1	-4.9	-6.7	-4.5	-2.0
1994/95	-1.4	-0.5	11.9	12.4	10.3	11.8
1995/96	6.3	10.7	4.6	7.6	11.1	19.1
1996/97	5.7	4.5	5.6	5.2	11.6	9.9
1997/98	10.7	10.5	15.8	11.5	28.2	23.2
1998/99	15.4	10.5	10.0	19.5	26.9	32.1
1999/00	13.3	10.8	-0.6	4.5	12.6	15.8
2000/01	-4.3	1.8	-5.7	4.7	-9.7	6.6
2001/02	3.9	8.1	-4.1	-5.3	-0.3	2.4
2002/03	-2.0	-1.3	5.5	8.6	3.4	7.1
2003/04	7.8	11.6	-2.0	-3.3	5.7	7.9
2004/05	7.7	8.7	0.4	0.2	8.1	8.9
2005/06	5.9	7.6	5.1	14.3	11.3	23.0
2006/07	3.0	3.1	5.8	6.8	9.0	10.1
2007/08	-4.4	-3.4	7.4	9.7	2.7	6.0
2008/09	6.4	7.1	9.2	6.1	16.2	13.7
2009/10	4.9	6.4	6.8	13.4	12.0	20.6
2010/11	6.4	8.1	4.0	4.9	10.6	13.5
2011/12	-2.1	-1.0	4.1	0.3	1.9	-0.7
Avg.	4.8 %	6.1 %	4.3 %	6.1 %	9.4 %	12.5 %
Fq > 0	78 %	83 %	74 %	83 %	87 %	91 %

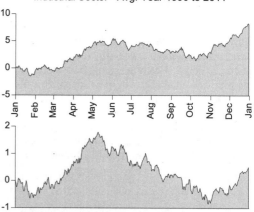

Industrial Sector - Avg. Year 1990 to 2011

Industrial / S&P 500 Rel. Strength - Avg Yr. 1990 - 2011

Ⓨ Alternate Strategy—
Investors can bridge the gap between the two positive seasonal trends for the industrials sector by holding from October 28th to May 5th. Longer term investors may prefer this strategy, shorter term investors can use technical tools to determine the appropriate strategy.

ⓘ The SP GICS Industrial Sector encompasses a wide range industrial based companies.
For more information on the information technology sector, see www.standardandpoors.com

2011-12 Strategy Performance

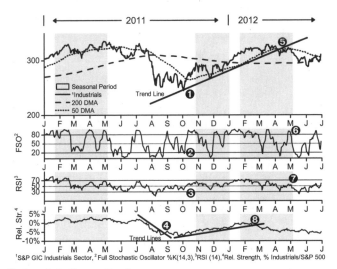

¹S&P GIC Industrials Sector, ²Full Stochastic Oscillator %K(14,3),³RSI (14),⁴Rel. Strength, % Industrials/S&P 500

Market Indices & Rates
Weekly Values**

Stock Markets	2010	2011
Dow	11,124	11,930
S&P500	1,190	1,236
Nasdaq	2,498	2,629
TSX	12,764	12,087
FTSE	5,739	5,466
DAX	6,766	5,896
Nikkei	9,894	8,493
Hang Seng	23,636	19,025

Commodities	2010	2011
Oil	82.20	99.27
Gold	1349.6	1755.7

Bond Yields	2010	2011
USA 5 Yr Treasury	1.51	0.91
USA 10 Yr T	2.89	2.02
USA 20 Yr T	3.94	2.73
Moody's Aaa	4.98	3.89
Moody's Baa	6.03	5.16
CAN 5 Yr T	2.35	1.37
CAN 10 Yr T	3.12	2.11

Money Market	2010	2011
USA Fed Funds	0.25	0.25
USA 3 Mo T-B	0.14	0.01
CAN tgt overnight rate	1.00	1.00
CAN 3 Mo T-B	0.94	0.89

Foreign Exchange	2010	2011
USD/EUR	1.36	1.35
USD/GBP	1.60	1.58
CAN/USD	1.02	1.02
JPY/USD	83.32	77.01

Industrials Sector Performance

After a weak summer performance in 2011, the industrials sector started to outperform in October as the S&P 500 started to show some positive results. It continued its outperformance until February. At that point, the sector became "flat" while the S&P 500 continued its upward ascent.

Technical Conditions– October 28th to May 5th, 2012
*Entry Date October 28th, 2011 –*Bullish*–* The industrials sector had started to outperform the S&P 500 in August, but this was too far ahead of its seasonal buy date to act upon❹. Nevertheless, it put the sector in good standing for the near future. The industrials sector continued to trade sideways into the beginning of October❶. At that time the FSO crossed back over 20❷, justifying an early entry. Supporting this position was the RSI crossing back over 50❸.

*Entry Strategy –*Buy Partial Position Early*–* The FSO crossed back over the 20 level and the RSI started to rise from a sub-50 position, justifying a partial early entry into the sector at the beginning of October.

*Exit Strategy –*Sell Partial Position Early*–* The industrials sector started to underperform the S&P 500 in mid-February, just after the second leg of the seasonal trade was getting underway❸. This was very early in the trade and if the underperformance continued, there would be cause to liquidate the trade. Further along in the trade, more cause was given to exit the trade as the industrials sector traded below its 50 day moving average and its upward trend line❺ and then the FSO and RSI turned down❻❼. The industrials sector continued to underperform the S&P 500 after the seasonal trade ended.

** Weekly avg closing values- except Fed Funds & CAN overnight tgt rate weekly closing values.

NOVEMBER

M	T	W	T	F	S	S
				1	2	3
4	5	6	7	8	9	10
11	12	13	14	15	16	17
18	19	20	21	22	23	24
25	26	27	28	29	30	

DECEMBER

M	T	W	T	F	S	S
						1
2	3	4	5	6	7	8
9	10	11	12	13	14	15
16	17	18	19	20	21	22
23	24	25	26	27	28	29
30	31					

JANUARY

M	T	W	T	F	S	S
	1	2	3	4	5
6	7	8	9	10	11	12
13	14	15	16	17	18	19
20	21	22	23	24	25	26
27	28	29	30	31		

At the macro level, the metals and mining (M&M) sector is driven by future economic growth expectations. When worldwide growth expectations are increasing, there is a greater need for raw materials– when growth expectations are decreasing, the need is less.

Within the macro trend, the M&M sector has traditionally followed the overall market cycle of performing well from autumn until spring. This is the time of year that investors have a positive outlook on the economy and as a result, the cyclical sectors tend to outperform, including the metals and mining sector.

14.7% gain and positive 74% of the time

The metals and mining sector has two seasonal "sweet spots" – the first from November 19th to January 5th and the second from January 23rd to May 5th. Investors have the option to hold and "bridge the gap" across the two sweet spots, but over the long-term, nimble traders have been able to capture extra value by being out of the sector from January 6th to the 22nd. During this period, the metals and mining sector produced an average loss of 2.9% and has only been positive 48% of the time.

From a portfolio perspective, it is important to consider reducing exposure at the beginning of May. The danger of holding on too long is that the sector tends not to do well in the late summer, particularly in September. For more detail on why the metals and mining sector underperforms in late summer, see the *September Pair Strategy - Long Gold and Short Metals and Mining Strategy*.

ⓘ *For more information on the metals and mining sector, see www.standardandpoors.com*

Metals & Mining Sector vs. S&P 500 1989/90 to 2011/12

Positive ▭

Year	Nov 19 to Jan 5 S&P 500	M&M	Jan 23 to May 5 S&P 500	M&M	Compound Growth S&P 500	M&M
1989/90	3.1%	6.3%	2.4%	-4.6%	5.6%	1.4%
1990/91	1.2	6.4	16.0	7.1	17.4	13.9
1991/92	8.9	1.0	-0.3	-1.7	8.5	-0.7
1992/93	2.7	12.5	1.9	3.2	4.7	16.1
1993/94	0.9	9.0	-4.9	-11.1	-4.1	-3.1
1994/95	-0.2	-1.2	11.9	-3.0	11.6	-4.1
1995/96	2.8	8.3	4.6	5.8	7.5	14.6
1996/97	1.5	-1.9	5.6	-1.2	7.2	-3.0
1997/98	4.1	-4.5	15.8	19.3	20.6	13.9
1998/99	8.8	-7.9	10.0	31.0	19.6	20.6
1999/00	-1.6	21.7	-0.6	-10.4	-2.2	9.1
2000/01	-5.1	17.0	-5.7	19.6	-10.5	40.0
2001/02	3.0	5.5	-4.1	12.8	-1.3	19.0
2002/03	0.9	9.3	5.5	3.2	6.4	12.8
2003/04	8.5	18.2	-2.0	-12.1	6.4	3.9
2004/05	0.0	-8.4	0.4	-4.0	0.4	-12.0
2005/06	2.0	17.3	5.1	27.3	7.2	49.4
2006/07	0.6	3.0	5.8	17.2	6.5	20.8
2007/08	-3.2	0.9	7.4	27.4	3.9	28.5
2008/09	8.0	43.8	9.2	30.6	17.9	87.8
2009/10	2.4	6.3	6.8	4.8	9.4	11.3
2010/11	6.7	15.0	4.0	-1.6	11.0	13.1
2011/12	5.4	1.2	4.1	-16.0	9.7	-15.0
Avg.	2.7%	7.8%	4.3%	6.2%	7.1%	14.7%
Fq > 0	83%	78%	74%	57%	83%	74%

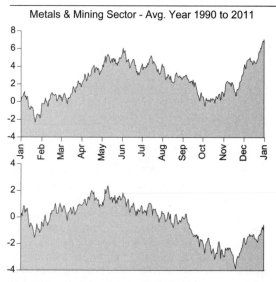

Metals & Mining Sector - Avg. Year 1990 to 2011

Metals & Mining / S&P 500 Rel. Strength- Avg Yr. 1990-2011

2011-12 Strategy Performance

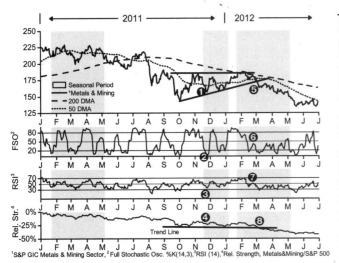

¹S&P GIC Metals & Mining Sector, ² Full Stochastic Osc. %K(14,3),³RSI (14),⁴Rel. Strength, Metals&Mining/S&P 500

Metals and Mining Sector Performance

The metals and mining sector traded steadily lower in the beginning part of 2011 and underperformed the S&P 500. In July the sector corrected strongly. When the market bounced strongly in October the metals and mining sector participated, but its performance relative to the S&P 500 was anaemic. When the broad market moves so strongly, typically a high beta sector such as metals and mining that has been beaten up badly, responds with very strong upside performance. This did not happen and after an initial period of slightly stronger performance, the metals and mining sector resumed its underperformance.

Technical Conditions– November 19th to May 5th, 2012

Entry Date November 19th, 2011 –Mildly Bullish– Just before the beginning of its period of seasonal strength, the metals and mining sector pulled back below its 50 day moving average❶, and the FSO crossed back below 20❷. Although this FSO level represents an oversold condition, a positive signal is only given when the sector crosses back up over 20. The RSI had just crossed back below 50❸ and the relative strength compared to the S&P 500 was neutral❹.

Entry Strategy –Buy Partial Position on Entry Date– It could be argued that when the metals and mining sector crossed back above a FSO reading of 20 in early October, that this represented an early buy signal, but this was some time before the start of the seasonal period. On the actual entry date, strong bullish or bearish signals did not exist, creating a situation where a partial allocation was appropriate.

Exit Strategy –Sell Position Early– After breaking through both the 200 and 50 day moving averages on the downside and then resistance, the trade was fundamentally broken and should have been exited❺. The FSO and the RSI provided little help in this decision as they traded lower early in the trade❻❼. Confirmation of an exit occurred when the sector started to underperform compared to the S&P 500 in March❽.

Market Indices & Rates
Weekly Values**

Stock Markets	2010	2011
Dow	11,124	11,383
S&P500	1,192	1,175
Nasdaq	2,526	2,487
TSX	12,893	11,620
FTSE	5,657	5,172
DAX	6,816	5,504
Nikkei	10,066	8,247
Hang Seng	23,075	17,993

Commodities	2010	2011
Oil	82.24	96.76
Gold	1367.0	1692.6

Bond Yields	2010	2011
USA 5 Yr Treasury	1.48	0.91
USA 10 Yr T	2.84	1.94
USA 20 Yr T	3.88	2.60
Moody's Aaa	4.90	3.81
Moody's Baa	5.95	5.11
CAN 5 Yr T	2.40	1.36
CAN 10 Yr T	3.13	2.07

Money Market	2010	2011
USA Fed Funds	0.25	0.25
USA 3 Mo T-B	0.16	0.02
CAN tgt overnight rate	1.00	1.00
CAN 3 Mo T-B	0.99	0.87

Foreign Exchange	2010	2011
USD/EUR	1.34	1.34
USD/GBP	1.58	1.55
CAN/USD	1.02	1.04
JPY/USD	83.55	77.20

NOVEMBER

M	T	W	T	F	S	S
				1	2	3
4	5	6	7	8	9	10
11	12	13	14	15	16	17
18	19	20	21	22	23	24
25	26	27	28	29	30	

DECEMBER

M	T	W	T	F	S	S
						1
2	3	4	5	6	7	8
9	10	11	12	13	14	15
16	17	18	19	20	21	22
23	24	25	26	27	28	29
30	31					

JANUARY

M	T	W	T	F	S	S
	1	2	3	4	5	
6	7	8	9	10	11	12
13	14	15	16	17	18	19
20	21	22	23	24	25	26
27	28	29	30	31		

THANKSGIVING
GIVE THANKS & TAKE RETURNS
Day Before and After – Two of the Best Days

We have a lot to be thankful for on Thanksgiving Day. As a bonus, the market day before and the market day after Thanksgiving have been two of the best days of the year in the stock market.

Each day by itself has produced spectacular results. From 1950 to 2011, the S&P 500 has had an average gain of 0.4% on the day before Thanksgiving and 0.3% on the day after.

The day before Thanksgiving and the day after have had an average cumulative return of 0.7% and together have been positive 84% of the time

To put the performance of these two days in perspective, the average daily return of the market over the same time period is 0.03%.

The gains the day before Thanksgiving and the day after are almost ten times better than the average market and have a much greater frequency of being positive.

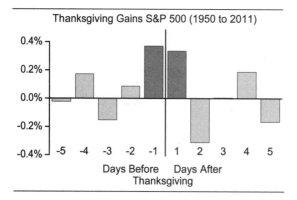

Thanksgiving Gains S&P 500 (1950 to 2011)

Days Before   Days After
Thanksgiving

Ⓨ *Alternate Strategy — Although the focus has been on the performance of two specific days, the day before and the day after Thanksgiving, the holiday occurs at the end of November which tends to be a strong month. December, the next month is also strong. Investors have a good option of expanding their trade out to include the "Santa Arrives Early & Stays Late" Strategy.*

ⓘ *History of Thanksgiving:
It was originally a "thanksgiving feast" by the pilgrims for surviving their first winter. Initially it was celebrated sporadically and the holiday, when it was granted, had its date changed several times. It was not until 1941 that it was proclaimed to be the 4th Thursday in November.*

S&P500	Day Before	Day After
		Positive
1950	1.4	0.8
1951	-0.2	-1.1
1952	0.6	0.5
1953	0.1	0.6
1954	0.6	1.0
1955	0.1	-0.1
1956	-0.5	1.1
1957	2.9	1.1
1958	1.7	1.1
1959	0.2	0.5
1960	0.1	0.6
1961	-0.1	0.2
1962	0.6	1.2
1963	-0.2	1.4
1964	-0.3	-0.3
1965	0.2	0.1
1966	0.7	0.8
1967	0.6	0.3
1968	0.5	0.6
1969	0.4	0.6
1970	0.4	1.0
1971	0.2	1.8
1972	0.6	0.3
1973	1.1	-0.3
1974	0.7	0.0
1975	0.3	0.3
1976	0.4	0.7
1977	0.4	0.2
1978	0.5	0.3
1979	0.2	0.8
1980	0.6	0.2
1981	0.4	0.8
1982	0.7	0.7
1983	0.1	0.1
1984	0.2	1.5
1985	0.9	-0.2
1986	0.2	0.2
1987	-0.9	-1.5
1988	0.7	-0.7
1989	0.7	0.6
1990	0.2	-0.3
1991	-0.4	-0.4
1992	0.4	0.2
1993	0.3	0.2
1994	0.0	0.5
1995	-0.3	0.3
1996	-0.1	0.3
1997	0.1	0.4
1998	0.3	0.5
1999	0.9	0.0
2000	-1.9	1.5
2001	-0.5	1.2
2002	2.8	-0.3
2003	0.4	0.0
2004	0.4	0.1
2005	0.3	0.2
2006	0.2	-0.4
2007	-1.6	1.7
2008	3.5	1.0
2009	0.5	-1.7
2010	1.5	-0.7
2011	-2.2	-0.3
Total Avg %	0.4%	0.3%
Fq > 0	77%	74%

2009-11 Strategy Performance

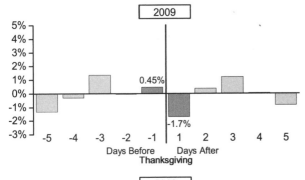

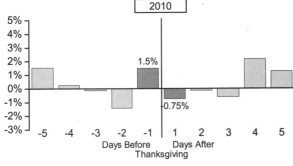

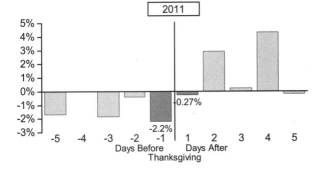

Market Indices & Rates
Weekly Values**

Stock Markets	2010	2011
Dow	11,212	11,833
S&P500	1,204	1,225
Nasdaq	2,549	2,583
TSX	13,068	11,953
FTSE	5,647	5,439
DAX	6,832	5,950
Nikkei	10,080	8,488
Hang Seng	23,239	18,465

Commodities	2010	2011
Oil	86.76	99.90
Gold	1383.7	1735.2

Bond Yields	2010	2011
USA 5 Yr Treasury	1.59	0.94
USA 10 Yr T	2.93	2.04
USA 20 Yr T	3.91	2.72
Moody's Aaa	4.90	4.00
Moody's Baa	5.95	5.28
CAN 5 Yr T	2.41	1.42
CAN 10 Yr T	3.14	2.13

Money Market	2010	2011
USA Fed Funds	0.25	0.25
USA 3 Mo T-B	0.16	0.02
CAN tgt overnight rate	1.00	1.00
CAN 3 Mo T-B	1.01	0.86

Foreign Exchange	2010	2011
USD/EUR	1.32	1.34
USD/GBP	1.56	1.56
CAN/USD	1.01	1.02
JPY/USD	83.70	77.84

NOVEMBER

M	T	W	T	F	S	S
				1	2	3
4	5	6	7	8	9	10
11	12	13	14	15	16	17
18	19	20	21	22	23	24
25	26	27	28	29	30	

DECEMBER

M	T	W	T	F	S	S
						1
2	3	4	5	6	7	8
9	10	11	12	13	14	15
16	17	18	19	20	21	22
23	24	25	26	27	28	29
30	31					

JANUARY

M	T	W	T	F	S	S
	1	2	3	4	5
6	7	8	9	10	11	12
13	14	15	16	17	18	19
20	21	22	23	24	25	26
27	28	29	30	31		

Thanksgiving Strategy Performance

When big events happen out of the blue, they will effect any strategy arbitrarily. Thanksgiving in 2011 is a perfect example. The trade was setting up very well on a technical basis, but unfortunately, Germany had an unsuccessful bond auction creating huge fear in the markets. As a result, the S&P 500 fell 2.2% the day before Thanksgiving.

Investors should remember that seasonal investing is a long-term discipline and not every trade works. The long-term statistics for the Thanksgiving trade are very strong and investors should not lose "faith" in the trade because of an uncontrollable event.

** Weekly avg closing values- except Fed Funds & CAN overnight tgt rate weekly closing values.

DECEMBER

	MONDAY	TUESDAY	WEDNESDAY
WEEK 49	**2** 29	**3** 28	**4** 27
WEEK 50	**9** 22	**10** 21	**11** 20
WEEK 51	**16** 15	**17** 14	**18** 13
WEEK 52	**23** 8	**24** 7	**25** 6 CAN Market Closed-Christmas Day USA Market Closed-Christmas Day
WEEK 01	**30** 1	**31**	1

THURSDAY		FRIDAY	
5	26	**6**	25
12	19	**13**	18
19	12	**20**	11
26	5	**27**	4
CAN Market Closed- Boxing Day			
2		3	

JANUARY

M	T	W	T	F	S	S
		1	2	3	4	5
6	7	8	9	10	11	12
13	14	15	16	17	18	19
20	21	22	23	24	25	26
27	28	29	30	31		

FEBRUARY

M	T	W	T	F	S	S
					1	2
3	4	5	6	7	8	9
10	11	12	13	14	15	16
17	18	19	20	21	22	23
24	25	26	27	28		

MARCH

M	T	W	T	F	S	S
					1	2
3	4	5	6	7	8	9
10	11	12	13	14	15	16
17	18	19	20	21	22	23
24	25	26	27	28	29	30
31						

APRIL

M	T	W	T	F	S	S
	1	2	3	4	5	6
7	8	9	10	11	12	13
14	15	16	17	18	19	20
21	22	23	24	25	26	27
28	29	30				

DECEMBER
S U M M A R Y

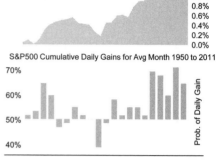

	Dow Jones	S&P 500	Nasdaq	TSX Comp
Month Rank	2	1	2	1
# Up	44	48	23	24
# Down	18	14	17	3
% Pos	71	77	58	89
% Avg. Gain	1.7	1.7	1.8	2.3

Dow & S&P 1950-2011, Nasdaq 1972-2011, TSX 1985-2011

♦ December is one of the best months of the year, having an average gain of 1.7% and a positive rate of 71% from 1950 to 2011. In 2011 the S&P produced a modest gain of 0.9%, while the TSX Composite lost 2%. ♦ Although the month tends to be positive, it is the second half of the month that tends to produce the biggest returns. ♦ The US dollar has a habit of weakening in December for a rally in January. ♦ Small cap stocks typically rally mid-December at approximately the same time that the Nasdaq also starts to outperform the S&P 500.

BEST / WORST DECEMBER BROAD MKTS. 2002-2011

BEST DECEMBER MARKETS
- ♦ Russell 2000 (2009) 7.9%
- ♦ Russell 2000 (2010) 7.8%
- ♦ Russell 3000 Value (2010) 7.7%

WORST DECEMBER MARKETS
- ♦ Nasdaq (2002) -9.7%
- ♦ Russell 3000 Gr (2002) -7.0%
- ♦ Dow (2002) -6.2%

Index Values End of Month

	2002	2003	2004	2005	2006	2007	2008	2009	2010	2011
Dow	8,342	10,454	10,783	10,718	12,463	13,265	8,776	10,428	11,578	12,218
S&P 500	880	1,112	1,212	1,248	1,418	1,468	903	1,115	1,258	1,258
Nasdaq	1,336	2,003	2,175	2,205	2,415	2,652	1,577	2,269	2,653	2,605
TSX	6,615	8,221	9,247	11,272	12,908	13,833	8,988	11,746	13,443	11,955
Russell 1000	896	1,143	1,251	1,306	1,480	1,538	938	1,176	1,340	693
Russell 2000	952	1,384	1,619	1,673	1,958	1,904	1,241	1,554	1,948	741
Russell 3000 Growth	1,413	1,831	1,939	2,018	2,184	2,406	1,460	1,966	2,279	2,295
Russell 3000 Value	1,713	2,191	2,502	2,610	3,116	3,009	1,860	2,164	2,459	2,397

Percent Gain for December

	2002	2003	2004	2005	2006	2007	2008	2009	2010	2011
Dow	-6.2	6.9	3.4	-0.8	2.0	-0.8	-0.6	0.8	5.2	1.4
S&P 500	-6.0	5.1	3.2	-0.1	1.3	-0.9	0.8	1.8	6.5	0.9
Nasdaq	-9.7	2.2	3.7	-1.2	-0.7	-0.3	2.7	5.8	6.2	-0.6
TSX	0.7	4.6	2.4	4.1	1.2	1.1	-3.1	2.6	3.8	-2.0
Russell 1000	-5.8	4.6	3.5	0.0	1.1	-0.8	1.3	2.3	6.5	0.7
Russell 2000	-5.7	1.9	2.8	-0.6	0.2	-0.2	5.6	7.9	7.8	0.5
Russell 3000 Growth	-7.0	3.1	3.8	-0.4	0.2	-0.4	1.9	3.3	5.6	-0.4
Russell 3000 Value	-4.5	5.7	3.0	0.3	1.9	-1.2	1.4	2.0	7.7	1.7

December Market Avg. Performance 2002 to 2011[1]

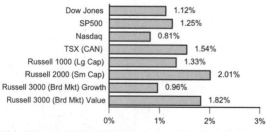

	Dow Jones	1.12%
	SP500	1.25%
	Nasdaq	0.81%
	TSX (CAN)	1.54%
	Russell 1000 (Lg Cap)	1.33%
	Russell 2000 (Sm Cap)	2.01%
	Russell 3000 (Brd Mkt) Growth	0.96%
	Russell 3000 (Brd Mkt) Value	1.82%

Interest Corner Dec[2]

	Fed Funds %[3]	3 Mo. T-Bill %[4]	10 Yr %[5]	20 Yr %[6]
2011	0.25	0.02	1.89	2.57
2010	0.25	0.12	3.30	4.13
2009	0.25	0.06	3.85	4.58
2008	0.25	0.11	2.25	3.05
2007	4.25	3.36	4.04	4.50

(1) Russell Data provided by Russell (2) Federal Reserve Bank of St. Louis- end of month values (3) Target rate set by FOMC (4)(5)(6) Constant yield maturities.

THACKRAY SECTOR THERMOMETER

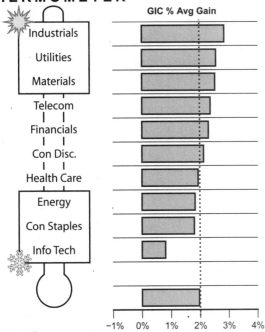

	GIC[2] % Avg Gain	Fq % Gain >S&P 500	SP GIC SECTOR 1990-2011[1]
	2.8 %	64 %	Industrials
	2.6	55	Utilities
	2.5	45	Materials
	2.4	59	Telecom
	2.3	59	Financials
	2.1	55	Consumer Discretionary
	1.9	55	Health Care
	1.8	41	Energy
	1.8	45	Consumer Staples
	0.8 %	36 %	Information Technology
	2.0 %	N/A %	S&P 500

Sector Commentary

♦ In December 2011, telecom, utilities and health care were the top performing sectors, producing gains of 3.7%, 3.0% and 2.8% respectively. ♦ On average it is only the utilities sector that is typically in the top three for the month, telecom and health care are typically fourth and seventh best sectors. ♦ The three sectors that performed the worst in December were information technology, energy and materials, producing loses of 0.9%, 1.0% and 2.4% respectively. ♦ On average, the energy and information technology sectors are at the bottom of the sector rank. ♦ The materials sector on the other hand, on average, is one of the top sectors. Performing so poorly in the month of December hinted at weaker results going forward for the cyclical sectors.

Sub-Sector Commentary

♦ In December 2011, the homebuilders sector was the second best performing sub-sector from the selected list of sectors. It produced a gain of 5.5%. On average from 1950 to 2011, it has been the best performing sub-sector with the amazing results of an average gain of 8.6% and a 91% frequency rate of success. ♦ The metals and mining and steel sectors did not perform positively, as they were expected, and indicated concern in the near future for these sectors.

SELECTED SUB-SECTORS 1990-2011[3]		
8.6 %	91 %	Homebuilders
5.3	68	Steel
4.5	55	Biotech (93-2011)
3.7	59	Metals and Mining
2.6	44	Chemicals
2.4	53	Agriculture (94-2011)
2.1	50	Silver (London)
2.0	55	Banks
1.7	45	Railroads
1.7	41	Software & Services
1.5	45	Pharmaceuticals
1.2	32	Retail
1.1	32	Transportation
0.2	32	Gold (London PM)

(1) Sector data provided by Standard and Poors (2) GIC is short form for Global Industry Classification (3) Sub Sector data provided by Standard and Poors, except where marked by symbol.

U.S. HIGH YIELD BONDS
November 24th to January 8th

Most investors are stock and bond investors, but the only bonds that they will hold are top rated corporations and government bonds. They are usually willing to take a lot of risk with some of their stocks, but not with their bonds.

3.5% gain & positive 100% of the time

For those investors that are willing to invest in securities that provide a diversification benefit by investing in securities that have characteristics of both bonds and stocks, a well diversified basket of high yield bonds can add value to a portfolio.

Nov 24 to Jan 8	S&P 500	HY Bonds	Positive Diff
1999	2.6%	0.9%	-1.7%
2000	-2.0	1.0	3.0
2001	0.9	1.4	0.5
2002	-2.2	5.1	7.3
2003	9.3	4.3	-5.0
2004	0.8	1.2	0.4
2005	1.6	2.2	0.6
2006	0.5	1.9	1.4
2007	-3.5	0.1	3.6
2008	13.7	15.9	2.2
2009	3.5	5.4	1.9
2010	7.7	2.3	-5.4
2011	10.0	4.3	-5.7
Avg	3.3%	3.5%	0.2%
Fq > 0	77%	100%	69%

U.S. High Yield Bonds Total Return* vs. S&P 500 1999 to 2011

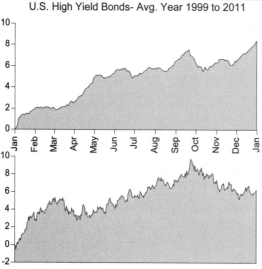

U.S. High Yield Bonds- Avg. Year 1999 to 2011

High Yield Bonds/S&P 500 Rel. Str. - Avg Yr. 1999 - 2011

High yield bonds have a period of seasonal performance and historically the best time to be invested in the sector has been from November 24th to January 8th. In this time period, from 1999 to 2011, high yield bonds have produced a average return of 3.5% and have been positive 100% of the time.

The fact that the high yield bond strategy has been successful 100% of the time, does not mean that it will be successful this year? No. Although the trend is very strong, it does not mean that the strategy will work again. There may be a higher seasonal probability that it will work, but there is no guarantee.

It is not a coincidence that the seasonal period for high yield bonds occurs at this time of the year, as this has historically been a good time to be in the equity market. In addition, government bonds tend to perform well at this time, just not as well as equities or high yield bonds.

The strength of the high yield trade lies in that not only does it provide a marginally higher average return than the S&P 500, but also that it helps to mitigate the damage from the losses in the down years. In other words, adding high yield bonds to the S&P 500 would have produced higher returns and less volatility than just holding the S&P 500.

The analysis on this page is based upon the Barclays Capital High Bond Index*. For individual investors, the best method to invest in this sector is to use an ETF that holds a well diversified basket of high yield bonds– please consult the prospectus of any fund in which you are contemplating making an investment.

* Source: Barclays Capital Inc. The U.S. High Yield Bonds is a total return index, which includes both interest and capital appreciation.

For more information on fixed income indices, see www.barcap.com.

2011-12 Strategy Performance

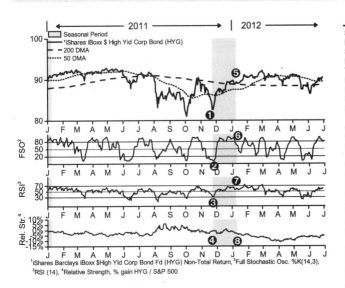

¹iShares Barclays iBoxx $High Yld Corp Bond Fd (HYG) Non-Total Return, ²Full Stochastic Osc. %K(14,3), ³RSI (14), ⁴Relative Strength, % gain HYG / S&P 500

Market Indices & Rates Weekly Values**

Stock Markets	2010	2011
Dow	11,375	12,125
S&P500	1,230	1,253
Nasdaq	2,611	2,640
TSX	13,217	12,067
FTSE	5,799	5,539
DAX	6,980	5,998
Nikkei	10,208	8,639
Hang Seng	23,219	19,011

Commodities	2010	2011
Oil	88.50	100.10
Gold	1397.5	1722.3

Bond Yields	2010	2011
USA 5 Yr Treasury	1.80	0.90
USA 10 Yr T	3.18	2.04
USA 20 Yr T	4.11	2.74
Moody's Aaa	5.03	4.02
Moody's Baa	6.09	5.30
CAN 5 Yr T	2.46	1.33
CAN 10 Yr T	3.23	2.07

Money Market	2010	2011
USA Fed Funds	0.25	0.25
USA 3 Mo T-B	0.14	0.01
CAN tgt overnight rate	1.00	1.00
CAN 3 Mo T-B	0.99	0.84

Foreign Exchange	2010	2011
USD/EUR	1.33	1.34
USD/GBP	1.58	1.57
CAN/USD	1.01	1.02
JPY/USD	83.58	77.70

U.S. High Yield Bonds Performance

U.S. High Yield bonds did not perform well in 2011 and ended up a bit lower than at the start of the year. There were two periods where the high yield bonds appreciated significantly. First, at the beginning of October, when the market rallied strongly. Second, in the seasonal period for high yield bonds.

Technical Conditions
Entry Date November 24th, 2011–Neutral– Up until the start of their seasonal period the technical conditions for high yield bonds were not positive. At the time the bonds were declining sharply and put in a bottom, right at the start of the seasonal period❶. The bounce triggered the FSO to cross back over 20❷ and RSI to bounce of 30❸. The bonds had been declining relative to the S&P 500, but the bounce brought them back to market performance❹.

Entry Strategy –Buy Partial Position on Entry Date– It is easy to look back and determine that a full position should have been bought on the entry date, but it was not until the entry date did the sector bounce. In reality, it would have taken a few days to get clear buy signal from the FSO. The full position would have been entered when the FSO turned above 20.

Exit Strategy –Exit Partial Position Early– A few days before the end of their seasonal period, high yield bonds turned to the 200 day moving average❺. Although this by itself would not trigger a sell signal, the action caused the FSO to fall below 80❻, giving an early sell signal. The RSI started to decline at the time❼ and the high yield bonds continued their underperformance relative to the S&P 500❽.

** Weekly avg closing values- except Fed Funds & CAN overnight tgt rate weekly closing values.

DECEMBER
M	T	W	T	F	S	S
						1
2	3	4	5	6	7	8
9	10	11	12	13	14	15
16	17	18	19	20	21	22
23	24	25	26	27	28	29
30	31					

JANUARY
M	T	W	T	F	S	S
	1	2	3	4	5
6	7	8	9	10	11	12
13	14	15	16	17	18	19
20	21	22	23	24	25	26
27	28	29	30	31		

FEBRUARY
M	T	W	T	F	S	S
					1	2
3	4	5	6	7	8	9
10	11	12	13	14	15	16
17	18	19	20	21	22	23
24	25	26	27	28		

SMALL CAP (SMALL COMPANY) EFFECT
Small Companies Outperform - Dec 19th to Mar 7th

At different stages of the business cycle, small capitalization companies (small caps represented by Russell 2000), perform better than large capitalization companies (large caps represented by Russell 1000).

Evidence shows that the small caps relative outperformance also has a seasonal component as they typically outperform large caps from December 19th to March 7th.

23 times out of 33 better than the Russell 1000

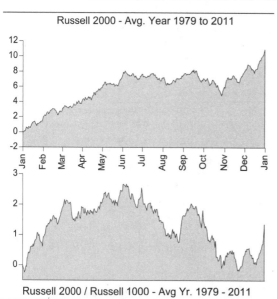

Russell 2000 - Avg. Year 1979 to 2011

Russell 2000 / Russell 1000 - Avg Yr. 1979 - 2011

Dec 19 - Mar7	Russell 1000	Russell 2000	Diff
79 / 80	-1.3 %	-0.4 %	0.9 %
80 / 81	-2.8	4.0	6.8
81 / 82	-12.4	-12.1	0.3
82 / 83	11.8	19.8	8.0
83 / 84	-6.4	-7.5	-1.1
84 / 85	7.7	17.1	9.4
85 / 86	8.2	11.7	3.5
86 / 87	17.2	21.3	4.1
87 / 88	8.3	16.4	8.0
88 / 89	6.9	9.1	2.5
89 / 90	-2.0	-1.9	0.2
90 / 91	14.6	29.0	14.4
91 / 92	6.0	16.8	10.8
92 / 93	1.4	5.0	3.5
93 / 94	0.5	5.7	5.3
94 / 95	5.3	5.5	0.2
95 / 96	8.3	7.8	-0.5
96 / 97	9.5	3.5	-6.0
97 / 98	10.2	10.3	0.1
98 / 99	7.3	0.2	-7.2
99 / 00	-1.7	27.7	29.4
00 / 01	-5.2	4.7	9.8
01 / 02	1.6	1.9	0.4
02 / 03	-6.7	-7.8	-1.0
03 / 04	6.4	9.6	3.3
04 / 05	2.8	0.3	-2.5
05 / 06	0.8	5.6	4.7
06 / 07	-1.6	-0.8	0.9
07 / 08	-10.9	-12.5	-1.5
08 / 09	-22.2	-26.7	-4.5
09 / 10	3.6	9.1	5.5
10 / 11	5.5	4.2	-1.3
11 / 12	11.3	10.2	-1.1
Avg.	2.5 %	5.7 %	3.2 %
Fq > 0	67 %	76 %	70 %

Russell 2000 vs. Russell 1000 Gains 19th Dec to Mar 7th 1979 to 2012
Positive

The core part of the small cap seasonal strategy occurs in January and includes what has been described as the January Effect (Wachtel 1942, 184).

This well documented anomaly of superior performance of stocks in the month of January is based upon the tenet that investors sell stocks in December for tax loss reasons, artificially driving down prices, and creating a great opportunity for astute investors.

In recent times, the January Effect starts mid-December and is more pronounced for small caps as their prices are more volatile than large caps.

At the beginning of the year, small cap stocks benefit from a phenomenon that I have coined, "beta out of the gate, and coast." If small cap stocks are outperforming at the beginning of the year, money managers will gravitate to the sector in order to produce returns that are above their index benchmark. Once above average returns have been "locked in," the managers then rotate from their small cap overweight positions back to index large cap positions and coast for the rest of the year with above average returns. The overall process boosts small cap stocks at the beginning of the year.

(i) *Russell 2000 (small cap index): The 2000 smallest companies in the Russell 3000 stock index (a broad market index). Russell 1000 (large cap index): The 1000 largest companies in the Russell 3000 stock index*

For more information on the Russell indexes, see www.Russell.com

Wachtel, S.B. 1942. Certain observations on seasonal movements in stock prices. The Journal of Business and Economics (Winter): 184.

2011-12 Strategy Performance

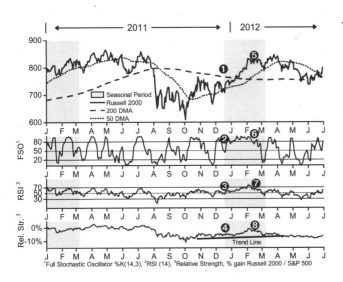

| | 2011 | 2012 |

¹Full Stochastic Oscillator %K(14,3), ²RSI (14), ³Relative Strength, % gain Russell 2000 / S&P 500

Market Indices & Rates
Weekly Values**

Stock Markets	2010	2011
Dow	11,471	11,907
S&P500	1,241	1,222
Nasdaq	2,630	2,565
TSX	13,238	11,670
FTSE	5,877	5,415
DAX	7,016	5,733
Nikkei	10,307	8,501
Hang Seng	23,022	18,338

Commodities	2010	2011
Oil	88.25	96.05
Gold	1382.8	1620.6

Bond Yields	2010	2011
USA 5 Yr Treasury	2.03	0.85
USA 10 Yr T	3.42	1.94
USA 20 Yr T	4.27	2.63
Moody's Aaa	5.08	3.92
Moody's Baa	6.18	5.20
CAN 5 Yr T	2.51	1.24
CAN 10 Yr T	3.27	1.95

Money Market	2010	2011
USA Fed Funds	0.25	0.25
USA 3 Mo T-B	0.14	0.01
CAN tgt overnight rate	1.00	1.00
CAN 3 Mo T-B	0.98	0.82

Foreign Exchange	2010	2011
USD/EUR	1.33	1.31
USD/GBP	1.57	1.55
CAN/USD	1.01	1.03
JPY/USD	83.84	77.93

DECEMBER

M	T	W	T	F	S	S
						1
2	3	4	5	6	7	8
9	10	11	12	13	14	15
16	17	18	19	20	21	22
23	24	25	26	27	28	29
30	31					

JANUARY

M	T	W	T	F	S	S
	1	2	3	4	5
6	7	8	9	10	11	12
13	14	15	16	17	18	19
20	21	22	23	24	25	26
27	28	29	30	31		

FEBRUARY

M	T	W	T	F	S	S
					1	2
3	4	5	6	7	8	9
10	11	12	13	14	15	16
17	18	19	20	21	22	23
24	25	26	27	28		

Small Cap Sector Russell 2000 Performance

After underperforming the S&P 500 in the summer of 2011, the small cap sector was settling into market performance as it entered its seasonal trade mid-December. The small cap sector managed to outperform the S&P 500 in the last half of January and the first half of February and then it resumed its underperformance once again.

Technical Conditions

Entry Date December 19th, 2011 –Mildly Bullish– On the seasonal entry date, the small cap sector had just fallen below its 50 day moving average❶ and the FSO had just turned down to its mid-level❷ and the RSI was at its mid-level❸. The small cap sector was performing at market❹.

Entry Strategy –Buy Partial Position Early– The FSO crossed back over 20 in late November at the same time as the RSI headed back up and crossed over 50. The action with the FSO justified an early entry into the small cap sector.

Exit Strategy –Sell Partial Position Early– When the small cap sector started to trade sideways in February❺, the FSO crossed below 80❻ and the RSI crossed below 70❼, justifying a partial early exit. Shortly afterwards, the small cap sector started to underperform the S&P 500❽. There was not a strong reason to stay in the trade after the end of the seasonal period.

** Weekly avg closing values- except Fed Funds & CAN overnight tgt rate weekly closing values.

DO THE "NAZ" WITH SANTA
Nasdaq gives more at Christmas – Dec 15th to Jan 23rd

One of the best times to invest in the major markets is Christmas time. What few investors know is that this seasonally strong time favors the Nasdaq market.

From December 15th to January 23rd, starting in 1972 and ending in 2012, the Nasdaq has outperformed the S&P 500 by an average 2.2% per year.

This rate of return is considered to be very high given that the length of favorable time is just over one month.

> ### *2.2% extra & 83% of time better than S&P 500*

Looking for reasons that the Nasdaq outperforms? Interestingly, the Nasdaq starts to outperform at the same time as small companies in December (see *Small Company Effect* strategy).

As investors move into the market to scoop up bargains that have been sold for tax losses, smaller companies and stocks with greater volatility tend to outperform.

Compared with the S&P 500 and Dow Jones, the Nasdaq market tends to be a much greater recipient of the upward move created by investors picking up cheap stocks at this time of the year.

Nasdaq vs. S&P 500 Dec 15th to Jan 23rd 1971/72 To 2010/11

Dec 15 to Jan 23	S&P 500	Positive Nasdaq	Diff
1971/72	6.1 %	7.5 %	1.3 %
1972/73	0.0	-0.7	-0.7
1973/74	4.1	6.8	2.8
1974/75	7.5	8.9	1.4
1975/76	13.0	13.8	0.9
1976/77	-1.7	2.8	4.5
1977/78	-5.1	-3.5	1.6
1978/79	4.7	6.2	1.4
1979/80	4.1	5.6	1.5
1980/81	0.8	3.3	2.5
1981/82	-6.0	-5.0	1.0
1982/83	4.7	5.5	0.8
1983/84	0.9	1.4	0.4
1984/85	9.0	13.3	4.3
1985/86	-2.7	0.8	3.5
1986/87	9.2	10.2	1.0
1987/88	1.8	9.1	7.3
1988/89	3.3	4.6	1.3
1989/90	-5.5	-3.8	1.7
1990/91	1.0	4.1	3.1
1991/92	7.9	15.2	7.2
1992/93	0.8	7.2	6.4
1993/94	2.5	5.7	3.2
1994/95	2.4	4.7	2.3
1995/96	-0.7	-1.0	-0.3
1996/97	6.7	7.3	0.6
1997/98	0.4	2.6	2.1
1998/99	7.4	18.9	11.6
1999/00	2.7	18.6	15.9
2000/01	1.5	4.1	2.6
2001/02	0.5	-1.6	-2.0
2002/03	-0.2	1.9	2.1
2003/04	6.3	9.0	2.7
2004/05	-3.0	-5.8	-2.9
2005/06	-0.7	-0.6	0.1
2006/07	0.2	-0.9	-1.1
2007/08	-8.8	-12.1	-3.3
2008/09	-5.4	-4.1	1.3
2009/10	-2.0	-0.3	1.7
2010/11	3.4	2.4	-1.0
2011/12	8.6	9.6	1.1
Avg	1.9 %	4.2 %	2.2 %
Fq > 0	68 %	71 %	83 %

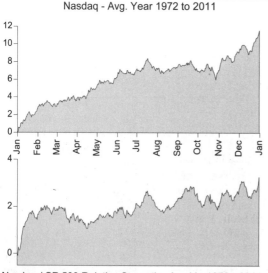

Nasdaq - Avg. Year 1972 to 2011

Nasdaq / SP 500 Relative Strength - Avg Yr. 1972 - 2011

> **(Y)** *Alternate Strategy — For those investors who favor the Nasdaq, an alternative strategy is to invest in the Nasdaq at an earlier date: October 28th. Historically, on average the Nasdaq has started its outperformance at this time. The "Do the Naz with Santa" strategy focuses on the sweet spot of the Nasdaq's outperformance.*

> **(i)** *Nasdaq is a market with a number of sectors. It is more focused on technology and is typically more volatile than the S&P 500.*

2011-12 Strategy Performance

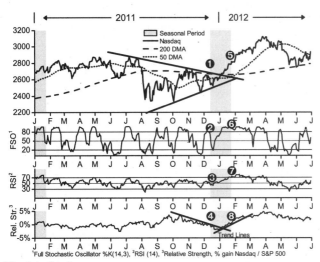

¹Full Stochastic Oscillator %K(14,3), ²RSI (14), ³Relative Strength, % gain Nasdaq / S&P 500

Stock Markets	2010	2011
Dow	11,536	12,088
S&P500	1,254	1,242
Nasdaq	2,664	2,585
TSX	13,339	11,763
FTSE	5,966	5,429
DAX	7,056	5,808
Nikkei	10,303	8,372
Hang Seng	22,883	18,315

Commodities	2010	2011
Oil	89.68	97.75
Gold	1380.9	1606.5

Bond Yields	2010	2011
USA 5 Yr Treasury	2.02	0.90
USA 10 Yr T	3.37	1.95
USA 20 Yr T	4.23	2.63
Moody's Aaa	5.01	3.88
Moody's Baa	6.10	5.24
CAN 5 Yr T	2.42	1.25
CAN 10 Yr T	3.17	1.94

Money Market	2010	2011
USA Fed Funds	0.25	0.25
USA 3 Mo T-B	0.14	0.01
CAN tgt overnight rate	1.00	1.00
CAN 3 Mo T-B	0.98	0.82

Foreign Exchange	2010	2011
USD/EUR	1.31	1.30
USD/GBP	1.54	1.56
CAN/USD	1.01	1.03
JPY/USD	83.38	78.05

Nasdaq Performance

The Nasdaq underperformed the S&P 500 starting in October 2011, forming a consolidation pattern. At the start of its seasonal period, the Nasdaq was poised to perform well, but it retraced its steps for a few weeks and then broke out of its consolidation pattern and started to strongly outperform the S&P 500. It maintained its strong performance well past the end of its seasonal period.

Technical Conditions

Entry Date December 15th, 2011 – <u>Mildly Bullish</u>– At the start of its seasonal period, the Nasdaq had just traded above its 50 day moving average and was up against its 200 day moving average and the top of its consolidating pattern❶. FSO had just turned below 80❷ and the RSI was just below 50❸. The Nasdaq was still underperforming the S&P 500, which was a concern❹. The situation changed very fast as the Nasdaq started to outperform the S&P 500 a short time later (beginning of January), the FSO and RSI rose sharply and a price-action breakout occurred as the Nasdaq broke out of its consolidating pattern. The situation became very bullish, very fast.

Entry Strategy – <u>Buy Partial Position Early</u>– A partial entry trade would have been indicated early when the FSO turned above 20 in late November. Ironically, it would have been better to stay in the S&P 500 and enter the Nasdaq a few weeks later.

Exit Strategy – <u>Sell Position Late</u>– At the end of the seasonal period, the Nasdaq continued to perform well. It was overbought but showed no signs of turning down❺. The FSO remained above 80❻ and the RSI remained above 70❼. In addition it continued to outperform the S&P 500❽. A sell signal was not triggered until late February, well past the end of the seasonal period for the Nasdaq.

** Weekly avg closing values- except Fed Funds & CAN overnight tgt rate weekly closing values.

DECEMBER
M	T	W	T	F	S	S
						1
2	3	4	5	6	7	8
9	10	11	12	13	14	15
16	17	18	19	20	21	22
23	24	25	26	27	28	29
30	31					

JANUARY
M	T	W	T	F	S	S
	1	2	3	4	5	
6	7	8	9	10	11	12
13	14	15	16	17	18	19
20	21	22	23	24	25	26
27	28	29	30	31		

FEBRUARY
M	T	W	T	F	S	S
					1	2
3	4	5	6	7	8	9
10	11	12	13	14	15	16
17	18	19	20	21	22	23
24	25	26	27	28		

January has the reputation of being a strong month. Since 1950, the S&P 500 has produced an average gain of 1.1% and been positive 62% of the time. One of the weaker sectors in the market in the month of January has been the consumer staples. From 1990 to 2011 the sector has produced an average monthly loss of 1.6% and has been negative 61% of the time.

-1.7% & negative 70% of the time

The worst performance for the sector is focused on the time period from January 1st to January 22nd. In this time period, the consumer staples sector has produced an average loss of 1.7% and has been negative 70% of the time.

Con. Staples vs. S&P 500 1990 to 2012

Jan 1 to Jan 22	S&P 500	Negative Staples	Diff
1990	-6.5 %	-8.3 %	-1.8 %
1991	-0.6	-1.1	-0.5
1992	0.3	-3.2	-3.4
1993	0.1	-3.5	-3.6
1994	1.8	-0.6	-2.4
1995	1.2	-1.1	-2.3
1996	-0.4	1.4	1.8
1997	6.1	6.2	0.0
1998	-0.8	-0.9	-0.1
1999	-0.3	-6.8	-6.4
2000	-1.9	-2.0	-0.1
2001	1.7	-8.4	-10.1
2002	-2.5	0.5	3.0
2003	-0.2	1.0	1.1
2004	2.9	-1.0	-3.9
2005	-3.6	0.4	4.1
2006	1.1	-0.8	-1.8
2007	0.3	1.7	1.4
2008	-10.8	-6.7	4.1
2009	-8.4	-4.9	3.5
2010	-2.1	-1.1	1.0
2011	2.0	0.2	-1.9
2012	4.6	-0.4	-5.0
Avg.	-0.7 %	-1.7 %	-1.0 %
Fq >0	48 %	30 %	39 %

Consumer Staples Sector - Avg. Year 1990 to 2011

Staples / S&P 500 Relative Strength - Avg Yr. 1990 - 2011

The Consumer Staples vs. S&P 500 table illustrates the relationship between the two sectors. In general, when the S&P 500 is positive or slightly negative, the consumer staples sector tends to underperform. On the other hand, when the S&P 500 suffers large losses the consumer staples sector tends to outperform the S&P 500.

The direction of the US dollar has an impact on the performance of the consumer staples sector. When the US dollar is rising, the sector tends to fall and when the dollar is falling, the sector tends to increase.

The reason that this relationship exists is that consumer staples companies receive a higher percentage of their revenues from offshore companies compared with the S&P 500.

This means that if the US dollar is falling, then consumer staples companies will benefit from increased revenues because of the lower exchange rate and vice versa. This relationship is important because the US dollar tends to rise in January and therefore put downward pressure on the consumer staples sector.

> (i) *The SP GICS Consumer Staples Sector encompasses a wide range consumer staples based companies.*
> *For more information on the information technology sector, see www.standardandpoors.com*

2010-11-12 Strategy Performance

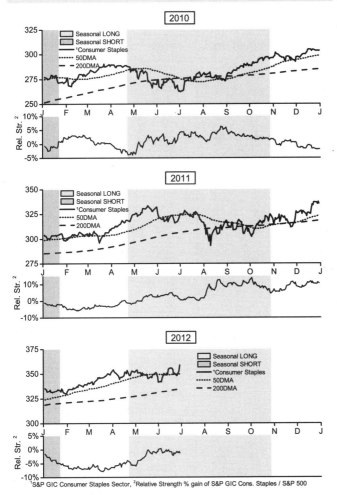

¹S&P GIC Consumer Staples Sector, ²Relative Strength % gain of S&P GIC Cons. Staples / S&P 500

Market Indices & Rates
Weekly Values**

Stock Markets	2010	2011
Dow	11,573	12,237
S&P500	1,258	1,259
Nasdaq	2,663	2,609
TSX	13,442	11,842
FTSE	5,956	5,549
DAX	6,963	5,852
Nikkei	10,306	8,440
Hang Seng	22,906	18,450

Commodities	2010	2011
Oil	90.97	99.80
Gold	1409.0	1551.0

Bond Yields	2010	2011
USA 5 Yr Treasury	2.07	0.90
USA 10 Yr T	3.38	1.94
USA 20 Yr T	4.21	2.62
Moody's Aaa	4.98	3.83
Moody's Baa	6.07	5.21
CAN 5 Yr T	2.45	1.29
CAN 10 Yr T	3.15	1.97

Money Market	2010	2011
USA Fed Funds	0.25	0.25
USA 3 Mo T-B	0.14	0.02
CAN tgt overnight rate	1.00	1.00
CAN 3 Mo T-B	0.97	0.82

Foreign Exchange	2010	2011
USD/EUR	1.32	1.30
USD/GBP	1.55	1.55
CAN/USD	1.00	1.02
JPY/USD	81.89	77.67

DECEMBER

M	T	W	T	F	S	S
						1
2	3	4	5	6	7	8
9	10	11	12	13	14	15
16	17	18	19	20	21	22
23	24	25	26	27	28	29
30	31					

JANUARY

M	T	W	T	F	S	S
		1	2	3	4	5
6	7	8	9	10	11	12
13	14	15	16	17	18	19
20	21	22	23	24	25	26
27	28	29	30	31		

FEBRUARY

M	T	W	T	F	S	S
					1	2
3	4	5	6	7	8	9
10	11	12	13	14	15	16
17	18	19	20	21	22	23
24	25	26	27	28		

Consumer Staples SHORT Performance– 2011-2012

Once again the consumer staples sector underperformed the S&P 500 and produced a loss in its seasonal short period in January. This trade was particularly successful in 2012 because the S&P 500 produced a gain of 4.6% at the time. In other words, shorting the consumer staples sector managed to provide positive returns even when the market was strongly moving up.

** Weekly avg closing values- except Fed Funds & CAN overnight tgt rate weekly closing values.

FINANCIALS (U.S.) YEAR END CLEAN UP
Outperform January 19th to April 13th

The U.S. financial sector often starts its strong performance in October and then steps up its performance in mid-December and then really outperforms starting in mid-January.

Extra 2.7% &
17 out of 23 times better than the S&P 500

If fundamental and technical indicators are favorable, then a justification to enter the market early can exist, otherwise a mid-January date represents the start of the seasonal sweet spot.

Financials Sector vs. S&P 500
1990 to 2012

Jan 19 to Apr 13	S&P 500	Positive Financials	Diff
1990	1.8 %	-4.3 %	-6.1 %
1991	14.5	27.7	13.2
1992	-3.1	-2.8	0.2
1993	2.8	11.3	8.5
1994	-5.9	-2.7	3.2
1995	8.4	10.4	1.9
1996	4.7	5.6	1.0
1997	-5.0	-2.6	2.4
1998	15.4	22.3	6.9
1999	8.6	13.2	4.6
1900	-1.0	5.9	6.9
2001	-12.2	-6.3	5.9
2002	-1.5	2.6	4.1
2003	-3.7	-5.2	-1.5
2004	-0.9	0.6	1.5
2005	-1.9	-6.2	-4.4
2006	0.9	1.1	0.2
2007	1.9	-3.1	-5.0
2008	0.6	-1.4	-2.0
2009	1.0	15.4	14.4
2010	5.4	11.2	5.8
2011	1.5	-2.1	-3.6
2012	4.8	8.3	3.6
Avg.	1.6 %	4.3 %	2.7 %
Fq > 0	61 %	57 %	74 %

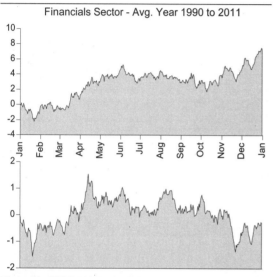

Financials Sector - Avg. Year 1990 to 2011

Financials / S&P 500 Relative Strength - Avg Yr. 1990-2011

In the 1990s and early 2000s, financial stocks benefited from the tailwind of falling interest rates. During this period, with a few exceptions, this sector has participated in both the rallies and the declines.

The real sweet spot on average each year, from 1989/90 to 2011/12, has been from mid-January to mid-April.

The main driver for the strong seasonal performance of the financial sector has been the year-end earnings of the banks that start to report in mid-January. A strong performance from mid-January has been the result of investors getting into the market early to take advantage of positive year-end earnings.

Interest rates are at historic lows and although they may move lower over the next few years, it is not pos-

sible for them to have the same decline that they have had since the 1980s. The Federal Reserve, through its quantitative easing policies is pushing down the rates on the long part of the yield curve and as a result flattening the curve and making difficult for banks to increase profits.

Given this situation, investors should concentrate their financial investments during the strong seasonal period.

It should be noted that Canadian banks have their year-ends at the end of October (reporting in November) and as such, their seasonally strong period starts in October.

(i) *Financial SP GIC Sector # 40:*
An index that contains companies involved in activities such as banking, mortgage finance, consumer finance, specialized finance, investment banking and brokerage, asset management and custody, corporate lending, insurance, financial investment, and real estate, including REITs.

2011-12 Strategy Performance

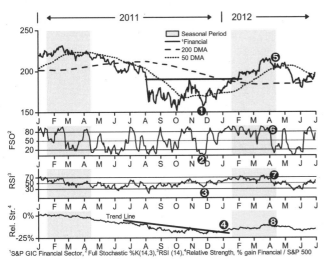

¹S&P GIC Financial Sector, ²Full Stochastic %K(14,3),³RSI (14),⁴Relative Strength, % gain Financial / S&P 500

Financial Sector Performance

Right from the start of 2011, the financial sector underperformed the S&P 500 until late December when it showed signs of starting to outperform. Many investors consider the financial sector a barometer of the stock market. If the financial sector is one of the top performing sectors, this is considered to be very healthy and the stock market has a higher likelihood of advancing. This proved to be true in the first quarter of 2012.

Technical Conditions

Entry Date January 19th, 2012 –<u>Bullish</u>– The financial sector had been advancing from late November❶. The FSO turned up above its 20❷ level at the end of November, justifying a partial early entry. At the time the RSI had a neutral rating❸. Most importantly, the financial sector had started to outperform the S&P 500 at the end of December, supporting an early entry decision and indicating strength ahead for the financial sector❹. At the beginning of financial seasonal trade, in mid-January, the sector had completed a double bottom pattern. A break-out of a double bottom is considered to be very bullish. The financial sector completed its breakout immediately after the start of the seasonal period, when it also crossed above its 200 day moving average.

Entry Strategy –<u>Buy Partial Position Early</u>– Although the sweet spot for the financial trade starts in mid-January, on an absolute basis the financial sector often bottoms mid-December. An early entry into the sector was justified, given the strength of the supporting technical indicators.

Exit Strategy– <u>Sell Partial Position Early</u>– The FSO had a number of crossovers below 80❺ before the seasonal exit date for the trade, but still the sector kept outperforming. At the beginning of April the sector turned down with the FSO and RSI confirming an early sell signal❻❼. At the end of the trade the financial sector resumed its underperformance❽.

** Weekly avg closing values- except Fed Funds & CAN overnight tgt rate weekly closing values.

JANUARY

M	T	W	T	F	S	S
	1	2	3	4	5	
6	7	8	9	10	11	12
13	14	15	16	17	18	19
20	21	22	23	24	25	26
27	28	29	30	31		

FEBRUARY

M	T	W	T	F	S	S
					1	2
3	4	5	6	7	8	9
10	11	12	13	14	15	16
17	18	19	20	21	22	23
24	25	26	27	28		

MARCH

M	T	W	T	F	S	S
					1	2
3	4	5	6	7	8	9
10	11	12	13	14	15	16
17	18	19	20	21	22	23
24	25	26	27	28	29	30
31						

APRIL

M	T	W	T	F	S	S
1	1	2	3	4	5	6
7	8	9	10	11	12	13
14	15	16	17	18	19	20
21	22	23	24	25	26	27
28	29	30				

MAY

M	T	W	T	F	S	S
			1	2	3	4
5	6	7	8	9	10	11
12	13	14	15	16	17	18
19	20	21	22	23	24	25
26	27	28	29	30	31	

JUNE

M	T	W	T	F	S	S
						1
2	3	4	5	6	7	8
9	10	11	12	13	14	15
16	17	18	19	20	21	22
23	24	25	26	27	28	29
30						

APPENDIX

STOCK MARKET RETURNS

S&P 500
PERCENT CHANGES

	JAN	FEB	MAR	APR	MAY	JUN
1950	1.7 %	1.0 %	0.4 %	4.5 %	3.9 %	− 5.8 %
1951	6.1	0.6	− 1.8	4.8	− 4.1	− 2.6
1952	1.6	− 3.6	4.8	− 4.3	2.3	4.6
1953	− 0.7	− 1.8	− 2.4	− 2.6	− 0.3	− 1.6
1954	5.1	0.3	3.0	4.9	3.3	0.1
1955	1.8	0.4	− 0.5	3.8	− 0.1	8.2
1956	− 3.6	3.5	6.9	− 0.2	− 6.6	3.9
1957	− 4.2	− 3.3	2.0	3.7	3.7	− 0.1
1958	4.3	2.1	3.1	3.2	1.5	2.6
1959	0.4	− 0.1	0.1	3.9	1.9	− 0.4
1960	− 7.1	0.9	− 1.4	− 1.8	2.7	2.0
1961	6.3	2.7	2.6	0.4	1.9	− 2.9
1962	− 3.8	1.6	− 0.6	− 6.2	− 8.6	− 8.2
1963	4.9	− 2.9	3.5	4.9	1.4	− 2.0
1964	2.7	1.0	1.5	0.6	1.1	1.6
1965	3.3	− 0.1	− 1.5	3.4	− 0.8	− 4.9
1966	0.5	− 1.8	− 2.2	2.1	− 5.4	− 1.6
1967	7.8	0.2	3.9	4.2	− 5.2	1.8
1968	− 4.4	− 3.1	0.9	8.0	1.3	0.9
1969	− 0.8	− 4.7	3.4	2.1	− 0.2	− 5.6
1970	− 7.6	5.3	0.1	− 9.0	− 6.1	− 5.0
1971	4.0	0.9	3.7	3.6	− 4.2	− 0.9
1972	1.8	2.5	0.6	0.4	1.7	− 2.2
1973	− 1.7	− 3.7	− 0.1	− 4.1	− 1.9	− 0.7
1974	− 1.0	− 0.4	− 2.3	− 3.9	− 3.4	− 1.5
1975	12.3	6.0	2.2	4.7	4.4	4.4
1976	11.8	− 1.1	3.1	− 1.1	− 1.4	4.1
1977	− 5.1	− 2.2	− 1.4	0.0	− 2.4	4.5
1978	− 6.2	− 2.5	2.5	8.5	0.4	− 1.8
1979	4.0	− 3.7	5.5	0.2	− 2.6	3.9
1980	5.8	− 0.4	− 10.2	4.1	4.7	2.7
1981	− 4.6	1.3	3.6	− 2.3	− 0.2	− 1.0
1982	− 1.8	− 6.1	− 1.0	4.0	− 3.9	− 2.0
1983	3.3	1.9	3.3	7.5	− 1.2	3.2
1984	− 0.9	− 3.9	1.3	0.5	− 5.9	1.7
1985	7.4	0.9	− 0.3	− 0.5	5.4	1.2
1986	0.2	7.1	5.3	− 1.4	5.0	1.4
1987	13.2	3.7	2.6	− 1.1	0.6	4.8
1988	4.0	4.2	− 3.3	0.9	0.3	4.3
1989	7.1	− 2.9	2.1	5.0	3.5	− 0.8
1990	− 6.9	0.9	2.4	− 2.7	9.2	− 0.9
1991	4.2	6.7	2.2	0.0	3.9	− 4.8
1992	− 2.0	1.0	− 2.2	2.8	0.1	− 1.7
1993	0.7	1.0	1.9	− 2.5	2.3	0.1
1994	3.3	− 3.0	− 4.6	1.2	1.2	− 2.7
1995	2.4	3.6	2.7	2.8	3.6	2.1
1996	3.3	0.7	0.8	1.3	2.3	0.2
1997	6.1	0.6	− 4.3	5.8	5.9	4.3
1998	1.0	7.0	5.0	0.9	− 1.9	3.9
1999	4.1	− 3.2	3.9	3.8	− 2.5	5.4
2000	− 5.1	− 2.0	9.7	− 3.1	− 2.2	2.4
2001	3.5	− 9.2	− 6.4	7.7	0.5	− 2.5
2002	− 1.6	− 2.1	3.7	− 6.1	− 0.9	− 7.2
2003	− 2.7	− 1.7	0.8	8.1	5.1	1.1
2004	1.7	1.2	− 1.6	− 1.7	1.2	1.8
2005	− 2.5	1.9	− 1.9	− 2.0	3.0	0.0
2006	2.5	0.0	1.1	1.2	− 3.1	0.0
2007	1.4	− 2.2	1.0	4.3	3.3	− 1.8
2008	− 6.1	− 3.5	− 0.6	4.8	1.1	− 8.6
2009	− 8.6	− 11.0	8.5	9.4	5.3	0.0
2010	− 3.7	2.9	5.9	1.5	− 8.2	− 5.4
2011	2.3	3.2	− 0.1	2.8	− 1.4	− 1.8
FQ POS*	38 / 62	33 / 62	40 / 62	43 / 62	35 / 62	31 / 62
% FQ POS*	61 %	53 %	65 %	69 %	56 %	50 %
AVG GAIN*	1.1 %	-0.2 %	1.1 %	1.5 %	0.2 %	− 0.1 %
RANK GAIN*	5	11	4	2	8	10

S&P 500 PERCENT CHANGES — STOCK MKT

JUL	AUG	SEP	OCT	NOV	DEC	YEAR	
0.8 %	3.3 %	5.6 %	0.4 %	— 0.1 %	4.6 %	**1950**	21.8 %
6.9	3.9	— 0.1	— 1.4	— 0.3	3.9	**1951**	16.5
1.8	— 1.5	— 2.0	— 0.1	4.6	3.5	**1952**	11.8
2.5	— 5.8	0.1	5.1	0.9	0.2	**1953**	— 6.6
5.7	— 3.4	8.3	— 1.9	8.1	5.1	**1954**	45.0
6.1	— 0.8	1.1	— 3.0	7.5	— 0.1	**1955**	26.4
5.2	— 3.8	— 4.5	0.5	— 1.1	3.5	**1956**	2.6
1.1	— 5.6	— 6.2	— 3.2	1.6	— 4.1	**1957**	— 14.3
4.3	1.2	4.8	2.5	2.2	5.2	**1958**	38.1
3.5	— 1.5	— 4.6	1.1	1.3	2.8	**1959**	8.5
— 2.5	2.6	— 6.0	— 0.2	4.0	4.6	**1960**	— 3.0
3.3	2.0	— 2.0	2.8	3.9	0.3	**1961**	23.1
6.4	1.5	— 4.8	0.4	10.2	1.3	**1962**	— 11.8
— 0.3	4.9	— 1.1	3.2	— 1.1	2.4	**1963**	18.9
1.8	— 1.6	2.9	0.8	— 0.5	0.4	**1964**	13.0
1.3	2.3	3.2	2.7	— 0.9	0.9	**1965**	9.1
— 1.3	— 7.8	— 0.7	4.8	0.3	— 0.1	**1966**	— 13.1
4.5	— 1.2	3.3	— 3.5	0.8	2.6	**1967**	20.1
— 1.8	1.1	3.9	0.7	4.8	— 4.2	**1968**	7.7
— 6.0	4.0	— 2.5	4.3	— 3.4	— 1.9	**1969**	— 11.4
7.3	4.4	3.4	— 1.2	4.7	5.7	**1970**	0.1
— 3.2	3.6	— 0.7	— 4.2	— 0.3	8.6	**1971**	10.8
0.2	3.4	— 0.5	0.9	4.6	1.2	**1972**	15.6
3.8	— 3.7	4.0	— 0.1	— 11.4	1.7	**1973**	— 17.4
— 7.8	— 9.0	— 11.9	16.3	— 5.3	— 2.0	**1974**	— 29.7
— 6.8	— 2.1	— 3.5	6.2	2.5	— 1.2	**1975**	31.5
— 0.8	— 0.5	2.3	— 2.2	— 0.8	5.2	**1976**	19.1
— 1.6	— 2.1	— 0.2	— 4.3	2.7	0.3	**1977**	— 11.5
5.4	2.6	— 0.7	— 9.2	1.7	1.5	**1978**	1.1
0.9	5.3	0.0	— 6.9	4.3	1.7	**1979**	12.3
6.5	0.6	2.5	1.6	10.2	— 3.4	**1980**	25.8
— 0.2	— 6.2	— 5.4	4.9	3.7	— 3.0	**1981**	— 9.7
— 2.3	11.6	0.8	11.0	3.6	1.5	**1982**	14.8
— 3.0	1.1	1.0	— 1.5	1.7	— 0.9	**1983**	17.3
— 1.6	10.6	— 0.3	0.0	— 1.5	2.2	**1984**	1.4
— 0.5	— 1.2	— 3.5	4.3	6.5	4.5	**1985**	26.3
— 5.9	7.1	— 8.5	5.5	2.1	— 2.8	**1986**	14.6
4.8	3.5	— 2.4	— 21.8	— 8.5	7.3	**1987**	2.0
— 0.5	— 3.9	4.0	2.6	— 1.9	1.5	**1988**	12.4
8.8	1.6	— 0.7	— 2.5	1.7	2.1	**1989**	27.3
— 0.5	— 9.4	— 5.1	— 0.7	6.0	2.5	**1990**	— 6.6
4.5	2.0	— 1.9	1.2	— 4.4	11.2	**1991**	26.3
3.9	— 2.4	0.9	0.2	3.0	1.0	**1992**	4.5
— 0.5	3.4	— 1.0	1.9	— 1.3	1.0	**1993**	7.1
3.1	3.8	— 2.7	2.1	— 4.0	1.2	**1994**	— 1.5
3.2	0.0	4.0	— 0.5	4.1	1.7	**1995**	34.1
— 4.6	1.9	5.4	2.6	7.3	— 2.2	**1996**	20.3
7.8	— 5.7	5.3	— 3.4	4.5	1.6	**1997**	31.0
— 1.2	— 14.6	6.2	8.0	5.9	5.6	**1998**	26.7
— 3.2	— 0.6	— 2.9	6.3	1.9	5.8	**1999**	19.5
— 1.6	6.1	— 5.3	— 0.5	— 8.0	0.4	**2000**	— 10.1
— 1.1	— 6.4	— 8.2	1.8	7.5	0.8	**2001**	— 13.0
— 7.9	0.5	— 11.0	8.6	5.7	— 6.0	**2002**	— 23.4
1.6	1.8	— 1.2	5.5	0.7	5.1	**2003**	26.4
-3.4	0.2	0.9	1.4	3.9	3.2	**2004**	9.0
3.6	— 1.1	0.7	— 1.8	3.5	— 0.1	**2005**	3.0
0.5	2.1	2.5	3.2	1.6	1.3	**2006**	13.6
— 3.2	1.3	3.6	1.5	— 4.4	— 0.9	**2007**	3.5
— 1.0	1.2	— 9.2	— 16.8	— 7.5	0.8	**2008**	-38.5
7.4	3.4	3.6	— 2.0	5.7	1.8	**2009**	23.5
6.9	— 4.7	8.8	3.7	— 0.2	6.5	**2010**	12.8
— 2.1	— 5.7	— 7.2	10.8	— 0.5	0.9	**2011**	0.0
33 / 62	34 / 62	27 / 62	37 / 62	40 / 62	48 / 62		45 / 62
53 %	55 %	44 %	60 %	65 %	77 %		73 %
1.0 %	0.0 %	— 0.6 %	0.8 %	1.5 %	1.7 %		8.6 %
6	9	12	7	3	1		

S&P 500 MONTH
CLOSING VALUES

	JAN	FEB	MAR	APR	MAY	JUN
1950	17	17	17	18	19	18
1951	22	22	21	22	22	21
1952	24	23	24	23	24	25
1953	26	26	25	25	25	24
1954	26	26	27	28	29	29
1955	37	37	37	38	38	41
1956	44	45	48	48	45	47
1957	45	43	44	46	47	47
1958	42	41	42	43	44	45
1959	55	55	55	58	59	58
1960	56	56	55	54	56	57
1961	62	63	65	65	67	65
1962	69	70	70	65	60	55
1963	66	64	67	70	71	69
1964	77	78	79	79	80	82
1965	88	87	86	89	88	84
1966	93	91	89	91	86	85
1967	87	87	90	94	89	91
1968	92	89	90	97	99	100
1969	103	98	102	104	103	98
1970	85	90	90	82	77	73
1971	96	97	100	104	100	99
1972	104	107	107	108	110	107
1973	116	112	112	107	105	104
1974	97	96	94	90	87	86
1975	77	82	83	87	91	95
1976	101	100	103	102	100	104
1977	102	100	98	98	96	100
1978	89	87	89	97	97	96
1979	100	96	102	102	99	103
1980	114	114	102	106	111	114
1981	130	131	136	133	133	131
1982	120	113	112	116	112	110
1983	145	148	153	164	162	168
1984	163	157	159	160	151	153
1985	180	181	181	180	190	192
1986	212	227	239	236	247	251
1987	274	284	292	288	290	304
1988	257	268	259	261	262	274
1989	297	289	295	310	321	318
1990	329	332	340	331	361	358
1991	344	367	375	375	390	371
1992	409	413	404	415	415	408
1993	439	443	452	440	450	451
1994	482	467	446	451	457	444
1995	470	487	501	515	533	545
1996	636	640	646	654	669	671
1997	786	791	757	801	848	885
1998	980	1049	1102	1112	1091	1134
1999	1280	1238	1286	1335	1302	1373
2000	1394	1366	1499	1452	1421	1455
2001	1366	1240	1160	1249	1256	1224
2002	1130	1107	1147	1077	1067	990
2003	856	841	848	917	964	975
2004	1131	1145	1126	1107	1121	1141
2005	1181	1204	1181	1157	1192	1191
2006	1280	1281	1295	1311	1270	1270
2007	1438	1407	1421	1482	1531	1503
2008	1379	1331	1323	1386	1400	1280
2009	826	735	798	873	919	919
2010	1074	1104	1169	1187	1089	1031
2011	1286	1327	1326	1364	1345	1321

S&P 500 MONTH CLOSING VALUES

JUL	AUG	SEP	OCT	NOV	DEC	
18	18	19	20	20	20	1950
22	23	23	23	23	24	1951
25	25	25	25	26	27	1952
25	23	23	25	25	25	1953
31	30	32	32	34	36	1954
44	43	44	42	46	45	1955
49	48	45	46	45	47	1956
48	45	42	41	42	40	1957
47	48	50	51	52	55	1958
61	60	57	58	58	60	1959
56	57	54	53	56	58	1960
67	68	67	69	71	72	1961
58	59	56	57	62	63	1962
69	73	72	74	73	75	1963
83	82	84	85	84	85	1964
85	87	90	92	92	92	1965
84	77	77	80	80	80	1966
95	94	97	93	94	96	1967
98	99	103	103	108	104	1968
92	96	93	97	94	92	1969
78	82	84	83	87	92	1970
96	99	98	94	94	102	1971
107	111	111	112	117	118	1972
108	104	108	108	96	98	1973
79	72	64	74	70	69	1974
89	87	84	89	91	90	1975
103	103	105	103	102	107	1976
99	97	97	92	95	95	1977
101	103	103	93	95	96	1978
104	109	109	102	106	108	1979
122	122	125	127	141	136	1980
131	123	116	122	126	123	1981
107	120	120	134	139	141	1982
163	164	166	164	166	165	1983
151	167	166	166	164	167	1984
191	189	182	190	202	211	1985
236	253	231	244	249	242	1986
319	330	322	252	230	247	1987
272	262	272	279	274	278	1988
346	351	349	340	346	353	1989
356	323	306	304	322	330	1990
388	395	388	392	375	417	1991
424	414	418	419	431	436	1992
448	464	459	468	462	466	1993
458	475	463	472	454	459	1994
562	562	584	582	605	616	1995
640	652	687	705	757	741	1996
954	899	947	915	955	970	1997
1121	957	1017	1099	1164	1229	1998
1329	1320	1283	1363	1389	1469	1999
1431	1518	1437	1429	1315	1320	2000
1211	1134	1041	1060	1139	1148	2001
912	916	815	886	936	880	2002
990	1008	996	1051	1058	1112	2003
1102	1104	1115	1130	1174	1212	2004
1234	1220	1229	1207	1249	1248	2005
1277	1304	1336	1378	1401	1418	2006
1455	1474	1527	1549	1481	1468	2007
1267	1283	1165	969	896	903	2008
987	1021	1057	1036	1096	1115	2009
1102	1049	1141	1183	1181	1258	2010
1292	1219	1131	1253	1247	1258	2011

DOW JONES PERCENT MONTH CHANGES

	JAN	FEB	MAR	APR	MAY	JUN
1950	0.8 %	0.8 %	1.3 %	4.0 %	4.2 %	− 6.4 %
1951	5.7	1.3	− 1.7	4.5	3.6	− 2.8
1952	0.6	− 3.9	3.6	− 4.4	2.1	4.3
1953	− 0.7	− 2.0	− 1.5	− 1.8	− 0.9	− 1.5
1954	4.1	0.7	3.1	5.2	2.6	1.8
1955	1.1	0.8	− 0.5	3.9	− 0.2	6.2
1956	− 3.6	2.8	5.8	0.8	− 7.4	3.1
1957	− 4.1	− 3.0	2.2	4.1	2.1	− 0.3
1958	3.3	− 2.2	1.6	2.0	1.5	3.3
1959	1.8	1.6	− 0.3	3.7	3.2	0.0
1960	− 8.4	1.2	− 2.1	− 2.4	4.0	2.4
1961	5.2	2.1	2.2	0.3	2.7	− 1.8
1962	− 4.3	1.2	− 0.2	− 5.9	− 7.8	− 8.5
1963	4.7	− 2.9	3.0	5.2	1.3	− 2.8
1964	2.9	1.9	1.6	− 0.3	1.2	1.3
1965	3.3	0.1	− 1.6	3.7	− 0.5	− 5.4
1966	1.5	− 3.2	− 2.8	1.0	− 5.3	− 1.6
1967	8.2	− 1.2	3.2	3.6	− 5.0	0.9
1968	− 5.5	− 1.8	0.0	8.5	− 1.4	− 0.1
1969	0.2	− 4.3	3.3	1.6	− 1.3	− 6.9
1970	− 7.0	4.5	1.0	− 6.3	− 4.8	− 2.4
1971	3.5	1.2	2.9	4.1	− 3.6	− 1.8
1972	1.3	2.9	1.4	1.4	0.7	− 3.3
1973	− 2.1	− 4.4	− 0.4	− 3.1	− 2.2	− 1.1
1974	0.6	0.6	− 1.6	− 1.2	− 4.1	0.0
1975	14.2	5.0	3.9	6.9	1.3	5.6
1976	14.4	− 0.3	2.8	− 0.3	− 2.2	2.8
1977	− 5.0	− 1.9	− 1.8	0.8	− 3.0	2.0
1978	− 7.4	− 3.6	2.1	10.5	0.4	− 2.6
1979	4.2	− 3.6	6.6	− 0.8	− 3.8	2.4
1980	4.4	− 1.5	− 9.0	4.0	4.1	2.0
1981	− 1.7	2.9	3.0	− 0.6	− 0.6	− 1.5
1982	− 0.4	− 5.4	− 0.2	3.1	− 3.4	− 0.9
1983	2.8	3.4	1.6	8.5	− 2.1	1.8
1984	− 3.0	− 5.4	0.9	0.5	− 5.6	2.5
1985	6.2	− 0.2	− 1.3	− 0.7	4.6	1.5
1986	1.6	8.8	6.4	− 1.9	5.2	0.9
1987	13.8	3.1	3.6	− 0.8	0.2	5.5
1988	1.0	5.8	− 4.0	2.2	− 0.1	5.4
1989	8.0	− 3.6	1.6	5.5	2.5	− 1.6
1990	− 5.9	1.4	3.0	− 1.9	8.3	0.1
1991	3.9	5.3	1.1	− 0.9	4.8	− 4.0
1992	1.7	1.4	− 1.0	3.8	1.1	− 2.3
1993	0.3	1.8	1.9	− 0.2	2.9	− 0.3
1994	6.0	− 3.7	− 5.1	1.3	2.1	− 3.5
1995	0.2	4.3	3.7	3.9	3.3	2.0
1996	5.4	1.7	1.9	− 0.3	1.3	0.2
1997	5.7	0.9	− 4.3	6.5	4.6	4.7
1998	0.0	8.1	3.0	3.0	− 1.8	0.6
1999	1.9	− 0.6	5.2	10.2	− 2.1	3.9
2000	− 4.5	− 7.4	7.8	− 1.7	− 2.0	− 0.7
2001	0.9	− 3.6	− 5.9	8.7	1.6	− 3.8
2002	− 1.0	1.9	2.9	− 4.4	− 0.2	− 6.9
2003	− 3.5	− 2.0	1.3	6.1	4.4	1.5
2004	0.3	0.9	− 2.1	− 1.3	− 0.4	2.4
2005	− 2.7	2.6	− 2.4	− 3.0	2.7	− 1.8
2006	1.4	1.2	1.1	2.3	− 1.7	− 0.2
2007	1.3	− 2.8	0.7	5.7	4.3	− 1.6
2008	− 4.6	− 3.0	0.0	4.5	− 1.4	− 10.2
2009	− 8.8	− 11.7	7.7	7.3	4.1	− 0.6
2010	− 3.5	2.6	5.1	1.4	− 7.9	− 3.6
2011	2.7	2.8	0.8	4.0	− 1.9	− 1.2
FQ POS	40 / 62	35 / 62	40 / 62	40 / 62	31 / 62	28 / 62
% FQ POS	65 %	56 %	65 %	65 %	50 %	45 %
AVG GAIN	1.0 %	0.0 %	1.1 %	2.0 %	0.0 %	− 0.4 %
RANK GAIN	6	9	5	1	8	11

DOW JONES PERCENT MONTH CHANGES — STOCK MKT

JUL	AUG	SEP	OCT	NOV	DEC	YEAR	YEAR
0.1 %	3.6 %	4.4 %	− 0.6 %	1.2 %	3.4 %	1950	17.6 %
6.3	4.8	0.3	− 3.2	− 0.4	3.0	1951	14.4
1.9	− 1.6	− 1.6	− 0.5	5.4	2.9	1952	8.4
2.6	− 5.2	1.1	4.5	2.0	− 0.2	1953	− 3.8
4.3	− 3.5	7.4	− 2.3	9.9	4.6	1954	44.0
3.2	0.5	− 0.3	− 2.5	6.2	1.1	1955	20.8
5.1	− 3.1	− 5.3	1.0	− 1.5	5.6	1956	2.3
1.0	− 4.7	− 5.8	− 3.4	2.0	− 3.2	1957	− 12.8
5.2	1.1	4.6	2.1	2.6	4.7	1958	34.0
4.9	− 1.6	− 4.9	2.4	1.9	3.1	1959	16.4
− 3.7	1.5	− 7.3	0.1	2.9	3.1	1960	− 9.3
3.1	2.1	− 2.6	0.4	2.5	1.3	1961	18.7
6.5	1.9	− 5.0	1.9	10.1	0.4	1962	− 10.8
− 1.6	4.9	0.5	3.1	− 0.6	1.7	1963	17.0
1.2	− 0.3	4.4	− 0.3	0.3	− 0.1	1964	14.6
1.6	1.3	4.2	3.2	− 1.5	2.4	1965	10.9
− 2.6	− 7.0	− 1.8	4.2	− 1.9	− 0.7	1966	− 18.9
5.1	− 0.3	2.8	− 5.1	− 0.4	3.3	1967	15.2
− 1.6	1.5	4.4	1.8	3.4	− 4.2	1968	4.3
− 6.6	2.6	− 2.8	5.3	− 5.1	− 1.5	1969	− 15.2
7.4	4.2	− 0.5	− 0.7	5.1	5.6	1970	4.8
− 3.7	4.6	− 1.2	− 5.4	− 0.9	7.1	1971	6.1
− 0.5	4.2	− 1.1	0.2	6.6	0.2	1972	14.6
3.9	− 4.2	6.7	1.0	− 14.0	3.5	1973	− 16.6
− 5.6	− 10.4	− 10.4	9.5	− 7.0	− 0.4	1974	− 27.6
− 5.4	0.5	− 5.0	5.3	3.0	− 1.0	1975	38.3
− 1.8	− 1.1	1.7	− 2.6	− 1.8	6.1	1976	17.9
− 2.9	− 3.2	− 1.7	− 3.4	1.4	0.2	1977	− 17.3
5.3	1.7	− 1.3	− 8.5	0.8	0.8	1978	− 3.2
0.5	4.9	− 1.0	− 7.2	0.8	2.0	1979	4.2
7.8	− 0.3	0.0	− 0.8	7.4	− 2.9	1980	14.9
− 2.5	− 7.4	− 3.6	0.3	4.3	− 1.6	1981	− 9.2
− 0.4	11.5	− 0.6	10.6	4.8	0.7	1982	19.6
− 1.9	1.4	1.4	− 0.6	4.1	− 1.4	1983	20.3
− 1.5	9.8	− 1.4	0.1	− 1.5	1.9	1984	− 3.7
0.9	− 1.0	− 0.4	3.4	7.1	5.1	1985	27.7
− 6.2	6.9	− 6.9	6.2	1.9	− 1.0	1986	22.6
6.4	3.5	− 2.5	− 23.2	− 8.0	5.7	1987	2.3
− 0.6	− 4.6	4.0	1.7	− 1.6	2.6	1988	11.9
9.0	2.9	− 1.6	− 1.8	2.3	1.7	1989	27.0
0.9	− 10.0	− 6.2	− 0.4	4.8	2.9	1990	− 4.3
4.1	0.6	− 0.9	1.7	− 5.7	9.5	1991	20.3
2.3	− 4.0	0.4	− 1.4	2.4	− 0.1	1992	4.2
0.7	3.2	− 2.6	3.5	0.1	1.9	1993	13.7
3.8	4.0	− 1.8	1.7	− 4.3	2.5	1994	2.1
3.3	− 2.1	3.9	− 0.7	6.7	0.8	1995	33.5
− 2.2	1.6	4.7	2.5	8.2	− 1.1	1996	26.0
7.2	− 7.3	4.2	− 6.3	5.1	1.1	1997	22.6
− 0.8	− 15.1	4.0	9.6	6.1	0.7	1998	16.1
− 2.9	1.6	− 4.5	3.8	1.4	5.3	1999	24.7
0.7	6.6	− 5.0	3.0	− 5.1	3.6	2000	− 5.8
0.2	− 5.4	− 11.1	2.6	8.6	1.7	2001	− 7.1
− 5.5	− 0.8	− 12.4	10.6	5.9	− 6.2	2002	− 16.8
2.8	2.0	− 1.5	5.7	− 0.2	6.9	2003	25.3
− 2.8	0.3	− 0.9	− 0.5	4.0	3.4	2004	3.1
3.6	− 1.5	0.8	− 1.2	3.5	− 0.8	2005	− 0.6
0.3	1.7	2.6	3.4	1.2	2.0	2006	16.3
− 1.5	1.1	4.0	0.2	− 4.0	− 0.8	2007	6.4
0.2	1.5	− 6.0	− 14.1	− 5.3	− 0.6	2008	− 33.8
8.6	3.5	2.3	0.0	6.5	0.8	2009	18.8
7.1	− 4.3	7.7	3.1	− 1.0	5.2	2010	11.0
− 2.2	− 4.4	− 6.0	9.5	0.8	1.4	2011	5.5
38 / 62	35 / 62	24 / 62	37 / 62	41 / 62	44 / 62		44 / 62
61 %	56 %	39 %	60 %	66 %	71 %		71 %
1.2 %	− 0.1 %	− 0.9 %	0.5 %	1.5 %	1.7 %		8.1 %
4	10	12	7	3	2		

DOW JONES
MONTH CLOSING VALUES

	JAN	FEB	MAR	APR	MAY	JUN
1950	202	203	206	214	223	209
1951	249	252	248	259	250	243
1952	271	260	270	258	263	274
1953	290	284	280	275	272	268
1954	292	295	304	319	328	334
1955	409	412	410	426	425	451
1956	471	484	512	516	478	493
1957	479	465	475	494	505	503
1958	450	440	447	456	463	478
1959	594	604	602	624	644	644
1960	623	630	617	602	626	641
1961	648	662	677	679	697	684
1962	700	708	707	665	613	561
1963	683	663	683	718	727	707
1964	785	800	813	811	821	832
1965	903	904	889	922	918	868
1966	984	952	925	934	884	870
1967	850	839	866	897	853	860
1968	856	841	841	912	899	898
1969	946	905	936	950	938	873
1970	744	778	786	736	700	684
1971	869	879	904	942	908	891
1972	902	928	941	954	961	929
1973	999	955	951	921	901	892
1974	856	861	847	837	802	802
1975	704	739	768	821	832	879
1976	975	973	1000	997	975	1003
1977	954	936	919	927	899	916
1978	770	742	757	837	841	819
1979	839	809	862	855	822	842
1980	876	863	786	817	851	868
1981	947	975	1004	998	992	977
1982	871	824	823	848	820	812
1983	1076	1113	1130	1226	1200	1222
1984	1221	1155	1165	1171	1105	1132
1985	1287	1284	1267	1258	1315	1336
1986	1571	1709	1819	1784	1877	1893
1987	2158	2224	2305	2286	2292	2419
1988	1958	2072	1988	2032	2031	2142
1989	2342	2258	2294	2419	2480	2440
1990	2591	2627	2707	2657	2877	2881
1991	2736	2882	2914	2888	3028	2907
1992	3223	3268	3236	3359	3397	3319
1993	3310	3371	3435	3428	3527	3516
1994	3978	3832	3636	3682	3758	3625
1995	3844	4011	4158	4321	4465	4556
1996	5395	5486	5587	5569	5643	5655
1997	6813	6878	6584	7009	7331	7673
1998	7907	8546	8800	9063	8900	8952
1999	9359	9307	9786	10789	10560	10971
2000	10941	10128	10922	10734	10522	10448
2001	10887	10495	9879	10735	10912	10502
2002	9920	10106	10404	9946	9925	9243
2003	8054	7891	7992	8480	8850	8985
2004	10488	10584	10358	10226	10188	10435
2005	10490	10766	10504	10193	10467	10275
2006	10865	10993	11109	11367	11168	11150
2007	12622	12269	12354	13063	13628	13409
2008	12650	12266	12263	12820	12638	11350
2009	8001	7063	7609	8168	8500	8447
2010	10067	10325	10857	11009	10137	9774
2011	11892	12226	12320	12811	12570	12414

DOW JONES
MONTH CLOSING VALUES
STOCK MKT

JUL	AUG	SEP	OCT	NOV	DEC	
209	217	226	225	228	235	1950
258	270	271	262	261	269	1951
280	275	271	269	284	292	1952
275	261	264	276	281	281	1953
348	336	361	352	387	404	1954
466	468	467	455	483	488	1955
518	502	475	480	473	500	1956
509	484	456	441	450	436	1957
503	509	532	543	558	584	1958
675	664	632	647	659	679	1959
617	626	580	580	597	616	1960
705	720	701	704	722	731	1961
598	609	579	590	649	652	1962
695	729	733	755	751	763	1963
841	839	875	873	875	874	1964
882	893	931	961	947	969	1965
847	788	774	807	792	786	1966
904	901	927	880	876	905	1967
883	896	936	952	985	944	1968
816	837	813	856	812	800	1969
734	765	761	756	794	839	1970
858	898	887	839	831	890	1971
925	964	953	956	1018	1020	1972
926	888	947	957	822	851	1973
757	679	608	666	619	616	1974
832	835	794	836	861	852	1975
985	974	990	965	947	1005	1976
890	862	847	818	830	831	1977
862	877	866	793	799	805	1978
846	888	879	816	822	839	1979
935	933	932	925	993	964	1980
952	882	850	853	889	875	1981
809	901	896	992	1039	1047	1982
1199	1216	1233	1225	1276	1259	1983
1115	1224	1207	1207	1189	1212	1984
1348	1334	1329	1374	1472	1547	1985
1775	1898	1768	1878	1914	1896	1986
2572	2663	2596	1994	1834	1939	1987
2129	2032	2113	2149	2115	2169	1988
2661	2737	2693	2645	2706	2753	1989
2905	2614	2453	2442	2560	2634	1990
3025	3044	3017	3069	2895	3169	1991
3394	3257	3272	3226	3305	3301	1992
3540	3651	3555	3681	3684	3754	1993
3765	3913	3843	3908	3739	3834	1994
4709	4611	4789	4756	5075	5117	1995
5529	5616	5882	6029	6522	6448	1996
8223	7622	7945	7442	7823	7908	1997
8883	7539	7843	8592	9117	9181	1998
10655	10829	10337	10730	10878	11453	1999
10522	11215	10651	10971	10415	10788	2000
10523	9950	8848	9075	9852	10022	2001
8737	8664	7592	8397	8896	8342	2002
9234	9416	9275	9801	9782	10454	2003
10140	10174	10080	10027	10428	10783	2004
10641	10482	10569	10440	10806	10718	2005
11186	11381	11679	12801	12222	12463	2006
13212	13358	13896	13930	13372	13265	2007
11378	11544	10851	9325	8829	8776	2008
9172	9496	9712	9713	10345	10428	2009
10466	10015	10788	11118	11006	11578	2010
12143	11614	10913	11955	12046	12218	2011

NASDAQ PERCENT MONTH CHANGES

	JAN	FEB	MAR	APR	MAY	JUN
1972	4.2	5.5	2.2	2.5	0.9	− 1.8
1973	− 4.0	− 6.2	− 2.4	− 8.2	− 4.8	− 1.6
1974	3.0	− 0.6	− 2.2	− 5.9	− 7.7	− 5.3
1975	16.6	4.6	3.6	3.8	5.8	4.7
1976	12.1	3.7	0.4	− 0.6	− 2.3	2.6
1977	− 2.4	− 1.0	− 0.5	1.4	0.1	4.3
1978	− 4.0	0.6	4.7	8.5	4.4	0.0
1979	6.6	− 2.6	7.5	1.6	− 1.8	5.1
1980	7.0	− 2.3	−17.1	6.9	7.5	4.9
1981	− 2.2	0.1	6.1	3.1	3.1	− 3.5
1982	− 3.8	− 4.8	− 2.1	5.2	− 3.3	− 4.1
1983	6.9	5.0	3.9	8.2	5.3	3.2
1984	− 3.7	− 5.9	− 0.7	− 1.3	− 5.9	2.9
1985	12.8	2.0	− 1.8	0.5	3.6	1.9
1986	3.4	7.1	4.2	2.3	4.4	1.3
1987	12.4	8.4	1.2	− 2.9	− 0.3	2.0
1988	4.3	6.5	2.1	1.2	− 2.3	6.6
1989	5.2	− 0.4	1.8	5.1	4.3	− 2.4
1990	− 8.6	2.4	2.3	− 3.5	9.3	0.7
1991	10.8	9.4	6.4	0.5	4.4	− 6.0
1992	5.8	2.1	− 4.7	− 4.2	1.1	− 3.7
1993	2.9	− 3.7	2.9	− 4.2	5.9	0.5
1994	3.0	− 1.0	− 6.2	− 1.3	0.2	− 4.0
1995	0.4	5.1	3.0	3.3	2.4	8.0
1996	0.7	3.8	0.1	8.1	4.4	− 4.7
1997	6.9	− 5.1	− 6.7	3.2	11.1	3.0
1998	3.1	9.3	3.7	1.8	− 4.8	6.5
1999	14.3	− 8.7	7.6	3.3	− 2.8	8.7
2000	− 3.2	19.2	− 2.6	− 15.6	− 11.9	16.6
2001	12.2	− 22.4	− 14.5	15.0	− 0.3	2.4
2002	− 0.8	− 10.5	6.6	− 8.5	− 4.3	− 9.4
2003	− 1.1	1.3	0.3	9.2	9.0	1.7
2004	3.1	− 1.8	− 1.8	− 3.7	3.5	3.1
2005	− 5.2	− 0.5	− 2.6	− 3.9	7.6	− 0.5
2006	4.6	− 1.1	2.6	− 0.7	− 6.2	− 0.3
2007	2.0	− 1.9	0.2	4.3	3.1	0.0
2008	− 9.9	− 5.0	0.3	5.9	4.6	− 9.1
2009	− 6.4	− 6.7	10.9	12.3	3.3	3.4
2010	− 5.4	4.2	7.1	2.6	− 8.3	− 6.5
2011	1.8	3.0	0.0	3.3	− 1.3	− 2.2
FQ POS	26/40	20/40	25/40	26/40	24/40	23/40
% FQ POS	65 %	50 %	63 %	65 %	60 %	58 %
AVG GAIN	2.6 %	0.3 %	0.6 %	1.5 %	1.0 %	0.7 %
RANK GAIN	1	9	8	4	5	6

JUL	AUG	SEP	OCT	NOV	DEC		YEAR
— 1.8	1.7	— 0.3	0.5	2.1	0.6	1972	17.2
7.6	— 3.5	6.0	— 0.9	— 15.1	— 1.4	1973	— 31.1
— 7.9	— 10.9	— 10.7	17.2	— 3.5	— 5.0	1974	— 35.1
— 4.4	— 5.0	— 5.9	3.6	2.4	— 1.5	1975	29.8
1.1	— 1.7	1.7	— 1.0	0.9	7.4	1976	26.1
0.9	— 0.5	0.7	— 3.3	5.8	1.8	1977	7.3
5.0	6.9	— 1.6	— 16.4	3.2	2.9	1978	12.3
2.3	6.4	— 0.3	— 9.6	6.4	4.8	1979	28.1
8.9	5.7	3.4	2.7	8.0	— 2.8	1980	33.9
— 1.9	— 7.5	— 8.0	8.4	3.1	— 2.7	1981	— 3.2
— 2.3	6.2	5.6	13.3	9.3	0.0	1982	18.7
— 4.6	— 3.8	1.4	— 7.4	4.1	— 2.5	1983	19.9
— 4.2	10.9	— 1.8	— 1.2	— 1.9	1.9	1984	— 11.3
1.7	— 1.2	— 5.8	4.4	7.4	3.5	1985	31.5
— 8.4	3.1	— 8.4	2.9	— 0.3	— 3.0	1986	7.4
2.4	4.6	— 2.4	— 27.2	— 5.6	8.3	1987	— 5.2
— 1.9	— 2.8	2.9	— 1.3	— 2.9	2.7	1988	15.4
4.2	3.4	0.8	— 3.7	0.1	— 0.3	1989	19.2
— 5.2	— 13.0	— 9.6	— 4.3	8.9	4.1	1990	— 17.8
5.5	4.7	0.2	3.1	— 3.5	11.9	1991	56.9
3.1	— 3.0	3.6	3.8	7.9	3.7	1992	15.5
0.1	5.4	2.7	2.2	— 3.2	3.0	1993	14.7
2.3	6.0	— 0.2	1.7	— 3.5	0.2	1994	— 3.2
7.3	1.9	2.3	— 0.7	2.2	— 0.7	1995	39.9
— 8.8	5.6	7.5	— 0.4	5.8	— 0.1	1996	22.7
10.5	— 0.4	6.2	— 5.5	0.4	— 1.9	1997	21.6
— 1.2	— 19.9	13.0	4.6	10.1	12.5	1998	39.6
— 1.8	3.8	0.2	8.0	12.5	22.0	1999	85.6
— 5.0	11.7	— 12.7	— 8.3	— 22.9	— 4.9	2000	— 39.3
— 6.2	— 10.9	— 17.0	12.8	14.2	1.0	2001	— 21.1
— 9.2	— 1.0	— 10.9	13.5	11.2	— 9.7	2002	— 31.5
6.9	4.3	— 1.3	8.1	1.5	2.2	2003	50.0
— 7.8	— 2.6	3.2	4.1	6.2	3.7	2004	8.6
6.2	— 1.5	0.0	— 1.5	5.3	— 1.2	2005	1.4
— 3.7	4.4	3.4	4.8	2.7	— 0.7	2006	9.5
— 2.2	2.0	4.0	5.8	— 6.9	— 0.3	2007	9.8
1.4	1.8	— 11.6	— 17.7	— 10.8	2.7	2008	— 40.5
7.8	1.5	5.6	— 3.6	4.9	5.8	2009	43.9
6.9	— 6.2	12.0	5.9	— 0.4	6.2	2010	16.9
— 0.6	— 6.4	— 6.4	11.1	— 2.4	— 0.6	2011	— 1.8
20/40	21/40	21/40	22/40	26/40	23/40		28/40
50 %	53 %	53 %	55 %	65 %	58 %		70 %
0.1 %	0.0 %	— 0.7 %	0.7 %	1.6 %	1.8 %		11.6 %
10	11	12	7	3	2		

NASDAQ MONTH CLOSING VALUES

	JAN	FEB	MAR	APR	MAY	JUN
1972	119	125	128	131	133	130
1973	128	120	117	108	103	101
1974	95	94	92	87	80	76
1975	70	73	76	79	83	87
1976	87	90	91	90	88	90
1977	96	95	94	95	96	100
1978	101	101	106	115	120	120
1979	126	123	132	134	131	138
1980	162	158	131	140	150	158
1981	198	198	210	217	223	216
1982	188	179	176	185	179	171
1983	248	261	271	293	309	319
1984	268	253	251	247	233	240
1985	279	284	279	281	291	296
1986	336	360	375	383	400	406
1987	392	425	430	418	417	425
1988	345	367	375	379	370	395
1989	401	400	407	428	446	435
1990	416	426	436	420	459	462
1991	414	453	482	485	506	476
1992	620	633	604	579	585	564
1993	696	671	690	661	701	704
1994	800	793	743	734	735	706
1995	755	794	817	844	865	933
1996	1060	1100	1101	1191	1243	1185
1997	1380	1309	1222	1261	1400	1442
1998	1619	1771	1836	1868	1779	1895
1999	2506	2288	2461	2543	2471	2686
2000	3940	4697	4573	3861	3401	3966
2001	2773	2152	1840	2116	2110	2161
2002	1934	1731	1845	1688	1616	1463
2003	1321	1338	1341	1464	1596	1623
2004	2066	2030	1994	1920	1987	2048
2005	2062	2052	1999	1922	2068	2057
2006	2306	2281	2340	2323	2179	2172
2007	2464	2416	2422	2525	2605	2603
2008	2390	2271	2279	2413	2523	2293
2009	1476	1378	1529	1717	1774	1835
2010	2147	2238	2398	2461	2257	2109
2011	2700	2782	2781	2874	2835	2774

NASDAQ MONTH CLOSING VALUES

JUL	AUG	SEP	OCT	NOV	DEC	
128	130	130	130	133	134	**1972**
109	105	111	110	94	92	**1973**
70	62	56	65	63	60	**1974**
83	79	74	77	79	78	**1975**
91	90	91	90	91	98	**1976**
101	100	101	98	103	105	**1977**
126	135	133	111	115	118	**1978**
141	150	150	136	144	151	**1979**
172	182	188	193	208	202	**1980**
212	196	180	195	201	196	**1981**
167	178	188	213	232	232	**1982**
304	292	297	275	286	279	**1983**
230	255	250	247	242	247	**1984**
301	298	280	293	314	325	**1985**
371	383	351	361	360	349	**1986**
435	455	444	323	305	331	**1987**
387	377	388	383	372	381	**1988**
454	469	473	456	456	455	**1989**
438	381	345	330	359	374	**1990**
502	526	527	543	524	586	**1991**
581	563	583	605	653	677	**1992**
705	743	763	779	754	777	**1993**
722	766	764	777	750	752	**1994**
1001	1020	1044	1036	1059	1052	**1995**
1081	1142	1227	1222	1293	1291	**1996**
1594	1587	1686	1594	1601	1570	**1997**
1872	1499	1694	1771	1950	2193	**1998**
2638	2739	2746	2966	3336	4069	**1999**
3767	4206	3673	3370	2598	2471	**2000**
2027	1805	1499	1690	1931	1950	**2001**
1328	1315	1172	1330	1479	1336	**2002**
1735	1810	1787	1932	1960	2003	**2003**
1887	1838	1897	1975	2097	2175	**2004**
2185	2152	2152	2120	2233	2205	**2005**
2091	2184	2258	2367	2432	2415	**2006**
2546	2596	2702	2859	2661	2652	**2007**
2326	2368	2092	1721	1536	1577	**2008**
1979	2009	2122	2045	2145	2269	**2009**
2255	2114	2369	2507	2498	2653	**2010**
2756	2579	2415	2684	2620	2605	**2011**

S&P/TSX MONTH PERCENT CHANGES

	JAN	FEB	MAR	APR	MAY	JUN
1985	8.1	0.0	0.7	0.8	3.8	— 0.8
1986	— 1.7	0.5	6.7	1.1	1.4	— 1.2
1987	9.2	4.5	6.9	— 0.6	— 0.9	1.5
1988	— 3.3	4.8	3.4	0.8	— 2.7	5.9
1989	6.7	— 1.2	0.2	1.4	2.2	1.5
1990	— 6.7	— 0.5	— 1.3	— 8.2	6.7	— 0.6
1991	0.5	5.8	1.0	-0.8	2.2	— 2.3
1992	2.4	— 0.4	— 4.7	— 1.7	1.0	0.0
1993	— 1.3	4.4	4.4	5.2	2.5	2.2
1994	5.4	— 2.9	— 2.1	— 1.4	1.4	— 7.0
1995	— 4.7	2.7	4.6	— -0.8	4.0	1.8
1996	5.4	— 0.7	0.8	3.5	1.9	— 3.9
1997	3.1	0.8	— 5.0	2.2	6.8	0.9
1998	0.0	5.9	6.6	1.4	— 1.0	— 2.9
1999	3.8	— 6.2	4.5	6.3	— 2.5	2.5
2000	0.8	7.6	3.7	— 1.2	— 1.0	10.2
2001	4.3	— 13.3	— 5.8	4.5	2.7	— 5.2
2002	— 0.5	— 0.1	2.8	— 2.4	— 0.1	— 6.7
2003	— 0.7	— 0.2	— 3.2	3.8	4.2	1.8
2004	3.7	3.1	— 2.3	— 4.0	2.1	1.5
2005	— 0.5	5.0	— 0.6	— 3.5	3.6	3.1
2006	6.0	— 2.2	3.6	0.8	— 3.8	— 1.1
2007	1.0	0.1	0.9	1.9	4.8	— 1.1
2008	— 4.9	3.3	— 1.7	4.4	5.6	— 1.7
2009	— 3.3	— 6.6	7.4	6.9	11.2	0.0
2010	— 5.5	4.8	3.5	1.4	— 3.7	— 4.0
2011	0.8	4.3	— 0.1	— 1.2	— 1.0	— 3.6
FQ POS	16/27	15/27	17/27	16/27	18/27	12/27
% FQ POS	59 %	56 %	63 %	59 %	67 %	44 %
AVG GAIN	1.0 %	0.9 %	1.3 %	0.8 %	1.9 %	-0.3 %
RANK GAIN	4	5	3	7	2	11

S&P/TSX MONTH PERCENT CHANGES

JUL	AUG	SEP	OCT	NOV	DEC		YEAR
2.4	1.5	— 6.7	1.6	6.8	1.3	**1985**	20.5
— 4.9	3.2	— 1.6	1.6	0.7	0.6	**1986**	6.0
7.8	— 0.9	— 2.3	— 22.6	— 1.4	6.1	**1987**	3.1
— 1.9	— 2.7	— 0.1	3.4	— 3.0	2.9	**1988**	7.3
5.6	1.0	— 1.7	— 0.6	0.6	0.7	**1989**	17.1
0.5	— 6.0	— 5.6	— 2.5	2.3	3.4	**1990**	— 18.0
2.1	— 0.6	— 3.7	3.8	— 1.9	1.9	**1991**	7.8
1.6	— 1.2	— 3.1	1.2	— 1.6	2.1	**1992**	— 4.6
0.0	4.3	— 3.6	6.6	— 1.8	3.4	**1993**	29.0
3.8	4.1	0.1	— 1.4	— 4.6	2.9	**1994**	— 2.5
1.9	— 2.1	0.3	— 1.6	4.5	1.1	**1995**	11.9
— 2.3	4.3	2.9	5.8	7.5	— 1.5	**1996**	25.7
6.8	— 3.9	6.5	— 2.8	— 4.8	2.9	**1997**	13.0
— 5.9	— 20.2	1.5	10.6	2.2	2.2	**1998**	— 3.2
1.0	— 1.6	— 0.2	4.3	3.6	11.9	**1999**	29.7
2.1	8.1	— 7.7	— 7.1	— 8.5	1.3	**2000**	6.2
— 0.6	— 3.8	— 7.6	0.7	7.8	3.5	**2001**	— 13.9
— 7.6	0.1	— 6.5	1.1	5.1	0.7	**2002**	— 14.0
3.9	3.6	— 1.3	4.7	1.1	4.6	**2003**	24.3
— 1.0	— 1.0	3.5	2.3	1.8	2.4	**2004**	12.5
5.3	2.4	3.2	— 5.7	4.2	4.1	**2005**	21.9
1.9	2.1	— 2.6	5.0	3.3	1.2	**2006**	14.5
— 0.3	— 1.5	3.2	3.7	— 6.4	1.1	**2007**	7.2
— 6.0	1.3	— 14.7	— 16.9	— 5.0	— 3.1	**2008**	— 35.0
4.0	0.8	4.8	— 4.2	4.9	2.6	**2009**	30.7
3.7	1.7	3.8	2.5	2.2	3.8	**2010**	14.4
— 2.7	— 1.4	— 9.0	5.4	— 0.4	— 2.0	**2011**	— 11.1
17/27	14/27	10/27	17/27	16/27	24/27		19/27
63 %	52 %	37 %	63 %	59 %	89 %		70 %
0.8 %	— 0.3 %	— 1.8 %	0.0 %	0.7 %	2.3 %		7.4 %
6	10	12	9	8	1		

S&P/TSX MONTH CLOSING VALUES

	JAN	FEB	MAR	APR	MAY	JUN
1985	2595	2595	2613	2635	2736	2713
1986	2843	2856	3047	3079	3122	3086
1987	3349	3499	3739	3717	3685	3740
1988	3057	3205	3314	3340	3249	3441
1989	3617	3572	3578	3628	3707	3761
1990	3704	3687	3640	3341	3565	3544
1991	3273	3462	3496	3469	3546	3466
1992	3596	3582	3412	3356	3388	3388
1993	3305	3452	3602	3789	3883	3966
1994	4555	4424	4330	4267	4327	4025
1995	4018	4125	4314	4280	4449	4527
1996	4968	4934	4971	5147	5246	5044
1997	6110	6158	5850	5977	6382	6438
1998	6700	7093	7559	7665	7590	7367
1999	6730	6313	6598	7015	6842	7010
2000	8481	9129	9462	9348	9252	10196
2001	9322	8079	7608	7947	8162	7736
2002	7649	7638	7852	7663	7656	7146
2003	6570	6555	6343	6586	6860	6983
2004	8521	8789	8586	8244	8417	8546
2005	9204	9668	9612	9275	9607	9903
2006	11946	11688	12111	12204	11745	11613
2007	13034	13045	13166	13417	14057	13907
2008	13155	13583	13350	13937	14715	14467
2009	8695	8123	8720	9325	10370	10375
2010	11094	11630	12038	12211	11763	11294
2011	13552	14137	14116	13945	13803	13301

S&P/TSX PERCENT CLOSING VALUES

JUL	AUG	SEP	OCT	NOV	DEC	
2779	2820	2632	2675	2857	2893	**1985**
2935	3028	2979	3027	3047	3066	**1986**
4030	3994	3902	3019	2978	3160	**1987**
3377	3286	3284	3396	3295	3390	**1988**
3971	4010	3943	3919	3943	3970	**1989**
3561	3346	3159	3081	3151	3257	**1990**
3540	3518	3388	3516	3449	3512	**1991**
3443	3403	3298	3336	3283	3350	**1992**
3967	4138	3991	4256	4180	4321	**1993**
4179	4350	4354	4292	4093	4214	**1994**
4615	4517	4530	4459	4661	4714	**1995**
4929	5143	5291	5599	6017	5927	**1996**
6878	6612	7040	6842	6513	6699	**1997**
6931	5531	5614	6208	6344	6486	**1998**
7081	6971	6958	7256	7520	8414	**1999**
10406	11248	10378	9640	8820	8934	**2000**
7690	7399	6839	6886	7426	7688	**2001**
6605	6612	6180	6249	6570	6615	**2002**
7258	7517	7421	7773	7859	8221	**2003**
8458	8377	8668	8871	9030	9247	**2004**
10423	10669	11012	10383	10824	11272	**2005**
11831	12074	11761	12345	12752	12908	**2006**
13869	13660	14099	14625	13689	13833	**2007**
13593	13771	11753	9763	9271	8988	**2008**
10787	10868	11935	10911	11447	11746	**2009**
11713	11914	12369	12676	12953	13443	**2010**
12946	12769	11624	12252	12204	11955	**2011**

10 BEST

YEARS

	Close	Change	Change
1954	36	11 pt	45.0 %
1958	55	15	38.1
1995	616	157	34.1
1975	90	22	31.5
1997	970	230	31.0
1989	353	76	27.3
1998	1229	259	26.7
1955	45	10	26.4
2003	1112	232	26.4
1985	211	44	26.3

MONTHS

	Close	Change	Change
Oct 1974	74	10 pt	16.3 %
Aug 1982	120	12	11.6
Dec 1991	417	42	11.2
Oct 1982	134	13	11.0
Aug 1984	167	16	10.6
Nov 1980	141	13	10.2
Nov 1962	62	6	10.2
Mar 2000	1499	132	9.7
Apr 2009	798	75	9.4
May 1990	361	30	9.2

DAYS

		Close	Change	Change
Mon	2008 Oct 13	1003	104 pt	11.6 %
Tue	2008 Oct 28	941	92	10.8
Wed	1987 Oct 21	258	22	9.1
Mon	2009 Mar 23	883	54	7.1
Thu	2008 Nov 13	911	59	6.9
Mon	2008 Nov 24	852	52	6.5
Tues	2009 Mar 10	720	43	6.4
Fri	2008 Nov 21	800	48	6.3
Wed	2002 Jul 24	843	46	5.7
Tue	2008 Sep 30	1166	60	5.4

10 WORST

YEARS

	Close	Change	Change
2008	903	− 566 pt	− 38.5 %
1974	69	− 29	− 29.7
2002	880	− 268	− 23.4
1973	98	− 21	− 17.4
1957	40	− 7	− 14.3
1966	80	− 12	− 13.1
2001	1148	− 172	− 13.0
1962	63	− 8	− 11.8
1977	95	− 12	− 11.5
1969	92	− 12	− 11.4

MONTHS

	Close	Change	Change
Oct 1987	252	− 70 pt	− 21.8 %
Oct 2008	969	− 196	− 16.8
Aug 1998	957	− 163	− 14.6
Sep 1974	64	− 9	− 11.9
Nov 1973	96	− 12	− 11.4
Sep 2002	815	− 101	− 11.0
Feb 2009	735	− 91	− 11.0
Mar 1980	102	− 12	− 10.2
Aug 1990	323	− 34	− 9.4
Feb 2001	1240	− 126	− 9.2

DAYS

		Close	Change	Change
Mon	1987 Oct 19	225	− 58 pt	− 20.5 %
Wed	2008 Oct 15	908	− 90	− 9.0
Mon	2008 Dec 01	816	− 80	− 8.9
Mon	2008 Sep 29	1106	− 107	− 8.8
Mon	1987 Oct 26	228	− 21	− 8.3
Thu	2008 Oct 09	910	− 75	− 7.6
Mon	1997 Oct 27	877	− 65	− 6.9
Mon	1998 Aug 31	957	− 70	− 6.8
Fri	1988 Jan 8	243	− 18	− 6.8
Thu	2008 Nov 20	752	− 54	− 6.7

10 BEST

10 WORST

YEARS

	Close	Change	Change
1954	404	124 pt	44.0 %
1975	852	236	38.3
1958	584	148	34.0
1995	5117	1283	33.5
1985	1547	335	27.7
1989	2753	585	27.0
1996	6448	1331	26.0
2003	10454	2112	25.3
1999	11453	2272	25.2
1997	7908	1460	22.6

YEARS

	Close	Change	Change
2008	8776	– 4488 pt	– 33.8 %
1974	616	– 235	– 27.6
1966	786	– 184	– 18.9
1977	831	– 174	– 17.3
2002	8342	– 1680	– 16.8
1973	851	– 169	– 16.6
1969	800	– 143	– 15.2
1957	436	– 64	– 12.8
1962	652	– 79	– 10.8
1960	616	– 64	– 9.3

MONTHS

	Close	Change	Change
Aug 1982	901	93 pt	11.5 %
Oct 1982	992	95	10.6
Oct 2002	8397	805	10.6
Apr 1978	837	80	10.5
Apr 1999	10789	1003	10.2
Nov 1962	649	60	10.1
Nov 1954	387	35	9.9
Aug 1984	1224	109	9.8
Oct 1998	8592	750	9.6
Oct 2011	11955	1042	9.5

MONTHS

	Close	Change	Change
Oct 1987	1994	– 603 pt	– 23.2 %
Aug 1998	7539	– 1344	– 15.1
Oct 2008	9325	– 1526	– 14.1
Nov 1973	822	– 134	– 14.0
Sep 2002	7592	– 1072	– 12.4
Feb 2009	7063	– 938	– 11.7
Sep 2001	8848	– 1102	– 11.1
Sep 1974	608	– 71	– 10.4
Aug 1974	679	– 79	– 10.4
Jun 2008	11350	– 1288	– 10.2

DAYS

		Close	Change	Change
Mon	2008 Oct 13	9388	936 pt	11.1 %
Tue	2008 Oct 28	9065	889	10.9
Wed	1987 Oct 21	2028	187	10.2
Mon	2009 Mar 23	7776	497	6.8
Thu	2008 Nov 13	8835	553	6.7
Fri	2008 Nov 21	8046	494	6.5
Wed	2002 Jul 24	8191	489	6.3
Tue	1987 Oct 20	1841	102	5.9
Tue	2009 Mar 10	6926	379	5.8
Mon	2002 Jul 29	8712	448	5.4

DAYS

		Close	Change	Change
Mon	1987 Oct 19	1739	– 508 pt	– 22.6 %
Mon	1987 Oct 26	1794	– 157	– 8.0
Wed	2008 Oct 15	8578	– 733	– 7.9
Mon	2008 Dec 01	8149	– 680	– 7.7
Thu	2008 Oct 09	8579	– 679	– 7.3
Mon	1997 Oct 27	8366	– 554	– 7.2
Mon	2001 Sep 17	8921	– 685	– 7.1
Mon	2008 Sep 29	10365	– 778	– 7.0
Fri	1989 Oct 13	2569	– 191	– 6.9
Fri	1988 Jan 8	1911	– 141	– 6.9

10 BEST

10 WORST

YEARS

	Close	Change	Change
1999	4069	1877 pt	85.6 %
1991	586	213	56.9
2003	2003	668	50.0
2009	2269	692	43.9
1995	1052	300	39.9
1998	2193	622	39.6
1980	202	51	33.9
1985	325	78	31.5
1975	78	18	29.8
1979	151	33	28.1

YEARS

	Close	Change	Change
2008	1577	– 1075 pt	– 40.5 %
2000	2471	– 1599	– 39.3
1974	60	– 32	– 35.1
2002	1336	– 615	– 31.5
1973	92	– 42	– 31.1
2001	1950	– 520	– 21.1
1990	374	– 81	– 17.8
1984	247	– 32	– 11.3
1987	331	– 18	– 5.2
1981	196	– 7	– 3.2

MONTHS

	Close	Change	Change
Dec 1999	4069	733 pt	22.0 %
Feb 2000	4697	756	19.2
Oct 1974	65	10	17.2
Jun 2000	3966	565	16.6
Apr 2001	2116	276	15.0
Nov 2001	1931	240	14.2
Oct 2002	1330	158	13.5
Oct 1982	1771	25	13.3
Sep 1998	1694	195	13.0
Oct 2001	1690	191	12.8

MONTHS

	Close	Change	Change
Oct 1987	323	– 121 pt	– 27.2 %
Nov 2000	2598	– 772	– 22.9
Feb 2001	2152	– 621	– 22.4
Aug 1998	1499	– 373	– 19.9
Oct 2008	1721	– 371	– 17.7
Mar 1980	131	– 27	– 17.1
Sep 2001	1499	– 307	– 17.0
Oct 1978	111	– 22	– 16.4
Apr 2000	3861	– 712	– 15.6
Nov 1973	94	– 17	– 15.1

DAYS

		Close	Change	Change
Wed	2001 Jan 3	2617	325 pt	14.2 %
Mon	2008 Oct 13	1844	195	11.8
Tue	2000 Dec 5	2890	274	10.5
Tue	2008 Oct 28	1649	144	9.5
Thu	2001 Apr 5	1785	146	8.9
Wed	2001 Apr 18	2079	156	8.1
Tue	2000 May 30	3459	254	7.9
Fri	2000 Oct 13	3317	242	7.9
Thu	2000 Oct 19	3419	247	7.8
Wed	2002 May 8	1696	122	7.8

DAYS

		Close	Change	Change
Mon	1987 Oct 19	360	– 46 pt	– 11.3 %
Fri	2000 Apr 14	3321	– 355	– 9.7
Mon	2008 Sep 29	1984	– 200	– 9.1
Mon	1987 Oct 26	299	– 30	– 9.0
Tue	1987 Oct 20	328	– 32	– 9.0
Mon	2008 Dec 01	1398	– 138	– 9.0
Mon	1998 Aug 31	1499	– 140	– 8.6
Wed	2008 Oct 15	1628	– 151	– 8.5
Mon	2000 Apr 03	4224	– 349	– 7.6
Tue	2001 Jan 02	2292	– 179	– 7.2

10 BEST

10 WORST

YEARS

	Close	Change	Change
2009	8414	2758 pt	30.7 %
1999	4321	1928	29.7
1993	5927	971	29.0
1996	8221	1213	25.7
2003	11272	1606	24.3
2005	2893	2026	21.9
1985	3970	500	20.8
1989	12908	580	17.1
2006	6699	1636	14.5
2010	13433	1697	14.4

YEARS

	Close	Change	Change
2008	8988	– 4845 pt	35.0 %
1990	3257	– 713	– 18.0
2002	6615	– 1074	– 14.0
2001	7688	– 1245	– 13.9
2011	11955	– 1488	– 11.1
1992	3350	– 162	– 4.6
1998	6486	– 214	– 3.2
1994	4214	– 108	– 2.5
1987	3160	94	3.1
1986	3066	173	6.0

MONTHS

	Close	Change	Change
Dec 1999	8414	891 pt	11.8 %
May 2009	8500	1045	11.2
Oct 1998	6208	594	10.6
Jun 2000	10196	943	10.2
Jan 1985	2595	195	8.1
Aug 2000	11248	842	8.1
Nov 2001	7426	540	7.8
Jul 1987	4030	290	7.8
Feb 2000	9129	648	7.6
Nov 1996	6017	418	7.5

MONTHS

	Close	Change	Change
Oct 1987	3019	– 883 pt	– 22.6 %
Aug 1998	5531	– 1401	– 20.2
Oct 2008	9763	– 1990	– 16.9
Sep 2008	11753	– 2018	– 14.7
Feb 2001	8079	– 1243	– 13.3
Nov 2000	8820	– 820	– 8.5
Apr 1990	3341	– 299	– 8.2
Sep 2000	10378	– 870	– 7.7
Sep 2001	6839	– 561	– 7.6
Jul 2002	6605	– 540	– 7.6

DAYS

		Close	Change	Change
Tue	2008 Oct 14	9956	891 pt	9.8 %
Wed	1987 Oct 21	3246	269	9.0
Mon	2008 Oct 20	10251	689	7.2
Tue	2008 Oct 28	9152	614	7.2
Fri	2008 Sep 19	12913	848	7.0
Fri	2008 Nov 28	9271	517	5.9
Fri	2008 Nov 21	8155	431	5.6
Mon	2008 Dec 08	8567	450	5.5
Mon	2009 Mar 23	8959	452	5.3
Fri	1987 Oct 30	3019	147	5.1

DAYS

		Close	Change	Change
Mon	1987 Oct 19	3192	– 407 pt	– 11.3 %
Mon	2008 Dec 01	8406	– 864	– 9.3
Thu	2008 Nov 20	7725	– 766	– 9.0
Mon	2008 Oct 27	8537	– 757	– 8.1
Wed	2000 Oct 25	9512	– 840	– 8.1
Mon	1987 Oct 26	2846	– 233	– 7.6
Thu	2008 Oct 02	10901	– 814	– 6.9
Mon	2008 Sep 29	11285	– 841	– 6.9
Tue	1987 Oct 20	2977	– 215	– 6.7
Fri	2001 Feb 16	8393	– 574	– 6.4

BOND YIELDS

BOND YIELDS 🇺🇸 10 YEAR TREASURY*

	JAN	FEB	MAR	APR	MAY	JUN
1954	2.48	2.47	2.37	2.29	2.37	2.38
1955	2.61	2.65	2.68	2.75	2.76	2.78
1956	2.9	2.84	2.96	3.18	3.07	3
1957	3.46	3.34	3.41	3.48	3.6	3.8
1958	3.09	3.05	2.98	2.88	2.92	2.97
1959	4.02	3.96	3.99	4.12	4.31	4.34
1960	4.72	4.49	4.25	4.28	4.35	4.15
1961	3.84	3.78	3.74	3.78	3.71	3.88
1962	4.08	4.04	3.93	3.84	3.87	3.91
1963	3.83	3.92	3.93	3.97	3.93	3.99
1964	4.17	4.15	4.22	4.23	4.2	4.17
1965	4.19	4.21	4.21	4.2	4.21	4.21
1966	4.61	4.83	4.87	4.75	4.78	4.81
1967	4.58	4.63	4.54	4.59	4.85	5.02
1968	5.53	5.56	5.74	5.64	5.87	5.72
1969	6.04	6.19	6.3	6.17	6.32	6.57
1970	7.79	7.24	7.07	7.39	7.91	7.84
1971	6.24	6.11	5.7	5.83	6.39	6.52
1972	5.95	6.08	6.07	6.19	6.13	6.11
1973	6.46	6.64	6.71	6.67	6.85	6.9
1974	6.99	6.96	7.21	7.51	7.58	7.54
1975	7.5	7.39	7.73	8.23	8.06	7.86
1976	7.74	7.79	7.73	7.56	7.9	7.86
1977	7.21	7.39	7.46	7.37	7.46	7.28
1978	7.96	8.03	8.04	8.15	8.35	8.46
1979	9.1	9.1	9.12	9.18	9.25	8.91
1980	10.8	12.41	12.75	11.47	10.18	9.78
1981	12.57	13.19	13.12	13.68	14.1	13.47
1982	14.59	14.43	13.86	13.87	13.62	14.3
1983	10.46	10.72	10.51	10.4	10.38	10.85
1984	11.67	11.84	12.32	12.63	13.41	13.56
1985	11.38	11.51	11.86	11.43	10.85	10.16
1986	9.19	8.7	7.78	7.3	7.71	7.8
1987	7.08	7.25	7.25	8.02	8.61	8.4
1988	8.67	8.21	8.37	8.72	9.09	8.92
1989	9.09	9.17	9.36	9.18	8.86	8.28
1990	8.21	8.47	8.59	8.79	8.76	8.48
1991	8.09	7.85	8.11	8.04	8.07	8.28
1992	7.03	7.34	7.54	7.48	7.39	7.26
1993	6.6	6.26	5.98	5.97	6.04	5.96
1994	5.75	5.97	6.48	6.97	7.18	7.1
1995	7.78	7.47	7.2	7.06	6.63	6.17
1996	5.65	5.81	6.27	6.51	6.74	6.91
1997	6.58	6.42	6.69	6.89	6.71	6.49
1998	5.54	5.57	5.65	5.64	5.65	5.5
1999	4.72	5	5.23	5.18	5.54	5.9
2000	6.66	6.52	6.26	5.99	6.44	6.1
2001	5.16	5.1	4.89	5.14	5.39	5.28
2002	5.04	4.91	5.28	5.21	5.16	4.93
2003	4.05	3.9	3.81	3.96	3.57	3.33
2004	4.15	4.08	3.83	4.35	4.72	4.73
2005	4.22	4.17	4.5	4.34	4.14	4.00
2006	4.42	4.57	4.72	4.99	5.11	5.11
2007	4.76	4.72	4.56	4.69	4.75	5.10
2008	3.74	3.74	3.51	3.68	3.88	4.10
2009	2.52	2.87	2.82	2.93	3.29	3.72
2010	3.73	3.69	3.73	3.85	3.42	3.20
2011	3.39	3.58	3.41	3.46	3.17	3.00

* Source: Federal Reserve Bank of St. Louis, monthly data calculated as average of business days

10 YEAR TREASURY  BOND YIELDS

JUL	AUG	SEP	OCT	NOV	DEC	
2.3	2.36	2.38	2.43	2.48	2.51	**1954**
2.9	2.97	2.97	2.88	2.89	2.96	**1955**
3.11	3.33	3.38	3.34	3.49	3.59	**1956**
3.93	3.93	3.92	3.97	3.72	3.21	**1957**
3.2	3.54	3.76	3.8	3.74	3.86	**1958**
4.4	4.43	4.68	4.53	4.53	4.69	**1959**
3.9	3.8	3.8	3.89	3.93	3.84	**1960**
3.92	4.04	3.98	3.92	3.94	4.06	**1961**
4.01	3.98	3.98	3.93	3.92	3.86	**1962**
4.02	4	4.08	4.11	4.12	4.13	**1963**
4.19	4.19	4.2	4.19	4.15	4.18	**1964**
4.2	4.25	4.29	4.35	4.45	4.62	**1965**
5.02	5.22	5.18	5.01	5.16	4.84	**1966**
5.16	5.28	5.3	5.48	5.75	5.7	**1967**
5.5	5.42	5.46	5.58	5.7	6.03	**1968**
6.72	6.69	7.16	7.1	7.14	7.65	**1969**
7.46	7.53	7.39	7.33	6.84	6.39	**1970**
6.73	6.58	6.14	5.93	5.81	5.93	**1971**
6.11	6.21	6.55	6.48	6.28	6.36	**1972**
7.13	7.4	7.09	6.79	6.73	6.74	**1973**
7.81	8.04	8.04	7.9	7.68	7.43	**1974**
8.06	8.4	8.43	8.14	8.05	8	**1975**
7.83	7.77	7.59	7.41	7.29	6.87	**1976**
7.33	7.4	7.34	7.52	7.58	7.69	**1977**
8.64	8.41	8.42	8.64	8.81	9.01	**1978**
8.95	9.03	9.33	10.3	10.65	10.39	**1979**
10.25	11.1	11.51	11.75	12.68	12.84	**1980**
14.28	14.94	15.32	15.15	13.39	13.72	**1981**
13.95	13.06	12.34	10.91	10.55	10.54	**1982**
11.38	11.85	11.65	11.54	11.69	11.83	**1983**
13.36	12.72	12.52	12.16	11.57	11.5	**1984**
10.31	10.33	10.37	10.24	9.78	9.26	**1985**
7.3	7.17	7.45	7.43	7.25	7.11	**1986**
8.45	8.76	9.42	9.52	8.86	8.99	**1987**
9.06	9.26	8.98	8.8	8.96	9.11	**1988**
8.02	8.11	8.19	8.01	7.87	7.84	**1989**
8.47	8.75	8.89	8.72	8.39	8.08	**1990**
8.27	7.9	7.65	7.53	7.42	7.09	**1991**
6.84	6.59	6.42	6.59	6.87	6.77	**1992**
5.81	5.68	5.36	5.33	5.72	5.77	**1993**
7.3	7.24	7.46	7.74	7.96	7.81	**1994**
6.28	6.49	6.2	6.04	5.93	5.71	**1995**
6.87	6.64	6.83	6.53	6.2	6.3	**1996**
6.22	6.3	6.21	6.03	5.88	5.81	**1997**
5.46	5.34	4.81	4.53	4.83	4.65	**1998**
5.79	5.94	5.92	6.11	6.03	6.28	**1999**
6.05	5.83	5.8	5.74	5.72	5.24	**2000**
5.24	4.97	4.73	4.57	4.65	5.09	**2001**
4.65	4.26	3.87	3.94	4.05	4.03	**2002**
3.98	4.45	4.27	4.29	4.3	4.27	**2003**
4.5	4.28	4.13	4.1	4.19	4.23	**2004**
4.18	4.26	4.20	4.46	4.54	4.47	**2005**
5.09	4.88	4.72	4.73	4.60	4.56	**2006**
5.00	4.67	4.52	4.53	4.15	4.10	**2007**
4.01	3.89	3.69	3.81	3.53	2.42	**2008**
3.56	3.59	3.40	3.39	3.40	3.59	**2009**
3.01	2.70	2.65	2.54	2.76	3.29	**2010**
3.00	2.30	1.98	2.15	2.01	1.98	**2011**

BOND YIELDS 5 YEAR TREASURY*

	JAN	FEB	MAR	APR	MAY	JUN
1954	2.17	2.04	1.93	1.87	1.92	1.92
1955	2.32	2.38	2.48	2.55	2.56	2.59
1956	2.84	2.74	2.93	3.20	3.08	2.97
1957	3.47	3.39	3.46	3.53	3.64	3.83
1958	2.88	2.78	2.64	2.46	2.41	2.46
1959	4.01	3.96	3.99	4.12	4.35	4.50
1960	4.92	4.69	4.31	4.29	4.49	4.12
1961	3.67	3.66	3.60	3.57	3.47	3.81
1962	3.94	3.89	3.68	3.60	3.66	3.64
1963	3.58	3.66	3.68	3.74	3.72	3.81
1964	4.07	4.03	4.14	4.15	4.05	4.02
1965	4.10	4.15	4.15	4.15	4.15	4.15
1966	4.86	4.98	4.92	4.83	4.89	4.97
1967	4.70	4.74	4.54	4.51	4.75	5.01
1968	5.54	5.59	5.76	5.69	6.04	5.85
1969	6.25	6.34	6.41	6.30	6.54	6.75
1970	8.17	7.82	7.21	7.50	7.97	7.85
1971	5.89	5.56	5.00	5.65	6.28	6.53
1972	5.59	5.69	5.87	6.17	5.85	5.91
1973	6.34	6.60	6.80	6.67	6.80	6.69
1974	6.95	6.82	7.31	7.92	8.18	8.10
1975	7.41	7.11	7.30	7.99	7.72	7.51
1976	7.46	7.45	7.49	7.25	7.59	7.61
1977	6.58	6.83	6.93	6.79	6.94	6.76
1978	7.77	7.83	7.86	7.98	8.18	8.36
1979	9.20	9.13	9.20	9.25	9.24	8.85
1980	10.74	12.60	13.47	11.84	9.95	9.21
1981	12.77	13.41	13.41	13.99	14.63	13.95
1982	14.65	14.54	13.98	14.00	13.75	14.43
1983	10.03	10.26	10.08	10.02	10.03	10.63
1984	11.37	11.54	12.02	12.37	13.17	13.48
1985	10.93	11.13	11.52	11.01	10.34	9.60
1986	8.68	8.34	7.46	7.05	7.52	7.64
1987	6.64	6.79	6.79	7.57	8.26	8.02
1988	8.18	7.71	7.83	8.19	8.58	8.49
1989	9.15	9.27	9.51	9.30	8.91	8.29
1990	8.12	8.42	8.60	8.77	8.74	8.43
1991	7.70	7.47	7.77	7.70	7.70	7.94
1992	6.24	6.58	6.95	6.78	6.69	6.48
1993	5.83	5.43	5.19	5.13	5.20	5.22
1994	5.09	5.40	5.94	6.52	6.78	6.70
1995	7.76	7.37	7.05	6.86	6.41	5.93
1996	5.36	5.38	5.97	6.30	6.48	6.69
1997	6.33	6.20	6.54	6.76	6.57	6.38
1998	5.42	5.49	5.61	5.61	5.63	5.52
1999	4.60	4.91	5.14	5.08	5.44	5.81
2000	6.58	6.68	6.50	6.26	6.69	6.30
2001	4.86	4.89	4.64	4.76	4.93	4.81
2002	4.34	4.30	4.74	4.65	4.49	4.19
2003	3.05	2.90	2.78	2.93	2.52	2.27
2004	3.12	3.07	2.79	3.39	3.85	3.93
2005	3.71	3.77	4.17	4.00	3.85	3.77
2006	4.35	4.57	4.72	4.90	5.00	5.07
2007	4.75	4.71	4.48	4.59	4.67	5.03
2008	2.98	2.78	2.48	2.84	3.15	3.49
2009	1.60	1.87	1.82	1.86	2.13	2.71
2010	2.48	2.36	2.43	2.58	2.18	2.00
2011	1.99	2.26	2.11	2.17	1.84	1.58

* Source: Federal Reserve Bank of St. Louis, monthly data calculated as average of business days

JUL	AUG	SEP	OCT	NOV	DEC	
1.85	1.90	1.96	2.02	2.09	2.16	**1954**
2.72	2.86	2.85	2.76	2.81	2.93	**1955**
3.12	3.41	3.47	3.40	3.56	3.70	**1956**
4.00	4.00	4.03	4.08	3.72	3.08	**1957**
2.77	3.29	3.69	3.78	3.70	3.82	**1958**
4.58	4.57	4.90	4.72	4.75	5.01	**1959**
3.79	3.62	3.61	3.76	3.81	3.67	**1960**
3.84	3.96	3.90	3.80	3.82	3.91	**1961**
3.80	3.71	3.70	3.64	3.60	3.56	**1962**
3.89	3.89	3.96	3.97	4.01	4.04	**1963**
4.03	4.05	4.08	4.07	4.04	4.09	**1964**
4.15	4.20	4.25	4.34	4.46	4.72	**1965**
5.17	5.50	5.50	5.27	5.36	5.00	**1966**
5.23	5.31	5.40	5.57	5.78	5.75	**1967**
5.60	5.50	5.48	5.55	5.66	6.12	**1968**
7.01	7.03	7.57	7.51	7.53	7.96	**1969**
7.59	7.57	7.29	7.12	6.47	5.95	**1970**
6.85	6.55	6.14	5.93	5.78	5.69	**1971**
5.97	6.02	6.25	6.18	6.12	6.16	**1972**
7.33	7.63	7.05	6.77	6.92	6.80	**1973**
8.38	8.63	8.37	7.97	7.68	7.31	**1974**
7.92	8.33	8.37	7.97	7.80	7.76	**1975**
7.49	7.31	7.13	6.75	6.52	6.10	**1976**
6.84	7.03	7.04	7.32	7.34	7.48	**1977**
8.54	8.33	8.43	8.61	8.84	9.08	**1978**
8.90	9.06	9.41	10.63	10.93	10.42	**1979**
9.53	10.84	11.62	11.86	12.83	13.25	**1980**
14.79	15.56	15.93	15.41	13.38	13.60	**1981**
14.07	13.00	12.25	10.80	10.38	10.22	**1982**
11.21	11.63	11.43	11.28	11.41	11.54	**1983**
13.27	12.68	12.53	12.06	11.33	11.07	**1984**
9.70	9.81	9.81	9.69	9.28	8.73	**1985**
7.06	6.80	6.92	6.83	6.76	6.67	**1986**
8.01	8.32	8.94	9.08	8.35	8.45	**1987**
8.66	8.94	8.69	8.51	8.79	9.09	**1988**
7.83	8.09	8.17	7.97	7.81	7.75	**1989**
8.33	8.44	8.51	8.33	8.02	7.73	**1990**
7.91	7.43	7.14	6.87	6.62	6.19	**1991**
5.84	5.60	5.38	5.60	6.04	6.08	**1992**
5.09	5.03	4.73	4.71	5.06	5.15	**1993**
6.91	6.88	7.08	7.40	7.72	7.78	**1994**
6.01	6.24	6.00	5.86	5.69	5.51	**1995**
6.64	6.39	6.60	6.27	5.97	6.07	**1996**
6.12	6.16	6.11	5.93	5.80	5.77	**1997**
5.46	5.27	4.62	4.18	4.54	4.45	**1998**
5.68	5.84	5.80	6.03	5.97	6.19	**1999**
6.18	6.06	5.93	5.78	5.70	5.17	**2000**
4.76	4.57	4.12	3.91	3.97	4.39	**2001**
3.81	3.29	2.94	2.95	3.05	3.03	**2002**
2.87	3.37	3.18	3.19	3.29	3.27	**2003**
3.69	3.47	3.36	3.35	3.53	3.60	**2004**
3.98	4.12	4.01	4.33	4.45	4.39	**2005**
5.04	4.82	4.67	4.69	4.58	4.53	**2006**
4.88	4.43	4.20	4.20	3.67	3.49	**2007**
3.30	3.14	2.88	2.73	2.29	1.52	**2008**
2.46	2.57	2.37	2.33	2.23	2.34	**2009**
1.76	1.47	1.41	1.18	1.35	1.93	**2010**
1.54	1.02	0.90	1.06	0.91	0.89	**2011**

BOND YIELDS  3 MONTH TREASURY

	JAN	FEB	MAR	APR	MAY	JUN
1982	12.92	14.28	13.31	13.34	12.71	13.08
1983	8.12	8.39	8.66	8.51	8.50	9.14
1984	9.26	9.46	9.89	10.07	10.22	10.26
1985	8.02	8.56	8.83	8.22	7.73	7.18
1986	7.30	7.29	6.76	6.24	6.33	6.40
1987	5.58	5.75	5.77	5.82	5.85	5.85
1988	6.00	5.84	5.87	6.08	6.45	6.66
1999	8.56	8.84	9.14	8.96	8.74	8.43
1990	7.90	8.00	8.17	8.04	8.01	7.99
1991	6.41	6.12	6.09	5.83	5.63	5.75
1992	3.91	3.95	4.14	3.84	3.72	3.75
1993	3.07	2.99	3.01	2.93	3.03	3.14
1994	3.04	3.33	3.59	3.78	4.27	4.25
1995	5.90	5.94	5.91	5.84	5.85	5.64
1996	5.15	4.96	5.10	5.09	5.15	5.23
1997	5.17	5.14	5.28	5.30	5.20	5.07
1998	5.18	5.23	5.16	5.08	5.14	5.12
1999	4.45	4.56	4.57	4.41	4.63	4.72
2000	5.50	5.73	5.86	5.82	5.99	5.86
2001	5.29	5.01	4.54	3.97	3.70	3.57
2002	1.68	1.76	1.83	1.75	1.76	1.73
2003	1.19	1.19	1.15	1.15	1.09	0.94
2004	0.90	0.94	0.95	0.96	1.04	1.29
2005	2.37	2.58	2.80	2.84	2.90	3.04
2006	4.34	4.54	4.63	4.72	4.84	4.92
2007	5.11	5.16	5.08	5.01	4.87	4.74
2008	2.82	2.17	1.28	1.31	1.76	1.89
2009	0.13	0.30	0.22	0.16	0.18	0.18
2010	0.06	0.11	0.15	0.16	0.16	0.12
2011	0.15	0.13	0.10	0.06	0.04	0.04

* Source: Federal Reserve Bank of St. Louis, monthly data calculated as average of business days

3 MONTH TREASURY  BOND YIELDS

JUL	AUG	SEP	OCT	NOV	DEC	
11.86	9.00	8.19	7.97	8.35	8.20	**1982**
9.45	9.74	9.36	8.99	9.11	9.36	**1983**
10.53	10.90	10.80	10.12	8.92	8.34	**1984**
7.32	7.37	7.33	7.40	7.48	7.33	**1985**
6.00	5.69	5.35	5.32	5.50	5.68	**1986**
5.88	6.23	6.62	6.35	5.89	5.96	**1987**
6.95	7.30	7.48	7.60	8.03	8.35	**1988**
8.15	8.17	8.01	7.90	7.94	7.88	**1999**
7.87	7.69	7.60	7.40	7.29	6.95	**1990**
5.75	5.50	5.37	5.14	4.69	4.18	**1991**
3.28	3.20	2.97	2.93	3.21	3.29	**1992**
3.11	3.09	3.01	3.09	3.18	3.13	**1993**
4.46	4.61	4.75	5.10	5.45	5.76	**1994**
5.59	5.57	5.43	5.44	5.52	5.29	**1995**
5.30	5.19	5.24	5.12	5.17	5.04	**1996**
5.19	5.28	5.08	5.11	5.28	5.30	**1997**
5.09	5.04	4.74	4.07	4.53	4.50	**1998**
4.69	4.87	4.82	5.02	5.23	5.36	**1999**
6.14	6.28	6.18	6.29	6.36	5.94	**2000**
3.59	3.44	2.69	2.20	1.91	1.72	**2001**
1.71	1.65	1.66	1.61	1.25	1.21	**2002**
0.92	0.97	0.96	0.94	0.95	0.91	**2003**
1.36	1.50	1.68	1.79	2.11	2.22	**2004**
3.29	3.52	3.49	3.79	3.97	3.97	**2005**
5.08	5.09	4.93	5.05	5.07	4.97	**2006**
4.96	4.32	3.99	4.00	3.35	3.07	**2007**
1.66	1.75	1.15	0.69	0.19	0.03	**2008**
0.18	0.17	0.12	0.07	0.05	0.05	**2009**
0.16	0.16	0.15	0.13	0.14	0.14	**2010**
0.04	0.02	0.01	0.02	0.01	0.01	**2011**

MOODY'S SEASONED CORPORATE Aaa*

	JAN	FEB	MAR	APR	MAY	JUN
1950	2.57	2.58	2.58	2.60	2.61	2.62
1951	2.66	2.66	2.78	2.87	2.89	2.94
1952	2.98	2.93	2.96	2.93	2.93	2.94
1953	3.02	3.07	3.12	3.23	3.34	3.40
1954	3.06	2.95	2.86	2.85	2.88	2.90
1955	2.93	2.93	3.02	3.01	3.04	3.05
1956	3.11	3.08	3.10	3.24	3.28	3.26
1957	3.77	3.67	3.66	3.67	3.74	3.91
1958	3.60	3.59	3.63	3.60	3.57	3.57
1959	4.12	4.14	4.13	4.23	4.37	4.46
1960	4.61	4.56	4.49	4.45	4.46	4.45
1961	4.32	4.27	4.22	4.25	4.27	4.33
1962	4.42	4.42	4.39	4.33	4.28	4.28
1963	4.21	4.19	4.19	4.21	4.22	4.23
1964	4.39	4.36	4.38	4.40	4.41	4.41
1965	4.43	4.41	4.42	4.43	4.44	4.46
1966	4.74	4.78	4.92	4.96	4.98	5.07
1967	5.20	5.03	5.13	5.11	5.24	5.44
1968	6.17	6.10	6.11	6.21	6.27	6.28
1969	6.59	6.66	6.85	6.89	6.79	6.98
1970	7.91	7.93	7.84	7.83	8.11	8.48
1971	7.36	7.08	7.21	7.25	7.53	7.64
1972	7.19	7.27	7.24	7.30	7.30	7.23
1973	7.15	7.22	7.29	7.26	7.29	7.37
1974	7.83	7.85	8.01	8.25	8.37	8.47
1975	8.83	8.62	8.67	8.95	8.90	8.77
1976	8.60	8.55	8.52	8.40	8.58	8.62
1977	7.96	8.04	8.10	8.04	8.05	7.95
1978	8.41	8.47	8.47	8.56	8.69	8.76
1979	9.25	9.26	9.37	9.38	9.50	9.29
1980	11.09	12.38	12.96	12.04	10.99	10.58
1981	12.81	13.35	13.33	13.88	14.32	13.75
1982	15.18	15.27	14.58	14.46	14.26	14.81
1983	11.79	12.01	11.73	11.51	11.46	11.74
1984	12.20	12.08	12.57	12.81	13.28	13.55
1985	12.08	12.13	12.56	12.23	11.72	10.94
1986	10.05	9.67	9.00	8.79	9.09	9.13
1987	8.36	8.38	8.36	8.85	9.33	9.32
1988	9.88	9.40	9.39	9.67	9.90	9.86
1989	9.62	9.64	9.80	9.79	9.57	9.10
1990	8.99	9.22	9.37	9.46	9.47	9.26
1991	9.04	8.83	8.93	8.86	8.86	9.01
1992	8.20	8.29	8.35	8.33	8.28	8.22
1993	7.91	7.71	7.58	7.46	7.43	7.33
1994	6.92	7.08	7.48	7.88	7.99	7.97
1995	8.46	8.26	8.12	8.03	7.65	7.30
1996	6.81	6.99	7.35	7.50	7.62	7.71
1997	7.42	7.31	7.55	7.73	7.58	7.41
1998	6.61	6.67	6.72	6.69	6.69	6.53
1999	6.24	6.40	6.62	6.64	6.93	7.23
2000	7.78	7.68	7.68	7.64	7.99	7.67
2001	7.15	7.10	6.98	7.20	7.29	7.18
2002	6.55	6.51	6.81	6.76	6.75	6.63
2003	6.17	5.95	5.89	5.74	5.22	4.97
2004	5.54	5.50	5.33	5.73	6.04	6.01
2005	5.36	5.20	5.40	5.33	5.15	4.96
2006	5.29	5.35	5.53	5.84	5.95	5.89
2007	5.40	5.39	5.30	5.47	5.47	5.79
2008	5.33	5.53	5.51	5.55	5.57	5.68
2009	5.05	5.27	5.50	5.39	5.54	5.61
2010	5.26	5.35	5.27	5.29	4.96	4.88
2011	5.04	5.22	5.13	5.16	4.96	4.99

* Source: Federal Reserve Bank of St. Louis, monthly data calculated as average of business days

MOODY'S SEASONED CORPORATE Aaa BOND YIELDS

JUL	AUG	SEP	OCT	NOV	DEC	
2.65	2.61	2.64	2.67	2.67	2.67	**1950**
2.94	2.88	2.84	2.89	2.96	3.01	**1951**
2.95	2.94	2.95	3.01	2.98	2.97	**1952**
3.28	3.24	3.29	3.16	3.11	3.13	**1953**
2.89	2.87	2.89	2.87	2.89	2.90	**1954**
3.06	3.11	3.13	3.10	3.10	3.15	**1955**
3.28	3.43	3.56	3.59	3.69	3.75	**1956**
3.99	4.10	4.12	4.10	4.08	3.81	**1957**
3.67	3.85	4.09	4.11	4.09	4.08	**1958**
4.47	4.43	4.52	4.57	4.56	4.58	**1959**
4.41	4.28	4.25	4.30	4.31	4.35	**1960**
4.41	4.45	4.45	4.42	4.39	4.42	**1961**
4.34	4.35	4.32	4.28	4.25	4.24	**1962**
4.26	4.29	4.31	4.32	4.33	4.35	**1963**
4.40	4.41	4.42	4.42	4.43	4.44	**1964**
4.48	4.49	4.52	4.56	4.60	4.68	**1965**
5.16	5.31	5.49	5.41	5.35	5.39	**1966**
5.58	5.62	5.65	5.82	6.07	6.19	**1967**
6.24	6.02	5.97	6.09	6.19	6.45	**1968**
7.08	6.97	7.14	7.33	7.35	7.72	**1969**
8.44	8.13	8.09	8.03	8.05	7.64	**1970**
7.64	7.59	7.44	7.39	7.26	7.25	**1971**
7.21	7.19	7.22	7.21	7.12	7.08	**1972**
7.45	7.68	7.63	7.60	7.67	7.68	**1973**
8.72	9.00	9.24	9.27	8.89	8.89	**1974**
8.84	8.95	8.95	8.86	8.78	8.79	**1975**
8.56	8.45	8.38	8.32	8.25	7.98	**1976**
7.94	7.98	7.92	8.04	8.08	8.19	**1977**
8.88	8.69	8.69	8.89	9.03	9.16	**1978**
9.20	9.23	9.44	10.13	10.76	10.74	**1979**
11.07	11.64	12.02	12.31	12.97	13.21	**1980**
14.38	14.89	15.49	15.40	14.22	14.23	**1981**
14.61	13.71	12.94	12.12	11.68	11.83	**1982**
12.15	12.51	12.37	12.25	12.41	12.57	**1983**
13.44	12.87	12.66	12.63	12.29	12.13	**1984**
10.97	11.05	11.07	11.02	10.55	10.16	**1985**
8.88	8.72	8.89	8.86	8.68	8.49	**1986**
9.42	9.67	10.18	10.52	10.01	10.11	**1987**
9.96	10.11	9.82	9.51	9.45	9.57	**1988**
8.93	8.96	9.01	8.92	8.89	8.86	**1989**
9.24	9.41	9.56	9.53	9.30	9.05	**1990**
9.00	8.75	8.61	8.55	8.48	8.31	**1991**
8.07	7.95	7.92	7.99	8.10	7.98	**1992**
7.17	6.85	6.66	6.67	6.93	6.93	**1993**
8.11	8.07	8.34	8.57	8.68	8.46	**1994**
7.41	7.57	7.32	7.12	7.02	6.82	**1995**
7.65	7.46	7.66	7.39	7.10	7.20	**1996**
7.14	7.22	7.15	7.00	6.87	6.76	**1997**
6.55	6.52	6.40	6.37	6.41	6.22	**1998**
7.19	7.40	7.39	7.55	7.36	7.55	**1999**
7.65	7.55	7.62	7.55	7.45	7.21	**2000**
7.13	7.02	7.17	7.03	6.97	6.77	**2001**
6.53	6.37	6.15	6.32	6.31	6.21	**2002**
5.49	5.88	5.72	5.70	5.65	5.62	**2003**
5.82	5.65	5.46	5.47	5.52	5.47	**2004**
5.06	5.09	5.13	5.35	5.42	5.37	**2005**
5.85	5.68	5.51	5.51	5.33	5.32	**2006**
5.73	5.79	5.74	5.66	5.44	5.49	**2007**
5.67	5.64	5.65	6.28	6.12	5.05	**2008**
5.41	5.26	5.13	5.15	5.19	5.26	**2009**
4.72	4.49	4.53	4.68	4.87	5.02	**2010**
4.93	4.37	4.09	3.98	3.87	3.93	**2011**

MOODY'S SEASONED CORPORATE Baa*

	JAN	FEB	MAR	APR	MAY	JUN
1950	3.24	3.24	3.24	3.23	3.25	3.28
1951	3.17	3.16	3.23	3.35	3.40	3.49
1952	3.59	3.53	3.51	3.50	3.49	3.50
1953	3.51	3.53	3.57	3.65	3.78	3.86
1954	3.71	3.61	3.51	3.47	3.47	3.49
1955	3.45	3.47	3.48	3.49	3.50	3.51
1956	3.60	3.58	3.60	3.68	3.73	3.76
1957	4.49	4.47	4.43	4.44	4.52	4.63
1958	4.83	4.66	4.68	4.67	4.62	4.55
1959	4.87	4.89	4.85	4.86	4.96	5.04
1960	5.34	5.34	5.25	5.20	5.28	5.26
1961	5.10	5.07	5.02	5.01	5.01	5.03
1962	5.08	5.07	5.04	5.02	5.00	5.02
1963	4.91	4.89	4.88	4.87	4.85	4.84
1964	4.83	4.83	4.83	4.85	4.85	4.85
1965	4.80	4.78	4.78	4.80	4.81	4.85
1966	5.06	5.12	5.32	5.41	5.48	5.58
1967	5.97	5.82	5.85	5.83	5.96	6.15
1968	6.84	6.80	6.85	6.97	7.03	7.07
1969	7.32	7.30	7.51	7.54	7.52	7.70
1970	8.86	8.78	8.63	8.70	8.98	9.25
1971	8.74	8.39	8.46	8.45	8.62	8.75
1972	8.23	8.23	8.24	8.24	8.23	8.20
1973	7.90	7.97	8.03	8.09	8.06	8.13
1974	8.48	8.53	8.62	8.87	9.05	9.27
1975	10.81	10.65	10.48	10.58	10.69	10.62
1976	10.41	10.24	10.12	9.94	9.86	9.89
1977	9.08	9.12	9.12	9.07	9.01	8.91
1978	9.17	9.20	9.22	9.32	9.49	9.60
1979	10.13	10.08	10.26	10.33	10.47	10.38
1980	12.42	13.57	14.45	14.19	13.17	12.71
1981	15.03	15.37	15.34	15.56	15.95	15.80
1982	17.10	17.18	16.82	16.78	16.64	16.92
1983	13.94	13.95	13.61	13.29	13.09	13.37
1984	13.65	13.59	13.99	14.31	14.74	15.05
1985	13.26	13.23	13.69	13.51	13.15	12.40
1986	11.44	11.11	10.50	10.19	10.29	10.34
1987	9.72	9.65	9.61	10.04	10.51	10.52
1988	11.07	10.62	10.57	10.90	11.04	11.00
1989	10.65	10.61	10.67	10.61	10.46	10.03
1990	9.94	10.14	10.21	10.30	10.41	10.22
1991	10.45	10.07	10.09	9.94	9.86	9.96
1992	9.13	9.23	9.25	9.21	9.13	9.05
1993	8.67	8.39	8.15	8.14	8.21	8.07
1994	7.65	7.76	8.13	8.52	8.62	8.65
1995	9.08	8.85	8.70	8.60	8.20	7.90
1996	7.47	7.63	8.03	8.19	8.30	8.40
1997	8.09	7.94	8.18	8.34	8.20	8.02
1998	7.19	7.25	7.32	7.33	7.30	7.13
1999	7.29	7.39	7.53	7.48	7.72	8.02
2000	8.33	8.29	8.37	8.40	8.90	8.48
2001	7.93	7.87	7.84	8.07	8.07	7.97
2002	7.87	7.89	8.11	8.03	8.09	7.95
2003	7.35	7.06	6.95	6.85	6.38	6.19
2004	6.44	6.27	6.11	6.46	6.75	6.78
2005	6.02	5.82	6.06	6.05	6.01	5.86
2006	6.24	6.27	6.41	6.68	6.75	6.78
2007	6.34	6.28	6.27	6.39	6.39	6.70
2008	6.54	6.82	6.89	6.97	6.93	7.07
2009	8.14	8.08	8.42	8.39	8.06	7.50
2010	6.25	6.34	6.27	6.25	6.05	6.23
2011	6.09	6.15	6.03	6.02	5.78	5.75

* Source: Federal Reserve Bank of St. Louis, monthly data calculated as average of business days

MOODY'S SEASONED CORPORATE Baa* BOND YIELDS

JUL	AUG	SEP	OCT	NOV	DEC	
3.32	3.23	3.21	3.22	3.22	3.20	1950
3.53	3.50	3.46	3.50	3.56	3.61	1951
3.50	3.51	3.52	3.54	3.53	3.51	1952
3.86	3.85	3.88	3.82	3.75	3.74	1953
3.50	3.49	3.47	3.46	3.45	3.45	1954
3.52	3.56	3.59	3.59	3.58	3.62	1955
3.80	3.93	4.07	4.17	4.24	4.37	1956
4.73	4.82	4.93	4.99	5.09	5.03	1957
4.53	4.67	4.87	4.92	4.87	4.85	1958
5.08	5.09	5.18	5.28	5.26	5.28	1959
5.22	5.08	5.01	5.11	5.08	5.10	1960
5.09	5.11	5.12	5.13	5.11	5.10	1961
5.05	5.06	5.03	4.99	4.96	4.92	1962
4.84	4.83	4.84	4.83	4.84	4.85	1963
4.83	4.82	4.82	4.81	4.81	4.81	1964
4.88	4.88	4.91	4.93	4.95	5.02	1965
5.68	5.83	6.09	6.10	6.13	6.18	1966
6.26	6.33	6.40	6.52	6.72	6.93	1967
6.98	6.82	6.79	6.84	7.01	7.23	1968
7.84	7.86	8.05	8.22	8.25	8.65	1969
9.40	9.44	9.39	9.33	9.38	9.12	1970
8.76	8.76	8.59	8.48	8.38	8.38	1971
8.23	8.19	8.09	8.06	7.99	7.93	1972
8.24	8.53	8.63	8.41	8.42	8.48	1973
9.48	9.77	10.18	10.48	10.60	10.63	1974
10.55	10.59	10.61	10.62	10.56	10.56	1975
9.82	9.64	9.40	9.29	9.23	9.12	1976
8.87	8.82	8.80	8.89	8.95	8.99	1977
9.60	9.48	9.42	9.59	9.83	9.94	1978
10.29	10.35	10.54	11.40	11.99	12.06	1979
12.65	13.15	13.70	14.23	14.64	15.14	1980
16.17	16.34	16.92	17.11	16.39	16.55	1981
16.80	16.32	15.63	14.73	14.30	14.14	1982
13.39	13.64	13.55	13.46	13.61	13.75	1983
15.15	14.63	14.35	13.94	13.48	13.40	1984
12.43	12.50	12.48	12.36	11.99	11.58	1985
10.16	10.18	10.20	10.24	10.07	9.97	1986
10.61	10.80	11.31	11.62	11.23	11.29	1987
11.11	11.21	10.90	10.41	10.48	10.65	1988
9.87	9.88	9.91	9.81	9.81	9.82	1989
10.20	10.41	10.64	10.74	10.62	10.43	1990
9.89	9.65	9.51	9.49	9.45	9.26	1991
8.84	8.65	8.62	8.84	8.96	8.81	1992
7.93	7.60	7.34	7.31	7.66	7.69	1993
8.80	8.74	8.98	9.20	9.32	9.10	1994
8.04	8.19	7.93	7.75	7.68	7.49	1995
8.35	8.18	8.35	8.07	7.79	7.89	1996
7.75	7.82	7.70	7.57	7.42	7.32	1997
7.15	7.14	7.09	7.18	7.34	7.23	1998
7.95	8.15	8.20	8.38	8.15	8.19	1999
8.35	8.26	8.35	8.34	8.28	8.02	2000
7.97	7.85	8.03	7.91	7.81	8.05	2001
7.90	7.58	7.40	7.73	7.62	7.45	2002
6.62	7.01	6.79	6.73	6.66	6.60	2003
6.62	6.46	6.27	6.21	6.20	6.15	2004
5.95	5.96	6.03	6.30	6.39	6.32	2005
6.76	6.59	6.43	6.42	6.20	6.22	2006
6.65	6.65	6.59	6.48	6.40	6.65	2007
7.16	7.15	7.31	8.88	9.21	8.43	2008
7.09	6.58	6.31	6.29	6.32	6.37	2009
6.01	5.66	5.66	5.72	5.92	6.10	2010
5.76	5.36	5.27	5.37	5.14	5.25	2011

COMMODITIES

OIL - WEST TEXAS INTERMEDIATE
CLOSING VALUES $ / bbl

	JAN	FEB	MAR	APR	MAY	JUN
1950	2.6	2.6	2.6	2.6	2.6	2.6
1951	2.6	2.6	2.6	2.6	2.6	2.6
1952	2.6	2.6	2.6	2.6	2.6	2.6
1953	2.6	2.6	2.6	2.6	2.6	2.8
1954	2.8	2.8	2.8	2.8	2.8	2.8
1955	2.8	2.8	2.8	2.8	2.8	2.8
1956	2.8	2.8	2.8	2.8	2.8	2.8
1957	2.8	3.1	3.1	3.1	3.1	3.1
1958	3.1	3.1	3.1	3.1	3.1	3.1
1959	3.0	3.0	3.0	3.0	3.0	3.0
1960	3.0	3.0	3.0	3.0	3.0	3.0
1961	3.0	3.0	3.0	3.0	3.0	3.0
1962	3.0	3.0	3.0	3.0	3.0	3.0
1963	3.0	3.0	3.0	3.0	3.0	3.0
1964	3.0	3.0	3.0	3.0	3.0	3.0
1965	2.9	2.9	2.9	2.9	2.9	2.9
1966	2.9	2.9	2.9	2.9	2.9	2.9
1967	3.0	3.0	3.0	3.0	3.0	3.0
1968	3.1	3.1	3.1	3.1	3.1	3.1
1969	3.1	3.1	3.3	3.4	3.4	3.4
1970	3.4	3.4	3.4	3.4	3.4	3.4
1971	3.6	3.6	3.6	3.6	3.6	3.6
1972	3.6	3.6	3.6	3.6	3.6	3.6
1973	3.6	3.6	3.6	3.6	3.6	3.6
1974	10.1	10.1	10.1	10.1	10.1	10.1
1975	11.2	11.2	11.2	11.2	11.2	11.2
1976	11.2	12.0	12.1	12.2	12.2	12.2
1977	13.9	13.9	13.9	13.9	13.9	13.9
1978	14.9	14.9	14.9	14.9	14.9	14.9
1979	14.9	15.9	15.9	15.9	18.1	19.1
1980	32.5	37.0	38.0	39.5	39.5	39.5
1981	38.0	38.0	38.0	38.0	38.0	36.0
1982	33.9	31.6	28.5	33.5	35.9	35.1
1983	31.2	29.0	28.8	30.6	30.0	31.0
1984	29.7	30.1	30.8	30.6	30.5	30.0
1985	25.6	27.3	28.2	28.8	27.6	27.1
1986	22.9	15.4	12.6	12.8	15.4	13.5
1987	18.7	17.7	18.3	18.6	19.4	20.0
1988	17.2	16.8	16.2	17.9	17.4	16.5
1989	18.0	17.8	19.4	21.0	20.0	20.0
1990	22.6	22.1	20.4	18.6	18.2	16.9
1991	25.0	20.5	19.9	20.8	21.2	20.2
1992	18.8	19.0	18.9	20.2	20.9	22.4
1993	19.1	20.1	20.3	20.3	19.9	19.1
1994	15.0	14.8	14.7	16.4	17.9	19.1
1995	18.0	18.5	18.6	19.9	19.7	18.4
1996	18.9	19.1	21.4	23.6	21.3	20.5
1997	25.2	22.2	21.0	19.7	20.8	19.2
1998	16.7	16.1	15.0	15.4	14.9	13.7
1999	12.5	12.0	14.7	17.3	17.8	17.9
2000	27.2	29.4	29.9	25.7	28.8	31.8
2001	29.6	29.6	27.2	27.4	28.6	27.6
2002	19.7	20.7	24.4	26.3	27.0	25.5
2003	32.9	35.9	33.6	28.3	28.1	30.7
2004	34.3	34.7	36.8	36.7	40.3	38.0
2005	46.8	48.0	54.3	53.0	49.8	56.3
2006	65.5	61.6	62.9	69.7	70.9	71.0
2007	54.6	59.3	60.6	64.0	63.5	67.5
2008	93.0	95.4	105.6	112.6	125.4	133.9
2009	41.7	39.2	48.0	49.8	59.2	69.7
2010	78.2	76.4	81.2	84.5	73.8	75.4
2011	89.4	89.6	102.9	110.0	101.3	96.3

* Source: Federal Reserve

OIL - WEST TEXAS INTERMEDIATE
CLOSING VALUES $ / bbl

COMMODITIES

JUL	AUG	SEP	OCT	NOV	DEC	
2.6	2.6	2.6	2.6	2.6	2.6	1950
2.6	2.6	2.6	2.6	2.6	2.6	1951
2.6	2.6	2.6	2.6	2.6	2.6	1952
2.8	2.8	2.8	2.8	2.8	2.8	1953
2.8	2.8	2.8	2.8	2.8	2.8	1954
2.8	2.8	2.8	2.8	2.8	2.8	1955
2.8	2.8	2.8	2.8	2.8	2.8	1956
3.1	3.1	3.1	3.1	3.1	3.0	1957
3.1	3.1	3.1	3.1	3.0	3.0	1958
3.0	3.0	3.0	3.0	3.0	3.0	1959
3.0	3.0	3.0	3.0	3.0	3.0	1960
3.0	3.0	3.0	3.0	3.0	3.0	1961
3.0	3.0	3.0	3.0	3.0	3.0	1962
3.0	3.0	3.0	3.0	3.0	3.0	1963
2.9	2.9	2.9	2.9	2.9	2.9	1964
2.9	2.9	2.9	2.9	2.9	2.9	1965
2.9	2.9	3.0	3.0	3.0	3.0	1966
3.0	3.1	3.1	3.1	3.1	3.1	1967
3.1	3.1	3.1	3.1	3.1	3.1	1968
3.4	3.4	3.4	3.4	3.4	3.4	1969
3.3	3.3	3.3	3.3	3.3	3.6	1970
3.6	3.6	3.6	3.6	3.6	3.6	1971
3.6	3.6	3.6	3.6	3.6	3.6	1972
3.6	4.3	4.3	4.3	4.3	4.3	1973
10.1	10.1	10.1	11.2	11.2	11.2	1974
11.2	11.2	11.2	11.2	11.2	11.2	1975
12.2	12.2	13.9	13.9	13.9	13.9	1976
13.9	14.9	14.9	14.9	14.9	14.9	1977
14.9	14.9	14.9	14.9	14.9	14.9	1978
21.8	26.5	28.5	29.0	31.0	32.5	1979
39.5	38.0	36.0	36.0	36.0	37.0	1980
36.0	36.0	36.0	35.0	36.0	35.0	1981
34.2	34.0	35.6	35.7	34.2	31.7	1982
31.7	31.9	31.1	30.4	29.8	29.2	1983
28.8	29.3	29.3	28.8	28.1	25.4	1984
27.3	27.8	28.3	29.5	30.8	27.2	1985
11.6	15.1	14.9	14.9	15.2	16.1	1986
21.4	20.3	19.5	19.8	18.9	17.2	1987
15.5	15.5	14.5	13.8	14.0	16.3	1988
19.6	18.5	19.6	20.1	19.8	21.1	1989
18.6	27.2	33.7	35.9	32.3	27.3	1990
21.4	21.7	21.9	23.2	22.5	19.5	1991
21.8	21.4	21.9	21.7	20.3	19.4	1992
17.9	18.0	17.5	18.1	16.7	14.5	1993
19.7	18.4	17.5	17.7	18.1	17.2	1994
17.3	18.0	18.2	17.4	18.0	19.0	1995
21.3	22.0	24.0	24.9	23.7	25.4	1996
19.6	19.9	19.8	21.3	20.2	18.3	1997
14.1	13.4	15.0	14.4	12.9	11.3	1998
20.1	21.3	23.9	22.6	25.0	26.1	1999
29.8	31.2	33.9	33.1	34.4	28.5	2000
26.5	27.5	25.9	22.2	19.7	19.3	2001
26.9	28.4	29.7	28.9	26.3	29.4	2002
30.8	31.6	28.3	30.3	31.1	32.2	2003
40.7	44.9	46.0	53.1	48.5	43.3	2004
58.7	65.0	65.6	62.4	58.3	59.4	2005
74.4	73.1	63.9	58.9	59.4	62.0	2006
74.2	72.4	79.9	86.2	94.6	91.7	2007
133.4	116.6	103.9	76.7	57.4	41.0	2008
64.1	71.1	69.5	75.6	78.1	74.3	2009
76.4	76.8	75.3	81.9	84.1	89.0	2010
97.2	86.3	85.6	86.4	97.2	98.6	2011

GOLD $US/OZ LONDON PM
MONTH CLOSE

	JAN	FEB	MAR	APR	MAY	JUN
1970	34.9	35.0	35.1	35.6	36.0	35.4
1971	37.9	38.7	38.9	39.0	40.5	40.1
1972	45.8	48.3	48.3	49.0	54.6	62.1
1973	65.1	74.2	84.4	90.5	102.0	120.1
1974	129.2	150.2	168.4	172.2	163.3	154.1
1975	175.8	181.8	178.2	167.0	167.0	166.3
1976	128.2	132.3	129.6	128.4	125.5	123.8
1977	132.3	142.8	148.9	147.3	143.0	143.0
1978	175.8	182.3	181.6	170.9	184.2	183.1
1979	233.7	251.3	240.1	245.3	274.6	277.5
1980	653.0	637.0	494.5	518.0	535.5	653.5
1981	506.5	489.0	513.8	482.8	479.3	426.0
1982	387.0	362.6	320.0	361.3	325.3	317.5
1983	499.5	408.5	414.8	429.3	437.5	416.0
1984	373.8	394.3	388.5	375.8	384.3	373.1
1985	306.7	287.8	329.3	321.4	314.0	317.8
1986	350.5	338.2	344.0	345.8	343.2	345.5
1987	400.5	405.9	405.9	453.3	451.0	447.3
1988	458.0	426.2	457.0	449.0	455.5	436.6
1989	394.0	387.0	383.2	377.6	361.8	373.0
1990	415.1	407.7	368.5	367.8	363.1	352.2
1991	366.0	362.7	355.7	357.8	360.4	368.4
1992	354.1	353.1	341.7	336.4	337.5	343.4
1993	330.5	327.6	337.8	354.3	374.8	378.5
1994	377.9	381.6	389.2	376.5	387.6	388.3
1995	374.9	376.4	392.0	389.8	384.3	387.1
1996	405.6	400.7	396.4	391.3	390.6	382.0
1997	345.5	358.6	348.2	340.2	345.6	334.6
1998	304.9	297.4	301.0	310.7	293.6	296.3
1999	285.4	287.1	279.5	286.6	268.6	261.0
2000	283.3	293.7	276.8	275.1	272.3	288.2
2001	264.5	266.7	257.7	263.2	267.5	270.6
2002	282.3	296.9	301.4	308.2	326.6	318.5
2003	367.5	347.5	334.9	336.8	361.4	346.0
2004	399.8	395.9	423.7	388.5	393.3	395.8
2005	422.2	435.5	427.5	435.7	414.5	437.1
2006	568.8	556.0	582.0	644.0	653.0	613.5
2007	650.5	664.2	661.8	677.0	659.1	650.5
2008	923.3	971.5	933.5	871.0	885.8	930.3
2009	919.5	952.0	916.5	883.3	975.5	934.5
2010	1078.5	1108.3	1115.5	1179.3	1207.5	1244.0
2011	1327.0	1411.0	1439.0	1535.5	1536.5	1505.5

* Source: Bank of England

GOLD $US/OZ LONDON PM MONTH CLOSE — COMMODITIES

JUL	AUG	SEP	OCT	NOV	DEC	
35.3	35.4	36.2	37.5	37.4	37.4	**1970**
41.0	42.7	42.0	42.5	42.9	43.5	**1971**
65.7	67.0	65.5	64.9	62.9	63.9	**1972**
120.2	106.8	103.0	100.1	94.8	106.7	**1973**
143.0	154.6	151.8	158.8	181.7	183.9	**1974**
166.7	159.8	141.3	142.9	138.2	140.3	**1975**
112.5	104.0	116.0	123.2	130.3	134.5	**1976**
144.1	146.0	154.1	161.5	160.1	165.0	**1977**
200.3	208.7	217.1	242.6	193.4	226.0	**1978**
296.5	315.1	397.3	382.0	415.7	512.0	**1979**
614.3	631.3	666.8	629.0	619.8	589.8	**1980**
406.0	425.5	428.8	427.0	414.5	397.5	**1981**
342.9	411.5	397.0	423.3	436.0	456.9	**1982**
422.0	414.3	405.0	382.0	405.0	382.4	**1983**
342.4	348.3	343.8	333.5	329.0	309.0	**1984**
327.5	333.3	326.5	325.1	325.3	326.8	**1985**
357.5	384.7	423.2	401.0	383.5	388.8	**1986**
462.5	453.4	459.5	468.8	492.5	484.1	**1987**
436.8	427.8	397.7	412.4	422.6	410.3	**1988**
368.3	359.8	366.5	375.3	408.2	398.6	**1989**
372.3	387.8	408.4	379.5	384.9	386.2	**1990**
362.9	347.4	354.9	357.5	366.3	353.2	**1991**
357.9	340.0	349.0	339.3	334.2	332.9	**1992**
401.8	371.6	355.5	369.6	370.9	391.8	**1993**
384.0	385.8	394.9	383.9	383.1	383.3	**1994**
383.4	382.4	384.0	382.7	387.8	387.0	**1995**
385.3	386.5	379.0	379.5	371.3	369.3	**1996**
326.4	325.4	332.1	311.4	296.8	290.2	**1997**
288.9	273.4	293.9	292.3	294.7	287.8	**1998**
255.6	254.8	299.0	299.1	291.4	290.3	**1999**
276.8	277.0	273.7	264.5	269.1	274.5	**2000**
265.9	273.0	293.1	278.8	275.5	276.5	**2001**
304.7	312.8	323.7	316.9	319.1	347.2	**2002**
354.8	375.6	388.0	386.3	398.4	416.3	**2003**
391.4	407.3	415.7	425.6	453.4	435.6	**2004**
429.0	433.3	473.3	470.8	495.7	513.0	**2005**
632.5	623.5	599.3	603.8	646.7	632.0	**2006**
665.5	672.0	743.0	789.5	783.5	833.8	**2007**
918.0	833.0	884.5	730.8	814.5	869.8	**2008**
939.0	955.5	995.8	1040.0	1175.8	1087.5	**2009**
1169.0	1246.0	1307.0	1346.8	1383.5	1405.5	**2010**
1628.5	1813.5	1620.0	1722.0	1746.0	1531.0	**2011**

FOREIGN EXCHANGE

US DOLLAR vs CDN DOLLAR MONTHLY AVG. VALUES*

	JAN		FEB		MAR		APR		MAY		JUN	
	US / CDN	CDN / US	US / CDN	CDN / US	US / CDN	CDN /US	US / CDN	CDN / US	US / CDN	CDN / US	US / CDN	CDN / US
1971	1.01	0.99	1.01	0.99	1.01	0.99	1.01	0.99	1.01	0.99	1.02	0.98
1972	1.01	0.99	1.00	1.00	1.00	1.00	1.00	1.00	0.99	1.01	0.98	1.02
1973	1.00	1.00	1.00	1.00	1.00	1.00	1.00	1.00	1.00	1.00	1.00	1.00
1974	0.99	1.01	0.98	1.02	0.97	1.03	0.97	1.03	0.96	1.04	0.97	1.03
1975	0.99	1.01	1.00	1.00	1.00	1.00	1.01	0.99	1.03	0.97	1.03	0.97
1976	1.01	0.99	0.99	1.01	0.99	1.01	0.98	1.02	0.98	1.02	0.97	1.03
1977	1.01	0.99	1.03	0.97	1.05	0.95	1.05	0.95	1.05	0.95	1.06	0.95
1978	1.10	0.91	1.11	0.90	1.13	0.89	1.14	0.88	1.12	0.89	1.12	0.89
1979	1.19	0.84	1.20	0.84	1.17	0.85	1.15	0.87	1.16	0.87	1.17	0.85
1980	1.16	0.86	1.16	0.87	1.17	0.85	1.19	0.84	1.17	0.85	1.15	0.87
1981	1.19	0.84	1.20	0.83	1.19	0.84	1.19	0.84	1.20	0.83	1.20	0.83
1982	1.19	0.84	1.21	0.82	1.22	0.82	1.23	0.82	1.23	0.81	1.28	0.78
1983	1.23	0.81	1.23	0.81	1.23	0.82	1.23	0.81	1.23	0.81	1.23	0.81
1984	1.25	0.80	1.25	0.80	1.27	0.79	1.28	0.78	1.29	0.77	1.30	0.77
1985	1.32	0.76	1.35	0.74	1.38	0.72	1.37	0.73	1.38	0.73	1.37	0.73
1986	1.41	0.71	1.40	0.71	1.40	0.71	1.39	0.72	1.38	0.73	1.39	0.72
1987	1.36	0.73	1.33	0.75	1.32	0.76	1.32	0.76	1.34	0.75	1.34	0.75
1988	1.29	0.78	1.27	0.79	1.25	0.80	1.24	0.81	1.24	0.81	1.22	0.82
1989	1.19	0.84	1.19	0.84	1.20	0.84	1.19	0.84	1.19	0.84	1.20	0.83
1990	1.17	0.85	1.20	0.84	1.18	0.85	1.16	0.86	1.17	0.85	1.17	0.85
1991	1.16	0.87	1.15	0.87	1.16	0.86	1.15	0.87	1.15	0.87	1.14	0.87
1992	1.16	0.86	1.18	0.85	1.19	0.84	1.19	0.84	1.20	0.83	1.20	0.84
1993	1.28	0.78	1.26	0.79	1.25	0.80	1.26	0.79	1.27	0.79	1.28	0.78
1994	1.32	0.76	1.34	0.74	1.36	0.73	1.38	0.72	1.38	0.72	1.38	0.72
1995	1.41	0.71	1.40	0.71	1.41	0.71	1.38	0.73	1.36	0.73	1.38	0.73
1996	1.37	0.73	1.38	0.73	1.37	0.73	1.36	0.74	1.37	0.73	1.37	0.73
1997	1.35	0.74	1.36	0.74	1.37	0.73	1.39	0.72	1.38	0.72	1.38	0.72
1998	1.44	0.69	1.43	0.70	1.42	0.71	1.43	0.70	1.45	0.69	1.47	0.68
1999	1.52	0.66	1.50	0.67	1.52	0.66	1.49	0.67	1.46	0.68	1.47	0.68
2000	1.45	0.69	1.45	0.69	1.46	0.68	1.47	0.68	1.50	0.67	1.48	0.68
2001	1.50	0.67	1.52	0.66	1.56	0.64	1.56	0.64	1.54	0.65	1.52	0.66
2002	1.60	0.63	1.60	0.63	1.59	0.63	1.58	0.63	1.55	0.65	1.53	0.65
2003	1.54	0.65	1.51	0.66	1.48	0.68	1.46	0.69	1.38	0.72	1.35	0.74
2004	1.30	0.77	1.33	0.75	1.33	0.75	1.34	0.75	1.38	0.73	1.36	0.74
2005	1.22	0.82	1.24	0.81	1.22	0.82	1.24	0.81	1.26	0.80	1.24	0.81
2006	1.16	0.86	1.15	0.87	1.16	0.86	1.14	0.87	1.11	0.90	1.11	0.90
2007	1.18	0.85	1.17	0.85	1.17	0.86	1.14	0.88	1.10	0.91	1.07	0.94
2008	1.01	0.99	1.00	1.00	1.00	1.00	1.01	0.99	1.00	1.00	1.02	0.98
2009	1.22	0.82	1.25	0.80	1.26	0.79	1.22	0.82	1.15	0.87	1.13	0.89
2010	1.04	0.96	1.06	0.95	1.02	0.98	1.01	0.99	1.04	0.96	1.04	0.96
2011	0.99	1.01	0.99	1.01	0.98	1.02	0.96	1.04	0.97	1.03	0.98	1.02

Source: Federal Reserve: Avg of daily rates, noon buying rates in New York City for cable transfers payable in foreign currencies

US DOLLAR vs CDN DOLLAR
MONTHLY AVG. VALUES

| JUL | | AUG | | SEP | | OCT | | NOV | | DEC | | |
US / CDN	CDN / US	US / CDN	CDN / US	US / CDN	CDN / US	US / CDN	CDN / US	US / CDN	CDN / US	US / CDN	CDN / US	
1.02	0.98	1.01	0.99	1.01	0.99	1.00	1.00	1.00	1.00	1.00	1.00	1971
0.98	1.02	0.98	1.02	0.98	1.02	0.98	1.02	0.99	1.01	1.00	1.00	1972
1.00	1.00	1.00	1.00	1.01	0.99	1.00	1.00	1.00	1.00	1.00	1.00	1973
0.98	1.02	0.98	1.02	0.99	1.01	0.98	1.02	0.99	1.01	0.99	1.01	1974
1.03	0.97	1.04	0.97	1.03	0.97	1.03	0.98	1.01	0.99	1.01	0.99	1975
0.97	1.03	0.99	1.01	0.98	1.03	0.97	1.03	0.99	1.01	1.02	0.98	1976
1.06	0.94	1.08	0.93	1.07	0.93	1.10	0.91	1.11	0.90	1.10	0.91	1977
1.12	0.89	1.14	0.88	1.17	0.86	1.18	0.85	1.17	0.85	1.18	0.85	1978
1.16	0.86	1.17	0.85	1.17	0.86	1.18	0.85	1.18	0.85	1.17	0.85	1979
1.15	0.87	1.16	0.86	1.16	0.86	1.17	0.86	1.19	0.84	1.20	0.84	1980
1.21	0.83	1.22	0.82	1.20	0.83	1.20	0.83	1.19	0.84	1.19	0.84	1981
1.27	0.79	1.25	0.80	1.23	0.81	1.23	0.81	1.23	0.82	1.24	0.81	1982
1.23	0.81	1.23	0.81	1.23	0.81	1.23	0.81	1.24	0.81	1.25	0.80	1983
1.32	0.76	1.30	0.77	1.31	0.76	1.32	0.76	1.32	0.76	1.32	0.76	1984
1.35	0.74	1.36	0.74	1.37	0.73	1.37	0.73	1.38	0.73	1.40	0.72	1985
1.38	0.72	1.39	0.72	1.39	0.72	1.39	0.72	1.39	0.72	1.38	0.72	1986
1.33	0.75	1.33	0.75	1.32	0.76	1.31	0.76	1.32	0.76	1.31	0.76	1987
1.21	0.83	1.22	0.82	1.23	0.82	1.21	0.83	1.22	0.82	1.20	0.84	1988
1.19	0.84	1.18	0.85	1.18	0.85	1.17	0.85	1.17	0.85	1.16	0.86	1989
1.16	0.86	1.14	0.87	1.16	0.86	1.16	0.86	1.16	0.86	1.16	0.86	1990
1.15	0.87	1.15	0.87	1.14	0.88	1.13	0.89	1.13	0.88	1.15	0.87	1991
1.19	0.84	1.19	0.84	1.22	0.82	1.25	0.80	1.27	0.79	1.27	0.79	1992
1.28	0.78	1.31	0.76	1.32	0.76	1.33	0.75	1.32	0.76	1.33	0.75	1993
1.38	0.72	1.38	0.73	1.35	0.74	1.35	0.74	1.36	0.73	1.39	0.72	1994
1.36	0.73	1.36	0.74	1.35	0.74	1.35	0.74	1.35	0.74	1.37	0.73	1995
1.37	0.73	1.37	0.73	1.37	0.73	1.35	0.74	1.34	0.75	1.36	0.73	1996
1.38	0.73	1.39	0.72	1.39	0.72	1.39	0.72	1.41	0.71	1.43	0.70	1997
1.49	0.67	1.53	0.65	1.52	0.66	1.55	0.65	1.54	0.65	1.54	0.65	1998
1.49	0.67	1.49	0.67	1.48	0.68	1.48	0.68	1.47	0.68	1.47	0.68	1999
1.48	0.68	1.48	0.67	1.49	0.67	1.51	0.66	1.54	0.65	1.52	0.66	2000
1.53	0.65	1.54	0.65	1.57	0.64	1.57	0.64	1.59	0.63	1.58	0.63	2001
1.55	0.65	1.57	0.64	1.58	0.63	1.58	0.63	1.57	0.64	1.56	0.64	2002
1.38	0.72	1.40	0.72	1.36	0.73	1.32	0.76	1.31	0.76	1.31	0.76	2003
1.32	0.76	1.31	0.76	1.29	0.78	1.25	0.80	1.20	0.84	1.22	0.82	2004
1.22	0.82	1.20	0.83	1.18	0.85	1.18	0.85	1.18	0.85	1.16	0.86	2005
1.13	0.89	1.12	0.89	1.12	0.90	1.13	0.89	1.14	0.88	1.15	0.87	2006
1.05	0.95	1.06	0.95	1.03	0.97	0.98	1.03	0.97	1.03	1.00	1.00	2007
1.01	0.99	1.05	0.95	1.06	0.95	1.18	0.84	1.22	0.82	1.23	0.81	2008
1.12	0.89	1.09	0.92	1.08	0.92	1.05	0.95	1.06	0.94	1.05	0.95	2009
1.04	0.96	1.04	0.96	1.03	0.97	1.02	0.98	1.01	0.99	1.01	0.99	2010
0.96	1.05	0.98	1.02	1.00	1.00	1.02	0.98	1.02	0.98	1.02	0.98	2011

FOREIGN EXCHANGE

U.S. DOLLAR vs EURO
MONTHLY AVG. VALUES

	JAN		FEB		MAR		APR		MAY		JUN	
	EUR / US	US / EUR	EUR / US	US / EUR	EUR / US	US / EUR	EUR / US	US / EUR	EUR / US	US / EUR	EUR / US	US / EUR
1999	1.16	0.86	1.12	0.89	1.09	0.92	1.07	0.93	1.06	0.94	1.04	0.96
2000	1.01	0.99	0.98	1.02	0.96	1.04	0.94	1.06	0.91	1.10	0.95	1.05
2001	0.94	1.07	0.92	1.09	0.91	1.10	0.89	1.12	0.88	1.14	0.85	1.17
2002	0.88	1.13	0.87	1.15	0.88	1.14	0.89	1.13	0.92	1.09	0.96	1.05
2003	1.06	0.94	1.08	0.93	1.08	0.93	1.09	0.92	1.16	0.87	1.17	0.86
2004	1.26	0.79	1.26	0.79	1.23	0.82	1.20	0.83	1.20	0.83	1.21	0.82
2005	1.31	0.76	1.30	0.77	1.32	0.76	1.29	0.77	1.27	0.79	1.22	0.82
2006	1.21	0.82	1.19	0.84	1.20	0.83	1.23	0.81	1.28	0.78	1.27	0.79
2007	1.30	0.77	1.31	0.76	1.32	0.75	1.35	0.74	1.35	0.74	1.34	0.75
2008	1.47	0.68	1.48	0.68	1.55	0.64	1.58	0.63	1.56	0.64	1.56	0.64
2009	1.32	0.76	1.28	0.78	1.31	0.77	1.32	0.76	1.36	0.73	1.40	0.71
2010	1.43	0.70	1.37	0.73	1.36	0.74	1.34	0.75	1.26	0.80	1.22	0.82
2011	1.34	0.75	1.37	0.73	1.40	0.71	1.45	0.69	1.43	0.70	1.44	0.69

Source: Federal Reserve: Avg of daily rates, noon buying rates in New York City for cable transfers payable in foreign currencies

US DOLLAR vs EURO
MONTHLY AVG. VALUES

JUL		AUG		SEP		OCT		NOV		DEC		
EUR / US	US / EUR	EUR / US	US / EUR	EUR / US	US / EUR	EUR / US	US / EUR	EUR / US	US / EUR	EUR / US	US / EUR	
1.04	0.96	1.06	0.94	1.05	0.95	1.07	0.93	1.03	0.97	1.01	0.99	**1999**
0.94	1.07	0.90	1.11	0.87	1.15	0.85	1.17	0.86	1.17	0.90	1.11	**2000**
0.86	1.16	0.90	1.11	0.91	1.10	0.91	1.10	0.89	1.13	0.89	1.12	**2001**
0.99	1.01	0.98	1.02	0.98	1.02	0.98	1.02	1.00	1.00	1.02	0.98	**2002**
1.14	0.88	1.12	0.90	1.13	0.89	1.17	0.85	1.17	0.85	1.23	0.81	**2003**
1.23	0.82	1.22	0.82	1.22	0.82	1.25	0.80	1.30	0.77	1.34	0.75	**2004**
1.20	0.83	1.23	0.81	1.22	0.82	1.20	0.83	1.18	0.85	1.19	0.84	**2005**
1.27	0.79	1.28	0.78	1.27	0.79	1.26	0.79	1.29	0.78	1.32	0.76	**2006**
1.37	0.73	1.36	0.73	1.39	0.72	1.42	0.70	1.47	0.68	1.46	0.69	**2007**
1.58	0.63	1.50	0.67	1.43	0.70	1.33	0.75	1.27	0.78	1.35	0.74	**2008**
1.41	0.71	1.43	0.70	1.46	0.69	1.48	0.67	1.49	0.67	1.46	0.69	**2009**
1.28	0.78	1.29	0.78	1.31	0.76	1.39	0.72	1.37	0.73	1.32	0.76	**2010**
1.43	0.70	1.43	0.70	1.37	0.73	1.37	0.73	1.36	0.74	1.32	0.76	**2011**